NEW ORLEANS

9th Edition

By Tami Fairweather
and Lavinia Spalding

FrommerMedia LLC

PREVIOUS PAGE: Some days it seems as if every street corner in the French Quarter features a talented musician entertaining passersby. THIS PAGE: It's not just tourist kitsch—a display of Voodoo masks explores the religion's roots in West Africa.

FROMMER'S STAR RATINGS SYSTEM

Every hotel, restaurant, and attraction listed in this guide has been ranked for quality and value. Here's what the stars mean:

★	Recommended
★★	Highly Recommended
★★★	A must! Don't miss!

AN IMPORTANT NOTE

The world is a dynamic place. Hotels change ownership, restaurants hike their prices, museums alter their opening hours, and buses and trains change their routings. And all of this can occur in the several months after our authors have visited, inspected, and written about these hotels, restaurants, museums, and transportation services. Though we have made valiant efforts to keep all our information fresh and up-to-date, some few changes can inevitably occur in the periods before a revised edition of this guidebook is published. So please bear with us if a tiny number of the details in this book have changed. Please also note that we have no responsibility or liability for any inaccuracy or errors or omissions, or for inconvenience, loss, damage, or expenses suffered by anyone as a result of assertions in this guide.

CONTENTS

Bourbon and Orleans streets meet at the heart of the fabled French Quarter.

A LOOK AT NEW ORLEANS

Tennessee Williams famously wrote "America has only three cities: New York, San Francisco, and New Orleans. Everything else is Cleveland." And while that may be an extreme viewpoint (and one that reflects an outdated view of Cleveland!), it's undeniable that NOLA, Crescent City, Nawlins, The Big Easy, or whatever other nickname you want to give it has a *joie de vivre* that's unmatched in the United States, if not the world. This is a city that raises the pursuit of pleasure to an art form—in its food, its music scene, its festivals, its embrace of culture, and the exquisite architecture that graces its streets. What follows in this section is a brief peek at just some of the scintillating sights and experiences that await you on your own trip.

—Pauline Frommer

During Mardi Gras season, masked performers and paraders take over New Orleans, and anyone who wants to can join the celebration.

FRENCH QUARTER

A second-line band leads its traveling street party past the elegant 19th-century Pontalba Buildings, rows of townhouses facing onto Jackson Square at the heart of the French Quarter. For a look inside, visit the 1850 House (p. 158).

The oldest active cathedral in the United States, St. Louis Cathedral (p. 157) presides over the French Quarter from the top of Jackson Square, with museums on either side in the historic Cabildo (p. 161) and Presbytère (p. 164).

The newly refurbished Audubon Aquarium of the Americas (p. 156) houses marine life from across the globe, with an emphasis on the Gulf of Mexico and the Mississippi River.

Pull up a stool to one of the food counters at the lively colonnaded French Market (p. 235) on Decatur Street. Dirty rice and gator burger, anyone?

The small New Orleans Historic Voodoo Museum (p. 164) is packed with displays of intriguing Voodoo objects from around the world.

Life-size statues of (left to right) Fats Domino, Al Hirt, and Pete Fountain hold court at Music Legends Park, a good spot to take a break along the famous (and infamous) Bourbon Street strip, known for live music and free-flowing booze.

ABOVE: Definitely the oldest bar, and possibly the oldest building, in the French Quarter, the atmospheric Lafitte's Blacksmith Shop (p. 225) is a popular place to down a brewskie and make new friends. BELOW: Established in 1840, Antoine's (p. 97) remains a New Orleans fine-dining classic, serving old-school Creole cuisine—oysters Rockefeller, baked Alaska— with formal flair.

A signature taste of New Orleans: the toasted muffuletta and Pimm's Cup at the historic Napoleon House bar (p. 226) on Chartres Street.

At elegant Arnaud's restaurant (p. 98), a century-old Quarter institution, the café brûlot cocktail is made with flaming brandy, spices, and citrus peel.

Expect to get dusted in powdered sugar when you indulge in a hot fried beignet and café au lait at the perennially popular Café du Monde (p. 148).

Perched on a barstool at the Monteleone Hotel's iconic rotating Carousel Bar (p. 224), enjoy a leisurely spin as you sip a trademark Vieux Carré cocktail.

MARDI GRAS & JAZZ FEST

Carnival season in New Orleans is always better if you plan ahead. Follow our advice in chapter 4 (p. 50) to grab the best sidewalk views of the many parades, each with its own flavor and distinctive elaborate floats.

With a little strategy and even more luck, you may score a sighting of one of the elusive Mardi Gras Indians (p. 55) in their intricate hand-beaded and -feathered ceremonial garb.

Even spectators join the spectacle on Fat Tuesday by donning costumes and glittering masks. To get yours, check out one of the costume shops on p. 242.

ABOVE: Roving Mardi Gras celebrations in the Cajun countryside (p. 60) call for colorful patch-work costumes, pointy hats, traditional music, and a gumbo feast. BELOW: At the New Orleans Jazz and Heritage Festival (p. 61), 14 stages present a broad range of music, from jazz and rock to zydeco, Delta blues, and folk music. Here, Cee Lo Green and band perform a sizzling tribute to James Brown.

And this being New Orleans, the "heritage" part of the Jazz and Heritage Festival (p. 61) must include a wide array of food booths featuring local delicacies.

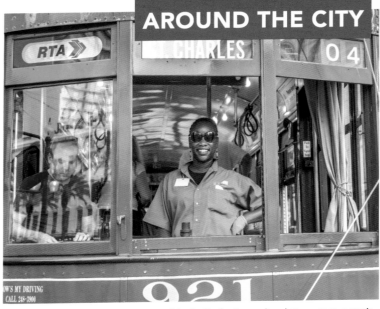

Clang clang! The historic green streetcars of the St. Charles Avenue line clatter uptown, a scenic way to escape the French Quarter and take in the beautiful Victorian and Greek Revival houses of the Garden District. Once you're there, hop off and take our walking tour on p. 261.

Bicycles are a great way to get around this relatively flat city—see p. 296 for rental options. A particularly nice path loops around under the live oaks uptown in Audubon Park (p. 182).

Exploring New Orleans also means exploring the Mississippi River. Docked along the riverfront, paddlewheel steamboats like the *Creole Queen* (p. 198) get you out on the water in style.

The National World War II Museum (p. 169) is one of the finest history museums in the United States. Descriptions don't do justice to its incredibly moving, interactive exhibits, which illuminate the personal side of war.

ABOVE: Some 40,000 works are owned by the New Orleans Museum of Art (p. 172), everything from pre-Columbian sculptures to paintings by European masters to the world's biggest collection of decorative glass. BELOW: Restored to its early 19th-century Creole glory overlooking Bayou St. John, Pitot House (p. 173) was originally a plantation home, before the city expanded outward and surrounded the bayou.

A Garden District walking tour pauses in front of the house used in the film *The Curious Case of Benjamin Button*. See p. 195 for a list of knowledgeable walking-tour guides.

Aboveground tombs at Lafayette Cemetery No. 1 (p. 188). New Orleans' unusual cities of the dead are a characteristic feature of the city's landscape.

A fascinating jumble of artifacts at the Southern Food and Beverage Museum (p. 173), in Central City, serves up the many cuisines of the American South.

It's a rite of passage for New Orleans kids: taking a whirl on the vintage 1906 wooden carousel—aka the "flying horses"—in City Park (p. 204).

Created by local artists, the immersive exhibits at JAMNOLA (p. 174) are like a cultural funhouse, refracting the city's history and icons in intriguing ways.

Meals are an event at the Warehouse District's Compère Lapin (p. 126), helmed by Nina Compton, a runner-up on TV's *Top Chef*.

There's no better place to while away an evening than on Frenchmen Street in the Marigny, especially at the always-hopping Spotted Cat Music Club (p. 220).

A slave cabin at Laura: A Creole Plantation (p. 279). The tour here offers a window into daily life on an 18th- and 19th-century sugar plantation and a cultural history of the Creole clan who owned it.

The splendid white "big house" at Oak Alley Plantation (p. 279) is complemented by re-created slave quarters that illuminate the other side of 19th-century plantation life.

The Evangeline Oak in St. Martinville (p. 290) commemorates the arrival of the Nova Scotian Acadians from whom modern Cajuns claim their descent.

Tours of the stunning, primeval Atchafalaya swamp (p. 290), near Lafayette, usually include encountering alligators in their native sloshing grounds.

Crawfish boils, andouille and boudin sausage, étouffée stew, pig-fat cracklings—welcome to the down-home tastes of Cajun food. See p. 282 for Cajun Country information, or chapter 6 for Cajun eateries in New Orleans.

Kayaking through the mysterious swamps outside New Orleans is vital to understanding the city's Mississippi Delta identity. See p. 197 for tours.

THE BEST OF NEW ORLEANS

By Lavinia Spalding

New Orleans should come with a warning label. No, no, not about hurricanes. That's like identifying Hawaii solely with erupting volcanoes. No, this is about the city itself. See, there's this group of residents known as the "never lefts." They are the people who first came to New Orleans as tourists, and the city worked its magic on them.

They became spellbound by the beauty of the French Quarter and the Garden District and marveled that history was alive right beneath their feet. They listened to music flowing from random doorways and street corners—jazz, soul, blues, whatever—and found themselves moving to a languorous rhythm. They kissed beneath flickering gas lamps and grooved to a brass band in a crowded club long past their usual bedtimes. They ate indulgent meals and indulged yet again hours later, with beignets at 3am, when the city's beguiling, sexy spookiness was cresting. They caught the scent of jasmine and sweet olive (with a whiff of the Caribbean, and a garlic top note, perhaps) wafting through the air.

That's what happened to the never lefts. They came for Mardi Gras, for a festival, conference, tryst, wedding, weekend—just came—and fell hard. Then they stayed forever. New Orleans does that to people.

What is it about this place? Well, New Orleans is where cultures and centuries commingle, perhaps not effortlessly but nowhere more captivatingly. It's where a barstool or bench becomes the opening salvo in a conversation you may never forget—raconteurship thrives here. It's a living masquerade party, a roving art exhibit, an everyone's-welcome family meal and dance party. It was the first U.S. city with a cocktail ratified by a state legislature—which speaks volumes to its state of mind. And it's where gumbo—the savory stew that is often (over-) used in describing the city's multicultural tableau—is actually an apt metaphor for a place that's deep, mysterious, rich with flavor, spiked with spice—and so much more than the hot, heady sum of its disparate parts.

Many a tourist leaves heart-struck with this magical, rare place. It's imperfect, but when you're falling in love it's easy to overlook flaws.

After a history of gut punches, New Orleans' storied resilience is a bit of a trope. And yet, it's proven true again and again. Most recently, Covid-19 and Hurricane Ida took a toll. But the city is all the way back. We're back. The music again reverberates from river to lake. We second-line in the streets every Sunday. New restaurants dazzle and delight. So, c'mon down and let the ineffable essence of New Orleans enchant you. Visit. See, hear, and taste for yourself. The best way to know New Orleans is to plunge in. Don't settle for the obvious. Sure, we've met people who never left Bourbon Street and had a terrific time, but the city offers so much more. Look over the advice that follows, and if New Orleans finds its way into your heart, perhaps you'll come to understand the never lefts. Perhaps you'll even come to be one.

THE best NEW ORLEANS EXPERIENCES

o **Do Festivals, Big & Small:** Yes to Jazz Fest, Mardi Gras, Essence, Southern Decadence, and French Quarter Fest, but also the smaller festivals in NOLA and nearby. With 400 fests in Louisiana, one is likely to be on while you're visiting. Seek it out. See p. 31.

o **Frequent Dive Bars and Corner-Grocery Back Counters:** If that's your thang, that is. For those whose thang it is, this town is siiick with deeply divey drinkeries (p. 227) and tasty tucked-away eateries (p. 111).

o **Check Out a Freebie Concert:** Grab a chair or blanket and join the locals. See what's up in **Armstrong Park, City Park,** the **French Market,** or at the CBD's **Lafayette Square** for music, food booths, and an all-around chill scene. And for outstanding indoor free concerts, head to the **New Orleans Jazz Museum** (www. nolajazzmuseum.org; p. 164).

o **Tour the Swamps:** Don't discount this because you think it's touristy (New Yorkers still go to Broadway, right?). The swamps are eerie, serene, and fascinating. The gators are spellbinding, and most guides are knowledgeable naturalists who will open your eyes to this unique ecoculture. Do, however, consider a responsible tour operator whose guides focus on the environment rather than on baiting the wildlife. See p. 196.

o **Ride a Bike:** NOLA is flat and compact, and you can see a lot on two wheels that you might otherwise miss. See p. 296 for rentals and p. 201 for tours.

o **Cheer the Saints:** In the Dome, if possible—ain't nothing like it, nowhere. Or at least from a barstool, like everyone who ain't in the Dome. See p. 180.

o **Look Around:** Pocket the phone and just take it all in: the architecture, flora, remnants of Spain and France, hint of Haiti, street tableaus weird and wonderful. As New Orleans swirls around you, let your eyes be your camera.

We dance even if there's no radio. We drink at funerals. We talk too much and laugh too loud and live too large and, frankly, we're suspicious of others who don't.

—*Chris Rose*

- **Go to Church:** Despite the reputation for decadence, this is a pretty pious city. Going to church is a wonderful way to hear some astounding gospel and mingle with welcoming locals. See p. 179.
- **Stroll the Galleries:** Look for openings with low-key revelry and flowing wine the first Saturday evening of each month on Julia Street, and the loosely organized second Saturdays on St. Claude Avenue. But any time will do. See p. 237.
- **Chat:** Discuss. Debate. Banter. In restaurants, bars, or shops. With people you've just met. We'll give you locals' topics: food, football, and city politics/ineptitude. Barring your expertise in those arenas, trading anecdotes about your observations as a tourist, discussing a recent activity or meal, or asking for recommendations for your next will get the convo started.
- **Eat with Your Hands:** Specifically, peel shrimp and crawfish (when in season), best done outdoors; slurp oysters, best done standing at a bar, chatting up the shucker; and try as many different po' boys (p. 112) as possible.
- **Loosen Up:** If a wailing trumpet catches your ear, follow the sound 'til you find it. If the swing band playing on a corner on Royal Street moves you, give your partner a whirl (and drop a fiver in the hat). If you normally track every calorie, lose count for a few days. And if you're lucky enough to happen upon a second-line parade passing by (easily accomplished by being in town on a Sunday—find out more on WWOZ's website), don't even think of watching from the sidewalk. Jump in and high-step it down the street. In other words, if there's something you wouldn't dare do elsewhere, now is your opportunity. You needn't lose *all* sense of propriety—but lose *some.* It's New Orleans, after all.

THE best PLACES TO EAT IN NEW ORLEANS

- **Best All-Around Dining Experience You Can Have in New Orleans:** They're world-famous for good reason at their respective ends of the spectrum: **Commander's Palace** (p. 136) and **Café du Monde** (p. 148). And a new shining star: **Dakar NOLA** (p. 138), with its spectacular tasting menu experience.
- **Best Classic French Quarter Restaurant:** Three old-line, fine-dining mainstays have been enjoyed for generations. **Arnaud's** (p. 98) is our choice for food; **Galatoire's** (p. 102) for the overall experience; and **Antoine's** (p. 97) for room after amazing room full of history.

o **Best Contemporary Creole or French:** An old favorite and a newish one, both well-deserved: lovely **Lilette** (p. 139) and sensational **Saint John** (p. 107). Add a little Afro-Caribbean influence and you've got the phenomenal **Compère Lapin** (p. 126).

o **Best Cajun:** Our votes go to playful fine-dining **Boucherie** (p. 141), long-timer **Brigtsen's** (p. 134), and **Mosquito Supper Club** (p. 140) for the intimate and memorable experience.

o **Best Italian:** We've fallen hard for the *nuovo* take by Uptown's sexy **Avo** (p. 134) and seafood specialist **San Lorenzo** (p. 140). **Irene's** (p. 110) represents New Orleans' traditional Creole Italian; **Mosca's** (p. 147) scores with classic food worth a half-hour's drive out of town.

o **Best Neighborhood Restaurants:** New Orleans tucks away some shockingly good restaurants on unassuming residential streets. Uptowners **Clancy's** (p. 136) and **High Hat** (p. 146) and Tremé's **Dooky Chase** (p. 119) show the range.

o **Best *Neighbahood* Restaurants:** These are old-school joints filled with locals who've been buddies since grade school (and act like you're their buddy, too). We'll go with **Lil Dizzy's** (p. 123) for gumbo and fried chicken, **Liuzza's by the Track** (p. 123) for barbecue shrimp po' boys, and **Charlie's** (p. 136) for sizzling steak and sass.

o **Most Innovative Restaurants:** Menu magic is made when talented chefs fuse traditional New Orleans ingredients and flavors with those of various cultures: **Mister Mao** (p. 143) surprises with its spectacular, spice-forward creations; **Maypop** (p. 131) mixes in Southeast Asian concepts with stellar results; and **Marjie's** (p. 120) blends heretofore uncommon ideas and essences.

o **Best Expense- or Savings-Account Blowouts:** Multi-course meals with fine wine pairings at **Restaurant R'evolution** (p. 106) or **Emeril's** (p. 127) are splurge-worthy indeed. The 10-course menu and wine pairing at lovely, novel **Saint-Germain** (p. 114) also impresses.

o **Best Bistro/Brasserie:** Tough choice given the richness of this category, but newcomer **MaMou** (p. 105) pulls out all the stops, while **La Petite Grocery** (p. 138) and **Bywater American Bistro** (p. 115) figure highly. **Zasu** (p. 118) and **Coquette** (p. 137) deserve a mention here too, with elevated cuisine that rises above the bistro norm.

o **Best Outdoor Dining:** On starry nights or balmy afternoons, we head for the pretty courtyards at **Bayona** (p. 99), **N7** (p. 117), and **Jewel of the South** (p. 225), or the unbeatable backyard vibes at **Bacchanal** (p. 115).

o **Best for Kids:** Everyone's sweet to kids here, especially at the big name, old-school fine-dining institutions. But on the casual side, we like the counter at **Camellia Grill** (p. 145) and the tolerance and something-for-everyone menu at **Joey K's** (p. 146). Don't skip **Acorn** when visiting the

Children's Museum (p. 205). Finally, this goes without saying: a **snoball** (p. 150).

o **Best Slightly Offbeat but Utterly New Orleanian Restaurants:** Fancy, fun **Justine** (p. 105) and colorful **Fritai** (p. 120) have their own special groove. Casual **Turkey and the Wolf** (p. 147) is also right up there.

o **Best Brunch:** Breakfast at **Brennan's** is rightly famed (p. 99). **Café Degas** (p. 119) or **Patois** (p. 140) can't miss, nor can **Miss River** (p. 99) with its tremendous Bloody Mary bar. All the fancy jazz brunches are great fun—as is the unfancy one at **Buffa's** (p. 220). Gotta give love to the drag brunch at **Country Club** (p. 231).

o **Best Global Cuisine:** You can't eat Creole and Cajun every day, right? Ok, maybe you can, but you'd miss some of the city's best restaurants, like **LUVI** (p. 133), whose "feed me" omakase menu is poetry on a plate. Our Mediterranean go-to is **Saba** (p. 144). **Saffron** serves hauntingly delicious Indian food (p. 144), **Lengua Madre** (p. 139) completely reframes Mexican cuisine, and **Queen Trini Lisa** (p. 124) is unanimously beloved for her Trinbagonian island soul food.

o **Best Seafood:** Upscale **GW Fins** sets a *very* high bar (p. 104), though **Pêche** (p. 129) and **Le Chat Noir** (p. 128) are strong contenders. Mid-City's **Bevi** (p. 122) covers the low-key, boiled-seafood angle. For oysters, **Casamento's** (p. 145) and **Pascal's Manale** (p. 143).

o **Best Desserts:** A meal at **Emeril's** (p. 127) is incomplete without banana cream pie; ditto **Commander's Palace**'s (p. 136) bread pudding soufflé, **Arnaud's** bananas Foster flambé (p. 98), and **Antoine's** (p. 97) baked Alaska. The pastry chefs at **Coquette** (p. 137) excel, as do the pie people at **High Hat** (p. 146) and **Gris Gris** (p. 142). Or head to a dessert specialist (p. 148).

THE best PLACES TO DRINK IN NEW ORLEANS

o **Best Old-School Cocktail Lounges:** There's just something about drinking a classic cocktail at the very bar where it was invented—a thrill you can experience at the **Sazerac Bar at the Hotel Roosevelt** (p. 230), where the city's official cocktail was first poured. You can also sip a Vieux Carré cocktail at its birthplace, the **Carousel Bar at the Hotel Monteleone** (p. 224)—the fact that it's a revolving bar just adds to the buzz. The landmark **Napoleon House** (p. 226) has been going strong for over a century; the signature drink here is a Pimm's Cup. And if the French 75 cocktail wasn't invented in the **French 75 Bar at Arnaud's** (p. 225), it should have been; despite being set in one of the city's most venerable restaurants, the outstanding bar program here never rests on its laurels.

- **Best New-School Cocktail Bars:** Among the new generation of mixologists who've revived New Orleans' cocktail culture in the past few years, the bar is set high by Neal Bodenheimer at his Freret Street mecca **Cure** (p. 228) and its sister lounge **Peychaud's** (p. 226), and Chris Hannah at charming **Jewel of the South** (p. 225). **Bar Marilou** (p. 228) serves tasty cocktails and small plates in a gorgeous, library-inspired setting, and **Bar Tonique** (p. 223) is what they call "a bartender's bar."

- **Restaurants with the Best Cocktail Programs:** From a looong (we mean, really: so long) list, we'll go with **Latitude 29** (p. 110), **Palm & Pine** (p. 110), sophisticated **Cane & Table** (p. 223) where rum is the star, and **Revel** (p. 121), with a nod to the surprisingly savory drinks at **Toups' Meatery** (p. 121).

- **Best Wine Lists:** Beyond the expensive three-star restaurants you'd expect to have vast cellars, we're consistently impressed with the smaller but smart wine list at **Herbsaint** (p. 127). For all its jazzy, eclectic vibe, **Bacchanal** (p. 115) is a serious contender, and a James Beard finalist for Outstanding Wine Program, no less. We're besotted with **The Tell Me Bar** (p. 230), a new spot with a vast list of natural wines and a lush, moody candlelit vibe. If what you really want is champagne, **Effervescence** (p. 224) is all about the bubbly.

- **Best Neighborhood Bars:** To spend an evening hanging with the locals, check out the friendly Irish pub **Erin Rose** (p. 224) in the French Quarter, Mid-City's **Bayou Beer Garden** and its next-door twin **Bayou Wine Garden** (p. 228), or the Lower Garden District's **Barrel Proof** (p. 228), with its vast menu of whiskies.

THE best PLACES TO STAY IN NEW ORLEANS

This is a little like deciding on a scoop of ice cream—so many tasty options to choose from, and different people like different flavors. We've tried to narrow down the selections based on specific criteria.

- **Best Moderately Priced Lodging:** You'll get the biggest bang in the off-season (including the heat of summer) and mid-week, when even luxury properties feature enticingly lower rates. In the French Quarter, **Olivier House** (p. 72) and **Place d'Armes** (p. 74) are fun and funky. The Marigny's **Auld Sweet Olive** (p. 81) is practically perfect. In the CBD, the **Pelham Hotel** (p. 80) is a clean, freshly remodeled boutique with surprisingly reasonable rates. Uptown, **Chimes B&B** (p. 92), a delightful family-owned guesthouse, has generated legions of loyal return guests.

- **Best Luxury Hotel:** At the intimate **Audubon Cottages** (p. 67), luxury commences when your 24-hour butler greets you at the private, unmarked entrance. For classic opulence, attention to your every need, and vast expanses of room, it's the **Windsor Court** (p. 77). A Club Level suite, of course. The new **Four Seasons** (p. 76) adds views-for-days to luxe detail; while boutique **Maison de la Luz** (p. 76) brings understated extravagance.

o **Best Service:** All those in the "Luxury" category above excel in the service category, as do the new **Virgin Hotel** (p. 79) and the **Ritz-Carlton** (p. 70). We're also continually impressed by the attentive **NOPSI Hotel** (p. 78). Of the more modest accommodations, congeniality and overall graciousness awards go to Uptown's **Maison Perrier** (p. 92), the **Chimes** (p. 92), and Mid-City's **1896 O'Malley House** (p. 85).

o **Most Romantic:** Romance is wherever you make it, but **Ashton's** (p. 84) encourages long, languid mornings, and the rooms in two new hotels, the **Hotel Saint Vincent** (p. 88) and **The Chloe** (p. 90), are swoony enough for you to stay in bed all day.

o **Best for Families:** While chain hotels are often the safest bet for travelers with kids, we favor family-pleasing local businesses. In the luxury category, the **Roosevelt Hotel** (p. 77) always makes kids feel extra-special (in Dec, the hotel's a magical wonderland) and the **Four Seasons** (p. 76) treats children to an adorable in-room camping setup. Among more moderately priced indies, we like low-key **Olivier House** (p. 72), with its pool, cats, and mysterious stairways to explore. Budget watchers might consider multi-bed rooms at newer hostels, like the **HI New Orleans** (p. 81).

o **Best Faaaabulous B&B:** A lot of B&Bs are crammed with over-the-top antiques, but the **Inn at the Old Jail** (p. 85) is pure restoration gorgeousness and warm service—and yes, it really was a jail. At the **Antebellum** (p. 85), we love the tawdry over-the-topness, hidden hot tub, and actual bordello bed.

o **Best for Hipness:** The **Hotel Peter & Paul** (p. 82) opened in 2018 to out-hip everything else, until the **Virgin Hotel** (p. 79) and **Hotel Saint Vincent** (p. 88) came to town. For action, it's still the **Ace** (p. 78).

o **Best Funky Spots:** The new **Frenchmen Hotel** (p. 83) is stylish and fun, especially if you're after lots of live music (Frenchmen St. can't be beat for that). We're also fond of Frenchmen-adjacent **Royal Street Inn** (p. 83). The hip, mid-century motel conversion **The Drifter** (p. 86) is altogether different for altogether different reasons (but not everyone will "get" it).

o **Best Hidden Gem:** The unobtrusive location of the **Henry Howard** (p. 87) belies its stunningly renovated interior and comfortable, hip vibe. The **Auld Sweet Olive** is a warm Marigny respite just far enough from the madding crowds (p. 81).

o **Best Spa Hotels:** If being pampered is integral to your travel experience, check into one of these luxury hotels or dip in for a dreamy day. The **Windsor Court** (p. 77) has infrared saunas, phenomenal facials, and we-cater-to-celebrities-level service. The **Four Seasons'** (p. 76) space looks and feels like one long exhale (and hello, the silhouette-slimming, Biologique Recherche lymphatic massage is . . . life changing). You'll feel cozy and cared for at the **Roosevelt Hotel**'s (p. 77) spa, with its low-lit, calm intimacy and highly skilled technicians. And finally, the **Ritz-Carlton** (p. 70) is home to the city's largest spa with an extensive treatment menu that includes a powerful 80-minute Voodoo-inspired massage with poultices of steamed herbs. (It *is* New Orleans, y'all).

THE best TRIP MEMENTOS

You'll always have your memories and IG posts. And nothing's wrong with T-shirts, caps, Mardi Gras beads, masks, a Voodoo doll, chicory coffee, or beignet mix. For something a little extra, consider these alternate ideas.

o **A Book from Faulkner House:** Many an author has tried, with varying success, to capture New Orleans on the page. Their efforts may help you know what it means to miss New Orleans. Pick up some reading material from this charming jewel on little Pirate's Alley, crammed with Louisiana-related tomes. See p. 241.

o **A Photo or Art Book from A Gallery for Fine Photography:** The owner calls his impressive shop "the only museum where you can buy the art." A photograph from one of the many famed photographers represented here is a souvenir to relish every day, not to mention a wise investment. If an original isn't feasible, consider a fine photo book. See p. 239.

o **A Southern Scent from Hové:** This classic perfumery (the city's oldest) creates its own perfumes and soaps. We're partial to sachet-favorite Vetivert, described as "smelling like the South." Locals also adore the scents made from the indigenous sweet olive, and the fine gentlemanly scents. See p. 246.

o **Local Art:** Take home a singular treasure from one of the many excellent galleries (p. 237), from the vendors around **Jackson Square,** or at a local art market like those at **Marsalis Harmony Park** (p. 234).

o **Tunes:** New Orleans' soundtrack is as essential to your experience as its sights and tastes. Some vinyl or a few CDs purchased (yes, bought) at gigs or a record shop (p. 248) will keep the good times rolling back home. See our recorded-music recommendations in chapter 2.

o **A Hat from Meyer:** We're mad about **Meyer the Hatter** for the selection, the service, and the 100-year-plus history. You're in the South, *darlin';* you can rock some class headgear. See p. 243.

o **A "be nice or leave" Sign:** Dr. Bob's colorful, bottle-cap-edged signs are true local works of folk art, handmade with found materials. Visiting his one-of-a-kind Bywater studio, **Dr. Bob Art** (p. 238), just adds to the sentimental value.

o **Fleur-de-Lis Jewelry:** Gold, silver, glass, cufflink, nose ring, pendant—the selection is unending. Consider something from **Mignon Faget** (p. 247) or **Saint Claude Social Club** (p. 247) or an inexpensive bauble from the flea-market stands at the **French Market** (p. 235).

o **Sazerac Glasses:** If you've taken a shine to the city's official cocktail, the **Roosevelt Hotel** (p. 77) has perfect reproductions of their original glasses.

- **Tipitina's Merch:** Catch a show at this classic venue and take home a T-shirt, hat, bandana, or koozie with the iconic banana-hand logo. See p. 223.
- **Pralines:** The choice for office gifts. And for home. Maybe one for the plane or car on the way there. (And remember, it's *prah,* not *pray.*) See p. 241.
- **A Custom-Writ Poem:** Why not a sonnet? Street poets set up their crusty, trusty typewriters most nights along Frenchmen Street and elsewhere, ready to plink out a verse or three based on your input.
- **A Forever Souvenir:** Get inked at **Electric Ladyland Tattoo,** 610 Frenchmen St. (electricladylandtattoo.com; ☏ **504/947-8286**), 10am to 10pm daily. If you can think it (and you should), they can ink it.

THE best OF OUTDOOR NEW ORLEANS

Not what you think of first—NOLA isn't Yellowstone, after all. But there are surprisingly wonderful outdoorsy things to do here that'll only enhance the vacation you envisioned. Besides, it can't all be about dark bars and decadent meals. Oh wait, it's New Orleans. Yes, it can. Still . . . these experiences provide a fine counterpoint and a different perspective. We've already sold you on touring the swamps and biking around, right? Here are more activities for you.

- **Kayak Bayou St. John:** A guided kayak tour of placid, pretty Bayou St. John is an entrancing way to see this historically significant waterway—and maybe work off a few bites of fried shrimp po' boy. See p. 197.
- **City Park It:** Whatever your outdoor thing, it's probably doable somewhere in the glorious, 1,300-acre **City Park** (p. 183), from pedal-boating to picnicking, birding to bicycling, golfing (mini or big) to art-gazing. It's great for a morning run, as is Uptown's **Audubon Park** (p. 182).
- **Ferry 'Cross the Mississippi:** It's not quite Huck Finn, but a brief "cruise" on the ferry to the historic Algiers neighborhood is an easy way to roll on the river and take in a different view. See p. 297.
- **Dine Alfresco:** We didn't say the best of *active* outdoor New Orleans, did we? A languid, courtyard dinner under the southern stars (or lunch under an umbrella) is an experience to be savored. See chapter 6.
- **Ascend to a Rooftop:** The Four Seasons' **Vue Orleans** (p. 171) offers the only 360-degree city view in town. Vistas with drinks also abound. We're partial to **Hot Tin** (go early, before it's a full-on scene; p. 88); **Alto,** atop the Ace Hotel (p. 78); and the Virgin Hotel's **Pool Club** (p. 79). It's a splurge, but **Chemin à la Mer** (p. 76) offers tasty cocktails overlooking the Mississippi.
- **Do Yoga in the Besthoff Sculpture Garden:** There may be no more sublime way to start a Saturday—especially when it's followed by beignets and

coffee (at the nearby branch of **Café du Monde**). A little yin, a little yang. It's Saturdays at 8am in City Park (© **504/482-4888;** p. 172).

o **Twerk in the Park:** New Orleans music accompanies the super fun **Move Ya Brass** (p. 299) twerk, bounce, and stretch classes, open to the community and held in public locales. Check the schedule at moveyabrass.com.

o **Walk. Walk. And Walk Some More:** This city is made for walking. It's truly the best way to take in the captivating sights, appreciate the silken air, and ogle (or join) the goings-on you will undoubtedly encounter. Wander lesser-traversed neighborhoods such as **Bayou Road** (p. 145) and **Bayou St. John** (p. 267). Shop. Talk to locals. Eat, drink, connect. Best to do most of your wandering during daylight hours, though, and bike or get a ride at night. Also, no texting while walking—these buckling old sidewalks require full attention, and New Orleans drivers aren't great at stopping for street-crossing pedestrians.

NEW ORLEANS' best MUSEUMS

New York, Chicago, Paris, Rome . . . great museum cities, all. New Orleans isn't included in that list, but it's a surprisingly excellent museum city. Museums also make stellar retreats when the elements become overbearing. *Note:* See also **Studio Be** (p. 174) and **M.S. Rau** (p. 237). Not technically museums, but may as well be.

o **Backstreet Cultural Museum:** Locals rejoiced at the recent reopening of this community center dedicated to Mardi Gras Indians, social aid and pleasure clubs, second-line parades, brass bands, and jazz funerals. See p. 175.

o **Historic New Orleans Collection:** A tech-forward, 2019 update has vaulted this treasured complex to the best museum list—and admission is free. See p. 162.

o **House of Dance and Feathers:** A beloved mini-museum, also recently reopened, it's an essential trove of cultural photos and artifacts from Mardi Gras krewes, Black Masking Indians, Bone Gangs, and more. See p. 176.

o **Louisiana Children's Museum:** Better than ever in its new City Park location, it offers so much hands-on, interactive fun (for all ages) you don't even realize you're also learning. See p. 205.

o **Le Musée de f.p.c.:** The history, plight, and stunning accomplishments of Free People of Color (f.p.c.) are not widely enough recognized. A guided tour of this house museum will do a fine job of changing that. See p. 175.

o **National World War II Museum:** It's the best museum of its kind. Period. Do not miss its world-class collection and interactive displays. See p. 169.

o **New Orleans Jazz Museum:** Try to time your visit to see the worthy collection along with a live performance. See p. 164.

- **New Orleans Museum of Art:** Consistently well-curated exhibits and an excellent permanent collection of all forms of fine art, housed in a stunning, neoclassical-meets-modernist building in beautiful City Park, with a gorgeous sculpture garden. See p. 172.
- **New Orleans Historical Pharmacy Museum:** Leeches and opium and Voodoo spells, oh my. A mightily worthwhile, off-the-wall diversion. See p. 163.
- **Ogden Museum of Southern Art:** A splendid collection of the art of the American South in a modern atrium between historic buildings. See p. 171.
- **The Presbytère:** The excellent exhibit on hurricanes captures their impact from all aspects; other rotating exhibits are consistently good. See p. 164.

NEW ORLEANS IN CONTEXT

By Lavinia Spalding

2

New Orleans has long been known for its jazz-infused joie de vivre; it's a place where life is lived fully and out loud. But the visitors who truly "get" the city are those who arrive eager to hear the *whole* story. New Orleans is complicated: Its joyful, high-stepping spirit emerged from centuries of struggle; it was built by enslaved people and rebuilt (and is still rebuilding) after multiple catastrophes. Learning the city's past is a path to touching its soul.

Louisiana's largest city (pop. 390,000) and one of the chief urban centers of the South, New Orleans—the ancient ancestral grounds of the Chitimacha, Choctaw, and Houma Indigenous people—lies nearly 100 miles above the mouth of the Mississippi River system, stretching along a low-lying strip of land 5 to 8 miles wide, between the Mississippi and Lake Pontchartrain. New Orleans, which celebrated the 300th anniversary of its founding in 2018, is an old city with untold layers of history. Yet it also upholds the "new" in its name, because while preserving its past, it's forever reinventing itself.

Think of this chapter as more than just a history lesson; it's an invitation to truly know New Orleans, so you can be part of its story.

NEW ORLEANS TODAY

New Orleans has earned its reputation as a hub of glorious music and food and beauty, a nonstop party with friendly locals, and a culture so deep that diving in might permanently alter you. But it's important to note that the city itself has been altered in recent years. New Orleans lies largely below sea level—its highest natural point, in City Park, is a whopping 35 feet above sea level—and that fact has indelibly impacted its history.

New Orleanians will forever mark time as "Before Katrina" or "After Katrina." While the city has rebounded palpably since then, the grim images that focused the world's eyes on New Orleans in August 2005 are not easily erased—nor should they be. Hurricane Katrina, a Category 5 hurricane, was downgraded to a Category 3 when it hit New Orleans, but the surge was too much for the city's federal levee system. The failure flooded 80% of the city, causing 1,836 recorded deaths and all forms of astounding, horrifying loss. Some 28,000 people took refuge in the Superdome, the unplanned refuge of last resort, and hundreds of thousands of locals were permanently displaced. The devastated city mourned, then began the work of cleaning up and restoring.

In 2006, 6 months later, New Orleans still celebrated Mardi Gras (albeit a smaller version). Jazz Fest returned that year, too, with one of the most meaningful musical events in the city's history. For many, participating wasn't just about upholding tradition or reveling or even proving to the world that New Orleans' spirit was alive. It was a respite from despair.

In 2010, 4½ years after Katrina, the Dome's home football team, the New Orleans Saints, at long last came marching in with their first-ever Super Bowl victory. The long-derided 'Aints restored what billions in rebuilding funds couldn't: civic pride. It may seem trivial, even disrespectful, to cite a football game as a turning point in the city's rebirth—but it isn't. The impact of this victory reached far beyond the ecstatic celebrations.

That year saw more high points: Mitch Landrieu won the mayoral race with 66% of the vote, a resounding response to the previous administration's fumbling, inertia, and corruption; and massive crowds poured into the city for festival after festival. HBO premiered its series *Tremé,* which portrayed authentic New Orleans with a (mostly) spot-on eye and a killer soundtrack. The good times were rolling again. And then, the whammy. One. More. Time. The Deepwater Horizon oil spill hit in April 2010, and although New Orleans was 150 miles from the spill, the disaster had great ramifications for its economy and the lives of many residents.

But if anything's true about this city, it's that it keeps on keeping on. The unprecedented development that followed Hurricane Katrina brought an influx of new residents and a massive tourism boom. Louisiana's visitor numbers set records year after year, and the hotel market grew like kudzu (and is growing still). In the decimated Lower 9th Ward, redevelopment chugs along slowly but proudly, with significant new developments. Other areas have also repopulated, redeveloped, and gentrified rapidly (threatening, many longtime locals believe, the very character that attracted the gentrifiers in the first place).

Yes, crime and the hobbled criminal justice system remain problems, and the city struggles to maintain and update an ancient pumping system and prevent (too-common) street flooding. And like so many American cities, New Orleans has unresolved issues with the racial divide, which flared up in 2017, when four of the city's prominent Confederate monuments were removed. Yet the next year, 2018, as New Orleans celebrated its 300th anniversary, LaToya Cantrell, a woman of color, was elected the city's first female mayor. Markers went up around town, finally memorializing the city's shameful history as the center of the domestic slave trade and recognizing the colossal influence of the enslaved on the region's development. Some 37 street names and a handful of parks have been (or are in the process of being) renamed, mostly because they were formerly named after white supremacists. In 2019, the dazzling $1-billion new terminal at Louis Armstrong International Airport was completed.

And then came . . . 2020. New Orleans, with its economy so reliant on tourism, was pummeled by the Covid-19 virus. In true form, locals responded with fortitude, community, and creativity. **The Krewe of Red Beans** (p. 52), a beloved Mardi Gras walking krewe, organized four grassroots campaigns that raised more than $2 million to feed local healthcare workers and culture bearers and to support struggling restaurants, musicians, artists, and bars. When Mardi Gras and Jazz Fest were canceled, two new traditions, house floats (aka Yardi Gras, p. 53) and "Festing in Place" (p. 62), lifted spirits and delivered hope.

The one-two punch came on August 29, 2021 (eerily, the 16th anniversary of Katrina), when Hurricane Ida made landfall as a Category 4 hurricane and barreled through Louisiana, causing about $900 million in damages. The levees held this time, but the power grid failed, and the storm took down many trees and roofs, destroyed a few historic sites, and caused catastrophic damage to the nearby river parishes.

Yet the Crescent City always springs back to life, much like the resurrection fern that covers the branches of its live oak trees. Most businesses have reopened, festivals have reported record attendance, music venues regularly sell out, and the restaurant scene thrives, continuing to win top awards. Once-untouristed streets like Oak, Freret, St. Claude Avenue, and Oretha Castle Haley Boulevard are hot spots. Stunning new "it-list" hotels have cropped up all over the city. New Orleans is one of the country's largest cruise ports, and cruises are back to pre-pandemic numbers. A massive waterfront revamp has brought the spectacular Four Seasons Hotel (and Vue Orleans, the only place you can get a 360-degree view of the city—see p. 171), a $34-million upgrade to the Audubon Aquarium, a snazzy new Canal Street Ferry Terminal, and more. Along the Tchoupitoulas Street Floodwall, a beautiful mile-long mural is in progress, illustrating New Orleans' story from its Indigenous history until today. When completed, it will be the longest mural in the U.S.

What Not to Call It

Call it New OR'linz. Call it New AW'linz. Call it New OR-lee-uhns, with four syllables. Call it New Or-LEENZ'. Or NOLA (in print). Even locals can't decide—you'll hear any of the above. But no one, save a true rube, calls it NAW-linz. Don't be a rube.

Phew. As if New Orleans weren't already pretty cool. Can you name another city in the U.S. with second-line parades every Sunday? You can't, because it doesn't exist. Is there a better street than Frenchmen for music, people-watching, and sheer exhilaration? We sure don't think so. New Orleans' indomitable spirit is intact. The oysters are still sweet, the jasmine-infused air still sultry. Bands still play in Jackson Square, and parades

Greater New Orleans

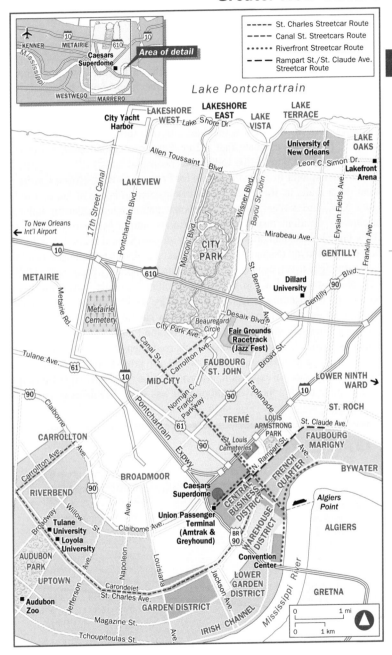

St. Charles Streetcar Route
Canal St. Streetcars Route
Riverfront Streetcar Route
Rampart St./St. Claude Ave. Streetcar Route

erupt at random. New Orleans is still the best city in America, and the *bons temps*—like those beloved Saints of field and song—go marching on. We're right there with them. You should be, too. Go, and be in that number.

HISTORY 101

New Orleans was originally called Bulbancha, a Choctaw word meaning "place of many tongues." Long before the French and Spanish arrived, the area was home to Indigenous peoples, with settlements in the present-day French Quarter, the Lower Garden District, and at the mouth of Bayou St. John. The French Market was once the site of a thriving intertribal trading grounds. Historians estimate that before European colonization, Louisiana was home to 13,000 to 15,000 Indigenous people.

The first explorer to claim the region for France was René-Robert Cavelier, Sieur de la Salle, in 1682; he named it Louisiana, in honor of his monarch, Louis XIV. (Just 5 years later, La Salle's navigational and leadership failures in other explorations resulted in his mutinous murder by his own party.) In 1699, French-Canadian brothers Pierre Le Moyne (Sieur d'Iberville) and Jean Baptiste Le Moyne (Sieur de Bienville) staked a claim at a dramatic bend in the Mississippi River, near where La Salle had stopped 17 years earlier. Iberville also established a fort at Biloxi. Brother Bienville stayed on there, becoming commanding officer of the territory while harboring thoughts of returning to the upriver spot to establish a new capital city.

Finally, Bienville got his chance. In 1718, the French monarch—eager to garner the riches Louisiana promised—charged Bienville with finding a suitable location for a settlement, one that would also protect France's New World holdings from British expansion. Bienville chose the easily defended high ground at the bend in the river. Although it was some 100 miles inland from

DATELINE

1682 La Salle stops near the present site after traveling down the Mississippi River from the Great Lakes. He claims the territory for Louis XIV.

1699 Pierre Le Moyne, Sieur d'Iberville, rediscovers and secures the mouth of the Mississippi on Mardi Gras day.

1718 Iberville's brother, Jean-Baptiste Le Moyne, Sieur de Bienville, founds New Orleans.

1719 First ships carrying enslaved people arrive in New Orleans.

1723 New Orleans replaces Biloxi as the capital of Louisiana.

1724 The Code Noir is established.

1762 Louis XV secretly cedes New Orleans and all of Louisiana west of the Mississippi to Spain.

1768 French residents in New Orleans banish Spanish commissioner Don Antonio de Ulloa.

1769 The Spanish return. A Spanish code replaces the Code Noir, and Native American slavery is outlawed.

the Gulf of Mexico, the site was near **Bayou St. John,** a waterway into Lake Pontchartrain. This "back door" was convenient for a military defense or escape, and as a trade route (as the Choctaw people, who called it Bayouk Choupic had long known)—allowing relatively easy access to the Gulf while bypassing a perilous section of the Mississippi.

The next year, in 1719, the first two ships carrying captive Africans arrived in Louisiana.

The new town was named La Nouvelle-Orléans in honor of the duc d'Orléans, then the regent of France. Following the plan of a late French medieval town, a central square (the Place d'Armes) was laid out with streets forming a grid around it. A church, government office, priest's house, and official residences fronted the square, and earthen ramparts dotted with forts were built around the perimeter. A tiny wooden levee was raised against the river, which still periodically turned the streets into rivers of mud. Today this area of original settlement is known as the Vieux Carré (old square) and the Place d'Armes as **Jackson Square.**

A Melting Pot

In its first few years, New Orleans was a community of French officials, adventurers, merchants, soldiers, prostitutes, convicts from French prisons, and the enslaved, all living in crude huts of cypress, moss, and clay. These were the first ingredients of the city's population gumbo. Commerce was mainly a matter of trading with Indigenous tribes and launching agricultural production. "Property development" was entrusted to John Law's Company of the West, which marketed the city as Heaven on Earth, full of boundless opportunities for wealth and luxury. Real estate values soared, and rich Europeans, merchants, exiles, soldiers, and a large contingent of German farmers arrived—to find only mosquitoes, a raw frontier existence, and swampy land.

1788–94 Fires destroy much of the city; brick buildings replace wood.	1812 Louisiana admitted as a U.S. state.
1800 Louisiana again becomes a French possession.	1815 Battle of New Orleans, the last battle of the War of 1812.
1803 United States purchases Louisiana.	1817 City restricts gatherings of enslaved people to Congo Square.
1805 New Orleans incorporates as a city; first elections are held.	1832–33 Yellow fever and cholera epidemics kill 10,000 people in 2 years.
1808 International slave trade banned; New Orleans becomes center of domestic slave trade.	1837 First newspaper coverage of Mardi Gras parade.
1809–10 10,000 Haitians arrive, doubling the city's population.	1850 Booming commerce totals $200 million; cotton accounts for 45% of total trade. City becomes largest slave market in the U.S.
1811 Largest slave uprising in U.S. history.	continues

Here Come the Brides

One significant barrier to the Louisiana colony's population growth was a lack of potential wives. In 1727, a small contingent of Ursuline nuns established a convent, and while the nuns themselves weren't eligible, they did provide shelter and education for many subsequent shiploads of *les filles à la cassette*. These "cassette girls" or "casket girls"—named for the casketlike trunks in which they carried their possessions— were virtuous young women sent to Louisiana by the French government to be courted and married by colonists. If we're to believe current city residents, the plan was remarkably successful: Nearly everyone in New Orleans claims descent from the casket girls or from Spanish or French nobility rather than from the colony's motley initial population of convicts and "fallen women," who therefore must have been wholly infertile. (Hmm . . .)

The scheme nearly bankrupted the French nation, but by 1721 the region was the most densely populated in the Gulf South. Half of its inhabitants were enslaved Africans.

In 1723, New Orleans replaced Biloxi as the capital of the Louisiana territory. In 1724, Bienville adopted the Code Noir, a set of laws controlling the lives of enslaved Africans and establishing Catholicism as the territory's official religion. While it codified slavery and banished Jews from Louisiana, the code did give enslaved people recognition and a very slight degree of legal protection, unusual in the South at that time. They were allowed to rest on Sundays and holidays, were given food and clothing allowances, and could petition a prosecutor if they were mistreated. Manumission was legalized, and young children could not be taken away from their mothers. The laws were meant to ensure the well-being of the enslaved (while simultaneously severely

1853 Yellow fever epidemic kills 12% of population in roughly 2 months.	1911 Razzy Dazzy Spasm Band performs in New York; another band takes its name, adjusts it to Razzy Dazzy Jazzy Band—first use of the word "jazz."
1861–62 Louisiana secedes from the Union; city captured by Admiral Farragut.	
1865–77 Reconstruction; city swarmed by "carpetbaggers."	
	1921 Inner-Harbor Navigational Canal built, connecting Lake Pontchartrain and the Mississippi.
1884–85 Cotton Centennial Exposition (World's Fair) held at present-day site of Audubon Park.	
	1928 Huey P. Long elected governor of Louisiana; 4 years later he is elected to U.S. Senate. Three years after that, he is shot dead.
1892 Creole of color Homer Plessy arrested on a train recently segregated by Jim Crow laws. He sues the state, culminating in the landmark U.S. Supreme Court decision *Plessy v. Ferguson*.	
	1939 French Quarter Residents Association formed as an agent for preservation.
1897 Storyville established.	

controlling them), but many enslavers ignored the laws and continued to horribly mistreat the enslaved.

By 1726, there were 1,385 enslaved Africans and 159 enslaved Indigenous people in New Orleans. They built the city's infrastructure, raising levees, digging drainage canals, and working as blacksmiths, carpenters, cooks, and farmers. They cleared swampland, tended livestock, and cared for their enslavers' children. By 1741, enslaved Africans outnumbered white people in the colony nearly four to one.

John Law's company relinquished its governance of Louisiana in 1731, and the French monarch regained control of the territory. In the following decades, planters established estates up and down the river. In the city, the upper crust began to develop a courtly atmosphere on the French model. Alongside their rough-and-tumble plantation existence, families competed to see who could throw the most opulent parties in their city town houses.

Meanwhile, colonization of a different sort began along the Gulf of Mexico. There, many French colonists, displaced by British rule from Acadia, Nova Scotia, made their way south from Canada and formed a rural outpost, where their descendants still live, farm, trap, and speak a unique brand of French. The Acadians' name has been Anglicized, and we know them today as **Cajuns.**

A Pawn of Empires

New Orleans' commercial development, however, was stymied by French restrictions requiring the colony to trade only with the mother country. To subvert these restrictions, smugglers and pirates provided alternative markets and transportation for local crops, furs, bricks, and tar. As the French saw it, their return on investment wasn't paying off, and so in 1762, Louis XV traded the city and all of Louisiana west of the Mississippi to his cousin Charles III

1956 Lake Pontchartrain Causeway, world's longest over-water bridge, completed.	2010 Saints win NFL Super Bowl for first time.
1960 New Orleans' public schools integrated.	2018 City of New Orleans' 300th anniversary. LaToya Cantrell elected city's first female mayor.
1975 Superdome opens.	2020 Covid-19 pandemic begins. Jazz Fest canceled for first time in history.
1977 Ernest N. "Dutch" Morial becomes first African-American mayor.	
1984 Louisiana World Expo spurs redevelopment of the riverside area.	2021 Mardi Gras celebrations canceled as Covid-19 cases surge; Hurricane Ida causes widespread damage.
2005 More than three-quarters of the city floods when levees fail following Hurricane Katrina.	

of Spain in the secret Treaty of Fontainebleau. It took 2 years for the news to reach a shocked New Orleans, and 2 more for Spain to send a governor, Don Antonio de Ulloa—who made few friends among local residents and was soon sent packing. For a time, New Orleans and Louisiana were effectively independent of any foreign power, and some proposed forming a Louisiana republic. That came to a crashing end in 1769 when the Spanish sent forth Don Alejandro "Bloody" O'Reilly and 2,000 soldiers. Local leaders of the relatively peaceful rebellion were executed, and Spanish rule was imposed again. With a Gallic shrug, French aristocracy mingled with Spanish nobility, intermarried, and helped to create a mingled "Creole" culture.

Thousands more enslaved Africans arrived. The Code Noir was replaced by a more liberal Spanish system that allowed the enslaved to earn money, to buy their own freedom, and to own property. This created an extensive population of free people of color, who enjoyed several privileges; many were artisans, musicians, and scholars who contributed enormously to the city's culture. The new code also outlawed the enslavement of Indigenous people.

A devastating 1788 fire destroyed more than 850 buildings; another in 1794 interrupted the rebuilding. From the ashes emerged a new architecture dominated by Spanish-style brick-and-plaster buildings designed with arches, courtyards, and cast-iron balconies (and, of course, attached slave quarters). Today you'll still see tile markers giving Spanish street names on French Quarter corners.

Imperial conflict among the Spanish, French, English, and Americans intensified, stoked by more trade restrictions (and more good times for pirates like the infamous brothers Pierre and Jean Lafitte). Spain had allowed some American revolutionaries to trade through the city in support of the colonists' fight against Britain, but in 1800 France regained possession of the territory with a surprisingly quiet transfer of ownership. The French held on for 3 years while Napoleon negotiated the **Louisiana Purchase** with the United States for the paltry sum of $15 million. (Not a lot of money, when you consider that the purchase doubled the size of the U.S.)

Forging a New Identity

By this time, there were 2,773 enslaved Africans and 1,335 free people of color in New Orleans. Together, they comprised 51% of the city's total population. In 1808, the United States banned the international slave trade, but if anything that gave new vigor to domestic sales, and New Orleans became a center of its activity, with human beings bought and sold all over the city. From 1809 to 1810, some 10,000 Haitians—both enslaved and free—arrived, fleeing the Saint-Domingue Revolution in their country. They approximately doubled the city's population. In 1811, inspired by the Haitian revolution, came the largest (and perhaps most-overlooked-by-history) slave rebellion in U.S. history, the German Coast Uprising. It was violently suppressed, and about 100 enslaved people fighting for their freedom were brutally killed.

For Creole society, a return to financially strapped French rule had been unpleasant enough, but a sale to uncouth America was anathema. To their minds, it meant the end of a European lifestyle in the Vieux Carré. Feeling shunned, the American upper classes installed showy new settlements across **Canal Street** (so named because a drainage canal was once planned along its route)—away from the old city and its insulated Creole society.

So it was that New Orleans came to be two parallel cities. The American Sector spread outward from Canal Street along **St. Charles Avenue;** business and cultural institutions centered in the **Central Business District;** and mansions rose in what is now the **Garden District,** which was a separate incorporated city until 1852. French and Creole society dominated the Quarter, extending toward Lake Pontchartrain along Esplanade Avenue. Soon, however, the Americans brought commercial success to the city, which quickly warmed relations. The Americans sought the vitality of downtown society, and the Creoles sought the profit of American business. They also had occasion to join forces against hurricanes, yellow fever epidemics, and floods.

The great turning point in Creole-American relations was the Battle of New Orleans during the War of 1812. To save the city, Andrew Jackson set aside his disdain for the pirate Jean Lafitte (and the Choctaw people and Black soldiers) to create a ragtag army, and Lafitte supplied the Americans with cannons and ammunition that helped swing the battle in their favor. When Jackson called for volunteers, some 5,000 citizens from both sides of Canal Street responded. During the battle on January 8, 1815, at **Chalmette Battlefield** (p. 183), a few miles downriver from the city, some 2,000 British troops and 20 Americans were killed or wounded. The course of history was changed, Louisiana was incorporated into the Union, and Jackson became a national hero—despite the treaty concluding the war having been signed a full 2 weeks before. Who knew?

In 1817, a city ordinance was put in place restricting enslaved people to a single gathering place: an open area on Rampart Street that would become known as **Congo Square.** On Sundays, the enslaved freely worshipped, sang, played instruments, danced, and sold food and wares there. Such gatherings were generally not allowed in the South, and not only did these gatherings shape New Orleans' diverse culture and jazz—they shaped all American music.

Colonial trade restrictions had evaporated with the Louisiana Purchase, and with the advent of steam-powered river travel, commerce burgeoned. By the 1840s, New Orleans' port was on par with New York's. Cotton and sugar made many local fortunes on the backs of enslaved people's labor; wealthy planters joined city merchants in building luxurious town houses and attending opera, theater, banquets, parades, and spectacular balls (including "Quadroon Balls," where beautiful biracial girls were peddled to the male gentry as possible mistresses). As always, politics and gambling were dominant pastimes.

By the middle of the 19th century, there were 17,000 enslaved people in New Orleans. Cotton-related business was responsible for nearly half of the total commerce in New Orleans, and the city housed the largest slave market in the U.S., where more than 130,000 humans were ultimately bought and

The Story of Storyville

In 1897, seeking to improve the city's tarnished image, Alderman Sidney Story moved all illegal (but highly profitable) activities into a restricted area along Basin Street next to the French Quarter. Quickly nicknamed **Storyville,** the district boasted "sporting palaces" with elaborate decor, entertainment, and all variety of ladies of pleasure. The *Blue Book* directory listed the names, addresses, and races of more than 700 prostitutes working everywhere from the "palaces" down to decrepit "cribs." Black musicians such as Jelly Roll Morton played in the more ornate bordellos, popularizing early forms of jazz. When the Secretary of the Navy decreed in 1917 that armed forces should not be exposed to such open vice, Storyville closed down and disappeared—with nary a trace beyond its immense cultural impact.

sold. Paradoxically, by this time New Orleans also had one of the largest populations of free people of color in the South. Racial distinctions within the city became increasingly difficult to determine; people could often trace their ancestry back to two or even three different continents. Adding to the diversity were waves of Irish and German immigrants, vital labor sources supporting the city's growth. The only major setbacks to the city's development were occasional mosquito-borne yellow fever epidemics, which killed thousands of residents and visitors, and persisted until late in the 19th century.

The Civil War & Reconstruction

The boom era ended rather abruptly with the Civil War. Louisiana seceded from the United States in 1861; Federal troops marched into the city in 1862 and stayed until 1877, through the bitter Reconstruction period. All over the South, this period saw violent clashes between armed white groups and the state's Reconstruction forces.

After the war, the city went about the business of rebuilding its economic life—without slavery. Lacking a free labor base, some fortunes crashed. By 1880, annexations had fleshed out the city limits, port activity had picked up, and railroads were establishing their economic importance. A new group of immigrants, Sicilians, arrived and put their unique mark on the city. Gambling thrived; there were hundreds of saloons and scores of "bawdy houses" engaged in prostitution (illegal, but largely unenforced). New Orleans was earning an international reputation for open vice, much to the chagrin of the city's polite society.

The 20th Century

In the early 20th century, New Orleans' port became the largest in the United States and the second-busiest in the world (after Amsterdam), with goods coming in by barge and rail. Electrification and other modern technology kept the port whirring. Drainage problems were conquered by means of high levees, canals, pumping stations, and great spillways, which directed floodwater away from the city. Bridges were built across the Mississippi River, including the Huey P. Long Bridge, named after Louisiana's infamous politician and demagogue. New Orleans' emergence as a regional financial center, with more than 50 commercial banks, led to the construction of soaring office buildings, mostly in the Central Business District. World War II spawned a thriving shipbuilding industry, which was replaced by expanded oil, gas, and petrochemical businesses after the war. Later in the 20th century, tourism became another primary economic driver.

As in most other American cities, the population spread outward, filling suburbs and nearby municipalities. A thriving community in New Orleans East was developed by Vietnamese refugees, who immigrated here in the 1970s. Unlike other cities, however, New Orleans was able to preserve its original town center and much of its historic architecture. And fortunately, it has also preserved the blend of cultures, races, and traditions that makes the city unique, always honoring its history—while welcoming whatever comes next.

NEW ORLEANS IN POPULAR CULTURE

Books

You can fill many bookcases with New Orleans literature and authors, so consider the following list a mere jumping-off point. Get more recommendations at the fine bookshops listed in chapter 9.

GENERAL FICTION

Many early fiction works provide a taste of old-time New Orleans life. George Washington Cable's stories are revealing and colorful, as in *Old Creole Days* (1879). Kate Chopin's works, including *The Awakening* (1899), are set in Louisiana and describe Creole society. Frances Parkinson Keyes, who lived on Chartres Street from 1945 to 1970, depicts life in the city at that time in her most famous work, *Dinner at Antoine's.*

Ellen Gilchrist's short-story collection *In the Land of Dreamy Dreams* (1981) portrays life in wealthy uptown New Orleans. Sheila Bosworth's tragicomedies *Almost Innocent* (1984) and *Slow Poison* (1992) perfectly sum up the city and its collection of characters. Michael Ondaatje's controversial *Coming Through Slaughter* (1976) is a wonderful fictionalized account of Buddy Bolden and the early New Orleans jazz era.

Newer favorites include Moira Crone's sci-fi thriller *The Not Yet,* set in a future even stranger than the present; Michael Zell's challenging but satisfying thriller *Errata;* and *King Xeno* by Nathaniel Rich, in which an ax murderer meets a Mafia kingpin in the early jazz age. In James Lee Burke's perennially popular mystery series, misfit Cajun detective Dave Robicheaux keeps the bad guys running and the pages turning.

New Orleans' Vietnamese community is the setting for Robert Olen Butler's 1993 Pulitzer Prize–winning collection, *A Good Scent from a Strange Mountain.* Maurice Carlos Ruffin's *The Ones Who Don't Say They Love You* (2021) is a bracing collection of short stories about local characters. Natalie Baszile's *Queen Sugar* (which became a great TV show) is a compelling novel about a Black woman from L.A. who inherits a sugar plantation in Louisiana.

And then there is the cottage industry known as Anne Rice, who undeniably ignited pop vampire culture in 1976 when *Interview with the Vampire* launched her now-classic *Vampire Chronicles,* which expertly capture the city's elegant, otherworldly essence.

HISTORY

Lyle Saxon, director of the writer's program under the WPA, wrote *Fabulous New Orleans*—a charming place to start learning about the city's past—and coauthored the folk-tale collection *Gumbo Ya-Ya.* Mark Twain visited the city often in his riverboat days, and his *Life on the Mississippi* has a number of tales about New Orleans and its riverfront life. *The WPA Guide to New Orleans* also contains excellent social and historical background and provides a fascinating picture of the city in 1938. *Beautiful Crescent,* by Joan Garvey and Mary Lou Widmer, is a solid reference book on the city's history. *Gangs of New York*'s author Herbert Asbury gave the same highly entertaining—if not terribly factual—treatment to New Orleans in *The French Quarter: An Informal History of the New Orleans Underworld.* New Orleans' favorite patroness, the Baroness de Pontalba, gets the biography treatment in Christina Vella's *Intimate Enemies.* In *The Last Madam: A Life in the New Orleans Underworld,* Christine Wiltz reveals a bawdy bygone era, conveyed through brothel owner Norma Wallace, who recorded her memoirs before her 1974 suicide. Before there was *Frommer's,* there was *The Bachelor in New Orleans,* a 1942 guide (reissued in 2017) for the coolest of visiting cats—charming, if anachronistic, and surprisingly informative.

Three eminently readable recent histories are Ned Sublette's *The World That Made New Orleans,* which focuses on the cultural influences of European, African, and Caribbean settlers; Lawrence Powell's *Accidental City,* a look back at the city's scrappy evolution; and the elegantly entangled *Unfathomable City,* a coffee-table atlas with essays by Rebecca Solnit and Rebecca Snedecker. Local historian Richard Campanella's works, including his essay

---

Focus on Mardi Gras

Of the many guides to Mardi Gras, Henri Schindler's *Mardi Gras New Orleans* reflects his knowledge as both a historian and a long-term producer of balls and parades. *Mardi Gras in New Orleans: An Illustrated History,* by *Mardi Gras Guide* publisher Arthur Hardy, describes the celebration's evolution. *I Wanna Do That!* by Echo Olander and Yoni Goldstein captures the extraordinary spirit of marching krewes. *The Big Book of King Cake* by Matt Haines tells the story of everyone's favorite Carnival-season dessert. Kim Vaz-Deville's *Walking Raddy* and *The "Baby Dolls": Breaking the Race and Gender Barriers of the New Orleans Mardi Gras Tradition* are essential introductions to the unique Baby Dolls culture.

collection *Cityscapes of New Orleans,* are quite insightful. Historian Douglas Brinkley's meticulous *The Great Deluge* may be the definitive postmortem examination of Katrina.

Lovers of the lurid will enjoy *Madame LaLaurie,* a biography of the notorious high-society murderess. Sara Roahen's charming *Gumbo Tales: Finding My Place at the New Orleans Table* explores the culture through its distinctive food and drink. Kim Marie Vaz's *The "Baby Dolls"* tells the story of the Baby Dolls, from Storyville brothels to their post-Katrina re-emergence. In *The Fish That Ate the Whale: The Life and Times of America's Banana King,* Rich Cohen recounts the rags-to-riches tale of fruit magnate Sam Zemurray. John Churchill Chase's *Frenchmen, Desire, Good Children . . . and Other Streets of New Orleans* is an intriguing tour of the city's street names. Emma Fick's brilliantly illustrated *Snippets of New Orleans* explores all sorts of insider secrets. Finally, check out ex-Mayor Mitch Landrieu's provocative 2017 memoir *In the Shadow of Statues: A White Southerner Confronts History*.

CLASSIC LITERATURE

William Faulkner penned *Soldiers' Pay* while living on Pirate's Alley, and several other Faulkner novels and short stories are set in New Orleans. Tennessee Williams, who lived in New Orleans on and off for many years, was inspired by the city to write *A Streetcar Named Desire,* one of the best-known New Orleans tales; he also set *The Rose Tattoo* here. Robert Penn Warren's classic 1946 novel *All the King's Men,* an exceedingly loose telling of the story of Louisiana governor Huey P. Long, portrays the performance art known as Louisiana politics. Walker Percy's novels, notably *The Moviegoer,* are classic portrayals of idiosyncratic New Orleans residents. Shirley Grau's *The Keepers of the House* won the Pulitzer Prize in 1964. John Kennedy Toole's posthumously published Pulitzer-winning *A Confederacy of Dunces* is a timeless New Orleans tragicomedy and probably the city's most beloved novel.

CONTEMPORARY PORTRAITS OF THE CITY

Tom Piazza's *Why New Orleans Matters* is a love letter to the city and a top choice for people trying to "get" New Orleans. His novel *City of Refuge* bisects Hurricane Katrina through the experiences of two families. *New Yorker* columnist Dan Baum deftly weaves together differing perspectives to illustrate the multihued city in *Nine Lives.* Sarah Broom won the National Book Award for *The Yellow House,* a stunning memoir about her relationship with the city. *Letters from New Orleans* by Rob Walker is packed with poignant just-moved-to-town observations. *My New Orleans,* edited by Rosemary James, collects essays by locals, from writers to restaurateurs and raconteurs, attempting to pin down what it is about this place that keeps them here. Fans of football and motivational memoirs may enjoy *Home Team* by Saints coach Sean Payton or Drew Brees' *Coming Back Stronger.*

For more insight on Katrina and its aftermath, *Times-Picayune* columnist Chris Rose collected his heartbreaking personal essays in *1 Dead in Attic,*

BOOKS ABOUT new orleans MUSIC

For a look at specific time periods, people, and places in the history of New Orleans jazz, you have a number of choices. They include William Carter's *Preservation Hall;* John Chilton's *Sidney Bechet: The Wizard of Jazz;* Gunther Schuller's *Early Jazz: Its Roots and Musical Development;* the excellent *A Trumpet Around the Corner: The Story of New Orleans Jazz,* by Samuel Charters; *New Orleans Jazz: Images of America,* by Edward Branley; and *New Orleans Style,* by Bill Russell. Al Rose's *Storyville, New Orleans* is an excellent source of information about the very beginnings of jazz; while *Up from the Cradle of Jazz* tells its story post-WWII. *Songs of My Fathers* is Tom Sancton's fine retelling of his boyhood at the feet of the great Preservation Hall musicians. If you prefer primary sources, read Sidney Bechet's autobiography *Treat It Gentle,* or Louis Armstrong's *Satchmo: My Life in New Orleans,* or *Satchmo: The Wonderful World and Art of Louis Armstrong,* a bio by way of his own artworks.

Ann Allen Savoy's *Cajun Music Vol. 1,* a combination songbook and oral history, features previously untranscribed Cajun music with lyrics in French and English—a definitive work and an invaluable resource. *The Kingdom of Zydeco* by Michael Tisserand delves into Black Creole music with equal parts depth and delight. Ben Sandmel's exhaustively researched *Ernie K-Doe: The R&B Emperor of New Orleans* can't help but be entertaining, given the subject. Mac Rebennack (aka Dr. John) recounts his wild life in the New Orleans music scene in *Under a Hoodoo Moon.* In *Blue Monday,* Rick Coleman convinces us that Fats Domino was more influential to rock 'n' roll than Elvis. And for a deep dive into the Nevilles, read *The Brothers* by all four brothers and co-author David Ritz.

written as he and his colleagues covered their flooded city. Pulitzer Prize–winning journalist Sherri Fink recounts the crisis in her harrowing *Five Days at Memorial* (which became a drama miniseries, as well). *Zeitoun,* Dave Eggers' gripping narrative nonfiction, recounts the tale of one man's horror and a nation's injustice.

Film & Television

With atmosphere and mystery to spare, not to mention generous tax incentives, film and TV production abound here in "Hollywood South." The city isn't a character in all of them, but it's the heart of the HBO series *Tremé.*

Seek out the stellar, hard-to-find comedy-drama series *Frank's Place* (1987–88). *True Blood* (2008–14) was filmed mostly in Baton Rouge, but important scenes were set in the gorgeous Marigny Opera House, among other New Orleans locations. The popular *NCIS: New Orleans* (2014–21), filmed on location, caught the city's lightning-in-a-bottle aura and tricky accents—with equally mixed results. Depending on your perspective, the raunchy *Girls Trip* (2017) did a better job. The creepy FX series *American Horror Story: Coven* was filmed in some of the city's oldest mansions, a notorious haunted house, and a possible fountain of youth in City Park. Beyoncé's thought-provoking 2016 long-form video "Lemonade" is also a strong local favorite.

Consider these for some pre- or post-visit flavor: classics like Marlon Brando in *A Streetcar Named Desire* (1951); Bette Davis in *Jezebel* (1938); the certified best Elvis film *King Creole* (1958); and counterculture Mardi Gras freakout *Easy Rider* (1969). A way-too-young Brooke Shields navigates a Storyville childhood in Louis Malle's *Pretty Baby* (1978).

Tom Waits bums around the city, the countryside, and jail in the indie *Down by Law* (1986); then there's the steamy but flawed (and locally derided) *The Big Easy* (also 1986). Brad Pitt goes fang to fang with Tom Cruise in *Interview with the Vampire* (1994) and then ages backwards in *The Curious Case of Benjamin Button* (2008). The Oscar-nominated *Beasts of the Southern Wild* (2012) set its powerful magic realism in the Louisiana bayous. Based on a true story and winner of three Oscars, *Twelve Years a Slave* (2013) was filmed on plantations near New Orleans.

Lighter fare: Disney's animated *The Princess and the Frog* (2009) is based on the late chef Leah Chase of **Dooky Chase** (p. 119). When *Abbott & Costello Go to Mars* (1953), they end up at Mardi Gras. Henry Griffin's wacky 1999 short, *Mutiny,* is a hoot, especially for fans of local band the Klezmer All-Stars.

All of the late, very great Les Blank's documentaries on Louisiana are worthy, but start with *Always for Pleasure* (1978). *Bayou Maharajah,* the excellent 2013 biodoc of noted pianist James Booker, also explains much about the New Orleans music scene in his day (and now).

Documentaries about the Katrina experience notably include Spike Lee's *When the Levees Broke;* the remarkable, Oscar-nominated *Trouble the Water;* the superb *Faubourg Tremé: The Untold Story of Black New Orleans;* Spike Lee's two-part *If God is Willing and da Creek Don't Rise;* and *Katrina Babies.*

More documentaries of note: *New Orleans: The First 300 Years, Bury the Hatchet, Tchoupitoulas, A Tuba to Cuba, The Whole Gritty City, Tootie's Last Suit, Up from the Streets, Make it Funky!, Piano Players Rarely Ever Play Together, Take Me to the River New Orleans,* and the Grammy-winning *Jazz Fest: A New Orleans Story.*

Recordings

Oh, boy. Well, the selections listed below should give you a good start, though we could fill pages more. We're barely even touching on the many fine pop, rock, or folky contributions (but we can't not mention the Revivalists, Lost Bayou Ramblers, and Hurray for the Riff Raff). Also check out the names listed in the Nightlife chapter (p. 209), and for more advice, consult the uber-helpful know-it-alls at **Louisiana Music Factory** and the other stores on p. 248.

CROSS-GENRE ANTHOLOGIES

There are many collections and anthologies of New Orleans and Louisiana music available, including the 1990s Alligator Stomp series by Rhino Records. The most comprehensive is 2004's acclaimed four-disc package *Doctors, Professors, Kings & Queens: The Big Ol' Box of New Orleans,* which touches all the bases of the diverse musical gumbo that is the Crescent City. The *Tremé, Season 1* soundtrack covers a bit of the same fertile, funky ground from recent years. Lovers of live music should grab Smithsonian Folkways' *Jazz Fest: The New Orleans Jazz & Heritage Festival,* a gorgeous box set that focuses on Louisiana-rooted live performances from Fests going all the way back.

JAZZ

A classic New Orleans jazz collection starts with the originators: King Oliver, Kid Ory, Sidney Bechet, Original Dixieland Jazz Band, and Jelly Roll Morton. Add early Louis Armstrong, with his Hot Five and Hot Seven bands.

Ken Burns' Jazz box covers the originators and more from New Orleans and beyond, and the anthologies *New Orleans* (Atlantic Jazz), *Recorded in New Orleans Volumes 1 and 2* (Good Time Jazz), and *New Orleans Jazz* (Arhoolie) are good choices. Baby Dodds Trio's *Jazz A La Creole* and Preservation Hall's *Preservation* cover classic territory; the recordings of Pete Fountain, Al Hirt (try *Honey in the Horn*), and Louis Prima (*The Wildest*) all swing things in new directions.

Wynton Marsalis, Terrance Blanchard, and Harry Connick, Jr., build on those traditions, and trumpeters Irvin Mayfield and Nicolas Payton push them forward. Terrific old-time revivalists like the New Orleans Jazz Vipers, Panorama Jazz Band, Meschiya Lake (check out *Lucky Devil*), the Smoking Time Jazz Club, Tuba Skinny, and Aurora Nealand are well worth the cost of a disc or a download. Pianist Jon Cleary is killing it on his Grammy-winning *Go Go Juice.* Allen Toussaint's final collection, *American Tunes,* is not at all a sentimental choice. Okay, it is. But it's also excellent, as is Jon Batiste's *Hollywood Africans.* And Batiste's phenomenal *We Are,* which won "Album of the Year" at the 2022 Grammys. (We also dig the *Soul* soundtrack, which garnered Batiste even more Grammys!)

BRASS BANDS

The age-old tradition of brass-oriented street bands underwent a spectacular revival in the 1980s and '90s with the revitalization of such long-term presences as the Olympia Brass Band and the arrival of newcomers like the Dirty Dozen Brass Band (try their monster anthology, *This Is the Dirty Dozen Brass Band*). They inspired a younger and funkier generation, including Grammy winners Rebirth Brass Band and New Orleans Nightcrawlers, plus New Birth, the Hot 8, the Stooges, up-and-comers TBC, hybridists the Brass-a-Holics, the Soul Rebels, and the Soul Brass Band, among the best of the crowd. *Bonerama Plays Zeppelin* (2019) is just plain fun, and 2013's *I Am a Brass-a-Holic* is irresistibly bumping. It's all better live, so get ye to the clubs or try *The Main Event: Live at the Maple Leaf,* or the loose, bumping *Rock with the Hot 8.*

RHYTHM, BLUES & SOUL

First things first: Get your Fats on with *My Blue Heaven.* Then get Dr. John's *Gumbo* or *Mos Scocious: The Dr. John Anthology.* Round out your legends collection with Professor Longhair's *'Fess: The Professor Longhair Anthology* and fellow keyboard wizard James Booker's *Classified: Remixed.* Go down funk road with The Meters' eponymous debut and *Rejuvenation,* Lee Dorsey's *Yes We Can,* and then *The Wild Tchoupitoulas* and *The Wild Magnolias* for Mardi Gras Indian funk. Ivan Neville's Dumpstaphunk band is keeping the funk alive, while Galactic might be funk, might be jazz, could be rock or jam—but is never uninteresting. Trombone Shorty rocks jazz, R&B, funk, and hip hop into his own thang, as on *Say That to Say This.* We're true to hometown heroes the Neville Brothers' *Yellow Moon* and *Treacherous: A History of the Neville Brothers, 1955–1985.* Producer/writer Allen Toussaint, who passed away in 2016 to tremendous shock and sadness, showed why he was a true icon and son of the city in *Southern Nights* and *Songbook.* Also get some soul crooners in, like Soul Queen Irma Thomas' *Time Is on My Side* and Johnny Adams' *Heart & Soul.* Worthwhile anthologies include *The Best of New Orleans Rhythm & Blues Volumes 1 and 2; Sehorn's Soul Farm;* and *The Mardi Gras Indians Super Sunday Showdown.* Bring it all current with multi-Grammy-winning PJ Morton or Tank and the Bangas' infectious, genre-busting *Green Balloon* (which could also fit in the next paragraph).

HIP HOP, BEATS & BOUNCE

New Orleans's distinctive hip hop and rap scene has produced numerous stars and a home-grown subgenre: booty-dropping, second-line-influenced, twerk-propagating bounce. It busted out with Big Freedia, who must be experienced live, but *Just Be Free* will do. Breakout dirty Southerner Juvenile's *400* is a classic, while rebounding hip-hop star Lil Wayne's breakout flow on *Tha Carter III* still holds up massively (really, any Hot Boyz cuts will do). The risqué rhymes on Mystikal's eponymous debut broke musical ground before jail time sidelined his career; he's out and back now. Also back is Choppa's infectious *Choppa Style,* which has fans shakety-shaking wid it years after its initial release on the album *Straight from the N.O.*

EATING & DRINKING

Where to start? Is there any other American city so revered, so identified with the glory of gluttony and the joy of the juice than New Orleans? Perhaps, but none with a truly indigenous cuisine (or two), none that lay claim (rightly or not) to inventing the cocktail, and surely none that goes about it with such unbridled gusto. As the oft-repeated homily goes: In most places, people eat to live; in New Orleans, people live to eat. Seriously, you're only visiting, so convince your tortured psyche that you can resume a sensible diet when you get home. Immerse yourself in the local culture and *indulge.* The most important thing to know? *Make reservations.* Another important thing to know: Restaurants are *still* short-staffed and yes, *still* struggling to recover from Covid-19 and Hurricane Ida; be patient and kind and tip your server and bartender well. Chapter 11 has much more about Cajun and Creole food. Chapter 8 has cocktailing info. And chapter 6 points you to the top troughs.

WHEN TO GO

With the possible exception of muggy July and August, just about any time is the right time to go to New Orleans. We love the jasmine-infused nights and warmer days of mid-fall and spring best, and even relish the occasional high drama of a good summer thunderstorm. Winter can be chilly, and in December New Orleans is gussied up with decorations, and special seasonal events abound. Eager hotels have good deals, and many restaurants offer prix-fixe "Réveillon" specials.

It's important to know *what's* going on *when,* because the city's landscape, hotel availability, and rates can change dramatically depending on events. Mardi Gras is, of course, the hardest time to get a hotel room, but it can also be difficult during major festivals (Jazz Fest, French Quarter Fest, Essence, Southern Decadence, etc.) and sporting events (Sugar Bowl, Saints and LSU Superdome games). See "Calendar of Events" below for dates.

The Weather

The average mean temperature in New Orleans is an inviting 70°F (21°C), but it can drop or rise considerably in a single day. (It can be 40°F/4°C and rain one day, 80°F/27°C and low humidity the next.) Conditions depend primarily on whether it rains and whether there is direct sunlight or cloud cover. Rain can provide slight and temporary relief on a hot day; it tends to hit in sudden (and sometimes dramatically heavy) showers, which disappear as quickly as they arrive. In unimpeded sun, it gets hot. The high humidity can intensify even mild warms and colds. Still, the semitropical climate is part of the city's appeal—there's just something about the lush, sensual air.

During the sweltering rainy summer months, follow the locals' example: Stay out of the midday sun, seek shade, and duck from one air-conditioned locale to another. August is a great time to visit museums, as the city offers "museum month" deals. June and September are still hot and humid; early spring and mid-fall are glorious. Winter is mild by American standards. Still, it's humid, so it feels colder than the official temperature, and the chill is punctuated by occasional freeze-level cold snaps. But *unpredictable* and

---

Hot Time in the City

If you can stand it, brave the city in summer. The tourist business slows down, leading to hotel bargains. On a recent July visit, high-end hotels were offering rooms from $89 to $129 (way below regular rates), sometimes with additional perks. A lot of hotels have great pools (and poolside bars), and you can often get upgrades to fancy suites for a song—ask when you check in.

From mid-July to early September, local restaurants run prix-fixe "COOLinary" specials (www.coolinaryneworleans.com), and some restaurants offer "temperature lunches" (if it's 96 out, your lunch is $9.60). Yeah, it's hot and humid, but there are always plenty of air-conditioned respites and, as you'll see below, fantastic festivals to distract you from the heat.

flexible are the watchwords. Hurricane season runs June 1 to November 30, and while severe storms are rare, the vagaries of climate change mean that anything is possible.

In the height of summer, T-shirts, shorts, and tissue-weight fabrics are acceptable everywhere except the finest restaurants. Just keep in mind that air-conditioning overcompensation chills rooms—especially restaurants—to meat-locker-like temps, so bring a light wrap even on warm nights. And pack a folding umbrella (though they're available everywhere, as are cheap rain ponchos for unexpected downpours). In the spring and fall, most days are lovely; in the winter, it can be surprisingly chilly; carry a coat and scarf.

New Orleans's Average Temperatures & Rainfall

	JAN	FEB	MAR	APR	MAY	JUNE	JULY	AUG	SEPT	OCT	NOV	DEC
HIGH (°F)	62	66	73	79	85	90	92	92	88	81	72	65
HIGH (°C)	17	18	23	26	29	32	33	33	31	27	22	18
LOW (°F)	43	45	51	57	65	71	73	78	69	58	48	43
LOW (°C)	6	8	11	14	18	22	23	26	21	16	10	6
DAYS OF RAINFALL	10	9	9	7	8	11	14	13	10	6	7	10

New Orleans Calendar of Events

There's lots more on **Mardi Gras** and **Jazz Fest** in chapter 4. Louisiana has some 400 festivals, so this is just a start. Check out www.neworleans.com/events/year-at-a-glance/ for additional NOLA fests and www.laffnet.org for others around the state. Times and dates are always subject to change. Check event websites to be safe. For general information, contact **New Orleans & Company,** 2020 St. Charles Ave., New Orleans, LA 70130 (www.new orleans.com; ℂ **800/672-6124** or 504/566-5011).

JANUARY

Allstate Sugar Bowl Classic. New Orleans' oldest yearly sporting occasion dates to 1934. The football game in the Superdome is the main event, but in the preceding days look for a kickoff second-line parade and a massive Fan Fest in the French Quarter. allstatesugarbowl.org. ℂ **504/828-2440.** January 1.

FEBRUARY

Lundi Gras. This tradition brings a free outdoor music-and-food celebration to Spanish Plaza (Poydras St. at the river), with the big event at 6pm: the ceremonial waterfront arrival of the Kings of Rex and Zulu, marking the start of Mardi Gras. They're welcomed by the mayor, fireworks, and much whoop-de-doo. www.lundigrasfestival.com. See p. 54. Monday before Mardi Gras.

Mardi Gras. The culmination of the 2-month-long Carnival season, Mardi Gras is the centuries-old annual blowout. Each year the eyes of the world are on New Orleans, as the entire city stops working and starts partying, and the streets are taken over by awe-inspiring parades. See chapter 4. Day before Ash Wednesday.

MARCH

St. Patrick's Day Parades. There are several, with dates (like the paraders) usually staggered. Instead of Mardi Gras beads, watchers are pelted with veggies, including coveted cabbages. **Molly's at the Market** usually hosts a black-tie limo pub crawl and a parade (www.mollysatthemarket.net; ℂ **504/525-5169**). On the preceding Sunday and on St. Patrick's Day, the party tends to go on all day between Tracey's and Parasol's bars in the Lower Garden District. On St. Patrick's Day (Mar 17), the downtown parade typically begins at 6pm at Burgundy and Piety in Bywater and stumbles to Bourbon Street. www.stpatricksdayneworleans.com.

St. Joseph's Day Parade. A fascinating, less well-known fete. Sicilians venerate St. Joseph, patron saint of families and working men, on his saint's day (Mar 19) with a parade and the creation of devotional altars, elaborate works of art featuring food, candles, and statues. They can be viewed at various churches, Italian restaurants, and private homes (where you might also get fed), and at the **American Italian Cultural Center** (537 S. Peters St.; americanitalianculturalcenter.com; ✆ **504/522-7294**). Locations are listed on www.nola.com prior to the event. March 19.

Super Sunday. At these annual Mardi Gras Indians gatherings, tribes garbed in full feathered regalia preen, parade, and engage in ritualized showdowns with traditional chants. The Uptown event takes place on the Sunday nearest St. Joseph's Day at A.L. Davis Park (Washington Ave. and LaSalle St.), from noon until late afternoon, with music and food booths. The looser Downtown street meeting is usually a few weeks later on Bayou St. John at Orleans Avenue. For details, check with the **Backstreet Cultural Museum** (p. 175) or www.wwoz.org/inthestreet. Mid-March to mid-April. More on p. 55.

Tremé Creole Gumbo & Congo Square Rhythms Festivals. It's two festivals for the price of one—and that price is free! This 2-day, family-friendly party in Armstrong Park celebrates the music, food, dance, and crafts of the enslaved Africans who made New Orleans the city it is. www.jazzandheritage.org. ✆ **504/558-6100**). Late March.

Tennessee Williams/New Orleans Literary Festival. This 5-day series celebrates New Orleans' rich literary heritage with theatrical performances, readings, discussions, master classes, musical events, walking tours, and the ever-popular Stella Shouting Contest. It's not exclusive to Williams, and the roster of writers and publishers participating is impressive. www.tennesseewilliams.net. ✆ **504/581-1144.** Late March.

APRIL

The Crescent City Classic. This scenic 10K race from the Superdome through the French Quarter to City Park brings in an international field of top (and lesser) runners. ccc10k.com. ✆ **504/861-8686.** Easter Saturday.

Easter Sunday. Expect posh restaurant brunches and three fabulous parades: The

bonneted one proceeds to St. Louis Cathedral in mule-drawn carriages and convertibles; then family-friendly floats roll down Bourbon Street; and lastly, drama and drag overrule decorum in the untraditional, fun-for-the-whole-fam gay parade. Easter Sunday.

Hogs for the Cause. Hogs is proof that New Orleans *is* a barbeque town. Proceeds from this plethora of porky goodness support pediatric brain cancer research. Some 90 cleverly named teams of talented pitmasters + 20 bands playing rootsy music = darn good times. *Tip:* Get tix early; Friday night is gloriously less crowded. www.hogsfest.org. Late March to early April.

French Quarter Festival. This 4-day festival, the world's largest showcase of Louisiana music and food, has become wildly popular, attracting an estimated 825,000 in 2022. Scores of free outdoor concerts, food booths, art shows, children's activities, tours, and seminars are set throughout the Quarter, making it easy to return to your hotel for a rest. Book travel early; this good time is becoming a victim of its own success. www.frenchquarterfest.org. ✆ **800/673-5725** or 504/522-5730. Mid-April.

Festival International de Louisiane. Some people split their festing between Jazz Fest and the popular Festival International in Lafayette, which focuses on French music and culture. The free 5-day street fair, held on the first weekend of Jazz Fest, dovetails nicely with the opening events of the bigger fest. www.festivalinternational.org. ✆ **337/232-8086.** Late April.

New Orleans Jazz & Heritage Festival (aka Jazz Fest). An incredible 8-day event that draws musicians, cooks, and craftspeople and their fans to celebrate music and life, Jazz Fest has been around for over half a century, and it rivals Mardi Gras in popularity. Get a full description in chapter 4. See www.nojazzfest.com or call ✆ **504/410-4100.** Late April to early May.

MAY

Mid-City Bayou Boogaloo. Another weekend, another laid-back New Orleans music, art, and food fest. This one's themeless, with the pretty location along Bayou St. John (and the rubber-ducky derby) the draw for a largely local crowd. Bring a blanket, parasol, and if you want to be on the water, your boat, float, canoe, kayak, or barge. It's cashless; buy your wristband online. And go now before it gets too huge. www.thebayou boogaloo.com. ℂ **504/488-3865.** Mid-May.

JUNE

New Orleans Wine & Food Experience. About 10,000 people attend this 3-day epicurean pleasure. Some 175 vintners and 75 restaurants feature wines and wares via tastings, seminars, and vintner dinners. The culmination is a grand tasting held at Generations Hall, but the party really hits its stride with the Royal Street Stroll, where revelers indulge their way from one tasting station to the next. www.nowfe.com. ℂ **504/655-5158.** Early June.

Creole Tomato Festival. This sweet, smallish free fest set in the French Market celebrates the humble tomato with cooking demos, tastings, a Tomato Parade, local music . . . and all manner of Bloody Marys. www.frenchmarket.org. ℂ **504/522-2621.** Mid-June.

Louisiana Cajun-Zydeco Festival. This free fest brings plenty of two-stepping, a few waltzes, and lessons for both at Armstrong Park in the Tremé. It also has art markets, kids' activities, and yes, food booths with a seafood focus. ℂ **504/558-6100.** Mid-June.

JULY

Essence Music Festival. This massive 3-day event sponsored by *Essence* magazine consistently presents a stellar lineup of first-name-only R&B, soul, and hip-hop musicians (like Mary J., Kendrick, Nas, Usher, Rihanna, Aretha, Beyoncé, Kanye, Prince [RIP], and Janet) in evening concerts on a main stage and clublike "Super Lounges." During the day, this "party with a purpose" has educational and empowerment seminars featuring A-list speakers (Michelle Obama! Oprah! Deepak!), plus crafts, merchandise, and trade fairs. www.essence.com/festival. Early July.

Go Fourth on the River. The Independence Day celebration culminates with a spectacular fireworks display from dueling barges in the Mississippi River at 9pm. www.go4thon theriver.com. ℂ **800/672-6124.** July 4.

Running of the Bulls. In perfectly imperfect New Orleans logic, Bastille Day, the famed Pamplona event, and the city's mixed French-Spanish heritage are celebrated with a reenactment of the manic dash, except the bulls are the all-gender roller-skating **Big Easy Roller Derby** (p. 205) and other roller derby clubs using plastic bats as horns. Pomp, parties, and hilarity accompany what is now the centerpiece of a 3-day **San Fermin in Nueva Orleans** fiesta. nolabulls.com. ℂ **800/672-6124.** Mid-July.

Tales of the Cocktail. This 20+-year-old 6-day mixtravaganza celebrates all things liquor. Based at the Monteleone Hotel but pouring over into other venues, it's a serious, sometimes scholarly gathering of upwards of 20,000 professional mixologists, brand ambassadors, and admirers of cocktail culture. (If you make your own bitters and take 10 min. to mix a drink, this might be for you.) The seminars, tastings, and "Spirited Dinners" (food and cocktail pairings at top restaurants) fill up fast. www.talesofthecocktail. com. ℂ **504/948-0511.** Late July.

AUGUST

Satchmo Summerfest. Louis Armstrong, hometown boy made very good, is celebrated with his own festival, held around his real birthday (he claimed to be born on July 4, but records say Aug. 4). There's food, music, kids' activities, and seminars, with the emphasis on jazz entertainment and education to ensure Satchmo lives on. www. satchmosummerfest.org. ℂ **504/522-5730.** Early August.

SEPTEMBER

Southern Decadence. This multi-day, multi-night dance/party/love-fest attracts some 275,000 gay, lesbian, bisexual, transgender, and straight participants who prove that even NOLA in September isn't too hot for leather. The annual "Gay Mardi Gras" peaks during a frenzied, bawdy, bar-studded parade. Book rooms early. www.southern decadence.net. Labor Day weekend.

Beignet Fest This one's pretty sweet! (And also savory.) Think fig and cream cheese beignets, bananas Foster beignets, creole crawfish beignets, jerk chicken beignets . . . Some 17 vendors gather in City Park to (try to) prove Café du Monde ain't the only game in town. Arts market & music, too. Late September.

OCTOBER

Crescent City Blues & BBQ Festival. A recent rash of credible barbecue restaurants might finally be changing the city's low profile in the pantheon of great barbecue destinations. 'Cue teams strut their stuff at this free fest, located in Lafayette Park in the CBD. Add two stages for blues tunes, a good lineup, a great arts market, and consider our folding chairs strapped on. Go soon, this one is set to blow up. www.bluesfest.jazzandheritage.org. ℭ **504/558-6100.** Mid-October.

Prospect. This contemporary art triennial features the works of leading and emerging international artists, interpreting New Orleans' expansive history and diverse culture in traditional and site-specific venues citywide. www.prospectneworleans.org. November 2, 2024–February 2, 2025.

Halloween. Halloween is celebrated especially grandly in this haunted city, rivaling Mardi Gras for costume outrageousness. The French Quarter is Halloween central (especially for the LGBTQIA+ crowd), where the **Krewe of Boo** parade rolls a week or so before Halloween (www.kreweofboo.com); another parade leaves **Molly's at the Market** (p. 225) on Halloween night. Other ghoulish action includes **Boo-at-the-Zoo** (last 2 weekends in Oct) for kids; the truly scary **Mortuary Haunted House** (www.themortuary.net); and City Park's interactive **Scout Island Scream Park.** October 31 and surrounding days.

NOVEMBER

Po-Boy Festival. You *could* just go to the participating restaurants any other day of the year, but you'd have to go 80 times to try each sandwich. And you'd miss the blessing of the po' boy. This Oak Street fest gets crazy crowded, but it's got some dang delish sandwiches plus tunes, and a fun locals' scene. www.facebook.com/poboyfest. Mid-November.

Celebration in the Oaks. More than a million holiday lights bedeck about 2 miles of City Park, and you can choose between a driving or walking tour (the latter includes access to the Carousel Amusement Park and Botanical Gardens, with marshmallow roasting, a "snow" area, hot chocolate, and a minitrain that lets you take in the charm and grandeur at your leisure), or you can do a combo. It's nostalgic winter wonderment for the whole fam. Buy all tickets in advance at www.neworleanscitypark.com. ℭ **504/482-4888.** Day after Thanksgiving–January 2.

DECEMBER

LUNA Fête. This incredible free, multi-night festival uses high-tech lighting, interactive artwork, illuminated sculptures, and video projections across 7½ acres of the new Convention Center Pedestrian Park and into Mississippi River Heritage Park, creating glowing, artistic awesomeness. (There's also a nightly arts market, live music, and food and drinks.) In recent years, it's drawn 100,000 fans. www.lunafete.com. Mid-December.

Christmas, New Orleans Style. The ever-celebratory New Orleanians do Christmas really well. The town is decorated to a fare-thee-well, with nightly concerts in St. Louis Cathedral and candlelit caroling in Jackson Square (the Sun before Christmas, Dec 20). The lobby of the **Roosevelt Hotel** (p. 77) dazzles. Christmasfest at the Convention Center gets everyone in the spirit (and exhausts the kids). Bonfires line the levees along River Road on Christmas Eve (to guide Papa Noël, in his alligator-drawn sled), and house tours offer glimpses of stunningly turned-out residences. The Running of the Santas adds hilarity whether you're a runner or watcher. www.neworleansonline.com/christmas. ℭ **504/522-5730.** Throughout December.

New Year's Eve. The countdown party takes place in Jackson Square and, in the New Orleans equivalent of Times Square, revelers watch a lighted fleur-de-lis drop from the top of Jackson Brewery. Fantastic fireworks ensue. December 31.

RESPONSIBLE TOURISM

Given the tribulations that New Orleans and Louisiana have undergone, one of the most important acts of responsible travel may simply be going, spending at local businesses, tipping generously, behaving respectfully, and encouraging others to do the same. Responsible tourism may start in the airport—if there's a brass band playing in the baggage claim area, tip them! The next day, ride one of the city's new fleet of biodiesel/electric hybrid buses. Most attractions are easily accessed by foot, streetcar, tour bus, pedicab, or bike. Renting a **Blue Bike** (p. 297) is where convenience marries sustainability.

Many dining establishments embrace the lake-, river-, Gulf-, bayou-, and farm-to-table movement, sourcing from local ingredients and purveyors; some even have their own farms and gardens. We love supporting restaurants that participate in the oyster shell recycling program by the **Coalition to Restore Coastal Louisiana** (www.crcl.org/osrp-restaurants). You can learn about Louisiana's rapidly shrinking coastline and restoration efforts on a tour with **Lost Lands** (p. 198) or **The Great Delta** (p. 196).

Infrastructure, fragility, and landmark regulations can make green improvements difficult and expensive, especially in the French Quarter. Many properties that suffered damages in Katrina's flooding expended their rebuilding resources just to get back on their feet, forsaking going green. That said, nearly every property has instituted programs like recycling and on-demand linen replacement. The **Virgin Hotel** (p. 79) is LEED-certified, with a goal of eventually making the hotel net-zero carbon and net-zero waste. **Hotel Monteleone** (p. 67) has also implemented a host of eco-friendly initiatives (and we love that they donate leftover food to a local nonprofit organization). And although our preferences lean away from major hotel chains, those with corporate-supported sustainability programs, like **Four Seasons, Kimpton, Hyatt, Sheraton, Marriott,** and **Loews,** are doing some of the better work in this arena. **HI Hostels** is a great choice for responsible budget travelers.

New Orleanians have become focused on the need to support local businesses as a means of economic rebuilding and cultural preservation. Responsible tourists, please remember that money spent in locally owned businesses (as opposed to big chains) has three times the community impact. **Donating to local causes** is a significant way to make a difference (and feel more connected to the city). **Voluntourism** is popular, especially with groups. The respected organization **Habitat for Humanity,** which created the Musicians Village for artists who lost their homes in the flood, offers volunteer opportunities (www.habitat-nola.org; ✆ **504/861-2077**). Or try **Common Ground** (www.commongroundrelief.org; ✆ **504/312-1729**). **Youth Rebuilding New Orleans,** which rehabs homes primarily for teachers, is geared toward teens and even younger kids—service hours, anyone?—(www.yrno.com; ✆ **504/264-3344**). **Green Light New Orleans** (www.greenlightneworleans.org; ✆ **504/324-2429**) helps homeowners make their properties more sustainable.

Groups of 25 to 1,000 can work through **Projects with Purpose** (www. projectswithpurpose.com; © **504/934-1000;** allow 2 weeks to complete applications and paperwork, volunteers may be responsible for expenses, equipment, and accommodations). If you can't give time, you can always give money: All these worthy organizations gratefully accept donations.

SUGGESTED ITINERARIES

By Lavinia Spalding

I t's easy to wander through New Orleans with your eyes wide, your mouth agape, and your hand holding someone else's (or your *Frommer's* guide). It's unlike any other place in the United States, so nearly everything you happen upon will be wondrous. You can easily duck into a restaurant or bar, or settle on a bench in Jackson Square or along the Mississippi River . . . and stay there for hours. Nothing wrong with that (we encourage it, in fact). But New Orleans has gobs of historic sites that can't be missed and countless curious nooks that shouldn't be.

3

The following itineraries are designed to help you make the most of your visit as you navigate the city. If you have the time, take our **walking tours** (see chapter 10) or sign up for a **guided tour**—see our recommendations on p. 192.

CITY LAYOUT

"Where y'at?" goes the traditional local greeting, in place of "How's it going?" "Where" is straightforward in the French Quarter, a 13-block-long grid between Canal Street and Esplanade Avenue from the Mississippi River to North Rampart Street. After that, fuggedaboutit. Because of the bend in the river (the "crescent" in the "Crescent City"), streets are laid out at angles and curves that render directions useless. Readjust your thinking to New Orleans' compass points: *lakeside, riverside, uptown,* and *downtown.* (Keep in mind that North Rampart Street is the *lakeside* boundary of the Quarter, and Canal Street is its *uptown* border.) And by all means, use the maps provided—you'll need them. *Note:* Street names change when they cross Canal Street: Bourbon Street becomes Carondelet, Royal becomes St. Charles Avenue, and so on.

Neighborhoods in Brief

The French Quarter (FQ) Made up of about 90 short square blocks in a 1-mile-square footprint, this section is also known as the Vieux Carré (Old Square). It's bordered by Canal Street, North Rampart Street, the Mississippi River, and Esplanade Avenue, with Jackson Square at its heart. Packed with hotels, restaurants, clubs, bars, stores, residences, and museums, the

The City at a Glance

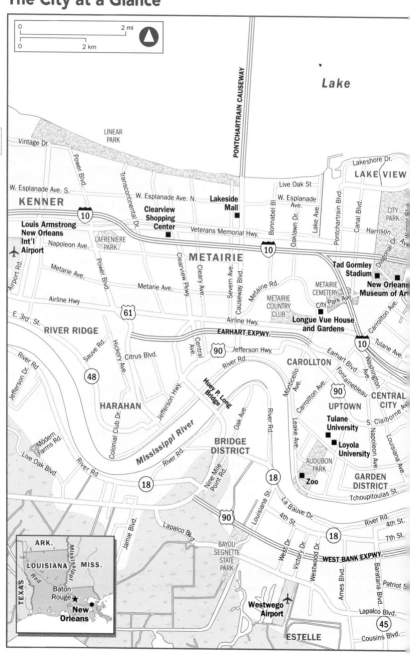

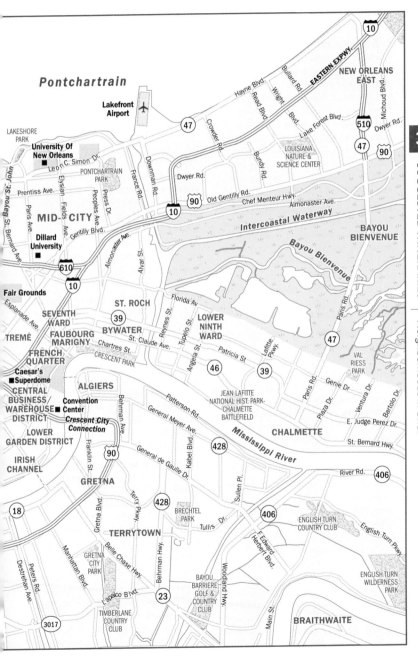

Quarter is the city's most historic and best-preserved area, and a natural starting point for first-time visitors. Use our French Quarter walking tour (p. 251) to explore it in detail.

Faubourg Marigny Bordering the French Quarter on the east, across Esplanade Avenue, the Marigny includes the city's premier nightlife center: Frenchmen Street, named for six French dudes who were hanged here for rebelling against colonial government (in 1768—8 years before the Declaration of Independence). It's a must for music lovers and scenesters. This small Creole suburb is home to old-time residents, young urban dwellers who've moved in recently, and a thriving LGBTQIA+ community.

Bywater A hotbed of gentrification, this riverside neighborhood downriver from the Faubourg Marigny was historically home to immigrants, free people of color, tradesmen, and artisans. Today, studios and old-school corner groceries still dot the area, alongside hipster bars, art galleries, upscale restaurants, many, many moustaches, and peaceful, scenic **Crescent Park** (p. 184).

Mid-City/Esplanade Ridge Stretching north from the French Quarter to City Park, Esplanade Ridge hugs either side of Esplanade Avenue, once Creole society's grand avenue (see walking tour, p. 267). Bisecting Esplanade, Bayou St. John lies adjacent to the lovely **Faubourg St. John** neighborhood. Booming **Mid-City** encompasses **City Park** (p. 183); its residential neighborhoods stretch up toward Lake Pontchartrain and include the BioDistrict research zone along Tulane Avenue.

Faubourg Tremé Directly across Rampart Street from the French Quarter, this dense 19th-century community is the country's oldest African-American neighborhood and the birthplace of jazz. For generations, many of the city's best-known musicians lived here, and the Tremé remains a massive musical incubator. Despite creeping gentrification, it continues to be an organic residential community with a fierce heritage (as highlighted in the eponymous HBO series). Once considered unsafe for tourists, it's much more welcoming now, but some sections have their share of crime—as you explore, go with a pal and heed your Spidey sense.

Central Business District (CBD) In the 19th century, **Canal Street** divided the French and American sections of the city. Today it's a far cry from its peak as an upscale shopping district, but several fine hotels, restaurants, and renovated theaters demonstrate Canal's ongoing renewal. Uptown of Canal Street is the **CBD**, roughly bounded by the elevated Pontchartrain Expressway (Business Rte. U.S. I-90) between Loyola Avenue and the Mississippi River. Here you'll find business and government offices, along with some of the city's coolest and most elegant hotels, best restaurants, and the **Caesars Superdome.** Within the CBD, the **Warehouse District,** once just a heap of abandoned warehouses, has evolved into a thriving neighborhood and lively arts district, with major museums and galleries along Julia Street (p. 167). **Note:** The CBD area is still growing; before booking, check with the hotel to see if nearby construction might impact your rest or the view.

Uptown/The Garden District Bounded by St. Charles Avenue (lakeside) and Magazine Street (riverside) between Jackson and Louisiana avenues, the picturesque **Garden District,** originally a plantation, was developed as a residential enclave for wealthy Americans. (See our walking tour, p. 261.) While the Garden District is *located* uptown, the neighborhood west of it is also *called* **Uptown.** There's also the **Lower Garden District (LGD),** lying between the Pontchartrain Expressway (I-90) and Jackson Avenue.

The Irish Channel Bounded by Magazine Street and the Mississippi River, between Jackson and Louisiana Avenues, this quiet residential neighborhood got its name in the 1800s when more than 100,000 Irish immigrated to New Orleans to work blue-collar jobs. Its streets are dotted with amazing churches, good local restaurants, cute shops, and a whole lotta dive bars.

Algiers Point Directly across the Mississippi River, quaint Algiers Point is an original Creole suburb, largely unchanged (if a little less lively now) since the boom days of the railroad and dry-docking industries. The lovely short ferry ride across the river (p. 297) is reason enough to visit.

Central City   In the early 1800s, this neighborhood of shotgun-style houses was home to Irish, German, and Jewish immigrants, alongside working-class African Americans (including jazz legends Jelly Roll Morton and Professor Longhair). Hard times fell, blight set in, and it has long been avoided by tourists. That's changing with creeping redevelopment, including the blossoming of **Oretha Castle Haley Boulevard** (aka O.C. Haley), now dotted with worthy eateries and attractions. It's an easy walk from the St. Charles streetcar (Euterpe St. stop), but to play it safe, don't stray far from O.C. Haley after dark.

Carrollton/Riverbend   Once a resort for French Quarter denizens (a whopping 5 miles away—an overnight train ride in the mid-1800s), this is now a charming middle- and upper-middle-class enclave. The St. Charles streetcar makes the big turn here, following the arching Mississippi River. The **Maple Street** and **Oak Street** stops both lead to sweet stretches for shopping, noshing, and hanging with the locals.

THE ICONIC QUARTER IN 1 DAY

You could spend days, weeks even, in the glorious, historic **French Quarter,** but if you only have 1 day to explore, you can't go wrong here. This very full day includes all the requisites for an ideal New Orleans visit: eating, walking, drinking, soaking in some history, eating more, listening to music, and dancing. *Tip:* As you stroll around, check out the building exteriors: Apart from the Spanish-style ironwork (mostly made by the enslaved), they're actually on the plain side: Creoles saved embellishments for their indoor living quarters. Many current residents outfit their courtyards with lush landscaping, so do peek discreetly through gates and down alleyways. *Start: Along the riverfront at St. Louis Street.*

Hour 1: A Riverfront Stroll in Woldenberg Park ★

Rise with the riverboats and take a walk along the **Moonwalk** pedestrian walkway (named for former Mayor Moon Landrieu), which parallels the river on one side and grassy, sculpture-dotted **Woldenberg Park** on the other. Stop to notice the public art installations and take in the sight of the vessels rounding the curving crescent in Ol' Man River, much as they have for centuries. **Oscar Dunn Park,** the platform above the steps just across from **Jackson Square** (named for General/President Andrew, not Michael or Janet), provides a perfect picture-taking perch.

Hour 2: Café du Monde ★★★

Downing a cup of creamy, chicory-laced *café au lait* (coffee with milk) and savoring beignets heaped with powdered sugar is the ideal way to start a New Orleans day. Watch this city come to lazy life as carriage drivers queue up across the street. Or take your order to go and enjoy it from a park bench in Jackson Square or along the river. *Hint:* Dark clothing and powdered sugar don't mix. More hints on p. 148.

Hour 3: St. Louis Cathedral ★

It's not the most inspiring ecclesiastical building, but it is the center of spiritual life for a town that is surprisingly devoutly Catholic (it's always

41

New Orleans Itineraries

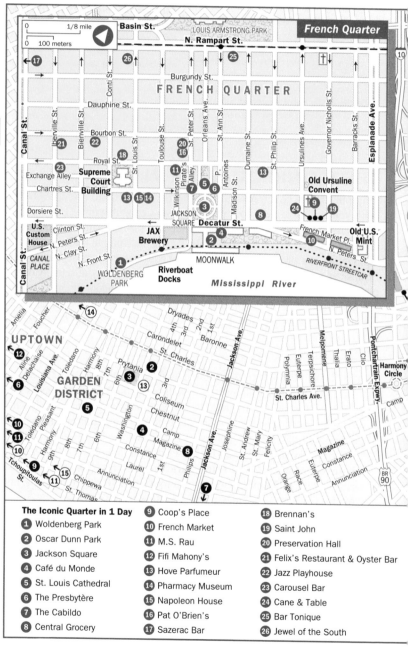

The Iconic Quarter in 1 Day

1 Woldenberg Park
2 Oscar Dunn Park
3 Jackson Square
4 Café du Monde
5 St. Louis Cathedral
6 The Presbytère
7 The Cabildo
8 Central Grocery
9 Coop's Place
10 French Market
11 M.S. Rau
12 Fifi Mahony's
13 Hove Parfumeur
14 Pharmacy Museum
15 Napoleon House
16 Pat O'Brien's
17 Sazerac Bar
18 Brennan's
19 Saint John
20 Preservation Hall
21 Felix's Restaurant & Oyster Bar
22 Jazz Playhouse
23 Carousel Bar
24 Cane & Table
25 Bar Tonique
26 Jewel of the South

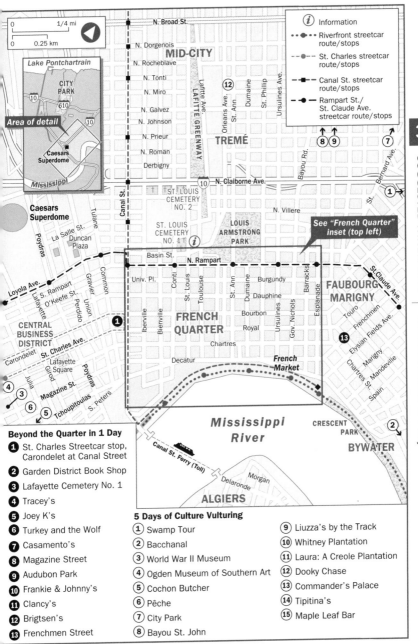

Beyond the Quarter in 1 Day

1 St. Charles Streetcar stop, Carondelet at Canal Street
2 Garden District Book Shop
3 Lafayette Cemetery No. 1
4 Tracey's
5 Joey K's
6 Turkey and the Wolf
7 Casamento's
8 Magazine Street
9 Audubon Park
10 Frankie & Johnny's
11 Clancy's
12 Brigtsen's
13 Frenchmen Street

5 Days of Culture Vulturing

1 Swamp Tour
2 Bacchanal
3 World War II Museum
4 Ogden Museum of Southern Art
5 Cochon Butcher
6 Pêche
7 City Park
8 Bayou St. John
9 Liuzza's by the Track
10 Whitney Plantation
11 Laura: A Creole Plantation
12 Dooky Chase
13 Commander's Palace
14 Tipitina's
15 Maple Leaf Bar

43

a shock to note how many foreheads bear ashes the day after Mardi Gras). Legend has it that the serene garden in the back was a favorite haunt of good Catholic Marie Laveau—better known as the Voodoo Queen. Not even the infamous Pere Antoine, sent to New Orleans by the Office of the Inquisition, could convince Madame Laveau to forsake Voodoo. The imposing statue of Jesus lost a thumb and finger to Katrina; at night, its shadow is otherworldly. See p. 157.

Hour 4: The Presbytère & the Cabildo ★★★

The former home of the priests who worked at St. Louis Cathedral has been turned into a museum housing a terrific "Living with Hurricanes" exhibit (p. 164). It's well worth an hour. If you still have time, the **Cabildo** museum (on the other side of St. Louis Cathedral; p. 161) is where the Louisiana Purchase was signed. Its exhibits illustrate New Orleans and Louisiana history and culture—including Napoleon Bonaparte's death mask. For real.

Hour 5: Muffuletta at Central Grocery ★★★

Ya gotta do it, if it's available (the building sustained damages in Hurricane Ida and at press time was still closed, but the owners plan to reopen soon). Get a classic muffuletta from **Central Grocery,** whose version of the celebrated Italian sandwich—filled with olive salad, Italian cold cuts, and cheese—is ginormous; half is more than enough for one hungry person. Eat in at the tiny tables in back or thread your way through the buildings across the street to chow down along the banks of the Mississippi (p. 114). If Central Grocery hasn't reopened, we got you: Its famed sandwiches are sold next door at **Sidney's Wine Cellar.** Other lunch options: **Coop's Place** (p. 112), up the street at 1109 Decatur, where the atmosphere is divey and the grub is solid; or across the street, any of several choices at the **French Market** (**Meals from the Heart** [p. 122] is consistently great, if not exactly speedy).

Hour 6: Strolling Royal & Chartres Streets ★★★

Royal Street is lined with swanky antiques, art, and clothing shops and has loads of pre-war architectural eye candy. Be sure to browse the sublime collection at **M. S. Rau,** at 622 Royal (p. 237)—the amazing 100+-year-old antiques store welcomes gawkers. We also love checking out the fabulous wigs at **Fifi Mahony's** (p. 242). Several blocks of Royal are usually closed to vehicles from 11am to 4pm, and myriad street performers entertain for tips. On **Chartres Street,** sniff out **Hové Parfumeur** (p. 246) and the **Pharmacy Museum** (p. 163) before enjoying a Pimm's Cup at **Napoleon House** (p. 226).

Hour 7: Bourbon Street ★

Truth: Bourbon Street is gaudy, loud, and pretty gross nowadays. For our money, if you do Bourbon, the best time to do it is at dusk, when it's neither too tame nor too rowdy. When music pours out the doors and dancers and barmen hawk their wares, it can be exhilarating. Everyone gets a pass to do it at least once. (As well as a pass to skip it entirely!) If you're ready to party it up, drink a legendary Hurricane on the always-lively patio at **Pat O'Brien's** (p. 224). For something (much) more refined, walk a few blocks off Bourbon and enjoy a Sazerac or a Ramos Gin Fizz at **The Roosevelt Hotel's** storied **Sazerac Bar** (p. 230).

Hour 8: Dinner at Brennan's or Saint John ★★★

Food is an intensely important part of your time in New Orleans, and you must dine well, several times daily. For your iconic French Quarter dinner, hit **Brennan's,** named for the famed first family of NOLA restaurants. It lives up to the mantle (p. 99). Or try new (but based on 18th-century recipes) Creole destination **Saint John** (p. 107). You've planned ahead and made reservations, right?

Hour 9: Let the Good Times Roll ★★★

Nightlife is essential to your day. Do not miss **Preservation Hall** (p. 216). It's affordable, and it's the real, traditional jazz McCoy. Late-night munchies? Head to **Felix's Restaurant & Oyster Bar** (p. 110) for a dozen raw. Still going? Slink into the swanky **Jazz Playhouse** (p. 216) for the city's finest jazz or a bit of burlesque, or **Hotel Monteleone**'s (p. 67) legendary Carousel Bar for drinks and (Wed–Sat) live music. A nightcap at **Cane & Table** (p. 223), **Bar Tonique** (p. 223), or **Jewel of the South** (p. 225) won't disappoint. And if you skipped **Café du Monde** (p. 148) earlier because the line was bonkers, now's an even better beignet-binging hour.

BEYOND THE QUARTER IN 1 DAY

You've had your day of exploring the Quarter. Now get out of the Quarter, *get out of the Quarter,* **get out of the Quarter!** Today we send you to the other side of the city for a completely different perspective. It's another full day of exploring, packed with great stuff to see and do. And eat. *Start: St. Charles streetcar line, Carondelet at Canal Street stop.*

Hour 1: St. Charles Avenue Streetcar ★★★

Hop on the country's oldest continuously operating wooden streetcar. Expect breezes through open windows, *not* air-conditioning, so riding in the cool of the morning is a good idea. Admire gorgeous homes and sprawling oaks dripping with Mardi Gras beads as you go, and remember which side of the car you sat on, so you can enjoy the other side on the ride back. Just don't expect to get anywhere fast—embrace leisure. (*Tip:* Get a **JazzyPass,** p. 298, for a full day of streetcar/bus transportation.)

Hours 2–3: The Garden District ★★★

Aside from its historical significance, this neighborhood of fabulous, meticulously preserved houses and lush greenery is just plain beautiful. Contrast the plain exteriors of the French Quarter with these grand, ornamented American district spectacles. Follow the walking tour on p. 261 or take a guided tour from **Historic New Orleans Tours** (p. 194). Start at the **Garden District Book Shop** (p. 241) at 2727 Prytania Street. Peek through the gates at the iconic **Lafayette Cemetery,** the city's first planned cemetery. One of the prettiest "little cities of the dead," it catered to Uptown folks, and has more foliage and room than others. See p. 188.

Hour 4: Magazine Street Lunch Break ★★

Magazine Street is loaded with good eats. For a cold beer and a very respectable roast beef po' boy, hit up **Tracey's,** just 2 blocks away on 2604 Magazine St. We're also fans of the fried catfish, fried chicken, and red beans at casual **Joey K's,** 3001 Magazine St. (p. 146). James Beard–lauded **Turkey and the Wolf** (p. 147) is also nearby, at 739 Jackson Ave. About a mile up, 100+-year-old **Casamento's** (p. 145) at 4330 Magazine is about as classic as an oyster bar gets; a cab or the no. 11 bus will get you there. (Call ahead to make sure they'll be open; lunch is served Thurs–Sat Sept–May.)

Hour 5: Magazine Street Shopping ★★★

Explore the fab boutiques, antiques, and galleries along **Magazine Street** (p. 236), where even non-shoppers can enjoy the quirky mix of upscale-downscale, old-meets-new. The souvenir options trounce those of the Bourbon Street T-shirt shops. Use that JazzyPass to hop on and off the no. 11 bus (it runs about every 20 min.); cabs or feet also work.

Hour 6: Audubon Park ★★

The #12 streetcar (or your feet) will deliver you to **Audubon Park,** where you can stroll the 2-ish-mile loop. On East Drive you'll find one of the city's sweetest spots of shade, the magnificent **Tree of Life** (officially named the Étienne de Boray Oak). Countless couples get engaged and wed beneath this 300-year-old giant. Nuptials aside, it's a serene place to rest your body and mind, snap some tree-hugging photos, and perhaps even spot a giraffe poking its head over the zoo fence. Up for more steps? "The Fly" (officially Audubon Riverview Park, but called that by no one) is a scenic riverside spot to picnic, laze, or toss a Frisbee as riverboats roll by. See p. 182.

Hour 7: Uptown Dinner, Two Ways ★★★

Your choice: lowbrow or highbrow. No wrong answer here; we love both. At nearby **Frankie & Johnny's** (321 Arabella St.), local families have devoured boiled seafood, gumbo, and oyster po' boys since 1942. For a very fine-dining experience, reserve in advance at **Clancy's** (p. 136), 6100 Annunciation St., a place of pure perfection. Or try to score a table at **Brigtsen's** (p. 134), at 723 Dante St., for a gorgeous meal in an intimate setting, and stellar pecan pie.

Hour 8: Frenchmen Street ★★★

Head back downtown and hit up the clubs and bars of **Frenchmen Street** in the Quarter-adjacent Faubourg Marigny. Wander, mingle, people-watch, heed the music pouring forth, and then pick a club or three in which to work your mojo. See p. 218.

5 DAYS OF CULTURE VULTURING

A trip to New Orleans is not just about eating, drinking, dancing, and admiring fancy houses (although that's a big part of it, *huge*). The city and environs are dripping with cultural coolness and historic eye-openers. Each of these day trips combines an enlightening activity with suggestions for nearby dining (and maybe another suggestion or two that we can't resist planting)—leaving time to discover the city as it's meant to be discovered—in serendipitous fashion. Do them all, or choose a couple of faves.

Day 1: Swamp Tour & Bacchanal ★★★

We scoff at those who scoff at swamp tours because they're too "touristy." Unless you're from Florida, you need to do this. Everyone knows about the gators, and they're cool enough. But the swamps themselves are mystical and otherworldly, and their ecological, cultural, historic, and economic relevance is fascinating. Get an early start so you have time for afternoon activities. Most tour companies can arrange round-trip transportation from your hotel. See p. 196.

Now that you're steeped in nature, we'll keep you outside for your afternoon-into-evening entertainment. Take a cab or Uber out to **Bacchanal** (p. 115) in the Lower 9th Ward to hang with locals under the stars and twinkle lights, enjoy a lovely meal, sip fine wine, and soak up great live music. Get dropped off and picked up right at the front door—the immediate area's seen a lot of crime lately, but the venue itself is magical.

Day 2: National World War II Museum ★★★

This historical jewel (p. 169) sprawls across a complex of buildings, each jam-packed with thought-provoking exhibits. Make sure to listen to some of the potent, personal oral histories, and if you see a veteran, volunteering or visiting, say thank you for us, please.

You could spend hours here, and you should. But you could also split your time appreciating the country's premier collection of Southern art (traditional and modern) at the stylish, airy **Ogden Museum of Southern Art,** just a block away (p. 171).

Have lunch at **Cochon Butcher** (p. 132), an upscale Cajun-inflected deli 2 blocks from the museum. Cured meats stand out, but just about everything is excellent (including the marinated Brussels sprouts).

Taste-test the muffaletta here—it's debatable, but Butcher's might just be the best in town. Or if it's impeccably prepared seafood you require, reserve a table at **Pêche** (p. 129).

Day 3: City Park & Bayou St. John ★★★

Full of nature's glories, City Park's 1,300 acres are also full of activities, from the splendid **New Orleans Museum of Art** (p. 172) to the outstanding **Besthoff Sculpture Garden** (p. 172). If you have kids in tow, visit the stellar **Louisiana Children's Museum** (p. 205), followed by a ride in a pedal boat in the lake, or a visit to the kids' amusement park and **Storyland.** The lush **Botanical Gardens** include the **Train Gardens,** a sort of melted Dr. Seuss replica of the city in miniature, complete with model trains and new *Star Wars* accessories (not to mention enormous lily pads). See p. 183.

Just outside the main entrance to City Park is **Bayou St. John,** the scenic site of the city's origins. A stroll here is one of the lesser-known, more peaceful delights of the city (see walking tour, p. 267), or plan your timing to coincide with a **kayak tour** of this mellow waterway (p. 197). Or just point yourself down Esplanade Avenue and turn left on Lopez for shivering-cold schooners of Abita and one of the city's best gumbos at **Liuzza's by the Track** (p. 123). Get the garlic oyster po' boy. You're welcome.

Day 4: River Road ★★★

To see an altogether different but vitally important side of the city's history, visit the **Whitney** and **Laura plantations** (p. 280 and p. 279). The extraordinary Whitney focuses entirely on the lives of the enslaved, and nearby Laura has long endeavored to include this history (as opposed to that of only the plantation owner). You'll need a car or tour company for this outing, a very worthwhile look at the pre– and post–Civil War eras, slavery, and Reconstruction.

For dinner back in the city, make a beeline for legendary **Dooky Chase** (p. 119). You'll not only enjoy a classic, casual meal, you'll pay homage to New Orleans' Creole cuisine queen, the late Leah Chase, who fed everyone from Martin Luther King, Jr., and presidents George W. Bush and Barack Obama to Ray Charles, James Baldwin, and Beyoncé. (Chase was also the inspiration for Disney's first African-American princess in the 2009 animated film *The Princess and the Frog*.) Get the gumbo. Get the fried chicken. Get a reservation. (And though casual attire is fine, do heed the dress code on the website—it's enforced.)

Day 5: Do It Up & Get on Down ★★★

Your iconic cultural event today is a meal at **Commander's Palace** (p. 136). Book in advance, and choose a long, luxurious dinner or a languid, martini-laden lunch. *When* you fit this into your schedule is up to you; just savor the experience in a leisurely fashion, one cocktail or course at a time. The world-famous establishment never rests on its laurels but continues to push Creole cuisine in new and exciting directions, while honoring its origins. It's fine dining done the New Orleans way: with a side of fun. Request a garden room table, and wear your Sunday best; don't hold back!

Later, check out **Tipitina's** (p. 223) or the **Maple Leaf Bar** (p. 221), both pillars of stellar NOLA tuneage (yes, you can wear your fancy-pants clothes to a club; you won't be alone, and besides, no one cares). This represents our perfect day in New Orleans: mixing high-society dining with down-and-dirty dancing, going from elegant manse to local joint. There isn't any *one* way to do New Orleans, but we can say with a degree of certainty that if you end your night at Tip's or the Maple Leaf, you've done something right.

MARDI GRAS & JAZZ FEST

By Lavinia Spalding

4

For many people, what they know about New Orleans begins and ends with its parties: Mardi Gras—the biggest street blowout in America—or Jazz Fest, the grand-mère of all other local music fests and still the best music event in the country. Here, where anything is an excuse for a celebration (there are festivals in Louisiana for swamps, gumbo, crawfish, frogs, tomatoes, daiquiris, hexes, pork, oysters, cracklins, po' boys, blues, burlesque, and on it goes), all you need to bring is a rollicking, party-ready attitude. New Orleans supplies the rest.

While **French Quarter Fest** (p. 32) and **Essence Fest** (p. 33) attract nearly as many (or more) visitors, they're somewhat more straightforward to navigate. This chapter, therefore, gives you some background, foreground, and tips to get you on your good foot for the two other biggies: Mardi Gras and Jazz Fest.

MARDI GRAS

The grandmother of all New Orleans celebrations is Mardi Gras. This massive, weeks-long (well, months-long, if you count all the small parades) street party rejoices in traditions new and old. It's the rare citywide event that's still remarkably, gloriously unsponsored and free of charge.

Thanks to sensationalized media accounts that zero in on the salacious aspects of this Carnival, its reputation persists as a Bourbon Street "Girls Gone Wild"-style spring break, drawing masses of wannabes for decadent, X-rated action rather than tradition. If that's your thang, by all means go forth and par-tay (just remember, the Internet is *eternal*).

But there is so much more to Carnival than media-hyped wanton action. Truth is, Mardi Gras remains one of the most exciting times to visit New Orleans, for *all* people, from toddlers to elders. Yes, you can hang in the Bourbon Street fratmosphere 'til you're falling down, but you can also spend days admiring and reveling in the city's rich traditions, or have a fun, memorable family vacation beyond what any mouse could offer.

Knowing some of its long and fascinating history helps put matters in perspective. First of all, Mardi Gras is just 1 day: French for "Fat Tuesday," Mardi Gras is the day before Ash Wednesday, when Lent begins. Though many people *call* it Mardi Gras, "Carnival" is the correct term for the 5- to 8-week "season" stretching from Twelfth Night (Jan 6) to Fat Tuesday. The idea was that good Christians would massively indulge while they still could, before their impending self-denial during Lent.

The party's origins can be traced to the Roman **Lupercalia** festival: 2 days when all sexual and social order disappeared, cross-dressing was mandatory, and the population ran riot (sound familiar?). The early Christian Church was naturally appalled by this, but unable to stop it. So Lupercalia was grafted onto the beginning of Lent, as a compromise to bribe everyone into observance.

Carnival (from a Latin word roughly meaning "farewell to flesh") and its lavish masked balls and other festivities became popular in Italy and France, and the tradition followed the French to New Orleans, where the first Carnival balls occurred in 1743.

The Birth of the Krewes

By the mid-1800s, Mardi Gras mischief had grown so ugly (the harmless habit of tossing flour on partiers gradually turned into throwing bricks at them) that everyone predicted the end of the tradition. Everything changed in 1856. Tired of being left out of the Creoles' Mardi Gras, a group of Americans who belonged to a secret society called Cowbellians formed the Mystick Krewe of Comus (named after the hero of a John Milton poem). On Mardi Gras evening, they presented a breathtakingly imaginative, torch-lit parade. And so a new tradition was born, with new rituals established. Mardi Gras marked the height of the social season for **"krewes,"** groups comprising prominent society and business types. After the Civil War put a temporary halt to things, two new enduring customs were added: Members threw trinkets to onlookers, and a queen reigned over their lavish balls.

As an elite Old South institution, Mardi Gras eschewed racial equality or harmony. African Americans participated in parades only by carrying torches to illuminate the route (the atmospheric if controversial *flambeaux,* as the torches are known). In 1909, a Black man named William Storey mocked the elaborately garbed Rex (aka King of Carnival) by prancing after his float wearing a lard can for a crown. Storey was promptly dubbed "King Zulu." Thus begat the Krewe of Zulu, which parodied the high-minded Rex krewe while mockingly condemning racial stereotypes. The Zulu parade quickly became one of the most popular aspects of Mardi Gras, famously crowning jazz legend Louis Armstrong as King Zulu in 1949.

Unfortunately, even as recently as the early 1990s, many krewes still excluded Blacks, Jews, and women. Anti-discrimination sentiment and laws (tied to parade permits) finally forced the issue. In a move that many old-liners still feel marked the beginning of the end of classic Mardi Gras, the mighty Comus canceled its parade in 1992 rather than integrate. Proteus and Momus followed. Proteus later relented and now parades again; Momus parties but no longer parades. Zulu itself—which was founded in response to racism—has seen a resurgent review of its controversial tradition of masking in black makeup.

The krewes of Mardi Gras change. Today there are dozens of unofficial krewes and "sub-krewe" spinoffs, and more crop up like roadside wildflowers (or weeds), some with hilarious or subversive themes. New "superkrewes" have emerged, like **Orpheus** (founded by local musical royalty and lifelong Mardi Gras enthusiast Harry Connick, Jr.), **Bacchus,** and **Endymion,** with nonexclusive memberships and block-long floats. (See "Parade Watch," p. 58.) Also keep a watch out for offbeat krewes and marching clubs like the sci-fi **Krewe of Chewbacchus,** the legume-adorned **Krewe of Red Beans,** or the severely spangled and side-burned, scooter-based **Krewe of Rolling Elvi.** Some of the best march early in Carnival season, including **Joan of Arc** and the stunning **Krewe Boheme.** And definitely keep your eyes peeled for **Mardi Gras Indians** (p. 55) and **Baby Dolls** (p. 54).

Parade Traditions

Parades were always things of spectacle and beauty, but as time passed, they grew bigger than the narrow French Quarter streets could accommodate and moved to various other sections of the city (see the map on p. 59). The largest parades might have dozens of floats, celebrity guests, marching bands, dance troupes, motorcycle or scooter (or even motorized reclining chair or bathtub) squads, and thousands of participants. Hilarity, irony, political and social commentary, and New Orleans–based inside jokes are often on blatant display on the floats and among the spectator costumes.

Traditionally, trinkets known as **throws** fly thick and fast from the floats, to the cry of "Throw me something, Mister!" (Or, in the case of all-women krewes, "Throw me something, Sister!") The ubiquitous strings of beads are mostly plastic nowadays, though they were originally glass, often from Czechoslovakia. (A tiny amount of glass beads are still thrown, and locals deem them a precious commodity.) **Doubloons**—oversize aluminum coins stamped with the year and the krewe's name or logo or coat of arms—are also collector's items for locals. Other throws include . . . well, you name it. Toys, stuffed animals, plastic krewe cups, tchotchkes, hats, moon pies, socks, and all things random and blingy and LED-blinky. Many krewes have signature hand-decorated throws, such as the cherished **Zulu coconuts,** glittery **Muses shoes, Carrollton shrimp boots, Iris sunglasses,** and **Tucks toilet plungers.**

And just as krewes change, times change—sometimes for the better. Many krewes, for instance, are leaning away from plastic beads as they embrace more sustainable throws, including items one might actually use, such as koozies, key chains, glitter, coffee beans, bottle openers, napkins, and games. New traditions also emerge. In 2021, after festivities were canceled due to the pandemic, thousands of residents decorated their homes instead, coining the terms "Yardi Gras" and "house floats." The Krewe of Red Beans spearheaded the hiring of local artists to create custom designs and raised more than $300,000 for the arts community. Some deep-pocketed residents hired **Kern Studios** (p. 169) to create giant, papier-mâché creations. Most folks just got crafty and DIY'd. The house-float movement soothed the soul of many a mournful local and gave us one more reason to love Carnival—and the phenomenon continues (in fact, some locals keep Yardi Gras going all year long). Look for a Google map of house floats, or just drive around. New Orleans always has and always will be a place where old and new traditions intertwine, and that's one of the reasons Carnival is the city's favorite season. Check **www.mardigrasguide.com** for up-to-date news.

Kickin' Up Your Heels: Mardi Gras Activities

Mardi Gras can be whatever you want. The entire city shuts down (including schools and many businesses) so that every citizen can join in the celebrations. Families and friends gather on the streets, on their stoops, or on balconies. They barbecue on the neutral ground (median strip) along the route and throw elaborate house parties. Bourbon Street is a parade of exhibitionism and drunkenness. Canal Street is a hotbed of bead lust. Royal and Frenchmen streets are a dance of costumed free spirits and fantasies come to life. St. Charles is a family affair of toddlers on ladders and kids tossing footballs down the middle of the avenue.

THE SEASON The date of Fat Tuesday is different each year, but Carnival season always starts on **Twelfth Night,** January 6, when the Phunny Phorty Phellows kick things off with a streetcar party cruise. Over the following weeks, the city celebrates, often with round purple, green, and gold **king cakes.** Each has a tiny plastic baby (representing the Baby Jesus) baked right in. Getting the slice with the baby is a good omen, and traditionally means you have to throw the next King Cake party. For the high-society crowd, the season brings parties and **masked balls,** where krewes introduce their royal courts.

In the weeks leading up to Mardi Gras itself, the parading (and parodying) begins. Adorable canines parade in the **Mystick Krewe of Barkus,** often with their humans in matching costumes. The riotous **Krewe du Vieux** outrages and delights with un-family-friendly decadence and political satire. Super family-friendly and sweetly insubordinate **'tit Rəx** features itsy-bitsy insurrectionary floats, shoebox-size stabs at the more established traditions (like those of *grande* Rex—'tit being an abbreviation of the French *petit,* meaning "wee"). To dip your toe into Mardi Gras, come for Mini Gras, the weekend 10 days before Fat Tuesday. You can count on at least 10 small-to-midsize parades, more manageable crowds, and better hotel rates.

The following weekend the parades and the crowds are *way* bigger—the massive party is *on.* It starts on Wednesday (yes, that's a weekend, when it's Carnival time), but Thursday is the bigger start, with **Muses,** a grand all-female super-krewe (and many people's favorite parade). Friday is somewhat mellower. Saturday's a blast, whether you're uptown with **Iris** and **Tucks** or downtown with **Endymion;** Sunday's day-long action is capped with the spectacular **Bacchus.**

LUNDI GRAS In a tradition going back to 1874, King Zulu arrives by boat (or train, sometimes) to meet King Rex on the Monday before Fat Tuesday. With the mayor presiding, this officially welcomes Mardi Gras day. Nowadays, there's (surprise!) an all-day music and food fest along the riverfront to celebrate the grand event (www.lundigrasfestival.com). Events start by noon (Feb 12, 2024; Mar 3, 2025); the kings meet around 5pm; major fireworks follow. That night, **Proteus** and the dazzling **Krewe of Orpheus** hold their parades, and a good portion of the city pulls an all-nighter.

MARDI GRAS DAY The two biggest parades, **Zulu** and **Rex,** run back-to-back to kick things off. Zulu starts at 8:30am; Rex starts at 10am. Across town, the bohemian **Societé of St. Anne** musters around 9am. This fantastical walking club (no floats) is known for incredibly creative, madcap, and occasionally risqué costumes. There's a very serious and sacred side to it, too, as there's a march to the Mississippi River to scatter the ashes of loved ones.

In between the parades, you can see other elaborately costumed Mardi Gras **walking** or **marching clubs,** such as the Jefferson City Buzzards, the Pete Fountain Half-Fast, and Mondo Kayo (identifiable by their tropical/banana theme). They walk (or stumble), accompanied by marching bands, along St. Charles Avenue. And throughout Carnival, look for **the Baby Dolls,** who carry on one of the oldest Mardi Gras Black masking traditions, started in 1912 by African-American women from the Storyville brothels. You'll see the Baby Dolls parading in ruffled satin skirts, bloomers, and bonnets, twirling parasols. They celebrate and preserve the history of a long line of powerful and subversive women who came before them and named themselves Baby Dolls . . . because, as the story goes, the men called them "baby." Reclaiming the name helped the women find freedom and exercise self-expression, while showing off their financial independence. In doing so, they launched a movement and cultural tradition for Black women that continues to this day.

The last parade each day (on both weekends) is loosely scheduled to end around 9:30pm but can run way later, and most krewes hold balls or parties after they parade. Some are members-only, but those of Bacchus, Endymion, Zulu, and Orpheus sell tickets to the public. Endymion's massive Extravaganza doubles as a concert—in 2022, Diana Ross and Maroon Five played to around 20,000 formally attired party people. In 2023, Darius Rucker and Foreigner headlined. At day's end (or the start of the next), expect exhaustion. If you're in the Quarter at midnight, you'll see another traditional marvel: The

pay respect TO THE MARDI GRAS INDIANS

On Mardi Gras day, keep an eye out for the elusive **Mardi Gras Indians** (also called Black Masking Indians), small communities of African Americans and Black Creoles (some of whom have Native American ancestors, others who pay homage to the Indigenous people who helped protect people escaping from enslavement). The tribes have an established hierarchy and deep-seated traditions that date back more than a century. They don enormous, exquisite, elaborate beaded and feathered suits made entirely by hand, each attempting to out-pretty the next. The men (and women, the queens) work on them all year, sewing thousands of tiny beads, in preparation for rituals and parades on Mardi Gras and St. Joseph's Day (p. 31); they're a great source of pride, and the intricate designs usually have deep personal meaning. Timing and locations of Indian gatherings are intentionally discreet, but traditionally tribes converge throughout the day at St. Augustine Church in the Tremé, and at main intersections along the Claiborne Avenue median (underneath the interstate). Crowds of locals mill around to see the spectacle: When two tribes meet, they'll stage a mock confrontation, resettling their territory. After marching in various parades, they reconvene around mid-afternoon on Claiborne, where a party gets going. Play it cool, however—this is not your neighborhood, nor a sideshow act. It is a ritual deserving of respect. Also, Indian suits are copyrighted works of art; photos of them can't be sold without permission. To find the Indians, ask locals, check **www.wwoz.org/inthestreet**, or head to Claiborne and Orleans avenues and listen for drums. You can also try to catch these fantastic cultural confrontations at **Super Sunday** near St. Joseph's Day, at parties, and at Jazz Fest. These are some of the city's greatest artists, and their culture is a treasure we're lucky to witness and experience; consider yourself blessed if you happen upon them.

police come en masse, on foot and horseback, and efficiently, effectively, shoo the crowds off—officially ending Mardi Gras. If you're tucked in, tune in to WYES (Channel 12) for live coverage of the Rex Ball—it's serious pomp.

Doing Carnival & Mardi Gras Day

LODGING   During Carnival season, accommodations in the city and the nearby suburbs are booked solid, *so book a room as early as possible*—a year in advance is quite common. Price-spike, minimum-stay requirements, and "no cancellation" policies often apply. Some hotels along the parade routes offer popular but pricey packages that include bleacher or balcony seats.

DINING   If you're planning to take time off from parade watching to dine out, be aware that some restaurants close on Mardi Gras day, so check ahead, and make reservations as early as possible. *Pay attention to those parade routes* (see the map on p. 59), because if there is one between you and your restaurant, you may not be able to drive or park nearby, or even cross the street, and you can kiss your dinner goodbye. This can also work to your advantage, however: Restaurants often have a high no-show rate during Mardi Gras, so a well-timed drop-in may unexpectedly snag you a table. Lots of restaurants offer Mardi Gras specials, and some even sell party-size to-go cocktails. You'll find food trucks, barbecue rigs, and enterprising homeowners-turned-delis along the parade routes.

CLOTHING For the parades before Mardi Gras day, dress comfortably (especially thy feets) and prepare for whatever weather is forecast (which can vary widely). You'll see lots of glitter and wigs, but most spectators don't dress up. Fat Tuesday is a different story. A **costume** and **mask** automatically make you a participant, which is the way to go. You needn't do anything fancy (though you certainly *can*). See p. 242 for costume shops or try the second-hand stores along Magazine Street or Decatur Street, and in the Bywater.

DRIVING & PARKING Don't. Navigating traffic during Mardi Gras is horrendous. Take a Lyft or Uber, walk, or pedal (arrange well in advance for bike-rental reservations; see p. 296). Parking along parade routes is not allowed 2 hours before and after the parade. Parking on the neutral ground (median strip) is illegal (despite what you may see), and you'll likely be towed. Streets in "the box" (the square blocks around parade routes) are blocked off. *Note:* Taxis and rideshares are hideously busy—surge pricing can cause sticker shock; and streetcar and bus schedules will be radically altered (none run on St. Charles Ave.). For more, go to the **Regional Transit Authority (RTA)** website (www.norta.com) or call ✆ **504/248-3900.** (All that said, it's *possible* to drive around; it's just a total pain.)

FACILITIES Restrooms are notoriously scant along the parade routes. The city brings in ever-popular Port-o-Lets. Most restaurants, bars, and hotels only allow paying guests to enter, and security is tight, but some establishments (and entrepreneurial homeowners) offer pay-to-pee passes. Some bars and restaurants sell wristbands for food, drinks, and toilet access, a Mardi Gras win-win-win. Bring tissues and take advantage of any facilities you come across. *Note: The vast majority of arrests on Mardi Gras day are for public urination. Just **don't**.*

> ### Save the Date
>
> **Mardi Gras** falls exactly 47 days before Easter: That's February 13, 2024, March 4, 2025, and February 17, 2026. (The Krewe of Oak also puts on a Mid-Summer Mardi Gras parade/costume party in late August, which kicks off at the Maple Leaf Bar on Oak Street, see p. 221.)

THE DAY (OR MULTI-DAY) PLAN It's not necessary to make a plan for the big day (or for the entirety of your Carnival season visit), but it might help. Get your hands on the latest edition of *Arthur Hardy's Mardi Gras Guide* through **www.mardigrasguide.com** or at nearly any store. Download the app; schedules and routes occasionally change at the last minute. Also download the real-time **parade-tracker app** from WWLTV.com or WDSU and queue up the city's helpful **routewise.nola.gov.** Because we're thorough, we also check **WWOZ.org** and **Gambit** (www.bestofneworleans.com) for coverage of some of the smaller and newer marching krewes. Resolve that you'll probably adjust the plan, or throw it out altogether, and that you'll chill and go with it. The fun is everywhere—but with limited transportation and facilities available, unless you're an old hand with a well-set routine, you'll have to make some choices about what to do in advance *and* on the fly. Read the rest of this section and check the route maps. Then decide if you want to head uptown, downtown, to the Quarter, the Bywater, Claiborne Avenue, or some combination of the above, as your shoes and stamina dictate.

SAFETY Many, many police officers are out, making the walk from uptown to downtown safer than at other times of year. All in all, it's a joyous occasion, but pickpockets come out at Mardi Gras, and rowdy revelers are known to go too far. Stay ever-aware, calm, cautious, and reasonably sober.

SEATING Some visitors buy cheap folding chairs at local drugstores, which typically don't make it home; others just bring a blanket or tarp. You might (*might*) find a spot to use them on the Uptown routes (especially if you stake a spot in the morning); downtown, you'll probably be standing. The longest parades can last 3-plus hours, so plan according to your staying power. A limited number of bleachers are erected along the downtown parade route, with seats sold to the public, which are actually not as pricey as you might expect (from $10 per person for the smaller, first-weekend parades; $80-ish for Mardi Gras day). Bleacher seats do sell out, though, so start checking **www.neworleansparadetickets.com** in September. Bleacher seats are general admission, so you still need to arrive early to stake out your turf. Most of these reserved areas come with designated Porta-Potties. On Bourbon Street, some bars sell VIP access to their balconies.

KIDS It may seem contrary to the common stereotype, but Mardi Gras *is* a family affair, and you can bring the kids (especially if you stick to the Uptown locales, where hundreds of local kids sit atop custom-rigged ladders . . . the better to catch throws). Many NOLA youngsters prefer Mardi Gras to Halloween. Why? The treats include Frisbees, Nerf footballs, plastic swords, hula hoops, stuffed animals, tiaras, and light sabers (pack extra bags to hold all their loot). Do bring supplies and diversions for between parades, however. It's worth all the schlepping involved, because the children's delight multiplies everyone's enjoyment. Just be sure to keep kids on the curb, safe from rolling floats and easily spooked horses.

WHAT ELSE TO BRING The usual dilemma applies: You'll want to stay unencumbered but well-supplied. Much depends on whether you plan to stay in one place or make tracks. A starter set of beverages and snacks is called for, or a full picnic if you desire. Toilet tissue and hand sanitizer are good ideas; don't forget a bag or backpack for those beads. Bring a hat and sunglasses. Locals often stake a spot in or near a favorite bar along Magazine Street or St. Charles Avenue, for drinks and restroom use.

How to Spend the Big Day

Your Carnival experience will depend on where you go and whom you hang out with. Here are three ways to do it: family style, costume party, and tourist trap. Us? We prefer the first two, traversed on two wheels.

FAMILY STYLE   Hang out exclusively Uptown with the families. Find a spot on St. Charles Avenue (which is closed to traffic that day) between Napoleon Avenue and Lee Circle and set up camp with a blanket and a picnic lunch for **Rex,** the walking clubs, and truck parades. Costumed families are all around. One side of St. Charles is for the parades and the other is open only to foot traffic, so you can wander about, admire the scene, and angle for an invitation to a barbecue or balcony party. The one downside is you may miss **Zulu,** which traditionally marches downriver; staking out a spot downtown is another option, but the crowds there are a bit thicker and rowdier. (In-between option: post up in the Lower Garden District, near **Avenue Pub,** p. 227.) For an utterly different experience, head to Claiborne Avenue at St. Bernard around 9am and look for the **Mardi Gras Indian** tribes' meeting (p. 55). It's a hit-or-miss proposition; the Indians themselves may not know in advance when or where the gatherings occur. But running across them on their own turf is one of the great sights and experiences of Mardi Gras.

COSTUME PARTY   Dress up (*at least* wear a wig), and rise early to be in the Tremé before dawn for the wake-up call of the **Northside Skull and Bones Gang,** who mask as skeletons and spread words of wisdom and cautionary tales. Around mid-morning, track down the **Societé de Sainte Anne:** no floats, just wildly creative, costumed revelers. At noon, try to be near the corner of Burgundy and St. Ann streets for the **Bourbon Street** awards. You may not get close enough to actually see the judging, but participants sporting all form of human expression (and sexuality) are everywhere, so you can gawk at their inventive, sometimes R- and X-rated costumes. It's boisterous and enthusiastic, but not (for the most part) obnoxious. Afterward, head to **Frenchmen Street,** where dancing and drum circles celebrate Carnival well into the night.

TOURIST TRAP   Despite the popular impression of Mardi Gras, the parades don't even go down **Bourbon Street,** but it has its own trademark action— and yep, it's every bit as crowded, booze-soaked, pee-smelling, and vulgar as you've heard. There are no fabulous floats. Instead, every square of street and overhanging balcony is packed with partiers. Those balcony dwellers pack piles of beads (some with X-rated anatomical features) ready to toss down in exchange for a glimpse of flesh (flashing is technically illegal). It's anything goes, which works for this crowd. It can also grow old fast; try starting with semi-madness on the parade route in the Central Business District and migrating later to the full madness of Bourbon Street, or vice-versa.

Parade Watch

A Mardi Gras parade works a spell on people. There's no other way to explain why thousands of otherwise rational grownups scream, plead, jostle, and sometimes (again, just on Bourbon St.) expose themselves for a plastic trinket. Nobody goes home empty-handed (even the trees end up laden with glittery goods), so don't forget to actually look at the amazing floats.

Major Mardi Gras Parade Routes

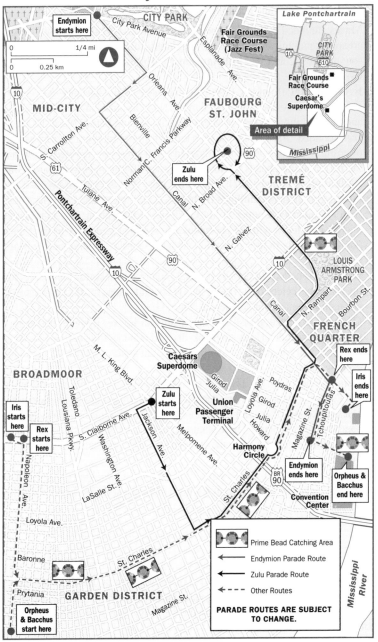

Below are just some of the major parades of the last days of Carnival. See the route map on p. 59, and check **www.mardigrasguide.com** for updated information on schedule and route changes.

o **Muses** (founded 2000): This popular all-gals krewe honors New Orleans' artistic community—and shoes. Its glittery, decorated pumps are highly sought throws, and its floats are superb. Thursday evening before Mardi Gras.

o **Krewe d'Etat** (founded 1996): Social satire is its specialty. No current event is left unscathed, and its hilarious float designs can fuel water-cooler and barstool discussions for weeks. Friday evening before Mardi Gras.

o **Iris** (founded 1917): This women's krewe follows traditional Carnival rules of costume and behavior. Its bedazzled sunglasses are a coveted throw, and the pastel-colored beads are lovely. Saturday afternoon before Mardi Gras.

o **Endymion** (founded 1967): One of the early 1970s "superkrewes," it features a glut of floats, millions of throws, 3,200 riders, and celebrity guests such as Anderson Cooper, Kelly Clarkson, Dolly Parton, and John Goodman. It concludes with an enormous black-tie party, usually in the Superdome (but lately in the convention center). Saturday evening before Mardi Gras.

o **Bacchus** (founded 1968): The original "superkrewe," it was the first to host international celebrities. Traditionally Bacchus runs from Uptown to the convention center. Sunday before Mardi Gras.

o **Orpheus** (founded 1993): Another youngish krewe, it was founded by a group that includes Harry Connick, Jr., and adheres to classic krewe traditions. Popular for its many stunning floats and generous throws. Lundi Gras evening.

o **Zulu** (founded 1916): The city's first African-American club to parade, Zulu's lively float riders are decked out in woolly wigs, grass skirts, and black makeup. Riders carry the most prized Mardi Gras souvenirs: glittery hand-painted coconuts. These status symbols must be placed in your hands, not tossed, so go right up to the float and do your best begging. Mardi Gras morning.

o **Rex** (founded 1872): Rex follows Zulu and various walking clubs down St. Charles. It features the King of Carnival and classic floats. Mardi Gras day.

Cajun Mardi Gras

For an entirely different experience, take the 2½- to 3-hour drive out to Cajun Country, where Mardi Gras traditions are just as strong but considerably more, er, traditional. **Lafayette** celebrates Carnival in a manner that reflects the Cajun heritage and spirit. The 3-day event is second in size only to New Orleans', with parades and floats and beads a-plenty, and the final pageant and ball are free and open to the general public. Don your formal wear and join right in!

MASKED MEN & A BIG GUMBO   In towns like Eunice and Mamou in the Cajun countryside, the Courir de Mardi Gras celebration is tied to the traditional French rural lifestyle. Bands of masked men (and women, now) dressed in raggedy patchwork costumes and peaked *capichon* hats set off on Mardi Gras morning on horseback, led by their *capitaine.* They ride from farm to farm, asking at each, *"Voulez-vous reçevoir le Mardi Gras?"* ("Will you receive the Mardi Gras?"). *"Oui,"* comes the invariable reply. Each farmyard then becomes a miniature festival of song, dance, antics, and much beer. As payment for their pageantry, they get "a fat little chicken to make a big gumbo" (or sometimes a bag of rice or other ingredients).

All meet back in town, where cooking, dancing, storytelling, and general merriment continue into the wee hours, and yes, there is indeed a very big pot of gumbo. Some are private events, but your best bet for particulars comes from the **Lafayette Convention & Visitors Commission** (www.lafayettetravel.com; ℂ **800/346-1958** in the U.S., 800/543-5340 in Canada, or 337/232-3737).

NEW ORLEANS JAZZ & HERITAGE FESTIVAL

What began in 1970 as a small gathering in Congo Square to celebrate the music and culture of New Orleans now ranks as one of the best attended, most respected, and most musically comprehensive festivals in the world, with more than 600 bands performing. Although everyone calls it Jazz Fest, the full name is **New Orleans Jazz & Heritage Festival.** The "Jazz" part hardly represents the scope of the musical fare. Each of the dozen or so stages spread around the mile-long Fair Grounds' horse-racing track showcases a musical genre or three. The "Heritage" part is why this fest rises above all others: 50+ years on, Jazz Fest remains rooted in its rich cultural traditions, while bringing new energy each year. If you've never attended, you can get a taste of what makes it so special by watching the Grammy-winning documentary *Jazz Fest, a New Orleans Story.*

Jazz Fest encompasses everything the city has to offer, in terms of music, food, and culture. That, and it's a hell of a party (even for kids and grandparents, since it takes place from 11am to 7pm). While headliners such as Lizzo, Ed Sheeran, Robert Plant, H.E.R., Ne-Yo, Jon Batiste, Alison Krauss, Santana, Mavis Staples, Dead & Company, The Lumineers, Jill Scott, Trombone Shorty, Ludacris, Mumford and Sons, and Galactic (just a handful of performers in 2023) draw huge crowds, serious Festers also savor the lesser-known acts, about 85% of which are Louisianan. They range from old-time Delta bluesmen, African artists making rare U.S. appearances, and avant-garde acts to street folkies, top zydeco players, and gospel choirs. And, of course, jazz in its many forms.

Filling the infield and outlying areas of the Fair Grounds' horse-racing track near City Park, the festival covers 2 long weekends, the last in April and the first in May. While Jazz Fest doesn't release the exact dates until closer to each Festival, the 2024 dates are suspected to be April 26 through May 5, and for 2025, April 25 through May 4. It's set up as well as a large event can be, with plenty of space to move about. Folks are friendly, and spirits stay high. And the music doesn't stop when the gates close; there are *hundreds* of stellar nighttime shows, all over town, all night long. Be it a hotspot or hole-in-the-wall, you never know what legendary artist might sit in with a musician pal and rock your world.

Musical and emotional epiphanies abound here. In 2006, after Shell Oil sponsored Jazz Fest's uncertain return after Katrina, a triumphant set by Bruce Springsteen sealed its resurrection. (Watch his powerful performance of "My City of Ruins" on YouTube. Bet ya cry. We did.) And even in 2020, when the pandemic caused Jazz Fest to be canceled for the first time in half a century, the music didn't stop. WWOZ, the beloved local community radio station, instituted "Festing in Place," airing past Jazz Fest shows that could be heard from open windows and doors in every neighborhood.

As for the **nonmusical aspects of Jazz Fest,** they're plentiful and exceptional. Hundreds of local craftspeople and juried artisans fill a huge area with artwork and products for show, demonstration, and purchase. Most vendors will pack and ship goods to your home (and there's a U.S. post office on-site, too). Some of the coolest experiences on the Jazz Fest grounds involve digging into New Orleans' heritage. In the **Louisiana Folklife Village,** artisans showcase their gorgeous work; in **Congo Square,** there's music, art, and culture from the African diaspora; in the **Native American Village,** Indigenous heritage is celebrated through dance, music, and food; and the **Cultural Exchange Pavilion** features bands from around the world. Meanwhile, experienced fest-goers know to duck into the **Grandstand** for art and folklore exhibits, cooking demonstrations, air-conditioning, a hideaway music stage, and (wait for it) **real bathrooms.** The upstairs **Allison Miner Music Heritage Stage** features interviews and short performances by top acts in a much more intimate setting.

And as always in New Orleans, there's food. Expect local standbys—not burgers and pizza but red beans and rice, jambalaya, étouffée, and gumbo. A few favorites are *cochon de lait* (a mouthwatering roast-pig sandwich); a fried softshell crab po' boy; quail and pheasant gumbo; buttery, crab-topped trout Bacquet; Ms. Linda's Ya-Ka-Mein; and all manner of oysters and crawfish—not to mention the various global or vegetarian dishes, or the desserts. (Don't skip the Mango Freeze—besides the icy deliciousness, sales benefit WWOZ.) Food ranges about $8 to $16. The terrific kids' area has PB&J, mac 'n' cheese, and other kid-pleasers. Try at least one new thing daily, and share, so you can sample more variety. At peak times, lines at the most popular of the 60-ish food booths look long, but they move quickly, and it's invariably worth any wait. *Tip #1:* There's copious cold beer, but those lines can be long. Smaller stages = shorter lines, and it's often worth it to trek there. *Tip #2:* Many hours of sun + many beers = premature crash.

Attending Jazz Fest means making some tough decisions. Hotels, restaurants, and flights fill up months (if not a year) in advance, but the schedule is not announced until a couple of months before the event. So reserving travel requires a leap of faith. Truth be told, every day at Jazz Fest is a good day regardless of who's playing. (Avoid the dilemma by attending both weekends.) The Thursday before the second weekend traditionally has more locals, on stage and in the audience, and smaller crowds. It's a great time to hit the most popular food booths and check out crafts areas.

Jazz Fest Pointers

"It's a marathon, not a sprint," as the saying goes. With music in every direction, you can plot out your day or just wander from stage to stage, catching a few songs by various acts—some of the best Jazz Fest experiences come from stumbling across an undiscovered musical gem. Or you can set up camp at one stage—from the big ones with famous headliners to the gospel tent, where musical miracles are pretty much a given. Everyone experiences *some* FOMO, so stage-hopping is standard (and again, many performers can be heard around town after hours). It's like choosing sit-down dining versus a buffet: Both have advantages, but the offerings are all incredible, so you really can't lose.

At your hotel, or as you're walking to the Fair Grounds, grab a free *Offbeat, Gambit,* or *Where Y'at* magazine (they're dispensed everywhere). You'll need the schedule "cubes" and performer descriptions. Also download the Jazz Fest and Offbeat apps. The official Fest program (available on-site; in 2022 it cost $10) also has the schedule, plus food coupons.

On a typical Jazz Fest day, arrive sometime after the gates open at 11am and stay until you are pooped or when they close at 7pm. The whole thing usually runs as efficiently as a Swiss train. After you leave, get some dinner and hit the town to pack in more music. (See chapter 8 for details.) Every venue in the city has top-notch bookings—of note are the late-night blow-outs at **Tipitina's** and intimate sets at **Preservation Hall.** Also, **Piano Night** at the House of Blues, the jam-heavy shows produced by **NolaFunk** (nolafunk.com), **Winter Circle** (wintercircleproductions.com), and **Backbeat** (backbeatfoundation.org). The **Jazz Fest Grids** (jazzfestgrids.com) is a very handy aggregate of the evening music options. You can also just listen to WWOZ and check out its music calendar (www.wwoz.org/calendar/livewire-music). Attending both weekends or have an extended stay? Consider getting tickets to **Daze Between New Orleans** at **Faubourg Brewery** (p. 229), a 2-day event between the two weekends,

Wear and bring as little as possible; you'll want to be comfy and unencumbered. Do pack sun protection—sunglasses and a wide-brimmed sunhat will be your best friends—and a poncho if rain is forecast (they sell them there, but at twice what you'll pay at a souvenir store), along with something that tells time, something that takes photos, and your credit cards—**the Fest has gone cashless**. (Festgoers who come with only cash can exchange for a prepaid credit card at booths on the Fair Grounds.) Wear supportive, well-broken-in shoes that you're willing to sacrifice to dirt or mud. Flip-flops + mud = fail. If serious rain or mud is forecast, lightweight waterproof boots are your saviors. This isn't the most fashion-forward event: dress fun and festive and you'll fit right in. Think shorts, tank tops, sundresses, and breathable cotton. Also, consider avoiding white pants or shoes—it's a dirt track, after all. The only beverage you can bring in is water, in an unopened bottle (one liter bottle per person maximum).

There are seats in the tented stages. Outside, a few of the bigger stages have a small VIP pit area; behind that is a standing-only (no-chair) zone; then grass. The two largest stages have bleachers way back. Generally, people stand or sit on the ground, a blanket, or a folding chair where allowed. When left vacant, these become annoying space hogs. Kind Fest-goers invite others to use their space when they leave temporarily—don't be shy about asking. VIPs also get covered, raised seating areas.

TICKETS   Purchase tickets right when they go on sale (generally after the start of the new year, when the lineup is announced); they're cheapest then. Tickets are available through www.nojazzfest.com or usually at the gate on festival days. Daily admission for adults ranges around $80 to $95 (ages 2–10 get in for $5); buy in advance online to get the best deals. Three-day weekend passes run $225 to $240; passes for the second 4-day weekend run $275 to $290. A lot of locals pony up for the $850 Brass Pass (available on www.wwoz.org), which not only covers admission for all 7 days of the festival but also generously supports beloved local radio station WWOZ. Various VIP packages, purchased by weekend, also come with a range of swanky seating, access, and amenities, from the $850 (or $950 for the second weekend) Krewe of Jazz Fest package to the $1,750 ($1,850 for the second weekend) Big Chief VIP pass. All sell out, so order early. For details, contact **New Orleans Jazz & Heritage Festival** (www.nojazzfest.com; ☏ **504/410-4100**).

PARKING & TRANSPORTATION   The only parking *at* the Fair Grounds is for VIP ticket holders to purchase or for people with disabilities, at $50 a day, first-come, first-served. E-mail access@nojazzfest.com or contact ☏ **504/410-6104.** Enterprising neighbors and nearby schools and businesses provide parking in their driveways or lots at $25 a day and up. Most people take public transportation or a shuttle. The **Regional Transit Authority** operates bus routes to the Fair Grounds from various pickup points; for schedules, contact ☏ **504/248-3900** (www.norta.com). Taxis, though busy and a bit harder to come by these days, charge a special-event rate to and from the Fair Grounds of $7 per person or the meter reading, whichever is higher (see p. 295). (All other fares around town, and to the airport, etc., remain unchanged.) Uber and Lyft are also in operation; expect surge rates, but if split among a few passengers it may even out. Gray Line's **Jazz Fest Express** (nojazzfest.com/official-shuttle; ☏ **800/233-2628** or 504/569-1401) operates shuttles from the steamboat *Natchez* dock in the French Quarter, the Sheraton at 500 Canal St., and Wisner Lot at City Park. You must have a Jazz Fest ticket to ride; shuttle tickets cost $24 round-trip or $61 and $82 respectively for weekend tickets. *Note:* The **Canal Street streetcar line** will be packed, but it's an option from the Quarter. Take cars destined for "City Park," not "Cemeteries." Fare is $1.25 (or 40¢ for seniors and 50¢ for kids 5-19) or use your multi-day **Jazzy-Pass** (p. 298). All these options have designated drop-off and pick-up locations outside the Fair Grounds. **Bicycling** is a great way to get to Jazz Fest (see p. 296 for rental info). Bike parking lots are located near the Gentilly and Sauvage streets entrances, and a few hundred pedal-assist Blue Bikes (p. 297) are usually available to rent, too (register through the mobile app in advance).

PACKAGE DEALS Check the "Travel" section of the Jazz Fest website for "On Location" package deals that include hotel accommodations, general admission or VIP festival tickets, and shuttle tickets to get you there. **Festival Tours International** (www.festival-tours.com; ✆ **310/749-2035**) offers a tour that includes accommodations and tickets to Jazz Fest, plus a midweek visit to Cajun Country for unique personal encounters with leading local musicians. In 2023 the tour included a crawfish boil with the Savoys (reigning first family of Cajun music), a bayou lunch and swamp tour, a barbecue and barn dance at zydeco master Geno Delafose's ranch, private Cajun dance lessons, a cooking class and gourmet lunch, and lots more. The company has been around since 1982. Their "nontours," which are filled with music lovers, are positively stellar. Tours start at around $2,500 but deliver a lot for the price.

4

New Orleans Jazz & Heritage Festival

WHERE TO STAY

By Lavinia Spalding

Accommodations in New Orleans range from your basic lodger to over-the-top luxurious: Like the city itself, there's something for every preference. Prices also vary widely. During the Covid years, many properties underwent extensive renovations or changed hands, and now it's a bit harder to find a bargain. They exist, though. Summer and winter are the best times to snag deals (and avoid 2- to 3-night minimum stays), especially when you purchase in advance (no canceling allowed). And of course, midweek stays are *way* cheaper than weekend. Note that the rates we list below don't reflect spikes during festival weekends, which can easily triple or quadruple regular rates. Book *super* early for those.

Note that while many hotels have restaurants, bars, gyms, and other bonuses, others have scant amenities. If perks are paramount to your lodging experience, we recommend calling to ask what's available. Why not just check the website, you ask? Because (trust us on this) many local businesses don't bother keeping websites updated. Best to chat with a real human!

If you're budget-conscious, consider staying outside the French Quarter or CBD, in neighborhoods where street parking may be available—parking fees can raise your day rate considerably (up to $50–$60 per day) and may not include ins-and-outs. Also be aware that by law, **all hotels are now nonsmoking,** although some provide an outdoor smoking area. *Note:* Loads of chain hotels exist in NOLA. You won't find many in this book, since we prefer smaller operations with local charm. But if chains are your preference, **Drury Plaza** (✆ **504/529-7800**) and **Homewood Suites** (✆ **504/581-5599**) are good.

FRENCH QUARTER

Called the Vieux Carré (Old Square), this is the picturesque soul of the city that most people envision. Visitors walk out of their hotels and feel wholly transported to the late 17th and early 18th centuries, when the French Quarter was built. In the Quarter, you're ensconced in the total N.O. experience—from serene to sybaritic.

(That said, there's some construction nowadays, so before you book, call to ask if you'll be in the middle of it. Also, you may prefer to play there than stay there, as quieter, cleaner, less expensive neighborhoods are plentiful.)

Best for: First-time visitors; short-term visitors; historians; architecture buffs; photographers; shoppers; foodies; partiers; travelers without cars.

Drawbacks: It can be bustling with tourists and goings-on. It's generally pricier than other areas, and parking can *seriously* add to the wallop.

Expensive

Audubon Cottages ★★★   Liz Taylor was once a guest here, and it still feels as if you're staying at her home (if she had lived in a sublime warren of 18th-century apartments). A subtly marked gate and leaf-canopied pathway lead to seven ultra-private one- and two-bedroom cottages with large courtyards (some private, some shared). Each is gracefully but not overly antiqued amid gorgeous brick walls and gleaming hardwood floors. The cottages surround a brick-lined heated swimming pool, and it's all attended to by an on-site butler. It's easy to imagine naturalist John James Audubon watching birds alight from his studio here (he did), inspiring him to capture their images in his historic paintings. If you prefer seclusion to services (since it's akin to a private home), by all means stay here. Some cottages sleep up to four, including children.

509 Dauphine St. www.auduboncottages.com. ✆ **504/206-4923.** 7 units. $250–$399 1-bedroom cottage; $369–$1,000 2-bedroom. Rates include bottled water, soda, coffee/tea. Parking nearby $36. **Amenities:** Butler service; outdoor pool; free Wi-Fi.

Hotel Monteleone ★★★   There is almost nothing modest about the venerable Monteleone, family-owned since 1886. Not the ornate lobby, not the hallowed literary tradition (Faulkner, Hemingway, Capote, Tennessee Williams, and Eudora Welty are just a few of the scribes who slept, drank, and/or wrote here—and if this is the main draw, book a "Literary Suite"), not the happy-hour scene or stellar view from the rooftop pool. And certainly not the fanciful, legendary, slowly rotating **Carousel Bar** (p. 224). Suites offer classic gentility (and sunken Jacuzzis in some, *swoon*). Rooms in the newly renovated Iberville tower cost more but are well worth the upgrade, with their brand-new, soothing elegance. The other two towers haven't yet been updated, and some rooms still lean toward the mumsy side of formal. Floors 7 and up have city views; those below have next-door-building views (but #56 and #59 are bigger and high-ceilinged). All suites are corner rooms, with river or city views (thankfully, the hotel has done away with its windowless rooms). The family ownership is reflected in gracious service—gentlemen should spring

5

WHERE TO STAY

French Quarter

New Orleans Hotels

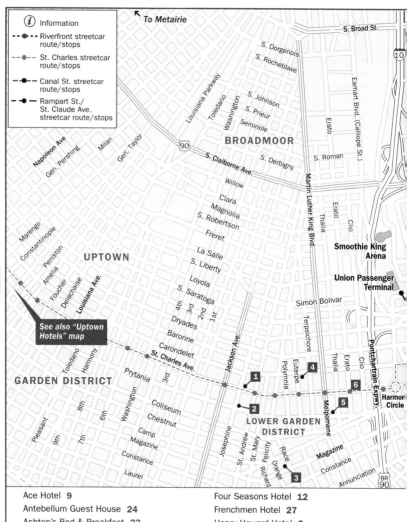

Ace Hotel **9**
Antebellum Guest House **24**
Ashton's Bed & Breakfast **23**
Auberge NOLA Hostel **4**
Auld Sweet Olive Bed & Breakfast **30**
The Brakeman **19**
Canal Street Inn **21**
Creole Gardens **5**
The Drifter **20**
1896 O'Malley House **21**
Eliza Jane **15**

Four Seasons Hotel **12**
Frenchmen Hotel **27**
Henry Howard Hotel **2**
HI New Orleans **18**
Hotel Kimpton Fontenot **11**
Hotel Peter & Paul **29**
Hotel Saint Vincent **3**
India House Hostel **21**
The Inn at the Old Jail **22**
The Lookout Inn **31**
Madame Isabelle's House in New Orleans **25**

Maison de la Luz **8**
NOPSI Hotel **16**
The Old No. 77 Hotel & Chandlery **10**
The Pelham **14**
Pontchartrain Hotel **1**
The Quisby **6**

The Roosevelt **17**
Royal Frenchmen **28**
Royal Street Inn & R Bar **26**
Virgin Hotel **7**
Windsor Court **13**

for a proper hot-towel, straight-razor shave in the barbershop, and everyone should spring for something from the pricy but so soothing full-service spa. The fitness equipment is notably good, and **Criollo Restaurant** is a big step up from standard hotel fare.

214 Royal St. www.hotelmonteleone.com. © **800/535-9595** or 504/523-3341. 523 units. $222–$499 double; $449 and up suite. Children 17 and under stay free in parent's room. Valet parking $54. Pets allowed ($100 + $25/night). **Amenities:** Restaurant; bar; concierge; fitness center; rooftop pool and bar; live entertainment Wed–Sat; 24-hr. room service; spa; free Wi-Fi.

Ritz-Carlton New Orleans ★★★   With all guest rooms completely renovated in 2020, this Ritz-Carlton got even ritzier. Expect luxury, service, and amenities, including a truly stellar spa (the city's largest) and the soignée **Davenport Lounge.** It's all quite gracious and stately, as was its previous incarnation as the landmark department store Maison Blanche (though the repurposed space can be a bit confusing to navigate). Decor leans toward traditional, with posh purple-and-gold fabrics; bedding is superb even in the smaller rooms. Try for a larger suite on the 14th and 15th floors, or better yet, the Maison Orleans club level (though at press time, the club tower was heading toward renovation and a 5-month closure). With its plush lounge, handsome library, spacious courtyard, concierge, and food and beverage service, it's among the best VIP sleeps in town.

921 Canal St. www.ritzcarlton.com/neworleans. © **800/522-8780** or 504/524-1331. 528 units. $224–$599 double; $638 and up suite. Valet parking $48. Pets allowed under 30 lbs. ($150 nonrefundable). **Amenities:** Restaurant; bar; spa; indoor pool; concierge; complimentary access to fitness center; 24-hr. room service; free Wi-Fi in lobby, in-room Wi-Fi $13–$15 (free for Marriot members or when booked through American Express).

Expensive/Moderate

Bourbon Orleans Hotel ★   If you're Bourbon Street–bound and don't mind noise, this location is perfect, smack in the middle of a busy part of the Quarter. This large, bustling property has decent service, amazing history (it was formerly an opera house *and* a convent), an impressive formal lobby, and a big pool. Under newish ownership, rooms are renovated with hardwood floors and updated furnishings; bathrooms are sexied-up in black marble. The smallest rooms are tight; bi-level loft suites with Bourbon-facing balconies are ideal for party people but way too loud for others (nearby bars blare tunes). Long hallways mean you might be walking your muffuletta off—for some that's a plus (otherwise, request elevator proximity). The **Bourbon O** bar has live jazz every night from 4pm to midnight, and a super cocktail list with light bites. For the price, this hotel isn't exactly the height of luxury, but if you're in town to live it up, it's unlikely to let you down.

717 Orleans St. www.bourbonorleans.com. © **800/935-8740** or 504/523-2222. 220 units. $150–$499 double; $400–$1,230 suite. Valet parking $48 plus tax. Dogs $75 (max 2). **Amenities:** Restaurant (breakfast only); bar; fitness room; outdoor saltwater pool; free Wi-Fi.

French Quarter Hotels

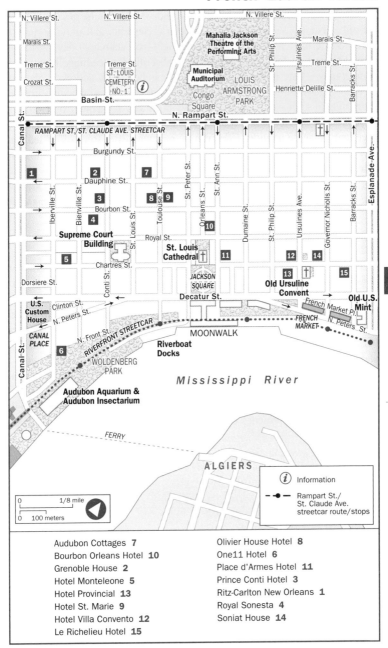

Audubon Cottages **7**
Bourbon Orleans Hotel **10**
Grenoble House **2**
Hotel Monteleone **5**
Hotel Provincial **13**
Hotel St. Marie **9**
Hotel Villa Convento **12**
Le Richelieu Hotel **15**

Olivier House Hotel **8**
One11 Hotel **6**
Place d'Armes Hotel **11**
Prince Conti Hotel **3**
Ritz-Carlton New Orleans **1**
Royal Sonesta **4**
Soniat House **14**

Olivier House Hotel ★★★ This family-owned collection of historic 1839 Creole houses is seriously packed with old French Quarter character. No two of the 42 rooms (former kitchens, laundry rooms, nurseries, and so on) are alike, but all feature funky architectural elements and unfussy antique decor. Some have high ceilings and wrought-iron staircases leading to loft beds. Others (tall folks take heed!) have absurdly low ceilings. Many have your granny's taste in linens. We adore the arched brick doorways, damask tapestries, gas lighting, unfinished barge wood, peeling paint, teeny-tiny elevator, hidden staircases, and three friendly hotel cats. It's a block off Bourbon, so request an interior-facing room for quietude. Service is warm, casual, and excellent. Imagine a quirky B&B run by pals who offer free coffee, tea, and snacks all day; add a peaceful courtyard and small swimming pool, and it's a splendid, decidedly un-cookie-cutter stay.

828 Toulouse St. www.olivierhouse.com. 𝒞 **504/525-8456.** 42 units. $149–$299 double; $349–$,1000 deluxe. Valet parking $42 (more during special events). **Amenities:** Free coffee, tea, hot chocolate, and snacks all day; free Wi-Fi.

One11 Hotel ★ When this former sugar refinery opened at the end of 2020, it was the first new French Quarter hotel in 50 years. We're pretty sweet on it. The boutique eight-story restoration is exceptionally clean and contemporary, with stunning old, faded brick and massive wood-and-metal beams. Next to the **Audubon Aquarium** (p. 156), it's a primo spot. Extra swoonworthy are the swimming pool, outdoor fireplace, and guests-only rooftop deck for chillaxing with a go-cup of sangria from on-site bistro/bar **Batture.** (Cheers to daily happy hour!) Rooms have a serene spa vibe, with natural light and sugary hues (think caramel and white). We prefer the rooms and suites—called "sweets," of course—in the historic wing, but the modern wing's no slouch. Either way, views from riverfront rooms dazzle. *One caveat:* Passing trains at night may disrupt your slumber, so this isn't an ideal choice for light sleepers. The hotel provides earplugs, but you may also want to download a white-noise app.

111 Iberville St. www.one11hotel.com. 𝒞 **504/699-8100.** 83 units. $164–$449 double; $390–$959 suite. Parking $48. **Amenities:** Pool; bar; bistro; concierge; complimentary access to fitness center; free Wi-Fi.

Also Check Out . . .

At press time, **Soniat House** (1133 Chartres St.; www.soniathouse.com)—one of the very finest luxury French Quarter hotels—was preparing to unveil the results of a lengthy renovation to its three lovely French Colonial houses that date from the 1800s. Details have been kept top-secret, but we suspect it will be nothing short of glorious. And on the next block, **Le Richelieu Hotel** (1234 Chartres St.; www.lerichelieuhotelnola.com), an old favorite of budget-minded travelers, has just finished a massive restoration, transforming it into an upscale boutique with great deals on rooms. We were going to press just as they were opening, so we don't have all the details, but check that one out, too.

Royal Sonesta ★★ You might forget you're right on Bourbon Street, what with all the graciousness inside. The Sonesta is large, busy, and classy, with outstanding service for the mix of tourists and business guests. Rooms are handsomely decorated in white and shimmery blue or purple; bathrooms, on the smaller side, are white-on-white. Some of the better suite options are here, or opt for added perks on the R Club floor. Rooms facing the inside courtyard avoid the Bourbon Street racket (though maybe that's what you're here for . . .); some rooms open onto the large courtyard pool, which is convenient but can get crowded. All amenity bases are covered; almost everything you could need is here, including the so-so **Desire Oyster Bar,** the terrific **Restaurant R'evolution** (p. 106), and the very good **Jazz Playhouse** (p. 216)—which adds to the luster and liveliness.

300 Bourbon St. www.sonesta.com/royalneworleans. ⓒ **800/766-3782** or 504/586-0300. 483 units. $169–$479 double; $400–$2,500 suite. Parking $60. Pets allowed ($75, 2 pets max). **Amenities:** 2 restaurants; 3 bars; cafe; concierge; 24-hr. fitness center; outdoor pool; free Wi-Fi.

Moderate

Grenoble House ★★ This midrange property has a lot of pluses that add up to a great choice. A heated pool, hot tub, and spacious courtyards link three 19th-century buildings with 17 big, apartment-style suites with full kitchens (if you're cereal eaters and leftovers snackers, the dining-out savings add up). Decor is comfy, with new beds and freshly redone bathrooms. Room sizes and configurations vary (some work well for families or small groups). Street noise can be an issue for front-facing rooms; third-floor rooms are cheaper for a reason—there are no elevators. But it's near Bourbon Street, it's clean, the air-conditioning rocks, and staff is friendly and helpful. The property uses a secure key-hold system (guests check keys at front desk when leaving).

323 Dauphine St. www.grenoblehouse.com. ⓒ **504/325-2271.** 17 units. $179–$399 suite (advance payment may be required). No children 11 and under. Parking nearby $35/night. **Amenities:** Pool; hot tub; free Wi-Fi.

Hotel St. Marie ★★ We've always been fond of **Vacherie,** the bar and restaurant in the St. Marie. After a renovation some years back, the rest of the property has caught up. Given its Bourbon Street proximity and choice of on- or off-street rooms, it's a terrific French Quarter location, and room rates can be downright bargains during low season. The staff has a friendly, helpful vibe, and rooms are clean and shockingly quiet. We especially like that 80% of the rooms have balconies overlooking the street or the modest pool.

827 Toulouse St. www.hotelstmarie.com. ⓒ **888/626-4812** or 504/561-8951. 103 units. $111–$323 double; $186–$409 suite. Children 12 and under stay free. Valet parking $47. **Amenities:** Bar; concierge; pool; free Wi-Fi.

Moderate/Inexpensive

Hotel Provincial ★★ This family-run hotel is a great budget pick for its healthy dose of character, from the flickering gas lamps and jumbly layout to the rumored ghosts (it's a former Civil War hospital). Rooms are fairly quiet, with high ceilings; those facing the street get a bit of noise but nothing serious. The better ones have nonworking fireplaces or huge windows; the best—on the upper floors, accessible only by stairs—reward climbers with peek-a-boo river views. We're also fond of those that open onto the courtyard and fountain; another courtyard is mostly pool. Rooms are regularly spruced, with a nod to modernity added to the mix of antiques, reproductions, and hotel traditional. (*Note:* Only the premium balcony-room windows open.) The lobby's **Ice House Bar** feels like your own private space, and busy on-site **Toast** (p. 113) serves a good, filling breakfast (or **Croissant D'or,** p. 149, is a half-block away).

1024 Chartres St. www.hotelprovincial.com. ℂ **800/535-7922** or 504/581-4995. 92 units. $135–$369 double; $219–$469 suite. Valet parking $39 ($29 if booking through hotel). **Amenities:** Bar; pool; restaurant; free Wi-Fi.

Place d'Armes Hotel ★★ This historic landmark (the site of Louisiana's first French Colonial school) is a fantastic choice for decently priced French Quarter lodging. You're a hop-skip from Jackson Square and Café du Monde, and it's hard to have a care when you're lounging by an amoeba-shaped pool shaded by palm trees, listening to the bells of St. Louis Cathedral. Several buildings are knit together by brick hallways and awfully pretty, awfully *vieux* courtyards. Rooms are clean and have freshly updated carpet, paint, and bedding. Bathrooms weren't recently renovated, but they're perfectly serviceable. If you live for light-filled mornings (or conversely, love sleeping in pitch blackness), know that some rooms are dark (or windowless, even). A few splendid rooms have terraces with a Jackson Square corner view (expect street noise with those because . . . French Quarter!)

625 St. Ann St. www.placedarmes.com. ℂ **800/626-5917** or 504/636-1023. 84 units. $118–$399 double; $169–$419 suite. Valet parking $42. **Amenities:** Pool; free Wi-Fi.

Prince Conti Hotel ★ Bourbon Street bound? Then convenience is the draw here—along with friendly, accommodating staff and prices in the $125 range during nonfestival weeks. Set in a historic building with rooms renovated in 2018, this isn't a chain experience. Some rooms are quite small, but they're comfy, with old-school decor and icy air-conditioning. If you aren't spending tons of time in the room, this heart-of-the-Quarter lodging delivers. Though a block from Bourbon, it's quiet (aside from thin guest-room walls), and all your needs are met nearby, from booze to beer to beignets. The **Bombay Club** offers live piano music, decent food, and 100+ martinis; and the day after all those martinis, **Café Conti** offers sustenance.

830 Conti St. www.princecontihotel.com. ℂ **504/529-4172.** 84 units. $100–$299 double; $150–$349 suite. Parking $42. **Amenities:** Bar; cafe; 24-hr. concierge; free Wi-Fi.

Inexpensive

Hotel Villa Convento ★ It belonged to the Ursuline nuns; it became a brothel; it's rumored to be the original House of the Rising Sun; Jimmy Buffett lived in room #305. But even without all that incredible history, the location can't be beat (a quiet Quarter spot 1½ blocks to Bourbon and 4 blocks to the French Market). It's an old charmer with hospitality so warm it's almost familial. Don't expect luxury—some rooms are sorely in need of TLC. But the prices are among the best in the Quarter, and free parking in this neighborhood is, well, otherwise unheard of. If you can, snag a balcony room with exposed brick and a balcony table. (If you're feeling splurgy, suite #401 is a quiet, spacious beauty with a superb view.) One proviso: Must love ghosts.

616 Ursuline St. www.villaconvento.com. © **504/491-7374.** 25 units. $80–$175 double; $103–$215 suite. Free garage parking (limited spaces). **Amenities:** Free coffee; microwave in lobby; free Wi-Fi.

CENTRAL BUSINESS DISTRICT

The "CBD" abuts the French Quarter along Canal Street and extends west to include the Warehouse District, with loft-conversion hotels, a thriving club scene, and the arts district. As the city's commerce center, it's a mix of modernity and history, where tourists and businesspeople mingle. Many of the city's finest restaurants and hotels are here, as are some good deals (especially on weekdays and off-season). Most of it is still walking distance to the French Quarter action.

Best for: Hipsters; foodies; conventioneers; Superdome attendees; museumgoers; art enthusiasts; families (lots of suite and chain hotels are here).

Drawbacks: It's not New York, but this is a city center, with people working and view-obstructing office buildings (and nonstop construction—ask what's nearby when making reservations). Parking is pricey; do without a car or save a few bucks and minutes by using a nearby private lot rather than the valet.

Expensive

Four Seasons Hotel ★★★ Transforming the World Trade Center into a five-star hotel (and private residences) was a 3-year, $530-million project. This is New Orleans, so it tracks that the hotel doors open into the bar. And it's a Four Seasons, so it tracks that above that bar hangs a fairytalelike chandelier of 15,000 hand-strung Czech crystals. No expense was spared here, and we appreciate the made-in-Louisiana touches: All art is local or locally inspired, and the food-and-beverage program stars revered locals. On the first floor, you'll find the aforementioned **Chandelier Bar,** featuring libations by expert mixologist Hadi Ktiri. Also on the first floor is **Miss River,** Alon Shaya's flawless ode to N.O. classic dishes. The fifth floor is home to **Chemin à la Mer,** Donald Link's spin on modern French cuisine, complete with oyster bar. That floor also houses a state-of-the-art fitness center, an extensive spa, and a 75-foot infinity pool overlooking the Mississippi River. A 34th-floor observation deck (separate entrance, admission charged) offers 360-degree city views. The rooms are sizeable with smart layouts, refined mid-century modern furnishings, sedate colors, and thoughtful *lagniappes* such as customized lighting and iPads for in-room controls—but the scene stealers are the floor-to-ceiling windows, many with glorious river and city views. Bathrooms are lovely, too: white Carrara marble with modern soaking tubs. It's a bevy of sophisticated gorgeousness.

2 Canal St. www.fourseasons.com/neworleans. ℂ **800/819-5053** or 504/434-5100. 341 units. $250–$990 room; $540–$2,100 and up suite. Valet parking $64. **Amenities:** 2 restaurants; bar/lounge; concierge; pool; gym; spa; room service; babysitting; free Wi-Fi.

Maison de la Luz ★★★ Opened in 2019, MdlL quickly staked its claim as one of NOLA's utmost luxury accommodations. Celeb fave designer Pamela Shamshiri artfully styled this stately former City Hall annex, built in 1908, for Atelier Ace, the Ace Hotel chain's luxury marque; its sister property (p. 78) is across the street, but miles away in spirit. (MdlL guests can access the Ace's pool, gym, eateries, and nightclub, while the Maison maintains its own more serene "Southern swoon" vibe and intimate guesthouse scale.) It's an enclave of care, comfort, and discretion, where finery is at your fingertips before you know you're reaching for it. The lobby honor bar, tiny speakeasy, and petite natty dining room are exclusive to Maison guests; only chic **Bar Marilou** (p. 228) welcomes outsiders—by separate entryway. Second-floor ceilings soar to 18 feet, while the third through sixth floors are still lofty, at 14 feet. Fabrics in midnight and ochre complement warm woods, pale lilac walls, hand-painted cabinetry, local art, and serpent shower handles. A regal embroidered crest crowns the velvet platform bed, where sumptuous sheets and spring-less mattresses define extravagance, as do the huge bathrooms with deep soaking tubs and multicolored marble floors. Chromecast, digital sound systems, stocked bars, and top-of-the-line, top-to-bottom service underscore the experience. Fresh morning coffee is silently delivered; concierges pay subdued attention and act accordingly. New Orleans awaits, but you might have trouble leaving such splendid, satiating repose.

546 Carondelet St. www.maisondelaluz.com. (C) **504/814-7720.** 67 units. $288 and up double; $513 and up suite. Valet parking $50. Pets under 25 lbs. allowed ($125). **Amenities:** Bar; concierge; access to nearby pool and gym; afternoon wine, cheese, and charcuterie reception; room service; breakfast (not included in rates); free Wi-Fi.

The Roosevelt ★★   This grandiose Waldorf property is regal throughout, but the movie-star-glamorous, block-long lobby is positively magnificent, and the history and pedigree equally impressive. Sizes and views in the well-appointed, traditional rooms vary: Luxury suites are more than ample, but the smallest rooms are simply too small for what you're probably paying, even if the upholstery is striped silk and/or deeply tufted. Some have tubs (even claw-foot); others on the upper floors overlook the city or the fourth-floor pool. All have luscious beds. But guest rooms really take a back seat to the exceptional lobby and other common areas: the sumptuous spa, **Domenica** restaurant (p. 130), and the historic **Sazerac Bar** (p. 230) and **Blue Room.** Check for occasional good package deals and seasonal rates. Holiday season here is dreamlike. (In 2022, for instance, the lobby was decorated with more than 112,000 twinkling lights, 4,000 glass ornaments on 42 trees, and 1,600 feet of garland.)

130 Roosevelt Way. www.therooseveltneworleans.com. (C) **800/925-3673** or 504/648-1200. 504 units, including 125 suites. $209–$599 double; $329–$999 suite. Valet parking $51. Pets under 25 lbs. allowed ($175). **Amenities:** 2 restaurants; coffee shop; bar; spa; concierge; fitness room; pool; room service; Wi-Fi (free in lobby and cafe; $15/day in-room; free for Hilton Honors members).

Windsor Court ★★★   There's a kind of hush at this ultra-fine hotel, for decades the center of New Orleans high society. Everything is tranquil and mannerly, from the proper high tea and mind-blowing hallway galleries of original 17th- to 19th-century fine art, to the restaurant—the highest-end **Grill Room.** The property completed a $15-million upgrade in 2018, and it looks and feels spiffier than ever. The spacious, handsome accommodations are traditional European in style but not at all stodgy, in serene pale aqua, cream, and silver (you can feel the luxe upon entry—those carpets have extra cush). Marble-laden bathrooms are roomy; suites are large-windowed, light-filled, and enormous. Those with balconies and river views are exceptional (though some "view" rooms are only partial views); a ritzy club level adds 24/7 concierge service. It has one of the city's best hotel spas. The outstanding rooftop pool is one of several superb places to enjoy a smart beverage, along with the chichi **Polo Club.** We've never loved the odd, 1980s exterior, but once inside we want to wrap ourselves in the Windsor Court and stay and stay and stay.

300 Gravier St. www.windsorcourthotel.com. (C) **888/596-0955** or 504/523-6000. 316 units. $290–$600 double; $340–$850 suite; $465–$899 club level. Kids 17 and under stay free with parent. Pets allowed ($150). Valet parking $59. **Amenities:** 2 restaurants; cafe; 2 lounges; pool cafe and bar; concierge; fitness center; pool; 24-hr. room service; spa; free Wi-Fi.

It's hot in the city! Are you swimsuit-ready, but your hotel isn't? No sweat: A number of the city's best hotels, including **Ace** (p. 78), **The Chloe** (p. 90), **NOPSI** (p. 78), and **Virgin** (p. 79) offer day passes to their splendid outdoor pools. **The Drifter** (p. 86) is a 21+ top-optional pool-party *scene*. Luxury hotels **The Roosevelt** (p. 77) and **Windsor Court** (p. 77) offer day passes to their rooftop pools—but better yet, book a treatment at one of their excellent spas, and you'll enjoy all-day pool access along with other perks like

champagne and validated parking. A spa treatment at **The Ritz-Carlton** (p. 70) includes access to its gym, sauna, steam room, and indoor resistance pool. At **Hotel Monteleone's** (p. 67) **Spa Aria,** treatment prices are a bit lower and include a $25 rooftop pool pass. Day pass prices start around $25, or $40 for reserved lounge chairs. *Note:* Not a hotel, but **The Country Club** (p. 231) also offers day passes for 21+ (then come back another day for its fab drag brunch.)

Expensive/Moderate

Ace Hotel ★ If a hotel could have a soul patch, the Ace would. Situated in a converted Art Deco building, this outpost of the Portland-based chain is a study in hipster bait, from photo booths, in-room turntables, and vintage vinyl, to room snacks of ramen and Bulleit bourbon. The chocolate-and-charcoal rooms look great, with their angular furnishings and custom-painted armoires, but they aren't built for deep comfort. No worry, cuz you be chillin' with the under-30 crowd in the action-packed lobby bar, excellent **Josephine Estelle** restaurant (p. 127), stellar rooftop pool and bar **Alto, Three Keys** club, and terrif **Seaworthy** oyster bar. The **Lovage Coffee** shop, **Parker Barber** barbershop, and **Local DNO** menswear shop further augment the hipness. Still, it can feel pricey for what it is, so hunt for deals.

600 Carondolet St. www.acehotel.com/neworleans. (C) **504/900-1180.** 234 units. $140–$709 double. Pets allowed ($25/night). Valet parking $50. **Amenities:** 2 restaurants; 3 bars; coffee cafe; music/performance venue; gym; rooftop pool; room service; free Wi-Fi.

NOPSI Hotel ★★ Ninety years after it first opened, this 1927 building got a massive renovation, transforming it into the NOPSI Hotel. Fortunately, the grandiose lobby—boasting 20-foot vaulted ceilings and stunning moldings—remains, reminding many locals of the electric services, bus passes, and appliances they once bought here (NOPSI stands for New Orleans Public Service Inc.). In contrast, the spacious, comfortable, well-appointed rooms are staid, with a yacht-y navy-white-and-tan scheme (this is a good thing). Perhaps marking NOPSI as a woman-owned property, the bathrooms rock: They're big, with double sinks, an enormous shower, and a separate lighted vanity tucked just outside the oft-steamy space. The well-thought-out spaces also have plenty of mirrors and storage space. The central CBD location is a big plus. The **Above the Grid** rooftop pool and bar has impressive Superdome views, and there's a decent on-site restaurant, **Public Service.** All-around pro service is the capper. It's also one of the city's only Black-owned hotels. *Note:* A $25-per-night "destination fee" is added to the room rate to cover amenities.

317 Baronne St. www.nopsihotel.com. ℂ **844/439-1463** or 504/962-6500. 217 units. $130–$467 double; $152–632 suite. Valet parking $47. Dogs allowed ($25). **Amenities:** Restaurant; 3 bars; concierge; fitness room; pool; free coffee; free Wi-Fi.

Virgin Hotel ★★★   We love a hotel that's stylish yet whimsical, so the fact that what you see first is a life-size, realistic (but not real) dude in a head-to-toe bunny suit playing chess or reading a book may tip you off: We *love* it. Opened in 2021, this boutique from Sir Richard Branson is high-design but easygoing, with living room–like public spaces and intimate nooks. The Shag Room has shag carpet and a fireplace; the Funny Library stocks books, sketching supplies, and board games (plus the aforementioned "Bunny Man") and a good cafe. We dig the local- and Matisse-inspired artwork and the breezy, tropical motif that pervades—including in the **Commons Club** restaurant (p. 126). You get killer city views from the 13th-floor rooftop's **Pool Club** (bar and pool) and the 14th-floor rooms, including two penthouses. Rooms are a nice size (not huge but big enough, with separate dressing rooms), and nine have terraces. The ergonomically designed red lounge beds are, um, perfection. The location's also spitting distance from loads of restaurants and museums. And finally, it's LEED certified, making it one of the city's most eco-friendly stays. Say hi to Bunny Man for us.

550 Baronne St. virginhotels.com/new-orleans. ℂ **504/603-8000.** 238 units. $160–$800 double; $464–$1,500 and up suite. Pets allowed free. Valet parking $48. **Amenities:** Restaurant; cafe; 2 lounges; poolside bar; concierge; fitness center; pool; room service, free Wi-Fi.

Moderate

Eliza Jane ★★   We love a place with a good story to tell, and they ooze from the walls of the Eliza Jane's seven conjoined warehouses. Once home to the Peychaud's Bitters factory (essential to the Sazerac cocktail), a munitions factory, and the *Daily Picayune* newspaper, it's named for Eliza Jane Nicholson, a poet who was the *Picayune's* first publisher, and the first woman in the U.S. to own a major newspaper. The guest rooms vary widely in configuration, natural light (those facing Magazine St. have huge windows; others are windowless), and size (first-floor rooms are small; fifth-floor ceilings are low). Decor is a goodly step above generic thanks to original exposed beams, joists, and brick, and rooms are well-appointed (except for those nonclosets . . . aka wardrobe racks), with Keurig coffeemakers, robe and slippers, and fluffy feather pillows. Check out those shower curtains—yes, there are beignets hidden in that custom toile pattern. Yet it's the Jane's common spaces that make it a good option, for Hyatt point collectors in particular (it's part of their individualized Unbound Collection): the **Press Room** lobby bar; a large, comfy sitting room with decorative nods to its newspaper heritage; terrific restaurant **Couvant** (whose brunch is among the tastiest in town); and a charming brick courtyard (whose fireplace was the original privy!).

315 Magazine St. www.theelizajane.com. ☏ **504/882-1234.** 196 units. $122–$327 double; $190–$434 suite. Service pets only. Valet parking $45. **Amenities:** Restaurant; bar; fitness center; free Wi-Fi.

Hotel Kimpton Fontenot ★★　An unusual assemblage of styles greets you in this freshly minted hotel. The lobby is all understated sophistication; the new **King Brasserie** is so sleek and modern it borders on cold (but service is warm, and the French Riviera–inspired food is sublime); on-site **Gospel Coffee and Boozy Treats** (where "anything can be spiked") is bright and cheery. And then . . . there's the **Peacock Room:** a lush, gardenlike gold and turquoise lounge where you can sip elevated cocktails among stuffed peacocks. (It sounds weird, but the space is exquisite.) On Thursdays you can catch live music there (there's decent food, too). Guest rooms offer yet another style: minimalist, with pops of soft pastels, plus attractive city and river views. There's plenty to like here, including a walkable location, hosted social hours, affable service, and free stays for pets (not just dogs, but "anything that can fit through the door").

501 Tchoupitoulas St. www.hotelfontenot.com. ☏ **504/571-1818.** 235 units. $135–$409 double; $279 and up suite. Valet parking $49. Pets allowed (free). **Amenities:** Restaurant; cafe; bar; fitness room; free Wi-Fi.

The Old No. 77 Hotel & Chandlery ★　Set in an 1854 warehouse formerly called the Old No. 77—a name borrowed from the former warehouse's ID number—this Warehouse Arts District hotel dishes history with original hardwood floors, exposed brick walls, and interesting ghost signs uncovered during the hotel's renovation. Most rooms are windowless and priced accordingly (book a premium room for sunlight), but in general the sleep space is comfortable and oozes charm. This hotel is all about local art and products from N.O. makers, including New Orleans Center for the Creative Arts and Where Y'art Gallery, for exhibits and artist-curated loft suites. Hotel service can be spotty, but chef Nina Compton's superb **Compère Lapin** restaurant (p. 126) is on-site, and guests get priority access, which is a major boon. *Note:* The hotel charges a $13 amenities fee.

535 Tchoupitoulas St. www.old77hotel.com. ☏ **504/527-5271.** 162 units. $95–$369 double; $271–$479 suite. Pets accepted ($55). Self-parking $33. **Amenities:** Coffee shop; fitness center; complimentary bikes; restaurant/bar; in-room fitness kit; free Wi-Fi.

The Pelham ★　This 1800s building newly remodeled in 2022 is filled with funky local art, retro-ish furniture, and cordial service. Amenities aren't the draw here (nor is the water pressure), but it's stylish, secure, and well cared for, at good rates. The quiet location is a quick walk to the Quarter, and at always-hopping local breakfast spot **Ruby Slipper** next door, Pelham guests get preferential seating. Beds are very comfortable, and though the clean, cute rooms aren't huge, 18-foot ceilings give the impression of spaciousness. Some units have 10-foot windows; others are windowless. Two more things: (1) the toiletries are Grown Alchemist, and (2) when we entered the room, a Victrola radio was tuned to WWOZ, both indicating that the Pelham clearly knows what's up.

444 Common St. www.thepelhamhotel.com. © **504/522-4444.** 65 units. $109–$311 double; $131–$316 studios. Valet parking from $52. **Amenities:** Free coffee; free Wi-Fi.

Moderate/Inexpensive

HI New Orleans ★★★ If you're not familiar with HI Hostels, this terrific, feature-laden lodging option might surprise you. Although it's still largely the purview of young travelers, all ages, families, and groups are welcome. Built in 1900, the fully converted five-story building retains some original architectural features (high ceilings on the fourth floor, wood floors where they've lasted) and is centrally located and clean. It has dorm, quad, and private queen-bed rooms (with TVs and en suite bathrooms; #414 has killer old windows); request an off-street room if you're sensitive to street hubbub. Sturdy, built-in bunk beds don't shift; they're extra-long and pretty comfy. Each has a curtain, bed light, charger station, and ample locked storage. There's also a gorgeous guest-use kitchen, a cafe, and well-decorated areas for hanging out or working. (BTW, no, that's not a giant whiskey barrel in the lobby near the custom mural—it's a cistern!) Individual, all-gender restrooms abound; it's eco-friendly; Wi-Fi is good throughout; and activities and helpful, friendly folk are plentiful.

1028 Canal St. www.hiusa.org/new-orleans. © **504/603-3850.** 146 beds; 24 private rooms. Dorms $34–$78; private rooms $154–$294. HI members get 5% discount. Parking nearby, about $20/day. **Amenities:** Restaurant; lockers; free breakfast, coffee, and tea; laundry facilities; bike storage; luggage storage; free Wi-Fi.

MARIGNY & BYWATER

A few inns and a slew of B&Bs (many newly minted) dot this gentrified-meets-working-class area. Artists' workshops, galleries, dive bars, and a fresh crop of fantastic restaurants are scattered throughout.

Best for: Artists and art appreciators; bohemians and alternative scenesters; B&B fans; people seeking a less-bustling neighborhood experience; LGBTQIA+; music lovers and street partiers who want to fall out of bed and onto Frenchmen Street.

Drawbacks: Some parts are walking distance to the French Quarter; others are too far from the action or from public transportation, warranting a car or bike. Dicey, rundown shotgun homes commingle with cool renovations.

Expensive/Moderate

Auld Sweet Olive Bed & Breakfast ★★★ "Sweet" is the operative word for this butter-yellow Creole cottage, from the laziness-inducing wicker porch chairs to the lovingly prepared hot breakfast to the walls custom-painted with pretty botanical patterns. But recent renovations make "gorgeous" the word, too. The eight airy, spiffed-up guest rooms include four spacious suites, one with a full kitchen and two with a kitchenette. The courtyard's lush, the neighborhood's walkable, the art and furnishings are refined, and the beds are comfy. It's delightful and warm, just like innkeeper Kate, whose regard for NOLA shows through her hospitality and fab local recommendations. And now, with the brand-new addition of a pool and hot tub, we'll go ahead and add the word "perfect."

2460 N. Rampart St. www.sweetolive.com. ℂ **877/470-5323** or 504/947-4332. 5 units. $145–$379 double/suite. No children 11 and under. Rates include buffet breakfast. Street parking. **Amenities:** Free Wi-Fi.

Hotel Peter & Paul ★★   This spectacular conversion—a former church, convent, rectory, and school—vies for the title of hippest hotel in New Orleans. Given its Marigny location, it may have the edge. Add the "Marie Antoinette's private picnic" design aesthetic, and all doubts dissolve. A stunning double wood staircase greets guests in the schoolhouse building, which houses most of the 71 rooms. Gingham, antiques, and church relics miraculously blend into a vibrant look, aided by high ceilings and huge windows on the second and third floors. We love the schoolhouse classic rooms, especially 311–314, which are entered via a stage. The fourth floor, the former attic, features skylights and original beams. Each room differs; some are pretty petite. But dashes of whimsy, like hand-painted armoires and "Cleanliness is Next to Godliness" hankies (as housekeeping request door hangers), tamp down any self-serious tendencies. In the convent's Mother Superior room, a huge tub set right in the shower made us guffaw (others have tubs in the bedroom). Firm-mattress people will be happy; those who like to sink into cushy loungers may go longing—those sexy antiques aren't always made for comfort. Frenchmen Street is a short stroll and the hotel's **Elysian Bar** (p. 116) has a terrific brunch and a lovely bar with tasty cocktails—but dinner and service are pretty mediocre (we know: womp, womp, but the rest of the hotel dazzles). If there's yoga, Pilates, a concert, or anything else going on in the exquisite 1860's church building, don't miss it.

2317 Burgundy St. www.hotelpeterandpaul.com. ℂ **504/356-5200.** 71 units. $150–$900 double; $309–$900 suite. Parking $10. Dogs allowed ($25). **Amenities:** Bar; restaurant; cafe; $10 pass to nearby gym; concierge; free Wi-Fi.

Royal Frenchmen ★★   If your plans include extensive Frenchmen Street music clubbing (p. 218), this is a good option. Renovated in 2017, the historic building (previously a Boys and Girls Club) is a moderately sophisticated respite from the street scene, yet within stumbling distance of the action. The building facing Frenchmen Street houses 13 rooms with double queens, or kings; those upstairs have French doors leading to small balconies where you can check out the street scene (and vice versa). Three suites are in a quieter back building, on the far side of a pleasant brick courtyard. Guest-room character comes from original or reproduced architectural touches like fireplaces (nonworking), crown moldings, and window shutters, which complement simple faux-antique furnishings and small but nicely updated bathrooms. The handsome white-marble-laden lobby features dramatic paintings by surrealist artist Vladimir Kush. Complimentary breakfast (fruit, yogurt, bagel, oatmeal) is a nice plus. Service is casual and friendly. The **bar** has daily happy hours and live music every night. Soundproofing is decent, but expect noise from the street and tunes from the bar. For many visitors, that's a plus—but if you're not in that number, march on.

700 Frenchmen St. www.royalfrenchmenhotel.com. ℂ **504/619-9660.** 16 units. $135–$359 double; $239–$489 suite. On-site parking $30. **Amenities:** Bar; free Wi-Fi.

Royal Street Inn & R Bar ★   The fact that the name of this all-suite guesthouse includes the name of the attached bar is not incidental. You're welcomed with complimentary drink tokens, and you should count on participating in the bar action (here or elsewhere) late into the night—lest you become its victim. As long as you know this is part of the experience (music, billiards, cigarette smoke), it's all good—including the actual rooms. They're a clever mix of platform bedding, Pottery Barn–ish leather seating, mood lighting, Sonos sound systems with Spotify (a classy touch to help muffle outside noise), and pops of color within the existing wood-and-brick vibe—all comfortable and worn-in but hip, like torn jeans. It's the free-spirited, decidedly Marigny attitude at play—which also describes the service and the clientele—but it's Quarter- and Frenchmen-close. Location and atmosphere help you feel a bit like a local—on Monday evenings you can get a shot and a haircut for $15, and there are free crawfish boils for guests on Fridays during crawfish season. (P.S. Fans of the TV show *NCIS: New Orleans*: You might also recognize this place as the Tru Tone Bar.)

1431 Royal St. www.royalstreetinn.com. ℂ **504/948-7499.** 5 units. $189–$559. Limited street parking. **Amenities:** Bar; free Wi-Fi.

Moderate

Frenchmen Hotel ★★   Frenchmen Street devotees: We give you a super vibey boutique with a fresh top-to-bottom renovation, on this city's (this country's?) finest stretch of live-music venues. Formed from three 1860 cottages, the posh design is inspired by avant-garde 1860s French surrealist artist Leonor Fini. In addition to 27 guest rooms, there's a plunge pool and hot tub in the courtyard (with oddly uncomfortable stone "cushions"), and, wait for it . . . a fab on-site tiki bar (**Tiki Tock**, p. 228). No, this hotel isn't the quietest. Yes, other guests may wake you, wobbling in late at night—but we don't visit New Orleans to sleep, do we? (And if we do, we don't stay on Frenchmen Street.) Some bathrooms are a tight fit, but rooms are clean and contemporary, with groovy wallpaper and bright, sexy touches—and so far (fingers crossed), this newbie isn't too pricey.

417 Frenchmen St. www.thefrenchmenhotel.com. ℂ **504/688-2900.** 27 units. $119–$221 double; $167–$365 suite. **Amenities:** Bar; concierge; free Wi-Fi.

Inexpensive

The Lookout Inn ★★   This small charmer is a helluva good deal, especially considering the lush back yard with pool, hot tub, barbecue, and cabana. The four super-spacious suites are nicely decorated but not overly serious (proof: the Elvis room, the Bollywood room). All told, it's a laid-back, friendly, owners-occupied situation. Don't expect breakfast or daily housekeeping, but your host Kelly will keep you in coffee and conversation, and her senior-citizen French bulldog will greet you with a wag. This pet- and kid-friendly oasis of an inn is in a residential area a block or two from some truly iconic drinking and dining establishments.

833 Poland Ave. www.lookoutneworleans.com. ✆ **504/947-8188.** 4 units. $105–$175 double. Street parking. Dogs $25. **Amenities:** Hot tub; pool; free Wi-Fi.

Madame Isabelle's House in New Orleans ★   The fact that it's within easy walking distance of the Quarter and Frenchmen Street is sufficient to make it attractive, but it's also a lovely, historic home run by friendly folks. With dorm rooms, a hot tub, loaner guitars, and social events (pub crawls, yoga, beer pong), it's party-positive but not (always) party central, thanks to private rooms, secure vibes, and a peaceful yard (not to mention a cute house cat). Breakfast included.

1021 Kerlerec St. www.isabellenola.com. ✆ **504/509-4422.** 7 units. $35 and up dorm; $120–$200 private double. Rates include breakfast. Street parking. **Amenities:** Lockers; hot tub; patio; shared kitchen; self-serve laundry; luggage storage; free Wi-Fi.

MID-CITY/ESPLANADE/TREMÉ

This thriving area encompasses diverse socio-economies and architectural styles amid quiet neighborhood streets and busy commercial corridors. It isn't replete with lodging options but does include a handful of wonderful B&Bs and a few decent hostels along the sometimes grand, sometimes shabby Esplanade Avenue.

Best for: Repeat visitors seeking to experience the city more like a resident; those who prefer B&Bs; Jazz Fest goers; budget backpackers; bike riders.

Drawbacks: You'll rely on a car, bikes, taxis, rideshares, or public transportation. It's a large area with some altogether lovely sections; other neighborhoods are more ramshackle.

Expensive/Moderate

Ashton's Bed & Breakfast ★★★   Ashton's stops just short of lavish, remaining comfortable rather than over-the-top. We might even call it homey— if home were a genteel Esplanade Avenue mansion. Once you sink into your comfy bed, you may not want to leave the romantic, pastel-walled, antiques-filled room. But you will, for stellar breakfasts like bananas Foster flambé and eggs *cochon de lait*. The main-house rooms are plenty spacious; ceilings are ridiculously high, sheets silky. Room #4 has a half-tester bed and an extravagant rain shower; #7 has a claw-foot whirlpool tub and rain shower. It's all light and bright, from the wide front gallery to the oak-shaded backyard, and the on-site hosts are most congenial. Excellence is in the details, and the owners have carefully attended to them.

2023 Esplanade Ave. www.ashtonsbb.com. © **504/942-7048.** 8 units. $218–$293 double. Rates include breakfast. On-site free parking. **Amenities:** Free snacks and beverages; free Wi-Fi.

The Inn at the Old Jail ★★★ It's exactly what the name implies—only far better. Built as a police jail and patrol station in 1902, this Queen Anne–style inn in the Tremé is a gem of a restoration, all old brick and wood and attention to detail. With a concert grand piano in the library (and occasional performances), vintage police memorabilia, and old black-and-white photos it feels just like a night at the (very comfortable, very hospitable) museum. The owners, brothers Todd and Nick, are generous with their time and knowledge, and the shared commercial kitchen rocks. (But **Gabrielle** [p. 118], **Dooky Chase** [p. 119], and **Willie Mae's Scotch House** [p. 125] are all nearby; you won't go hungry.)

2552 St. Philip St. innattheoldjail.com. © **504/301-5743.** 9 units. $200–$350 double; $350–$550 suite. Street parking. **Amenities:** Rooftop deck; free coffee and tea; shared kitchen; free Wi-Fi.

Moderate

1896 O'Malley House ★★ A quiet, nondescript Mid-City neighborhood unexpectedly houses this splendid B&B, antiqued but not frilly, steps from the Canal Street streetcar line. Stunning woodwork and a gorgeous fireplace add architectural flair. A tasty full breakfast is in the formal dining room. The largest guest rooms are on the second floor, though their impressive decor ends at the bathroom door (though some have Jacuzzi tubs, so we'll deal). Smaller, garretlike rooms on the third floor make clever use of their odd shapes. Ghost hunters should request the haunted room.

120 S. Pierce St. www.1896omalleyhouse.com. © **866/226-1896** or 504/488-5896. 8 units. $155–$200 double. Rates include breakfast. Discounts for military and veterans. Limited free off-street parking. **Amenities:** Free snacks and beverages; free Wi-Fi.

Antebellum Guest House ★★★ The name's problematic; the lodging is not. Grandiosity, check. Antiques everywhere. High ceilings. Elaborate breakfast. Check, check, check. The real difference is the experience, and the hosts. You could spend your entire visit chatting with them about New Orleans, art, travel, history, and whatever far-flung topics arise. They're interesting and interested, which describes much of New Orleans' population, but now you're at home with them—home being a tarted-up 1830s Esplanade Avenue glamour gal. Lavish restaurant-quality breakfasts (such as an 1830s Creole poached eggs recipe, served with boudin) are included in room rates. There's nothing to complain about here. (Well, the anachronistic, 1970s bathrooms are a bit ho-hum.) But when you step into the moss-hung backyard, with its hot tub and secret garden, magic begins.

1333 Esplanade Ave. www.antebellumguesthouse.com. ℘ **504/943-1900.** 3 units. $150–$185 double; $260–$350 suite. Rates include full breakfast. Street parking. **Amenities:** Hot tub; free Wi-Fi.

Canal Street Inn ★★   In this carefully restored 1912 Greek Revival, each of the 11 rooms is unique; you might score hardwood floors, exposed beams, a high ceiling, a claw-foot tub or whirlpool, a stained-glass window, or a courtyard view; in room #6, you score a private, screened-in veranda. And everyone scores access to the pretty parlor room, gourmet breakfast, attentive hospitality, and manicured, photogenic gardens (a popular wedding venue). Some foodie favorites like **Mandina's** (p. 120) and **Angelo Brocato** (p. 148) are an easy walk, and the streetcar stops across the way. With rooms from $155, it's a deluxe stay at a moderate (for NOLA) rate.

3620 Canal St. www.canalstreetinn.com. ℘ **504/483-3033.** 11 units. $155–$300 double. Limited on-site parking. **Amenities:** Breakfast; free coffee and tea; small gym; free Wi-Fi.

Moderate/Inexpensive

The Brakeman ★★   We enjoy a good historic building repurposing, so this new Tremé boutique, opened in 2020 in the old Norfolk train station (the last in the city, ca. 1904), is right on track. Designed to evoke railroad travel, rooms are spacious and refined, with exposed brick and comfortable beds. Even the windowless interior rooms are charming (and economical). A coffee bar, gift shop, train exhibits, and the Hop-On Hop-Off Bus's visitor center are all in the lobby. If it sounds like a lot going on, you're not wrong—but it's convenient, and the friendly staff keeps things calm. It's French Quarter–adjacent (next to the famed **St. Louis Cemetery No. 1,** p. 188), but far from the chaos. More food would be nice, but nearby dining options abound, including spectacular **Jewel of the South** (p. 225). All Aboard!

501 Basin St. www.brakemanhotel.com. ℘ **504/207-6400.** 18 units. $116–$270 double. Parking $22. **Amenities:** 24-hr. concierge; coffee bar; grab-n-go snacks; free Wi-Fi.

The Drifter ★   The Drifter is just barely removed from its previous life as a boxy mid-century modern, no-tell motel on an as-yet-untrammeled stretch of Tulane Avenue (5–15 Lyft minutes to the Warehouse or Marigny). Yet it's eons beyond that blah existence. The understated high design of the hotel engages without engulfing, from the lobby's wall-size crawling ivy sculpture and '60s furniture to the retro-looking tiled floor and outdoor mirror balls. Beds have Casper mattresses and Frette linens, and though the smallish cement-walled rooms have no TVs and few amenities beyond a minifridge, a couple of swank magazines, and a Tivoli radio/speaker, it's deliberate . . . because life here revolves around the ample bar and spacious "toptional" (topless-optional) pool area, where local parties large and small happen year-round (in winter, they spark up the fire pits and set the water heater at 95°F/35°C). It's a wacky and wild locals' scene, and you're invited: to the techno pool parties with DJs, the burlesque, the food trucks and pop-ups—even the odd music fest. And then sometimes (depending on weather and the other guests), it can be spookily quiet. By 7 or 8pm, the staff goes home and the bar closes, so if you arrive after that, you're on your own (with emailed instructions and a key in a lockbox). There's a great coffee bar that opens at 10:30am. A stay at the Drifter can be hit or miss, but it brings the pool party to you at a good price point, so maybe you do want to hit it.

3522 Tulane Ave. www.thedrifterhotel.com. ℂ **504/605-4644.** 20 units. $103–$250 double; $150–$400 bunk (4 full beds). Not appropriate for kids. Free street parking. **Amenities:** Coffee bar; cocktail bar; pool; free Wi-Fi.

Inexpensive

India House Hostel ★   Foreign travelers and students 18 and over (passport or student ID required) looking for budget dorms and an instant party, welcome home. Along with standard bunk-bed dorms, the four buildings also house private rooms (some with their own bathrooms) for out-of-state visitors 18 or older (no Louisiana residents allowed). A pool, deck stage, usable kitchen, and outdoor bar make for a ready-made social scene. It's half a block to the Canal Street streetcar, and tour companies pick up here regularly. It's friendly, funky but not filthy, and backpacker-ready. Also, a lazy, fluffy cat is available for petting. Book directly for the best rates, and pack earplugs—there's no curfew here.

124 S. Lopez St. www.indiahousehostel.com. ℂ **504/821-1904.** 168 beds. $25–$120. Street parking. **Amenities:** Kitchen use; laundry use; pool; courtyard; barbecue; free Wi-Fi.

LOWER GARDEN DISTRICT

Much more residential than the Central Business District, the Lower Garden District has some lovely blocks of colonnaded houses, vintage cottages, and stately trees, as well as plenty of excellent shops and restaurants along the Magazine Street strip. It's only a few streetcar stops from the French Quarter.

Best for: Style-seeking shoppers (for nearby Magazine St.); Warehouse District museumgoers who prefer less bustle.

Drawbacks: You're not in the thick of the action or near the city's top attractions (though there are some fun restaurants and bars).

Expensive/Moderate

Henry Howard Hotel ★★★   This stunning 1867 townhouse with classic columns and soaring ceilings is a drop-dead gorgeous, super-stylish choice, where crisp white-black-blue decor and sleek custom touches meet classy antiques. Second-line instruments as artwork and (limited) amenities like a small, butler-style bar in the polished parlor keep it friendly; the wide front gallery, complete with dawdle-ready wicker rockers, keeps it welcoming. Second-floor rooms with private balcony spaces feel positively Southern-chic, and a few hours on that front porch are very well spent. The Lower Garden District is a nice central locale and convenient to the streetcar line.

2041 Prytania St. www.henryhowardhotel.com. ✆ **504/313-1577.** 18 units. $159–$519 double; $749 and up suite. Street parking. **Amenities:** Concierge; parlor bar; free Wi-Fi.

Hotel Saint Vincent ★★★ Built in 1878, this property was originally the Saint Vincent's Infant Asylum, a historic orphanage. In 2021 the building was fully reimagined with a distinctly posh European girlcation vibe. (The design inspiration was "The kids inherited a castle." Nailed it!) It's filled with vintage glass and groovy art and dreamy, lush velvety furniture (custom-made Art Deco, mid-century modern, and 20th-century imported Italian). Rooms are next-level stylish, with muted grey paint against bright tile and marbled wallpaper (think trippy hot pinks and bold teals). About a third have outside patios. Bathrooms are appointed with gorgeous tubs. Mattresses are Wink, robes are silk, phones are vintage. We kinda wish they'd sourced more locally for design and food, but aside from that, it's *divine.* The neighborhood is great, too, on a sweet stretch of Magazine Street across from Mojo Coffee and steps from Coliseum Square, a two-fountained dog-friendly park. (In fact, bring your pup, since this is that rare swanky hotel that's also kid- and canine-friendly.) Adult humans will appreciate the very pretty sunken pool with bar and courtyard, and solid drinking and dining options: two inside bars, gorgeous (and guests-only) **Chapel Club** and cheerful **Paradise Lounge,** plus two restaurants, **San Lorenzo** (upscale coastal Italian, p. 140) and **Elizabeth Street Café** (French Vietnamese). Chef's kiss to this new glamour gal.

1507 Magazine St. www.saintvincentnola.com. ✆ **504/350-2450.** 75 units. $219–$619 double; $365–$1,699 suite. Pets accepted ($50). Valet parking $50 or street parking. **Amenities:** 2 restaurants; 2 bars; pool; concierge; room service; free Wi-Fi.

Pontchartrain Hotel ★★ This 1920s apartment building was reborn in the '40s as a high-end hotel, hosting presidents, movie stars, and Tennessee Williams (who wrote parts of *A Streetcar Named Desire* here) and throwing storied parties for the likes of The Doors and many a well-heeled local. The latest post-slump redo, a $10-million job, is splendid. Guest-room decor maintains a throwback feel with traditional furnishings, crystal chandeliers, and luxe fabrics (leather, velvet); patterns and accessories evoke the tropics. Modern needs are well met with the expected comforts and conveniences and spaciousness (even more so in the impressive suites). The busy St. Charles Avenue location, outside more touristed areas and a pleasant walk from some stunning manses, is part of the experience. But it's the common areas that really reel us in, from the foyer forward: the sweet **Silver Whistle** cafe, gentlemanly **Bayou Bar** (where Sinatra and Capote imbibed *and* where the deal to create the Saints was signed—who dat!), and the swank lounge area outside fab **Jack Rose** restaurant, where a wall of campy floral still-lifes surround an enormous Ashley Longshore painting of Lil' Wayne chowing a slice of the hotel's legendary Mile High Pie. And then there's **Hot Tin** on floor #11 (arguably the city's most see-and-be-seen rooftop bar) styled after a 1940s writer's salon. If only these walls could talk. (Ok, we'll talk, though: A family member once ran into Katy Perry here.)

2031 St. Charles Ave. thepontchartrainhotel.com. ✆ **504/323-1400.** 106 units. $143–$424 double; $250–$939 suite. Valet parking $34. **Amenities:** Restaurant; bar; cafe; access to nearby fitness center; rooftop bar; concierge; free Wi-Fi.

Moderate

Creole Gardens ★★   This brightly painted, colorful guesthouse is beyond cute, with individually themed mansion and cottage rooms (we're enamored of the red bordello rooms) and a laid-back courtyard. With a DJ or live music in its Roadhouse event space some weekend nights; adult beverages sold in the front office; complimentary breakfast (pastries, quiche, fruit, coffee, and so forth); pets allowed for a reasonable fee; kind service; and a quiet, central spot in the LGD (one of our fave neighborhoods) near the streetcar, it's a primo *pied-à-terre.*

1415 Prytania St. www.creolegardens.com ✆ **504/569-8700.** 24 units. $139–$329 double. Rates include breakfast. Street parking. **Amenities:** Courtyard; free Wi-Fi.

Inexpensive

Auberge NOLA Hostel ★★   Backbackers, looking for your peeps? Here you go! The clean youth hostel has a helpful staff, a decent shared kitchen, and standard-issue metal bunk beds in mixed and female-only dorms. It's a friendly party hub with nightly social events (translation: fun & noisy). A big selling point is location: It's a few blocks off the St. Charles streetcar line and a few blocks the other direction from the heart of the CBD. There's a cozy courtyard, and a bit of old NOLA character in the converted home. A small apartment has a private kitchen and bathroom and two double-bunk beds. *Note:* Guests must show a foreign passport or out-of-state ID, and proof of travel may be required.

1628 Carondolet St. www.aubergenola.com. ✆ **504/524-5980.** 60 beds. $32–$66 bunk bed; $149–$162 private room. Rates include linens. Street parking. **Amenities:** Shared kitchen and TV room; luggage storage; free Wi-Fi.

The Quisby ★★   The newer youth hostels are, as they say, lit. Unlike the derelict dives of yore, some are super-sleek and even—yes—clean. The Quisby is one of the best. Opened in 2017 after a gut-rehab of a long-shuttered historic building, the Quisby and its techno lobby area—sleek bar, sculpted industrial lighting, and graphical mural—sets the poppin' social scene. There, $3 well drinks rule at happy hour, and trivia nights on Wednesday are—as they also say—legion. The beds offer the best evidence that the Quisby is something special: no rickety Ikea-style pole kits, but handsome, sturdy, XL beech bunks built by a noted local wood craftsman, with memory-foam mattresses. Each has an adjacent book light, charging outlet, accessory cubby, and oversize storage locker. Configurations include two- and four-person private rooms and four- and six-person co-ed or female-only dorms. Perhaps the Quisby's single best feature is its streetcar-adjacent St. Charles Avenue location (to snag a window-laden room overlooking the avenue during Mardi

Gras, book 8–12 months ahead) and its 24/7 bar. Guests under age 18 must stay in a private room with a parent.

1225 St. Charles Ave. www.thequisby.com. ✆ **504/208-4881.** 120 beds. $23–$40/bed, $60–$100 during events; private rooms $70–$350. Rates include breakfast. Street parking. **Amenities:** 24-hr. bar with snacks and coffee; on-site laundry room; free Wi-Fi.

UPTOWN/GARDEN DISTRICT

The Garden District offers iconic Southern charm, complete with moss-laden greenery and palatial, columned homes. Not all of Uptown is as grandiose as the name might suggest—there are many more modest, no less charming properties—but the best sections are both spacious and gracious. Public transportation is easy, and street parking is usually easy to find.

Best for: Repeat visitors; romantics; history buffs; claustrophobes; garden lovers; Tulane and Loyola parents.

Drawbacks: Allow a little extra time to get around—it's sure pretty, but you're not in the thick of the action. You'll likely be close to inexpensive public transportation but may prefer a car or bike.

Expensive

The Chloe ★★   This new boutique hotel might initially remind you of that older, cooler cousin you had growing up—the moody, brooding one. The Chloe is impressively decked, with its dark teal paint, red and purple furniture, provocative art, hidden nooks—but belly up to the bar for a welcome beverage and you'll find it's also friendly. Built in 1891, the once-private mansion has 14 elegant guest rooms with nice natural light and hipster touches like turntables, vinyl from **Peaches** (p. 248), and Marshall speakers. Toss in Italian Bellino sheets, covetable bird-shaped lamps, and local Piety & Desire chocolates, and we're sold. (Narnia fans, please report to one of the Uptown King rooms or the Picard suite, where you enter the bathroom *through the wardrobe*.) The only drag is the off-limits balconies. Sigh: I suppose we'll adjourn to the pristine pool, where guests enjoy unlimited 24/7 access (and mixed-to-perfection cocktails at the pool bar), or the **restaurant** (p. 142), led by inimitable chef Todd Pulsinelli, with its exceptional modern Creole fare and dizzying wine list. Bonuses: Full breakfast included, and the streetcar stops just across the street.

4125 St. Charles Ave. www.thechloenola.com. ✆ **504/541-5500.** 14 units. $343–$949 double. Rates include breakfast. Discounts on extended stays. Street parking. Dogs allowed ($25/night, 1 max). **Amenities:** Restaurant; 2 bars; rental bikes; pool; room service; free Wi-Fi.

Expensive/Moderate

The Columns ★★   We'd be remiss to not point you to the newly revamped version of an old classic—and not just because we've spent countless afternoons on its patio, sipping Sazeracs. The Columns of yesteryear was beleaguered, but the new one? Blammo. It's back, baby. Built in 1884, the mansion

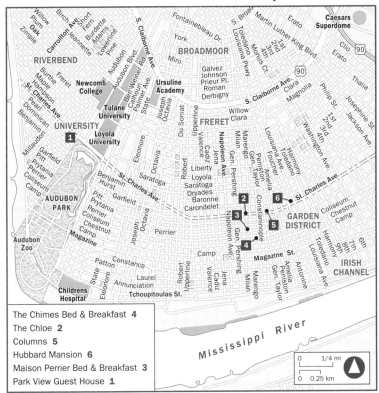

The Chimes Bed & Breakfast **4**
The Chloe **2**
Columns **5**
Hubbard Mansion **6**
Maison Perrier Bed & Breakfast **3**
Park View Guest House **1**

hotel changed hands in 2019 and got spruced up, complete with a spacious second-floor balcony and an elegant cocktail bar. Some modern-meets-antique rooms have dainty toile wallpaper; others are brightly painted. All are equipped with custom beds and Parachute linens. Fifteen-foot ceilings in the second-floor rooms heighten the experience. The kitchen is run by the **Coquette** (p. 137) team. (Breakfast not included, but the cafe has pastries, and there's brunch on weekends.) With a streetcar rumbling by like you're on a movie set, you're bound to be charmed.

3811 St. Charles St. www.thecolumns.com. ✆ **504/899-9308.** 18 units. $200–$390 double; $375–$586 suite. Street parking. **Amenities:** Bar/restaurant; cafe; free Wi-Fi.

Hubbard Mansion ★★★ Who says we could never be royals? This stunner of a Greek Revival mansion on St. Charles Avenue says otherwise. Five gracefully decorated, immaculate suites house museum-quality furnishings and heirloom antiques, such as velvety settees and claw-foot tubs, marble-topped dressers, and canopy beds. The treatment is royal, too. Sheila & Don are the consummate hosts, and the Uptown location is convenient and peaceful, right on the streetcar line, 1 block from a large grocery store, 2 blocks from **The Columns** (p. 90), where we never tire of cocktail-sipping, and across from **The Delachaise,** a must-visit wine bar. Lovely courtyard and continental breakfast included.

3535 St. Charles St. www.hubbardmansion.com. © **504/897-3535.** 6 suites. $215–$355 double. 2-night minimum. Rates include breakfast. Street parking. **Amenities:** Free Wi-Fi.

Moderate

The Chimes Bed & Breakfast ★★★   Reasons why this is a perennial favorite: constant upgrades and upkeep to the rooms, grounds, and common spaces; the tasteful, unfussy, unpretentious mix of antiques, modernity, creature comforts, and thoughtful amenities; the striking black-and-white photographs of local musicians decorating the rooms (the work of one of many repeat guests); and the individually cooked $15 breakfasts (eaten in the dining room, your own room, or in the pretty courtyard). But mainly it's because there are no grand airs, just pure charm and contentment in a true neighborhood setting. You'd be hard-pressed to find hosts who are more gracious, friendly, welcoming, and helpful—their 35+ years of hospitality experience (they built the Chimes themselves) shows in the details. (Also, sometimes on weekends, top local bands play on nearby porches, delivering true New Orleans spirit and soul to an otherwise quiet neighborhood.)

1146 Constantinople St. www.chimesneworleans.com. © **504/899-2621** or 504/453-2183. 5 units. $156–$219 double. Street parking. **Amenities:** Free Wi-Fi.

Maison Perrier Bed & Breakfast ★★★   The impressive exterior is frillier than inside, though there is still plenty to impress here. Antiques abound, and a smattering of country touches help create genuine, warm

---

NOT YOUR MOTHER'S room & board

Wherever you stay in New Orleans, good food is close by. But if that's just not close enough—if you're one of those who selects your accommodations based on its culinary offerings—here are a few hotels with outstanding restaurants:

- **Compère Lapin** (p. 126) in Old No. 77 Hotel & Chandlery (CBD)
- **The Chloe Restaurant** (p. 142) in the Chloe (Uptown)
- **Couvant** in Eliza Jane (CBD)
- **Domenica** (p. 130) in the Roosevelt Hotel (CBD)
- **The Grill Room** in the Windsor Court (CBD)

- **Jack Rose** in the Ponchartrain Hotel (LGD)
- **Josephine Estelle** (p. 127) in the Ace Hotel (CBD)
- **King Brasserie** in the Kimpton Hotel Fontenot (CBD)
- **Latitude 29** (p. 110) in the Bienville House (FQ)
- **Lüke** in the Hilton St. Charles (CBD)
- **Miss River** (p. 128) in the Four Seasons (CBD)
- **Restaurant R'evolution** (p. 106) in the Royal Sonesta (FQ)
- **San Lorenzo** (p. 140) in Hotel Saint Vincent (LGD)

comfort. The beds are deep and piled with soft linens, and room configurations are amenable to couples and families. All the well-appointed bathrooms have tubs—two of which are whirlpools. There's a full breakfast with mini-quiches and Southern specialties. A nonalcoholic honor bar, an ample supply of homemade sweets, and gracious hosts round out the very pleasing experience here. Check the website for seasonal deals. ***Bonus:*** The leafy, quiet residential neighborhood is close to Magazine Street shopping, the St. Charles streetcar, and Constantinople Stage, where you can occasionally catch terrific low-key weekend porch concerts.

4117 Perrier St. www.maisonperrier.com. ✆ **888/610-1807** or 504/897-1807. 9 units. $145–$295 double. Rates include breakfast. 2-4 day minimum-stay requirements. Limited free on-site parking or street parking. **Amenities:** Concierge; free Wi-Fi.

Park View Guest House ★   For Tulane and Loyola visitors and others staying far uptown, this late-1800s boardinghouse with easy streetcar access is a splendid choice. Views of verdant Audubon Park from the wide front porch, large breakfast room, or park-facing guest rooms add serenity and spaciousness. Antique-laden decor is Victoriana-meets-reproduction; smaller and nonview rooms can feel cramped, but all have updated bathrooms, some with walk-in showers, most with deep tubs. The hot ample breakfast also ranks high. Daily cookies and snacks add delightfulness; warm, helpful staff multiplies it. A cozy new inside/outside, open-to-the-public bar, **The Gilded Perch,** is a big bonus.

7004 St. Charles Ave. www.parkviewguesthouse.com. ✆ **504/861-7564.** 22 units. $199–$304 double. Rates include breakfast. Street parking and limited on-site parking. **Amenities:** Free afternoon snacks; bar; free Wi-Fi.

WHERE TO EAT

By Tami Fairweather

The late New Orleans restaurant matriarch Ms. Ella Brennan once said that whereas in other places, one eats to live, "In New Orleans, we live to eat." It seems that as soon as you step foot in this city, your appetite for just about everything somehow increases: adventure, romance, joy . . . and food food food.

Here, we don't call a friend and ask, "How are you?" Instead, it's either the colloquial "Where y'at?" or, more often, "What're you eatin'?" Here, cuisine is community, cuisine is culture, cuisine is a way of expressing love. Food forms the crucial threads of the city's multicolored fabric: It weaves through the people, the music, the history, the parties, the traditions. A style of gumbo can define a neighborhood. A conversation (or debate) about roux techniques could go on for an hour (we've seen it).

New Orleans has always been recognized by food lovers, but with the advent of the foodie movement, the restaurant scene has positively erupted, and the city has rightfully taken its place as a global food destination. When the post-Katrina population fell to three quarters of the pre-K population, the number of restaurants doubled. Some closed during the pandemic, but more opened.

There's goodness in every direction and on every level: in centuries-old grande-dame restaurants and corner po' boy shops, in a gas station with shockingly good steam-table food, and in the many bars, nightclubs, and roving pop-ups serving stellar snacks. Fourth-generation chefs work backstreet dives whose menus and ingredients haven't varied since, well, forever. Meanwhile, the pipeline for new cooks and chefs is supported by places like **Café Reconcile** (1631 Oretha Castle Haley Blvd.; www.cafereconcile.org; *©* **504/568-1157**) and **Liberty's Kitchen** (300 N. Broad St.; www.libertyskitchen.org; *©* **504/822-4011**), where you can eat lunch prepared and served by young people training for careers in food service. (Liberty's also hosts regular guest chef nights—an extra-local way to have a fancy dinner with some of the top chefs in town while supporting the community.) **New Orleans Culinary and Hospitality Institute** (NOCHI) offers "enthusiast classes" that deep dive into things like cheese tasting and oyster shucking with local chefs (go to www.nochi.org/enthusiast for upcoming classes).

Also Check Out . . .

A number of much-anticipated restaurants were *about* to open as we were turning in this book; we were not able to review them in time, but they should be open by the time you travel and will no doubt be worth checking out. They include northern Italian **Osteria Lupo** (4609 Magazine St.; www.osterialupo. com; *C* **504/273-1268**) and restaurateur and promoter Larry Morrow's **Sun Chong,** a Korean-inspired, hip hop–vibed love letter to his maternal grandmother (240 Decatur St.; www. sunchongnola.com; *C* **504/355-0022;** see Morrow's, p. 117).

You are going to want to eat a lot here. And you are going to want to eat here a lot. And then you are going to talk about it. You'll probably adopt the local custom of talking about dinner while you're at lunch (and lunch while you're breakfasting). The food here is utterly, unashamedly regional, which isn't to say that (in some cases) it's not also utterly of the moment, sophisticated, and/or redolent of other influences as well. But it's ingredient- and chef-driven, which makes it uniquely New Orleanian: Michelin-style frippery is irrelevant here, and it doesn't want (or need) to be anything else. While nearly all restaurateurs source fresh ingredients from local purveyors, butter phobia has never taken hold here (thankfully). Flavor comes first. That said, it's not hard at all to find healthy foods, including vegetarian and vegan options (p. 122).

So, indulge and enjoy. It's what you do here. Try some of everything. We're particularly big on lunching, as many of the best restaurants have terrific prix-fixe lunch deals that include dishes that'd cost twice as much during dinner; and Friday Lunches are events themselves (that go on for hours).

Please keep in mind that all prices, hours, and menu items in the listings are subject to change according to season, availability, or whim. Staffing remains a challenge since the pandemic, so add an extra dollop of patience. Reservations are recommended; call in advance to ensure the accuracy of anything of import to you (dietary restrictions or otherwise). Make sure to check out our **"Best of"** recommendations in chapter 1.

Of Beignets, Boudin & Dirty Rice

Many of the foods in New Orleans are unique to the region and consequently may be unfamiliar. This list should help you navigate local menus:

andouille (ahn-doo-*we*)   A spicy Cajun sausage made with pork.

bananas Foster   Bananas sautéed in liqueur, brown sugar, cinnamon, and butter, drenched in rum, set ablaze, served over vanilla ice cream.

barbecued shrimp   Not actually grilled or BBQ-sauced, but a butter-soaked, garlicky, pepper-shot peel-and-eat Gulf specialty.

beignet (ben-*yay*)   A big, puffy, deep-fried, square and hole-free dough-nut, liberally sprinkled with powdered sugar.

boudin (boo-*dan*)   Cajun pork-and-rice sausage of varying spice levels.

café au lait (cah-*fay* oh-*lay*)   Coffee with hot milk, usually flavored with chicory, a ground root.

CREOLE COOKING 101

In many restaurants—certainly in the more traditional ones—dishes are based largely on variations of Creole recipes, a cuisine created by the inhabitants of New Orleans. **Creole food** originally developed from cooking techniques brought by the French colony settlers, blended with the beans, herbs, and *filé* (ground sassafras leaves) used by Indigenous people; saffron and peppers were introduced by the Spanish, along with breads baked and vegetables farmed by German immigrants; new vegetables, spices, and sugar cane were brought from the Caribbean via trading routes. The West African and Afro-Caribbean influence runs the deepest, though it is often overlooked: It came from the enslaved cooks who prepared and created Creole food using local ingredients, melding French techniques with those of their homelands. The late Leah Chase (p. 119) once said that "There isn't one famous Creole dish that didn't pass through the hands of a Black chef or cook before it came to be written down." In recent years, a boom of pop-up chefs brought the Caribbean and African influences of Creole cuisine into sharper focus; many of them have now settled into permanent locations, staking their distinctive (and delicious) claim in the city's dining-scape.

café brûlot (cah-*fay* brew-*low*)   A boozy coffee, served flaming.

calas (keh-*lah*)   Sweet rice fritters, considered the precursor to beignets.

crawfish   A tiny, lobster-like freshwater crustacean with sweet and tender tail meat, most famously boiled whole with spices, potatoes, and corn and peeled by hand. (Also called *mudbugs*—but never *crayfish*.)

debris   The rich, juicy bits of meat that fall off during roasting and carving, often served in a gravy.

dressed   A "dressed" po' boy comes with lettuce, tomato, mayonnaise, and sometimes pickles.

étouffée (ay-too-*fay*)   A shellfish and roux-based stew (usually containing crawfish or shrimp) served over rice.

filé (*fee*-lay)   Ground sassafras leaves, frequently used to thicken gumbo.

gumbo   A richly-flavored soup of poultry, seafood, and/or sausage, with roux base, thickened with okra or *filé,* served with rice. **Gumbo z'herbes,** a Maundy Thursday tradition (before Easter Sunday), eschews meat for greens.

holy trinity   Onions, bell peppers, and celery: the flavor base of most Louisiana Creole and Cajun dishes.

Hurricane   A local cocktail of rum and passion-fruit punch.

jambalaya (jum-ba-*lie*-ya)   A simmer of yellow rice, sausage, seafood, poultry, vegetables, and spices.

king cake   A sweet, oval-shaped, cake-size pastry with lots of sugar on top and a tiny plastic baby (Baby Jesus) hidden inside. It's sacrilege to eat it out of season (Jan. 6 "King's Day" through Mardi Gras day, though you won't be struck down for eating a leftover on Ash Wednesday).

lagniappe (lan-*yap*)   A little something extra: a bonus freebie.

maque choux (mock-shoe) A corn-based side dish originating from Indigenous peoples, adapted by Cajun French.

mirliton (*mur*-li-tawn) A pear-shaped green squash, also called chayote.

muffuletta (muff-a-*let*-ta or muff-fuh-*lot*-ta) A mountainous sandwich made with Italian deli meats, cheese, and olive salad, piled onto a specially made seeded round bread (see box, p. 114).

oysters Rockefeller Oysters on the half shell in a creamy spinach sauce, so called because Rockefeller was the only name rich enough to match the taste.

po' boy/po-boy/poor boy A stuffed sandwich on long French bread, similar to submarines and hoagies (see "The Po' Boy Lowdown," p. 112).

pralines (*praw*-leens) A sweet confection of brown sugar and pecans.

Rémoulade (*rum*-a-lawd) A mayonnaise-based dressing with horseradish and Creole mustard, usually served over shrimp.

roux A mixture of flour and fat that's slowly cooked over low heat, used as a concentrated base for stews, soups, and sauces.

Sazerac The official cocktail of New Orleans, consisting of rye whiskey, Herbsaint liqueur, sugar, Peychaud's bitters, and lemon peel. (Sometimes with cognac instead of whiskey, or absinthe in place of Herbsaint.)

> ### Impressions
>
> In America, there might be better gastronomic destinations than New Orleans, but there is no place more uniquely wonderful. . . . It's a must-see city because there's no explaining it, no describing it. You can't compare it to anything.
> —Anthony Bourdain

shrimp Creole Shrimp in a tomato sauce, with a holy trinity base.

snoball Fluffy shaved ice drenched in flavored sugarcane syrup, plus condensed milk if you really want to go for it (p. 150).

THE FRENCH QUARTER

Expensive

Antoine's ★★ CLASSIC CREOLE We're sentimental about Antoine's, it being one of the first French-Creole fine-dining restaurants in the city, and the oldest. It's been owned and operated by the same family for going on 185 years; some of the chefs and servers have been there for 4 decades. It's as classic as classic New Orleans dining gets. Truth be told, the food isn't mind-blowing, but the experience is well worth it. The best strategy: Go for conviviality and classics. Order the charbroiled oysters and the hallowed soufflé potato puffs with your entree. If there are at least two of you, finish with a *café brûlot* and the frivolous football-size baked Alaska. Don't miss asking for a peek at the private rooms in the back, filled with paraphernalia from the founding Mardi Gras krewes—like the Twelfth Night Revelers and Rex—they will leave your head spinning. The seasonal two-course weekday lunch at $24

bars & clubs WITH NOTABLE FOOD

Folks in New Orleans love to linger at their bars, so savvy drinking spots generally enable such lingering by serving something more than pretzels and beer nuts. Though technically bars and clubs rather than proper restaurants, the following establishments serve bar food that's right up there with the best.

In the French Quarter, standouts include the Latin/Caribbean small plates at **Cane & Table** ★★★ (p. 223), sophisticated nibbles at champagne bar **Effervescence** ★★ (p. 224), tapas and caviar at cocktail specialist **Jewel of the South** ★★★ (p. 225), a pressed Cubano at **Manolito** ★★ (p. 225), and the famous hot muffulettas at **Napoleon House** ★★ (p. 226).

Hitting the music clubs on Frenchmen Street? You can chow down on topnotch burgers with a baked potato side at **Snug Harbor** ★★★ (p. 219), Asian-inflected comfort food at **Three Muses** ★★ (p. 220), or Cajun bar snacks around the corner at **Buffa's** ★★ (p. 220).

In the Lower Garden District, the beer-centric **Avenue Pub** ★★ (p. 227) is famed for its beef-fat tater tots and other pub grub, while the **Bakery Bar** ★★ (p. 227), just like the name says, will convince you that you do want cake with your cocktail. Swanky **Bar Marilou** ★★★ (p. 228) in the Central Business District serves French-ified small plates.

And among the city's top meccas of mixology, you'll find seasonal, global small plates accompanying the craft cocktails at Mid-City's **Revel** ★★ (p. 121) and Freret Street's **Cure** ★★★ (p. 228).

is worth every penny. The attached **Hermes Bar** offers more casual access. Make dinner or jazz brunch reservations well in advance during peak periods.

713 St. Louis St. www.antoines.com. © **504/581-4422.** Entrees $20–$46 lunch, $22–$57 dinner, $18–$46 brunch. Mon–Fri 11:30am–2pm and 5–9pm; Sat 10am–2pm and 5–9pm; Sun 10am–2pm. No shorts, flip-flops, or baseball hats; collared shirts strongly suggested.

Arnaud's ★★★ CLASSIC CREOLE   Arnaud's isn't the best-known of the old New Orleans restaurants, but it tops them in quality, and far exceeds them in the cocktail arena. It's classically atmospheric with white tile floors and dark wood accents, and the recipes are classics as well. Have the signature shrimp Arnaud appetizer (topped with a spicy rémoulade sauce) and the spicy pompano Duarte or the definitive *filet au poivre*. A pre- or post-meal stop in the classic **French 75** bar (p. 225) is required (with some puffy soufflé potatoes), and a more casual **jazz bistro room** features nighttime entertainment (a $6 cover goes to the band). The Sunday jazz brunch is also a worthy classic. Ask to see the vintage collection of Count Arnaud's daughter and successor Germaine's lavish Carnival ball gowns behind glass in the slightly haunting museum upstairs.

813 Bienville St. www.arnaudsrestaurant.com. © **866/230-8895** or 504/523-5433. Entrees $27–$45 dinner, $36–$49 brunch. Tues–Sat 5:30–9pm; Sun jazz brunch 10am–1:30pm. Reservations suggested. No shorts, T-shirts, or flip-flops; collared shirts required for brunch, jackets for dinner.

Bayona ★★ CONTEMPORARY SOUTHERN   After celebrating 30+ years, chef/owner Susan Spicer's multi-award-winning modern classic restaurant is more classic than modern, but the food, cocktails, and wine list are still thoughtful and inspired. The Creole cottage ambience inside and out is positively lovely, the staff attentive and warm. Always begin with the signature cream of garlic soup. Entrees are influenced by Spain, Italy, France, India, the Mediterranean, and Asia, often centering on rabbit, duck, and fresh Gulf fish; ever-changing preparations of locally-sourced vegetables are consistently superb, as are the desserts featuring seasonal fruits. The famed smoked duck with cashew butter and pepper jelly is a flavor bomb. Reservations required for dinner; book early.

430 Dauphine St. www.bayona.com. ✆ **504/525-4455.** Entrees $17–$12 lunch, $33–$44 dinner. Thurs–Sat 11:30am–1:30pm; Tues–Sat 5–9pm.

Brennan's ★★★ MODERN CREOLE   After a fall to lesser heights, ownership change, and $20-million-plus renovation 60 years in, Brennan's reclaimed its legendary restaurant-family name (it's owned by the Ralph Brennan limb of the family tree) about a decade ago and is back in all its pink glory and then some. Its elegant dining room, charming courtyard, and attentive service all scream old New Orleans, but there's nothing tired on the plate: Twists on classics turn updated dishes into newfound awesome. Breakfast at Brennan's is a celebration, like the airport billboards promise. First course: cocktails, as in a rum-spiked milk punch or a Ramos Fizz. They do well with breakfast meats, and the famed Brennan's-original egg preparations are pretty perfect. At dinner, seasonally-varied entrees are flourished with all things local: Sazerac glaze, Creole tomato gravy, Louisiana lump crab, sugar cane syrup. The signature turtle soup is well sherried, but the turtles living in the fountains have names (and the kids love 'em). Bananas Foster, born here in 1951 and prepared tableside, makes for a flaming fun finale. If your mood

---

Catch 'Em If You Can

What other cities might refer to as street food vendors are called **pop-ups** in New Orleans, and they come in various forms: food truck, pickup truck, someone else's restaurant kitchen, a folding table and a propane tank, or even a bike (See Taco Bike NOLA, www.instagram.com/taco bikenola). They're temporary, informal, and—just like a brass-band second-line parade—they signal that you serendipitously found yourself in the right place at the right time (and often on the cutting edge; some of our favorite restaurants started as pop-ups). Instagram can help with the fun of tracking them down through the bars that regularly host them; check **Barrel Proof** (p. 228, @barrelproofnola); **Miel Brewery** (p. 229, @mielbrewery); **Pete's Out in the Cold** (p. 227, @petesirishchannel); **Zony Mash** (p. 229, @zonymashbeer); **Pal's Lounge** (@palsloungenola); and **Pepp's Pub** (@peppspubnola). If you find Ms. Linda Green (@cheflindagreen), aka **The Ya-Ka-Mein Lady,** you've reached the pinnacle. Her brothy, salty, noodley, secret-recipe, Chinese-meets-Southern, nick-namesake soup is an iconic New Orleans original guaranteed to "fix whatever ails you right up" (especially a hangover).

Addis NOLA **20**
Angelo Brocato's Ice Cream
& Confectionery **8**
Annunciation **48**
Arabella Casa de Pasta **68**
Bacchanal **88**
Bakery Bar **52**
Bar Marilou **37**
Barrel Proof **50**
Bearcat **44**
Bésame **33**
Bevi Seafood **9**
Budsi's Authentic Thai **66**
Buffa's **65**
Bywater American Bistro **81**
Bywater Bakery **86**
Café Degas **14**
Café du Monde **4**
Cajun Seafood **63**
Carmo **46**
Chemin a la Mer **60**
Cleo's **84**
Cochon **53**
Cochon Butcher **53**
Coco Hut **17**
Coffee Science **24**
Commons Club **36**
Compére Lapin **57**
Country Club **82**
Domenica **34**
Dooky Chase **26**
Drago's **61**
Elizabeth's **85**

Elysian Bar **72**
Emeril's **55**
Frady's **84**
French Truck
   Coffee **38, 51**
Fritai **30**
Froot Orleans **19**
Gabrielle **25**
Gianna **39**
Green Room Kuhnya **64**
Herbsaint **41**
I-tal Garden **31**
The Joint BBQ **87**
Josephine Estelle **40**
Junction **79**
La Boca **54**
Le Chat Noir **42**
Liberty's Kitchen **22**
Lil' Dizzy's **29**
Liuzza's by the Track **15**
Loretta's Authentic
   Pralines **67**
Maïs Arepas **49**
Mammoth Espresso **43**

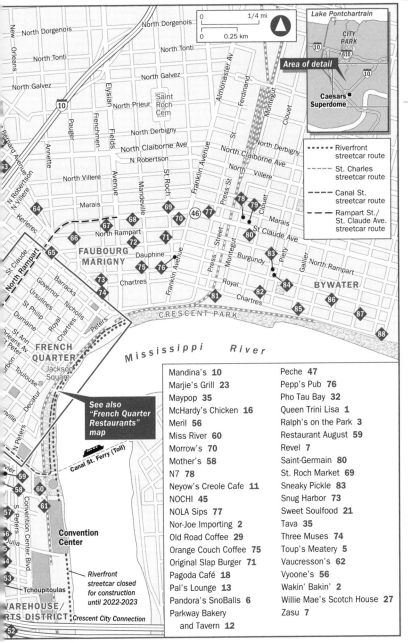

Lake Pontchartrain

CITY PARK

Area of detail

Caesars
Superdome

······ Riverfront
streetcar route

----- St. Charles
streetcar route

--- Canal St.
streetcar route

-- Rampart St./
St. Claude Ave.
streetcar route

New Orleans

North Dorgenois

North Dorgenois

North Tonti

North Tonti

North Galvez

Elysian

North Prieur

Saint
Roch
Cem

North Derbigny

North Claiborne Ave

N Robertson

North Villere

Marais

Kerlerec

FAUBOURG
MARIGNY

North Rampart

Dauphine

Chartres

FRENCH
QUARTER

Jackson
Square

See also
"French Quarter
Restaurants"
map

Canal St. Ferry (Toll)

Convention
Center

Convention Center Blvd

Riverfront
streetcar closed
for construction
until 2022-2023

Tchoupitoulas

WAREHOUSE/
ARTS DISTRICT

Crescent City Connection

North Galvez

Almonaster Av

Ferdinand

Montegut

Clouet

North Derbigny

St

North Claiborne Ave

North
Villere

Marais

St Claude Ave

Burgundy

Royal

Chartres

CRESCENT PARK

Mississippi River

BYWATER

North Rampart

Galjier

Piety

Mandina's **10**

Marjie's Grill **23**

Maypop **35**

McHardy's Chicken **16**

Meril **56**

Miss River **60**

Morrow's **70**

Mother's **58**

N7 **78**

Neyow's Creole Cafe **11**

NOCHI **45**

NOLA Sips **77**

Nor-Joe Importing **2**

Old Road Coffee **29**

Orange Couch Coffee **75**

Original Slap Burger **71**

Pagoda Café **18**

Pal's Lounge **13**

Pandora's SnoBalls **6**

Parkway Bakery
  and Tavern **12**

Peche **47**

Pepp's Pub **76**

Pho Tau Bay **32**

Queen Trini Lisa **1**

Ralph's on the Park **3**

Restaurant August **59**

Revel **7**

Saint-Germain **80**

St. Roch Market **69**

Sneaky Pickle **83**

Snug Harbor **73**

Sweet Soulfood **21**

Tava **35**

Three Muses **74**

Toup's Meatery **5**

Vaucresson's **62**

Vyoone's **56**

Wakin' Bakin' **2**

Willie Mae's Scotch House **27**

Zasu **7**

calls for a bottle of champagne, come for the sabering in the courtyard Thursday through Monday at 5pm.

417 Royal St. www.brennansneworleans.com. © **504/525-9711.** Entrees $22–$45 breakfast/lunch, $28–$50 dinner. Thurs–Mon 9am–2pm and 6–10pm. Smart casual dress; no shorts or tank tops for the gents.

Court of Two Sisters ★ CLASSIC CREOLE   No doubt about it, this is one of the prettiest places around, thanks to its huge wisteria-shaded courtyard in a 200-year-old building. Though the food is nothing special, its daily jazz brunch buffet is popular because it does the trick, especially with kids: There are plenty of items available, it's fairly priced, and you get all that jazz and atmosphere—so fill up and enjoy the company. Make brunch reservations in advance.

613 Royal St. www.courtoftwosisters.com. © **504/522-7261.** Dinner entrees $28–$37; brunch buffet $33 adults, $14 children 5–12. Daily 9am–3pm and 5:30–10pm.

Doris Metropolitan ★★ STEAK   Upscale Doris audaciously displays its dry-aging beef in the front window like the diamonds at Tiffany's. Besides the distinctive, slightly pungent flavor of dry-aged steaks (sourced from raised-to-specification cattle), the Israeli-run restaurant brings some Middle Eastern touches to its menu, like a charred eggplant appetizer with glossy tahini. Servers are warm and knowledgeable. The room's presentation is indisputably handsome. Locals have embraced the hopping bar with its beguiling wines and open-kitchen view, and a luxe, chill vibe permeates the moneyed air in the comfortable dining rooms. A juicy pan-glazed chicken knocked us over, and the silken tuna tartare is superb, but ultimately, it's about the beef. Great happy hour Tuesday through Thursday 5 to 6:30pm with shareable cocktails, that tuna tartare, and a primo $18 burger.

Price Categories
Meal per person, not including drinks or tip:
Inexpensive: $20 and under
Moderate: $20–$40
Expensive: $40 and above

620 Chartres St. www.dorismetropolitan.com. © **504/267-3500.** Entrees $22–$90 (Wagyu more). Tues–Sun 5–10pm; Fri noon–2:30pm.

Galatoire's ★★ CLASSIC CREOLE   Considered New Orleans' consummate old-line Creole French restaurant, Galatoire's is a time-honored, fine-dining classic beloved by generations—perhaps because their families are beloved by Galatoire's. Or perhaps because Tennessee Williams supped here, as did his characters Stella and Blanche in *A Streetcar Named Desire.* It oozes tradition: Ceiling fans whir, bentwood chairs strain, mirrored walls reflect the civilized frivolity. Things are a tad more somber in the (lesser, but perfectly fine) upstairs dining room. Either way, the drinking commences upon arrival, and doesn't let up for a few hours, especially at the fabled Friday Lunch, with a brass band rolling through and toasts made with the attention of the full

Acme Oyster House **12**
Antoine's **18**
Arnaud's **8**
Backatown Coffee **1**
Bayona **10**
Brennan's **17**
Café Amelie **40**
Café Beignet **9, 16**
Café du Monde **35**
Café Maspero **29**
Café Sbisa **45**
Cane & Table **48**
Central Grocery **44**
Cleo's **21**
Clover Grill **39**
Coop's Place **47**
Court of Two Sisters **19**
Croissant D'Or **42**

Dian Xin **23, 50**
Dickie Brennan's Bourbon
  House Seafood **11**
Doris Metropolitan **32**
Effervescence **37**
Felix's Restaurant
  & Oyster Bar **13**
French Truck Coffee **22**
Galatoire's **4**
Galatoire's 33 **5**
GW Fins **7**
Irene's **24**
Italian Barrel **51**
Jewel of the South **3**
Johnny's Po-Boys **28**
Justine **22**
Killer Po'Boys **6**
Latitude 29 **25**
Loretta's Authentic Pralines **52**

MaMou **36**
Meals From the Heart **53**
Mr. B's Bistro **14**
Muriel's **33**
Napoleon House **27**
Palace Café **20**
Palm & Pine **2**
Port of Call **54**
QuarterMaster **41**
Restaurant R'evolution **15**
Saint John **49**
Stanley **34**
Sylvain **30**
Tableau **31**
Toast **46**
Tujague's **26**
Verti Marte **43**
Wakin' Bakin' **38**

dining room. If you aren't offered a menu when you sit down, consider yourself a local (but it's okay if you do get one). No one comes here for great gastronomy, but Galatoire's does know fish (it's had 115 years of practice, after all). Go with a classic shrimp rémoulade, crab maison, or the eggplant fingers. Ask the waiter which fish is best today, get it a la meunière and topped with crabmeat; or order the soft-shell crab if available and some creamed spinach. Worth mentioning: Galatoire's regulars have known for years that these seafood specialists grill a mean steak. That's the specialty at the offshoot next door, **Galatoire's 33** (215 Bourbon St.; ✆ **504/335-3932**), which also corners the Galatoire's bar scene.

209 Bourbon St. www.galatoires.com. ✆ **504/525-2021.** Entrees $17–$52. Wed–Sat 11:30am–9pm; Sun noon–9pm. No shorts, flip-flops, or T-shirts; collared shirts always; jackets required after 5pm and all day Sun.

GW Fins ★★★ SEAFOOD   Polished from the top down, this modern seafood shrine is one of the city's best restaurants, period (and a leader in seafood sustainability education and practices). The day's freshest catches from the Gulf and beyond hit the kitchen by 4pm, changing the menu daily. The exceptions are the innovative (and phenomenal) dry-aged-in-house prime seafood cuts that Chef Michael Nelson says are best 2 weeks after the full moon (a testament to his deep knowledge of fishing related to the tides, rather than astrology). Stylish preparations include the signature "scalibut" (thin-sliced scallop "scales" atop grilled halibut), delicate calamari "fettucine" (shaved thin in white wine cream), "seacuterie" plates (with fish skin cracklins and swordfish bacon), and the startlingly rich and savory tempura-fried "wings"—aka fish fins, a sustainability-minded reimagining of a traditionally throwaway fish part. The wine list is thoughtfully complementary, with a good range of mid-priced bottles and an extensive array of finer pours by the glass. Order dessert, even if you only have room for a bite. The large, tiered dining room is conversation conducive, and we particularly love those high-backed gangster booths along the back wall. *Tip:* Vegan, gluten-free, and other special diets are accommodated with gusto.

808 Bienville St. www.gwfins.com. ✆ **504/581-3467.** Entrees $28–$75. Sun–Thurs 5–9:30pm; Fri–Sat 5–10pm. Collared shirts for men; no shorts, flip-flops, or hats in the dining room.

Italian Barrel ★★ ITALIAN   If longevity and popularity are solid measures, Italian Barrel shares the banner with Irene's (p. 110) for best Italian food in the French Quarter, covering the downtown end. Northern Italian is the focus, and the menu is full of familiar favorites. We're partial to the veal dishes and scampi, but pastas are generally winners (ask for sauce on the side if you like yours lightly sauced). Its popularity with locals and tourists alike also stems from the excellent wine selection and "friendly white tablecloth" ambiance; sidewalk tables offer a different take on romantic, even if the view faces the scruffier end of the Quarter.

1240 Decatur St. www.theitalianbarrel.com. ✆ **504/569-0198.** Entrees $25–$69. Sun–Thurs 11am–10pm; Fri–Sat 11am–10:30pm.

YOU GOT cajun IN MY CREOLE!

The murky difference between Cajun and Creole cuisine lies chiefly in distance between city and country. Cajun cooking came from the Acadians who settled in the swamps and bayous of rural Louisiana and adapted the recipes of their French-Canadian heritage to their new location's food sources, drawing on the indigenous Houma tribe's techniques (like boiling crawfish). Their cuisine is like their music: robust and full of flavor (and despite the reputation, not necessarily spicy), focused on single-pot stews that fed large families and farms. Creole, on the other hand, is a cuisine reflecting the various inhabitants of the city of New Orleans—something influenced by many cultures, and yet entirely new. (See "Creole Cooking 101," p. 96). Today, the two cuisines are often blurred on menus, and though both have jambalaya, gumbo, and liberal use of the holy trinity (p. 96), the distinctions are largely based in regional pride and tradition (though don't mess with gumbo outside of Louisiana). Our advice? Try it all, have fun asking questions to get locals going, and decide what dishes *you* prefer on your own.

Justine ★★ CONTEMPORARY FRENCH   This is dining as event and for events, a neo-nod to the Moulin Rouge reset in the French Quarter, just short of raucous and a definite *fête* for the eyes, where French antiques flirt with color-saturated modern decor (*j'adore* the multimedia murals, which mix historic and current local imagery). The straightforward French cuisine isn't as exuberant, nor is it on par (yet) with proprietors/chef Justin and Mia Devillier's flagship **La Petite Grocery** (p. 138). Still, the food is no second thought (and priced accordingly), and it's a worthy accompaniment to the overall fabulousness of a night here. Brunch is a blast with mimosa service, and the bar is a fun hang.

225 Chartres St. www.justinenola.com. ✆ **504/218-8533.** Entrees $24–$65 dinner, $19–$30 brunch. Sun–Thurs 5–9:30pm; Fri–Sat 5–10:30pm; Fri–Sat brunch 10:30am–2:30pm.

MaMou ★★★ CONTEMPORARY FRENCH   Since it bears the nickname of executive chef Tom Branighan's great-grandma, she must have made him feel as special as we feel here: A fresh flower tucked into our folded napkin, two sommeliers replenishing wine glasses from a one-of-a-kind decanter, the *Côte de Bouef* brought tableside in a skillet with a bundle of dried herbs and roasted lemons, and that rum cake flambé—prepared on a tiny cart, flames doused by a madeleine-shaped dollop of pistachio cream, joyfully placed center table. All this in a blissfully floral, flirty, Parisian-vibed brasserie space that feels like it's been here forever (it hasn't, they opened in Nov 2022). Branighan's menu mingles his Southern roots, French training, and locally-sourced ingredients to a (dare we say) nouveau-Creole result. A loosely woven bundle of julienned celery root tossed in a cool dill- and blue-crab-claw-infused rémoulade served atop a thick, warm wedge of *pain perdu* is a disarmingly delicious starter (we want it again right now). Partner and head sommelier Molly Wismeier and her team have applied their approachable charm to the wine list, and also to the cocktail menu—leading with moody flavor profiles like the Suze-based Golden Sage's "lush, velvety, bittersweet, savory"—that pretty much describes how we felt when the meal was over. Reservations will be necessary, though lucky walk-ins could nab a seat at the bar.

942 N Rampart St. www.mamounola.com. ✆ **504/381-4557.** Entrees $29–$44. Thurs–Sun 5–10pm.

Mr. B's Bistro ★★ CONTEMPORARY CREOLE   The "B is for Butter." Barbecue shrimp is the claim to fame here, and that's what you should get. Other dishes tempt as well (the gleaming ginger-glazed pork chop is terrific, for example), but the plump, peppery house special is the standout and indeed the distinguishing feature here. The hunt-club motif draws a businessman's lunch crowd for strong drinks and attentive service; the roving-band jazz brunch is a hit with all ages.

201 Royal St. www.mrbsbistro.com. ✆ **504/523-2078.** Entrees $22–$34 lunch, $28–$53 dinner, $22–$34 brunch. Wed–Sat 11:30am–2pm and 5–9pm; Sun 10:30am–2pm and 5–9pm. Upscale casual; men must wear sleeves.

Muriel's ★ CONTEMPORARY CREOLE   The dreaded "fine." That's how we feel about perennially popular Muriel's. We want to fall in love with its romantic, red-walled dining rooms, and pose on the elegant balconies overlooking Jackson Square. We want to *ooh* over the crawfish and goat-cheese crêpes, like others seem to do. But except for the admittedly fab atmosphere, there's just nothing especially inspired or inspiring here, on the plate or working the floor. That said, there's no denying that the table d'hôte menus are good value ($49.95); we'd opt for the safety of the pan-roasted half-chicken. Visit the ghost's table, and ask to see the séance room upstairs—it's worth it. Muriel's is popular with groups, so reserve in advance during peak periods.

801 Chartres St. (at St. Ann). www.muriels.com. ✆ **504/568-1885.** Entrees $19–$29 lunch/brunch, $27–$39 dinner. Sun–Thurs 5–9:30pm; Fri–Sat 10:30am–2pm and 5–10pm; bar opens daily at 3pm. Smart casual; no hats or tank tops for men.

Palace Café ★★ CONTEMPORARY CREOLE   A good standby for low-key, non-intimidating Creole dining, this historic two-story restaurant (formerly the Werlein's music store) has sidewalk seating for people-watching and a craft rum bar upstairs. It comes with the stamp of New Orleans authenticity that Brennan-family ownership conveys, and the crabmeat cheesecake appetizer makes people pound the table. Andouille-crusted fish is a winner, and the pleasantly familiar rotisserie chicken is done well. White-chocolate bread pudding was invented here, so opt for that (we like coming just for dessert at the streetside tables).

605 Canal St. www.palacecafe.com. ✆ **504/523-1661.** Entrees $16–$32. Wed–Fri 11am–3pm and 5–10pm; Sat–Sun 10:30am–3pm and 5–10pm.

Restaurant R'evolution ★★★ CONTEMPORARY CREOLE   This extravagant spot, helmed by food-world icons John Folse and Rick Tramonto, keys the cuisine to New Orleans' globe-hopping cultural influences. Go big at this big-idea, big-ticket spot in a fanciful but refined setting, with unpretentious service and beautiful plating. Tour the rooms (better yet, book one, like the stunning Storyville Parlor, or come for the festive jazz brunch). Indulge in something marvelous from the wine list, so enormous that only an iPad can contain it; select from the caviar, salumi, cheese, and potted meat sub-menus; and augment your order with sides, sauces, and toppings. Lead with the rich "Death by Gumbo" and gently crisped blue crab beignets, each with a different rémoulade dollop. Heaven. A jewelry box of tiny cookies is a darling lagniappe (get an after-dinner cognac or amaro to go with it). Service can be a bit casual for a restaurant of this caliber and cost, but it doesn't lag, and we'll take that over snooty. Do relish the luxe bar before or after dining, or hit it for happy hour (with a sampling menu).

777 Bienville St. (in Royal Sonesta Hotel). www.revolutionnola.com. ℂ **504/553-2277.** Entrees $26–$35 brunch, $29–$65 dinner. Sun and Wed–Thurs 5–9pm; Fri–Sat 5–10pm (happy hour 4:30–6:30pm). Reserve well in advance for dinner. No tank tops, T-shirts, flip-flops, or ballcaps.

Saint John ★★★ MODERN CREOLE   Born and raised in New Orleans, Chef Eric Cook helms two of the best restaurants in the city, **Gris Gris** (p. 142) and now the sleek and energetic Saint John, opened in late 2021. Cook and his chef de cuisine Daren Porretto (also locally born and raised) dug deep in researching old-school Creole family dinner-in-the-Quarter standards for Saint John, and the kitchen's skill and modern oomph turn those recipes into anything but traditional. Our favorite spot is right at the open kitchen counter, where you can see the fun the team has, cranking out dishes even they seem enamored by, such as grilled brown-butter corn on the cob or Southern greens braised in cane vinegar and syrup. You truly can't go wrong with anything, but we'll cite the oysters three ways (the double-cream poached version has us feeling *some type of way*) and the French-style beef daube (wine-braised short ribs) as two standouts. Cocktails rock and so do Porretto's personal playlists, which inspired Saint John's Sunday Bounce brunch. The wine selection—and the service—is solid and fun; lunch and brunch are great deals for the quality. Raised booths with a kitchen view and the front room bar are great options too.

1117 Decatur St. www.saintjohnnola.com. ℂ **504/581-8120.** Entrees $16–$25 lunch/ brunch, $20–$45 dinner. Sun–Mon and Wed–Thurs 11am–9pm; Fri–Sat 11am–10pm. Reservations recommended.

Tableau ★★ CLASSIC CREOLE   Tableau's pristine white space and high-arched entries are impressive, and its airiness conversation conducive . . . but that balcony view overlooking Jackson Square is peerless. Relish an afternoon here with a well-balanced classic cocktail, slices of the addictive tart bread, and a "Demi Royale" appetizer trio of seafood starters. In cooler weather, opt for a hearty red and the hopped-up onion soup or sage brown-butter gnocchi with pecans. Entrees are well-seasoned and perfectly balanced, like the juicy dark and white portions of chicken Tableau in a rich béarnaise sauce. Service occasionally hits overwhelm, but the overall experience is classic New Orleans, turned up enough to honor gastronomy in 1880 as well as today.

675 St. Peter St. www.tableaufrenchquarter.com. ☏ **504/934-3463.** Entrees $16–$32 brunch, $24–$48 dinner. Wed 5–9pm; Thurs–Sun 11am–9pm.

Tujague's ★★ CLASSIC CREOLE Tujague's holds the silver medal for oldest New Orleans restaurant (Antoine's has the gold), and tradition still reigns here, despite a move from its long-held location down the block. Some things changed for the better: Both food and decor are archetypal but spiffed up; others fell victim to the real estate transaction that pre-empted the move (trek to 823 Decatur to check the fab original neon sign and famed wooden bar and mirror) though the light fixtures and art made it. The bar still makes a perfect Sazerac, as well as Tujague's own invention, the frothy minty Grass-hopper. The traditional five-course table d'hôte menu is the way to go for classics: tenderly tossed house salad, sinus-clearing shrimp rémoulade, and warm bread pudding with rum sauce included. Soft-shell crab meunière (when in season) and off-menu baked garlic chicken Bonne Femme are good entree choices. You'll enjoy solid, if not earth-shattering, authentic Creole cooking at this true classic, whether brunch or dinner.

429 Decatur St. www.tujaguesrestaurant.com. ☏ **504/525-8676.** Entrees $16–$32 brunch, $26–$49 dinner; for 5-course dinner add $32 to entree price. Mon–Thurs 5–9pm; Fri 10:30am–2:30pm and 5–10pm; Sat 10am–2:30pm and 5–10pm; Sun 10am–2:30pm and 5–9pm; bar opens 2:30pm every day.

Moderate

Acme Oyster House ★★ SEAFOOD/CREOLE Is it worth the wait, you ask, eyeing the block-long lineup? They're Gulf oysters, people, and this is the oldest oyster bar in the French Quarter. In other words, yes (unless you're famished—then just go across the street to **Felix's;** see p. 110). The oysters are tastiest when you're standing at the bar, talking tourist trash with the shucker, piling up shells to be tallied later, knocking back some oyster shooters (chilled vodka, cocktail sauce, bivalve, gullet). But if you sit at a checked-cloth-covered table, you can also order a dozen or two of the garlicky chargrilled oysters, which may change your life. Or po' boys served in red plastic baskets, and Creole standbys (jambalaya, gumbo, red beans and sausage) good enough for those who do not slurp oysters. It's boisterous and there's much waiter scurrying, so things do move fast once you're inside.

724 Iberville St. www.acmeoyster.com. ☏ **504/522-5973.** Oysters $21/dozen raw, $29 chargrilled; po' boys and platters $11–$26. Thurs–Mon 11am–10pm; Wed noon–7pm. No reservations.

Café Amelie ★★ CONTEMPORARY SOUTHERN The greenery-laden brick courtyard was Amelie's calling card for years, and many hearts broke when it closed mid-2022. Proof that you can't keep a casual fine-dining legend with a good courtyard down lies in its resurrection on the corner of the ol' block in early 2023, romantic brick and greenery-laden courtyard included (just quainter). Go for properly-prepared Southern classics with a twist like shrimp and grits with corn *maque choux* (p. 97); an approachable, French-inspired wine list (by the glass and bottle); and a refreshing cocktail program (selection of mocktails included). Nothing here is fried (what a novelty!) and the new brunch menu offers a tasting option for the table, so no one has to make decisions they're not ready for—you're here to relax. If it rains, not to worry, there's a table (or a bar stool) ready for you in the warm and inviting dining room.

900 Royal St. www.cafeamelie.com. ℂ **504/412-8065.** Entrees $15–$29. Thurs–Sun 10:30am–2:30pm and 5:30–9:30pm; bar open between service.

Café Maspero ★ SOUTHERN

Why is it always so crowded here? We'll give you five good reasons: the big menu with something for everyone, decent food, reasonable prices, convenient location, and a seat to watch the action on Decatur Street. It's nothing to post home about, but it's an easy stop for a standard breakfast, burger, jambalaya, or muffuletta (regular or veggie).

601 Decatur St. www.cafemaspero.com. ℂ **504/523-6250.** Entrees $17–$25. Daily 8am–10pm. Breakfast menu until 4pm.

Café Sbisa ★★ CREOLE

Established in 1899, this atmospheric stunner sashays with original wood, intimate balcony, and courtyard patio dining. Chef Alfred Singleton, who worked his way up from busboy to chef until Katrina devastated the restaurant, took over as partner and chef in 2016. His outstanding French-Creole cuisine includes blue crab cakes and an amazing turtle soup laced with sherry, served under the watchful eyes of a bawdy George Dureau mural (which somehow survived the mold that bloomed after the flood). During Sunday brunch, live jazz fills the restaurant, providing a wonderful ambience in which to enjoy Creole classics like crawfish and andouille omelet, cheese grits, and smoked-salmon Benedict. Reserve a table on the balcony for alfresco dining.

1011 Decatur St. www.cafesbisanola.com. ℂ **504/522-5565.** Entrees $19–$32 brunch, $20–$38 dinner. Thurs–Sat 5:30–10pm; Sun 10:30am–2:30pm.

Dickie Brennan's Bourbon House Seafood ★★ SEAFOOD

Although it looks a bit sprawling and formulaic from the street, this modern version of a classic New Orleans fish house has much to recommend it. Hang out at the super-fresh raw bar or order the head-turning *fruits du mer* platter. A simple grilled redfish is perfect (top it with fresh lump crabmeat for $15 more, a worthy addition). In a city of good barbecue shrimp dishes (p. 95), we love the bourbon-finished version here. Leave room for a frozen bourbon milk punch, a dreamy booze-shake. (Naturally they're committed to and knowledgeable about all things bourbon.)

144 Bourbon St. www.bourbonhouse.com. ℂ **504/522-0111.** Entrees $11–$15 breakfast, $15–$25 lunch, $18–$32 dinner. Daily 8–10am (in lobby bar); Sun–Thurs 11am–9pm; Fri–Sat 11am–10pm. No tank tops or sweatpants.

Felix's Restaurant & Oyster Bar ★★ SEAFOOD/CREOLE Seventy-year-old Felix, the friendly across-the-street rival to **Acme Oyster House** (p. 108), has two rooms: the original, a down-home, nuthin'-fancy oyster bar/diner (entrance on Iberville), and a new spiffier spot around the corner (entrance on Bourbon St.). Oyster dozens come out fresh and bitterly chilled, needing nothing more than a spritz of lemon. You can also have them in stews, soups, pastas, or omelets, broiled, fried, or baked. And if it's crawfish season, order up a spicy pile. It's not nearly as much of a scene as Acme (a big plus), and the shuckers have fast hands and quick wit. *Tip:* If there's a line at the Iberville entrance, check the Bourbon Street entrance. They seat separately. Or, take a drive to the Lakefront location.

739 Iberville St. www.felixs.com. ✆ **504/522-4440.** Oysters $23/dozen raw; po' boys $15–$18; entrees $12–$28. Sun–Thurs 11am–9pm; Fri–Sat 11am–10pm. Also at 7400 Lakeshore Dr. on Lake Pontchartrain, ✆ **504/304-4125.**

Irene's ★★★ ITALIAN Consider Irene's if you're invariably enticed by the scent of simmering garlic. Owned and run by Irene DiPiertro, whose family moved from Sicily to New Orleans in 1956, this relatively underground French Quarter institution serves delectable house-made pastas and sauces, unfussy French Provincial and Creole-Italian dishes that have been on the menu for literally decades. There's the Duck St. Phillip (with raspberry-pancetta demi-glace), shrimp and crawfish fettucine, plus the seemingly simple *pollo rosemarino*—marinated, par-cooked, re-marinated, and roasted—that is nearly perfect. Smallish, warmly lit rooms (designed to resemble the beloved original location) engender a genial time, and chat between the closely set tables is common. Plan for a wait, even with reservations.

529 Bienville St. irenesnola.com. ✆ **504/529-8811.** Entrees $22–$35. Tues–Sat 5–9:30pm.

Latitude 29 ★★ HAWAIIAN When rumors first arose that Jeff "Beachbum" Berry was moving to New Orleans and opening up a bar/restaurant at the start of the tiki renaissance, the bartending community was ablaze. After all, Berry literally wrote the book on tiki. That the cocktails would deliver was never in doubt, but Lat 29 succeeds because it's all the tiki you could hope for and less: There's bamboo-wood-and-thatch decor, but it's understated; the fun, made-for-sharing rum bombs, in bowls and giant clamshells, are nuanced and ingredient-driven. The fare is less cloyed, with solid classic Hawaiian (Spam musubi, macaroni salad, and Loco Moco). There are pork ribs, a burger, and fries too. Wait for a cozy bar stool that you'll want to sit in for a while.

321 N. Peters St. (in the Bienville House hotel). www.latitude29nola.com. ✆ **504/609-3811.** Entrees $15–$28. Sun–Thurs 4–10pm; Fri–Sat 4–11pm.

Palm & Pine ★★★ SOUTHERN/LATIN This former pop-up leapt to the top of our "love" list shortly after opening in 2019. We're fond of its often-indefinable flavor hybrids that span the menu (Southern U.S. and south of that: Latin, Caribbean) and its easy-going, new-school vibe, in line with many other "edge of the Quarter" restaurants. Dishes are creative enough for those

CORNER STORE bites

Back-room deli counters in unassuming corner stores are prevalent throughout the city, serving up fast, cheap, and surprisingly good New Orleans cuisine. In the French Quarter, it's how many residents eat, because it's also mostly available 'round-the-clock. True locals eat their takeout while leaning against a wall or seated on someone's front stoop, but you can get it delivered too.

○ **Cleo's** (see p. 133)
○ **QuarterMaster** ★ (1100 Bourbon St.; ℭ **504/529-1416**; open 24 hr.). Best choices: basic po' boys,

especially the French-fry po' boy, and greasy burgers.

○ **Verti Marte** ★★ (1201 Royal St.; ℭ **504/525-4767**; open 24 hr.). Best choices: anything in the deli case or from the mother lode of a menu, especially the day's specials, like Grandma's Boardinghouse Meat Loaf or catfish Bienville.

For a destination spot, head to **Frady's** ★★ (in the Bywater at 3231 Dauphine St.; ℭ **504/949-9688**; Mon–Fri 9am–6pm, Sat 9am–3pm). Best choices: a hot plate or a hot sausage or oyster po' boy.

---

who want to push their palates beyond the usual, and the menu changes seasonally and frequently. It's best to share—everyone will want to try everything (look out for the spicy). One of the rare restaurants open late nights until 1am Friday and Saturday (accompanied by burlesque twice a month). Cocktails are outstanding; a winner for Sunday brunch, too.

308 N. Rampart St. www.palmandpinenola.com. ℭ **504/814-6200.** Entrees $25–$30. Mon and Wed–Thurs 5:30–9pm; Fri–Sat 5:30pm–1am; Sun 10:30am–2pm and 5:30–9pm.

Sylvain ★★ SOUTHERN   The tradition-bound French Quarter is surprisingly devoid of coolness, save for a few spots like this gastropub (and its sister **The Will & The Way** at 719 Toulouse St.). The allure of its side-alley entrance, Civil-War-meets-SoHo vibe, sexy courtyard, and literary heritage (it was once the home of a tall, feisty Storyville madam who was the inspiration for Miss Reba in Faulkner's *Sanctuary* and *The Reivers*) is irresistible. Though it's seen some wear and chef rotations, it's still delicious, friendly, and unexpectedly unpretentious, even when packed and loud. The signature fried chicken sandwich is a sure bet, and the $90 fries and champagne party pack is a good time; though the fries and "Champagne of Beers" (aka Miller High Life) for $25 might be even better.

625 Chartres St. www.sylvainnola.com. ℭ **504/265-8123.** Entrees $14–$20 brunch, $19–$32 dinner. Mon–Thurs 4–11pm, Fri–Sun 10:30am–2:30pm and 4–11pm (Sun closes 10pm); Fri–Sun bar stays open between brunch and dinner.

Inexpensive

Café Beignet ★★ CAFE   Some swear the beignets here are better than those at Café du Monde, and we can attest that they're usually fresh out of the deep fryer. You won't find insane lines here, and you will find brioche French toast, omelets, gumbo, sandwiches, and salads. All locations except Decatur

Often filled with fried seafood (oyster, shrimp, catfish, soft-shell crab), roast beef, hot sausage (a local's favorite), or famously with French fries and gravy, po' boys can be stuffed with most anything (see Parkway's Thanksgiving version). The story goes that they were originally a free sustenance offered to striking transit workers, working-class "poor boys." After decades of apostrophe and hyphen use, some purists are returning to the full "poor boy" name. They're delish in any spelling, and best eaten "dressed" (p. 96). Do yourself a favor—taste and compare at some of the classics: **Domilise's** ★★ (p. 146), **Guy's** ★★ (5259 Magazine St.; www.facebook.com/guyspoboynola; ℂ **504/891-5025**), **Johnny's** ★★ (below), **Killer** ★★★ (219 Dauphine St.; www.killerpoboys.com; ℂ **504/439-7445**), **Liuzza's by the Track** ★★★ (p. 123), **Parasol's** ★★ (2533 Constance St.; www.facebook.com/parasolsnola; ℂ **504/354-9079**), **Parkway** ★★★ (p. 124), and **Vaucresson's** ★★ (1800 St. Bernard Ave.; www.vaucresson sausage.com; ℂ **855/727-3653**).

Street have nice patios; there's even live jazz from 10am to 9:30pm at the Bourbon Street location, a respite from the street's insanity.

334 Royal St.; 311 Bourbon St.; 600 Decatur St.; 622 Canal St. www.cafebeignet.com. ℂ **504/500-4370**. Most items under $15. Daily, hours vary per location.

Clover Grill ★ DINER   The burger here is just a frozen patty thrown on the grill, but it's cooked under a hubcap (the better to seal in the juices), available at 4am, costs $9.79, and is served by a sassy queen in a "Clever Girl" T-shirt, making it so very worthwhile. Basic egg breakfasts and standard diner fare are also available. Bonus points for: excellent '80s jukebox, Formica counter, red vinyl stools you can spin around on, pie. But mostly for aforementioned sass, which they have in spades here, 24/7 (sleeping on the table not allowed).

900 Bourbon St. www.clovergrill.com. ℂ **504/598-1010**. Most items under $10. Daily 24 hr.

Coop's Place ★ SOUTHERN   This divey locals' hangout has long since been discovered by tourists, which may mean an unjustifiably long wait: It's good, but not OMG good—except for the well-known rabbit-and-sausage jambalaya, and the fried chicken, both of which really are pretty awesome. Decent food, friendly prices, late hours, and a menu that covers all the bases make this a good fallback if the line isn't crazy prohibitive.

1109 Decatur St. www.coopsplace.net. ℂ **504/525-9053**. Entrees $12–$22. Mon and Thurs 11am–10pm; Fri–Sun 11am–11pm. 21 and older only.

Johnny's Po-Boys ★ BREAKFAST/CASUAL   Johnny's is the standard-bearer for po' boys in the French Quarter, as old school as it gets. They'll put almost anything on that crunchy, fluffy Leidenheimer bread pretty much the way they've done it for nearly 75 years, but they're best known for their roast beef po' boy. We have a soft spot for their Italian chicken parm. The line moves fast; don't be discouraged. Little-known insider fact about the family-owned fave: It's also a good, cheap breakfast spot. Other little-known fact: They deliver in the Quarter.

511 St. Louis St. ✆ **504/524-8129.** Most items $9–$15. No credit cards. Daily 8am–3:30pm.

Port of Call ★ CASUAL   Port of Call's half-pound monster burger has been drawing hordes for decades, so you're probably going to wait a while for it. So, what's the appeal? Besides the capricious baked potato side in lieu of fries, it's the toppings (we like the wine-soaked sautéed mushrooms), the fruity tiki drinks, and the dark ship-themed den of a dining room (and packed bar). There are steaks on the menu, but they're irrelevant. Sometimes you just need a good burger, and even with other serious contenders around town (if the line is hideous, head into the Bywater for **The Original Slap Burger ★★** in the delightfully divey **Marie's Bar & Kitchen,** 2483 Burgundy, www.originalslapburger.com).

838 Esplanade Ave. www.portofcallnola.com. ✆ **504/523-0120.** Cheeseburger $12, rib-eye $23. Sun–Mon and Wed 11am–10pm; Thurs–Sat 11am–midnight. No reservations.

Stanley ★★ SOUTHERN   It's cute and convenient (Jackson Square–adjacent) and serves well-prepared "regular" food that kids and grown-ups like (pancakes, good burgers, and an old-fashioned soda fountain serving home-made ice cream). So naturally it's popular as all get-out; try to go during off-peak hours. If you need a po' boy fix, the cornmeal-crusted oyster is a good way to go. For breakfast (served all day), those oysters come Benedict style, with poached eggs and hollandaise. Yum.

547 St. Ann St. (corner of Jackson Sq. and St. Ann). www.stanleyrestaurant.com. ✆ **504/587-0093.** Everything under $20. Mon and Thurs 8am–3pm; Fri–Sun 8am–4pm.

Toast ★★★ CAFE   Breakfast, thy name is Toast. Lunch, too. This darling French Quarter offshoot of one of our fave spots near the Fair Grounds has rolled omelets, sweet or savory crepes, waffles, and yes, French toast (including a decadent king cake version with cinnamon cream filling); also thick toast with inventively savory toppings (fried oysters or herbed ricotta). Start with *abelskivers* for the table (we like 'em with Nutella or lemon sauce) and go from there, as you watch the Decatur Street action through enormous windows (or sit at the old-fashioned counter). Most everything, including larger entrees like a fried chicken biscuit sandwich or hanger steak, is tasty and generously sized.

1035 Decatur St. ✆ **504/300-5518.** Everything under $15. Daily 8am–3pm.

Wakin' Bakin' ★★ CAFE   Headline: "Neighborhood breakfast fave finds new French Quarter home. Tourists approve." We've always loved this quiet bi-level corner space, and it suits Wakin's down-home friendly, familiar fare just fine. Don't come for innovation, do come for pancakes, shrimp étouffée

WHOLE LOTTA muffuletta GOIN' ON

Muffulettas are sandwiches of (pardon the pun) hero-ic proportions, enormous concoctions of round seeded Sicilian bread, Italian cold cuts, cheese (usually aged provolone and swiss), and olive salad. One person cannot eat a whole one—at least not in one sitting. A half makes a good meal; a quarter is a filling snack. They may not be as famous as their New Orleans–sandwich sibling, the po' boy, but once you try one, you'll be hooked.

Though a few places in town claim to have invented the muffuletta, no one disputes it being born in "Little Palermo" near the river docks in the French Quarter, which, in the late 19th century, was a working-class neighborhood of mostly Sicilian immigrants. Now you can find it on menus across the city; comparison-shopping is a worthy (and rewarding) pastime.

The world-famous **Central Grocery** ★★★, 923 Decatur St. (© **504/523-1620**), is the undisputed muffuletta mecca; though damage from 2021's Hurricane Ida shut the storefront down, it should be reopened by press time (and the sandwiches are sold next door at Sidney's Wine Cellar in the meantime, $30 for a whole). They're made and wrapped early in the day, letting flavors soak through. Expect some seating, but it's more romantic to walk across the street and eat on the banks of the Mississippi anyway.

Are the hot muffulettas at **Napoleon House** ★★ (p. 226) better or blasphemy? It's a heated debate (it's the former if you're a toasted bread fan). Feeling experimental? Drive to **Nor-Joe's Importing Co.** ★★, 505 Friscoe, in Metairie (© **504/833-9240**), where the ginormous muffulettas, constructed with iconoclastic ingredients like prosciutto and mortadella, have their own cult following. Feeling fancy? The upcycled version at newcomer **Miss River** ★★ (p. 128) is pretty terrific. Then there's **Cochon Butcher** ★★★ (p. 132), where house-cured meats top a mini 'letta, and the ever-inventive **GW Fins** ★★★ (p. 104) seafood version.

and grits, the breakfast bowls and burrito, all with homemade touches (including biscuits and sourdough bread). Well-priced and kid-friendly but BYOB. 900 Dumaine St. www.wakinbakin.com. © **504/233-3877.** Entrees $10–$17. Daily 7am–2pm. Also Uptown at 3625 Prytania St. and in Mid-City at 4408 Banks St.

THE FAUBOURG MARIGNY & BYWATER

Expensive

Saint-Germain ★★★ CONTEMPORARY FRENCH Proposing? Whether or not, consider this romantic 16-seat dining room in a converted shotgun house, which transports you from gritty St. Claude Avenue to a country inn outside Lyon, perhaps. The nightly menu is based on availability and chef's whim; you're wise to put yourself in his hands for 10 courses. At various times here we've enjoyed a lean venison tartare with a rich gorgonzola sauce; our first guodong clam with cantaloupe; and a less exotic but no less lovely salmon, delicately herbed and accompanied by buttered shitakes. There's verve to the cooking, vitality to the components, and a bit of chef madness, with French roots lurking. If you can't get a dining room reservation, a basket of magical frites with a glass of wine (or a cocktail) in the adjacent bar are an excellent also-ran. Wines are natural; service is gracious. Alert for vegans and vegetarians: The third week of every month, the menu is meat-free.

3054 Saint Claude Ave. www.saintgermainnola.com. ℭ **504/218-8729.** 10-course menu $125–$135; wine discounts on Wed. Wed–Sun 5:30–10:30pm. Reservations essential. No children.

Moderate

Bacchanal ★★★ SPANISH/MEDITERRANEAN   It's a ramshackle old building and a big backyard. It's a wine store. It's a bar. It's a jazz club, and a small-plates restaurant. Its everything-at-once epitomizes New Orleans, and it's one of our favorite spots anywhere. The unusual, European-leaning wine selection, creative cocktails, and funky twinkle-lit outdoor garden with live music (day and evening) attracts locals kicking back in mismatched chairs, steampunk wine snobs in deep discussion, and—as of late—mostly out-of-towners seeking the "real" New Orleans on weekends. Get wine bottles inside, glasses out. Find a table, order at the window, and get a number. Or better yet, choose and buy your cheese from the wine shop fridge, and pay the upcharge to have the kitchen transform it into a charcuterie plate. A converted attic bar with extra tables means it's available even on rainy days, but ahh, that garden. It won't be the best meal you have in New Orleans (the food is two stars), but it's tasty, never boring, and ultra-atmospheric. It all seems thrown together, but it melds into something much greater than the sum of its parts (thus the three stars).

600 Poland Ave. www.bacchanalwine.com. ℭ **504/948-9111.** Tapas and small plates $10–$13, entrees $20–$38. Mon–Thurs noon–10pm; Fri–Sun noon–11pm (kitchen closes 1 hr. earlier). 21+ only. No reservations.

Bywater American Bistro ★★★ CONTEMPORARY SOUTHERN   About a week after opening BABs, as Nina Compton's second New Orleans restaurant is known, she snagged the James Beard award for Best Chef South for **Compère Lapin** (p. 126), her flagship locale. No pressure. And still she persists . . . and rises to meet her own high bar. This more casual spot is no less inventive, featuring flavor profiles that spark the palate in ways both newfound and comforting, taking techniques and ingredients from New Orleans and the Caribbean by way of Europe, with appetizers leading the way (order 2-3). The handful of entrees each evening will feature Gulf fish, meat, or house-made pasta, with perfect flavor balances like brown-butter hazelnut and coconut celery-root puree, or polenta with English peas and charred spring onions. That said, the biggest hit is the simple spaghetti pomodoro: It's perfection. The bar program is solid, and a seat there is a fun hang in the warm and artsy warehouse space.

2900 Chartres St. www.bywateramericanbistro.com. ℭ **504/605-3827.** Entrees $18–$30. Wed–Sat 5:30–10pm; Sun 10am–2pm and 5:30–9pm.

The Country Club ★★ MODERN CREOLE   See review, p. 231.

Elizabeth's ★ SOUTHERN   Elizabeth's was driving the bacon truck long before the bandwagon hooked on, and it's rightly famous for its brown-sugar-coated praline version. If the quality's dropped a bit since that heyday and service leans toward perfunctory, it's still a solid choice for Southern breakfast and brunch faves—like fried chicken livers with pepper jelly or old-fashioned calas (p. 96). The bananas Foster *pain perdu* is a perennial winner.

601 Gallier St. www.elizabethsrestaurantnola.com. ℂ **504/944-9272.** Entrees under $16; brunch $12–$24. Thurs–Mon 8am–2:30pm.

Elysian Bar ★★ CONTEMPORARY SOUTHERN   In a converted church that houses the ultra-hip **Hotel Peter & Paul** (p. 82), the stage is set for an eclectic vibe and menu. Expectations are met. Fortunately, it's also good, especially for brunch (served daily). The bar's overgrown cypress tree sculpture (crafted by Mardi Gras float builders) is worth a look, and the two parlor-style rooms are well-suited for a bottle of wine with your meal. The sunshine yellow "breakfast room" is the most practical for dining. Menus are limited but enticing, veggie-forward, and made for sharing. Desserts aren't much but justify another selection from the wine list's fine curiosities.

2317 Burgundy St. www.theelysianbar.com. ℂ **504/356-6769.** Entrees $16–$24 brunch, $18–$28 dinner. Daily 11am–3pm and 5–10pm ('til 11pm Fri–Sat); coffee cafe 7am–1pm, bar snacks 3–5pm.

st. claude ICONOCLASTS

There's talent in the clubs *and* the kitchens of St. Claude Avenue (p. 219), where a burgeoning homegrown restaurant scene is incubating some crushing creativity at modest prices. Anchoring the avenue is **St. Roch Market** ★★, a food hall trendsetter showcasing varied vendors (2381 St. Claude Ave.; www.strochmarket.com; ℂ **504/267-0388;** dining Sun–Thurs 11am–9pm, Fri–Sat 10am–11pm; coffee daily 7am–7pm). Other faves nearby:

○ **Arabella Casa di Pasta** ★★   At the counter, order mixy-matchy style from skillfully house-made pastas and sauces, plus veggie, shrimp, or sausage add-ins. Consulting Italian Grandma Nettie says check YES box next to the meatballs; ditto the filled-to-order cannoli. 2258 St. Claude Ave.; www.arabellanola.com;

ℂ **504/517-5540;** Mon–Thurs 4–9pm, Fri–Sat 4–10pm.

○ **Budsi's Authentic Thai** ★★   This Thai standard-bearer's proof of quality is its leap from pop-up to brick and mortar restaurant; its food is still all flavor and freshness. 1760 Rampart St.; budsisthai.com; ℂ **504/381-4636;** Tues–Thurs and Sun 11am–9pm, Fri–Sat 11am–10pm.

○ **Junction** ★★   High-quality burgers (beef sourced from a local small-production cattle farm) on soft, sweet brioche buns baked by Dong Phuong (p. 147). Straight up or with specialty toppings plus one of 40 tap craft beers. 3021 St. Claude Ave.; www.junctionnola.com; ℂ **504/272-0205;** daily 11am–2pm.

○ **Morrow's**   See full review, p. 117.

Morrow's ★★ SOUL FOOD/KOREAN   Two traditions meet in this mother-son operation. Mom Lenora is in charge of Korean dishes (Bibim Bop, short ribs, sesame ginger wings); son Larry handles the straight-up New Orleans Creole-meets-soul dishes (po' boys, charbroiled oysters, crawfish pasta). There's not much fusion going on, just two-in-one goodness with fair prices, always dope vibes, and a well-dressed crowd out for a night on the town, snapping selfies to prove it. Order the Oysters Morrow immediately. (Event and club promoter Larry also owns the **Treehouse** hookah and music club in Central City—1840 Thalia St; www.treehousenola.co.)

2438 St. Claude Ave. www.morrowsnola.com. ⟂ **504/827-1519.** Entrees $12–$26. Mon–Thurs 11am–10pm; Fri–Sat 11am–11pm; Sun 10:30am–4pm.

N7 ★★★ FRENCH   On a balmy eve, there may be no better place than under N7's pergola. This idyllic setting secreted behind an unmarked door in the St. Claude neighborhood feels as if you've dropped into a backyard in Laurel Canyon—or Avignon—circa 1967. As we languidly sipped an aromatic viognier at one of the mix-and-match patio tables, while noshing mussels steamed in sake and roasted beets with pistachios and smoked yogurt, it made perfect sense that the couple at the table on our left were practicing card tricks; the well-shod middle-agers at a bottle-laden picnic table were sampling pours; and the scruffy dudes across the room were polishing off escargot and frites between intense chess moves. During more inclement weather, house-made charcuterie and onion soup in the *charmant* dining room is nearly as dreamy.

1117 Montegut St. www.N7nola.com. No phone. Entrees $13–$17 lunch; dinner small plates $12–$18, large plates $20–$35. Mon–Thurs 5–9pm; Fri–Sat 11:30am–2:30pm and 5–10pm. 18+ only. Reservations advised (up to 30 days in advance).

Inexpensive

Bywater Bakery ★★★ CAFE/BAKERY   The only bad thing about Bywater Bakery is that it closes too early. This casual Bywater breakfast-lunch cafe is a multi-threat, with delicious pastries, scrumptious savories, really cool local art, a rotating variety of local musical talents playing on weekends, and occasional block parties. We're fond of the "breakfast Gumbo" served over grits with scrambled eggs; the Ya-Ka-Mein soup (with Ms. Linda's blessing, see p. 99); anything from the bakery case; and bagel Fridays (Fri only, and they sell out by midday). Surprisingly, it's only been open since 2017 rather than forever, like it feels. That's all the love for community and baking that chef/owner Chaya and her husband Alton put into it: You can taste it in every bite.

3624 Dauphine St. www.bywaterbakery.com. ⟂ **504/336-3336.** Everything under $14. Thurs–Mon 8am–3pm.

The Joint ★★★ BARBECUE   When you think of barbecue, you might conjure up Memphis, St. Louis, Texas, the Carolinas . . . well, the Joint stands up to the best of them. Its location in an old corner store is less joint-like and more roadhouse, with picnic tables inside and out back, and wood chopping for the enormous smoker on ready view. The luscious baby back ribs and lean, smoldering brisket are sublime; for something local, try the house-made green onion sausage. Save room for peanut butter pie. Some cuts sell out, so get there early for the best selection.

701 Mazant St. www.alwayssmokin.com. © **504/949-3232.** Entrees $10–$19. Mon–Thurs 11:30am–9pm; Fri–Sat 11:30am–10pm.

MID-CITY/TREMÉ/BAYOU ST. JOHN
Expensive

Gabrielle ★★★ CONTEMPORARY CAJUN   It took 12 years for this charming neighborhood gem to return from its watery (Katrina) demise, and one bite for us to be all in. The warm French-blue exterior in the midst of Orleans Avenue in the Tremé is a welcoming beacon to the creative Cajun and Creole riffs within (for example, why have applesauce with your pork chops when you can have *root beer glazed* apples?). Regulars table-hop between bowls of smoked guinea hen gumbo, an insanely good concoction coaxed from the delicious depths of a near-black roux. The barbecue shrimp/sweet potato pie appetizer positively works, and it leads directly to the signature dusky sweet roast duck (with orange-sherry sauce), or cassoulet stewed with craw-fish, shrimp, lobster, smoked fish, *and* a fried oyster (*plus* a seared sea scallop? See what we mean?). And then, all the desserts. We mean it. We can't pick.

2441 Orleans Ave. www.gabriellerestaurant.com. © **504/603-2344.** Entrees $27–$42. Thurs–Sat 5–9:30pm.

Ralph's on the Park ★★★ CONTEMPORARY CREOLE   Huge pic-ture windows look out on Spanish moss–draped oaks in City Park. Live piano seeps from the lounge and across the cream-upholstered dining room. You're sipping a French 75, gazing upon the setting sun, glistening rain, or your sweetheart's lips. Whatevs—it's dreamy here. The fare is traditional fine Cre-ole with a pinch of global inspiration. Grilled tuna comes with green tomato chow chow; jambalaya is made into arancini. Desserts are crowd-pleasing: Just say strawberry doberge cake. The whole experience epitomizes Southern elegance—a vacation within a vacation, it's easily reachable by car ride or the City Park streetcar, and there are usually multi-course specials at lunch and brunch, plus a happy hour.

900 City Park Ave. www.ralphsonthepark.com. © **504/488-1000.** Entrees $16–$33 lunch/brunch, $24–$43 dinner. Tues 5:30–9pm; Wed–Fri 11:30am–2pm and 5:30–9pm (Fri until 9:30pm); Sat–Sun 10:30am–2pm and 5:30–9pm (Sat until 9:30pm).

Zasu ★★★ SEAFOOD/GLOBAL   One of our favorite newish fine dining restaurants is this petite, sophisticated bistro. Music is low; walls an urbane asparagus green; service informed and affable; plating striking. Whip-smart preparations are just atypical enough to stretch the palate's expectations yet gentle enough to spotlight the fine ingredients. Proof is in a seared halibut in a graceful mushroom-ginger broth, surrounded by crisp peas and haricot verts—a simple, perfect melding of textures, components, and flavor. The sumptuous Korean pork cheeks starter satisfies more robust cravings; delicate pierogies (!) are a "for the table" requisite. Drinks are equally well prepared; wines well selected; desserts, too, are swell (we're smitten with the brown sugar tart with satsuma marmalade).

127 N. Carrollton Ave. www.zasunola.com. ℂ **504/267-3233.** Entrees $23–$35. Mon and Wed–Thurs 5:30–9:30pm; Fri–Sat 5:30–10pm. Reservations advised.

Moderate

Addis NOLA ★★ WEST AFRICAN/ETHIOPIAN Family-owned Addis is the bustling hub of the African diaspora on Bayou Road, thanks to its stunning, sensual space and expertly prepared family-style Ethiopian dishes, sopped up just right by the spongy injera bread (house-made daily). We can't resist the spicy, honey-glazed Mar Mitmita shrimp; or the fried sambusa hand pies filled with lentils, meat, or collard greens (we go for the greens). A traditional Ethiopian coffee ceremony for four comes with a respectable pomp and delicious ice cream for the table. Black-owned brands and spirits are highlighted at the bar, and though the Ethiopian coffee martini is a standout, we're big fans of the Prince's TEJ Ethiopian honey wine.

2514 Bayou Rd. www.addisnola.com. ℂ **504/218-5321.** Entrees $16–$35. Wed–Mon 5–10pm (closed Tues).

Café Degas ★★★ FRENCH Every neighborhood in every city should have a charming, casual French bistro that serves a perfect salad Niçoise and has a tree growing in the middle of the indoor/outdoor dining room. But only Faubourg St. John can claim it. Café Degas is darling, perfectly suited to a romantic dinner or a gals' lunch. Favorites like escargot, hanger steak, and rack of lamb are straightforward, flavorful, and generous; a delicate roast quail starter is tempting to double as an entree. It's a popular spot, particularly for brunch and 30-percent-off bottled wine Thursdays, so reserve ahead.

> ### Impressions
>
> You've got to live life to the fullest. You just enjoy every beautiful thing there is to enjoy.
> —*Chef Leah Chase of Dooky Chase*

3127 Esplanade Ave. www.cafedegas.com. ℂ **504/945-5635.** Entrees $13–$27 lunch/brunch, $26–$35 dinner. Wed–Fri 11am–3pm and 5–9:30pm (until 10pm Fri); Sat–Sun 10:30am–3pm and 5–9:30pm (until 10pm Sat). Reservations advised.

Dooky Chase ★★ SOUL FOOD/CREOLE The late Leah Chase—chef, hostess, art curator, activist, educator, unifier, mother, and proprietress of Dooky Chase since the 1940s (founded with her late husband Dooky) was a visionary who knew that food and grace could unite the divided, impel justice, and ultimately change the world. The Chases created a welcoming place for Rev. Dr. King and other civil rights leaders to dine and work; Dooky's was where Sarah Vaughn, Nat King Cole, Ray Charles, and other musicians hung out at all hours; they hosted Obama, and Bush II. Ms. Leah was the model for

Tiana in Disney's delightful *The Princess and the Frog*. She won just about every culinary award in existence, and after Katrina decimated the restaurant (they lived in a FEMA trailer across the street for years while rebuilding) and Dooky passed, she persevered, "cooking with love" and making immeasurable contributions to New Orleans and the whole country. After her passing at age 96 in 2019 and the traditional second-line jazz funeral that made national news, the younger Chases are continuing the tradition of Creole standards and a handsome, art-filled, neighbor-saturated dining room. Come on a pilgrimage for the hallowed history and stay for the fried chicken, a contender for the city's best.

2301 Orleans Ave. www.dookychaserestaurants.com. ✆ **504/821-0535.** Lunch buffet $18, dinner entrees $20–$25. Tues–Thurs 11am–3pm; Fri 11am–3pm and 5:30–9:30pm; Sat 5:30–9:30pm. Business casual attire (no tank tops, ballcaps, short-shorts, or crop tops).

Fritai ★★★ HAITIAN   This bright, warm, and vibrant space is filled with island energy befitting New Orleans' status as the northernmost city in the Caribbean. Chef Charly Pierre's delectable foray into Haitian cuisine honors the deep cultural connection between the two places, cemented when Haitian immigrants doubled the city's population after the Haitian Revolution in 1809. The menu is often rotating, but we can always count on our favorites: the charred beet salad with avocado and a minty orange zest, baked crab mac 'n' cheese, and the signature Fritai sandwich with your choice of filling between two fried plantains. An outstanding bar menu centers on fruit-, spirit-, and coconut cream-forward choices, plus our favorite: a tropical take on a DIY "setup" cocktail for the table, a NOLA neighborhood bar staple. Haitian art paintings are for sale.

1535 Basin St. www.fritai.com. ✆ **504/264-7899.** Entrees $16–$29. Wed–Mon 4–10pm (closed Tues).

Mandina's ★★ CREOLE ITALIAN   Dis is da ultimate Sicilian-Creole neighborhood restaurant, owned by the same family since the late 1800s—and largely unchanged, as it should be. Nothing innovative here, just heart, soul, and comfort food the way Nonna made it (including canned veggies—skip 'em), served by someone who looks like her. If the daily specials aren't to your liking, get some butter-soaked garlic bread to share, and the right and true seafood gumbo or Italian salad (with anchovies). Then go for the sweet Italian sausage and spaghetti combo, or the brown-buttery trout meunière. The cocktails are strong here; so is the air-conditioning. Bring a sweater.

3800 Canal St. www.mandinasrestaurant.com. ✆ **504/482-9179.** Entrees $13–$28. Sun–Thurs 11am–9pm; Fri–Sat 11am–9:30pm.

Marjie's Grill ★★ CONTEMPORARY SOUTHERN/ASIAN   Eclectic menu, off-cuts of meats and poultry, offbeat location, playful flavor mashups. It works. Adventurous Marjie's mashes Southeast Asian bar food flavors (Vietnamese, Laotian, Thai) with Southern Gulf bounty and, in many cases, smokes them over coal or wood. It's not all beef tongue and pork skin (just some of it); less-novel options might include a deeply succulent pork shoulder or tuna basted with miso honey butter. Cool it down with smashed cucumbers and buttered cornbread. A side of roasted sweet potatoes (with cane syrup) is necessary. Service and space are mismatched-dish-style casual; in good weather, the outdoor deck is a sweet spot.

320 S. Broad St. www.marjiesgrill.com. ℭ **504/603-2234.** Entrees $15–$32. Mon–Sat 5–10pm.

Neyow's Creole Café ★★ CREOLE/SOUL FOOD

When you mention Neyow's around here, someone is going to yell out a dish with enthusiasm, followed by, "Oh my God" (Big Freedia [p. 29] included, this is one of her faves). You'll hear about the char-grilled oysters (wood fired in the window), file gumbo, stuffed crab, crab claws, "Pasta on the Bayou" (shrimp and crawfish in a spicy cream sauce); and the sides: carrot souffle, sweet potato tots, and cornbread dressing. If decisions seem too overwhelming, consider the Extravaganza Dinner for two ($65) to make it easy. There's usually a line, but people get in and out fast (air-conditioning on blast or DJ-volume music, could be either), and it's always friendly, even if you don't know anyone like everyone else seems to.

3332 Bienville St. www.neworleans.neyows.com. ℭ **504/827-5474.** Entrees $15–$32. Mon–Thurs 11am–9pm; Fri–Sat 11am–11pm.

Revel ★★ CONTEMPORARY SOUTHERN

When Chris McMillian, renowned OG craft bartender and globally revered liquor historian, opens his own place, we come and imbibe. There's nothing frou-frou here: Revel is a regular neighborhood hang, and that's the atmosphere to expect. Although it's a cocktail mecca (the drinks menu is a great read), the food is no second thought. The best way to "Revel" is to start at happy hour (daily until 7pm) and just keep going. We're hesitant to cite specific dishes since they change frequently, but the tempura-battered Creole crawfish corndog is a staple for a good reason. Chef plays New Orleans food well with Mediterranean and North African flavors, so we tend to trust the extensive menu's mashups and ask to pair drinks.

133 N. Carrolton Ave. www.revelcafeandbar.com. ℭ **504/309-6122.** Snacks and small plates $6–$13, large plates $16–$29. Tues–Thurs 4–11pm; Fri–Sat 11am–11pm.

Toups' Meatery ★★ CONTEMPORARY CAJUN

Just another neighborhood spot with killer food that speaks our oinky language. Order some hearty cracklins to warm up for what's ahead. One should no doubt order the charcuterie board here (it's exceptional). Another should get the cheese board, just to even things out (ditto). Despite the meat-centricity, making a meal of the brine-forward small plates is actually a ton of fun for meat, seafood, and vegetable-lovers alike. But if you really want to go all-in, oh, it's there: tender lamb neck on a bed of sweet pea risotto; seared duck breast with tasso jam; or mustard-crusted rack of elk. A rich confit of chicken thighs and the lunchtime-only chicken sandwich are also worthy. Cocktails are aptly savory-leaning

PLANT-BASED AND vegalicious

Despite its reputation for all things seafood, pork, butter, and cream, there's substantial culinary creativity happening in New Orleans' plant-based food scene. You can find scrumptious meat-free offerings at most of the city's top-rated restaurants, though some, like **Addis NOLA** (p. 119), **Bearcat Café** (p. 132), **Green Room Kukhnya** (p. 133), **Saint-Germain** (p. 114), and any Afro-Caribbean spot (p. 145) have entire sections of their menus devoted to vegan/vegetarian options. (Most can accommodate other special diets too, like gluten free or vegan, just ask.) Here are a few places whose inventive and sustainably-minded chefs are giving herbivores a seat at the head of the table:

○ **Breads on Oak** ★★: Organic, plant-based bakery and cafe for breakfast and lunch, veggie burgers and beer. 8640 Oak St.; www.breads onoak.com; ℂ **504/324-8271;** also downtown at 222 Carondelet St.

○ **Carmo** ★★: "Tropical" soups, salads, beans, rice, curry . . . and Brazilian jazz. 527 Julia St.; www. cafecarmo.com; ℂ **504/875-4132.**

○ **I-tal Garden** ★★: Totally vegan New Orleans–style soul food

lunches, pancake breakfasts, and killer barbecue jackfruit. 810 N. Claiborne Ave. (Tremé); www.italgarden nola.com; ℂ **504/515-7321.**

○ **Meals from the Heart** ★★: Vegan crab cakes, hot sausage, and gumbo alongside hearty breakfasts, salads, sandwiches, and tacos. Served with love. 1100 N. Peters St. Bay #13 (French Market); www. mealsfromtheheartcafe.com; no phone.

○ **Sneaky Pickle** ★★★: Always from scratch and always changing veggie plates, rice bowls, tacos, ridiculous vegan mac 'n' cheese, and sandwiches (smoked tempeh reuben is a fave). At night, it transforms into saucy Bar Brine. 3200 Burgundy St. (Bywater); www.yousneakypickle. com; ℂ **504/218-5651.**

○ **Sweet Soulfood** ★★: Totally vegan and soy-free soul food dishes served cafeteria-style, rotating daily. Pick one to four (or more, you can), a side of cornbread, and a brownie, and you'll be set through the evening. 1025 N. Broad St.; www. sweetvegansoulfood.com; ℂ **504/821-2669.**

("ring my bell" features bell-pepper-infused tequila with umami bitters), but surprisingly refreshing.

845 N. Carrollton Ave. www.toupsmeatery.com. ℂ **504/252-4999.** Entrees $14–$34 lunch, $18–$48 dinner. Mon–Thurs 11am–3pm and 5–10pm; Fri–Sat 11am–3pm and 5–11pm; Sun 10am–3pm.

Inexpensive

Bevi Seafood ★★★ SEAFOOD/CASUAL   Bevi is a smidge more proper and pricier than a divey corner seafood shack, but make no mistake, these folks know how to berl (boil) and fry up a downright fine batch of shrimp, oysters, crab, or crawfish. The seafood is fresh, seasonal, and local—and the spice is right, even in the tangy slaw. Carnivores have excellent options, too. Consider meeting in the middle with a Peacemaker po' boy (half fried shrimp, half roast beef debris with Swiss). It's counter service with just a few tables, but don't get fried stuff to go: A concise fryer-plate-mouth interval is essential. ***Bonus:*** It's a few doors from **Angelo Brocato** (p. 148), thus amortizing the Mid-City Lyft ride.

236 N. Carrollton Ave. www.beviseafoodco.com. ✆ **504/488-7503.** Everything under $20. Tues–Sat 11am–8pm; Sun–Mon 11am–4pm.

Cajun Seafood ★★ SEAFOOD/CAJUN Those intrepid travelers who ask, "Where can I eat like the locals do?" will find their just rewards at Cajun Seafood, which is where to go if you like substantial spice—in your food and in your urban travel adventures. Order at the counter and take it to go or sit at one of the rudimentary tables. If it's crawfish season (roughly mid-Feb to mid-May), that's what everyone comes for. First-timers can order a starter pound or two per person, though you might get some side-eye—experienced Louisianans can inhale the weight of a toddler in crawfish. If the nearby table heaped with 10 times your order stares at your timid pile, admit you're a newbie and ask them for a crawfish eating lesson. For sides, add some potatoes, sausage, and corn, and be warned: Corn and taters soak up the heat. Peel-and-eat boiled shrimp or grilled or fried catfish work any time of year, or try whatever else strikes your fancy from the extensive menu, though we're true to the boiled goods here. You want plenty of cold drinks and paper towels: This ain't for the dainty. Dig in.

1749 N. Claiborne Ave. www.cajunseafoodnola.com ✆ **504/948-6000.** Boiled seafood market price, platters and po' boys mostly under $16. Mon–Sat 10:30am–8:30pm; Sun 11am–8:30pm. Also at 2730 S. Broad Ave. (Uptown), ✆ **504/821-4722;** and 1091 Alamonster Ave. (St. Roch), ✆ **504/945-5447.**

Lil' Dizzy's ★★ CREOLE/SOUL FOOD This Tremé mainstay is another quintessential family-owned neighborhood restaurant that was resurrected (to the city's great relief) by Wayne Jr. and his wife Arkesha after founder Wayne Baquet, Sr.'s retirement in 2021. It's warm and lively with locals and home-comers sitting elbow-to-elbow, satiating their cravings for fried chicken, seafood gumbo, bread pudding, greens, and candied yams under photos of celebrity visitors Obama, Oprah, and more. Trout Baquet is a standout daily special, a delicate fillet topped with garlic-butter sauce and lump crabmeat.

1500 Esplanade Ave. www.lildizzyscafe.net. ✆ **504/766-8687.** Entrees $9.25–$20.25. Mon–Sat 11am–3pm.

Liuzza's by the Track ★★★ CREOLE/CASUAL When friends fly in for a visit, we stop here on the way home to get them in the gumbo groove. Liuzza's by the Track has one of the best in town. The barbecue-shrimp po' boy is its signature, stuffed and soaking in peppery butter sauce and tails-off shrimp, but we're partial to the garlic oyster sammie. We'll often get the cup of gumbo and half po' boy deal for well-roundedness. Specials can be pretty special, so check the board. Locals swear by the Reuben, but the veggie-deprived should opt for the portobello salad, and everyone should strike up a conversation with whoever's nearby. It's that sort of place. Avoid prime week-day lunch hours if you can.

1518 N. Lopez St. www.liuzzasbtt.com. 📞 **504/218-7888.** Everything under $17. Mon–Sat 11am–8pm. Open on Sun for Saints' games.

McHardy's Chicken and Fixin' ★★★ SOUL FOOD

Popeye's will do when we're far from New Orleans, but if we're in town, it's gotta be this take-out fried chicken joint owned and run by three generations of the Mogille family. They're good people who make good chicken—as in moist, tender, slightly crispy-skinned, perfectly seasoned, hot, and cheap. We never have a party without it, and often *make* a party *just* to have it. Fried catfish and other "fixins" do the trick—the mustardy, nearly mashed homemade potato salad and smoky green beans are standouts—but the bird is the word here. We're looking forward to their planned expansion upstairs, with table service and an even bigger menu.

1458 N. Broad St. www.facebook.com/pages/McHardys-Chicken-Fixin/176427879083461. 📞 **504/949-0000.** 5-piece box $6; 100-piece $128. Mon–Sat 11am–5pm; closed Sun.

Parkway Bakery and Tavern ★★★ CASUAL

This corner shop began life as a bakery more than a century ago; was shuttered for decades; reopened; and was underwater in 2005. Now, after heaps of love from magazines and travel- and food-channel shows (plus a visit from the Obamas), people come by the literal busload. Try to sit inside or on the original deck; either has more charm than the massive picnic area now required to accommodate its fame. What matters is that the po' boys are still terrific. Claims to fame are the fried shrimp and NOLA-style roast beef (our favorite in the city)—slow roasted to the point of nothing beyond a juicy, shredded heap of beefy deliciousness (use a fork and knife). We're fond of the Reuben or lighter caprese, and oysters (Mon and Wed only). Don't neglect the excellent sides (killer potato salad, chili and sweet potato fries) and squeeze in the lip-smacking, old-school banana pudding. Round it all out with a bottled Barq's and a stroll along nearby Bayou St. John. There may be a line. It may be daunting. The line actually moves pretty fast, more so with a beer in hand, so hit up the bar. *Pro tip:* If you can score a stool at the teensy bar, do. Order your po' boy from the bartender, thereby skipping the food line.

538 Hagan Ave. www.parkwaypoorboys.com. 📞 **504/482-3047.** Everything under $23. Wed–Sun 10am–6pm.

Queen Trini Lisa ★★★ AFRO CARIBBEAN/SOUL FOOD

Owner and Chef Lisa Nelson fittingly brings the African, East Indian, and Asian flavors of her native Trinidad and Tobago to what many refer to as the northernmost city in the Caribbean. She opened this bright and airy brick-and-mortar with a friendly tropical vibe in early 2022, after years of popping-up around town. Her barbecue chicken is the reigning champ of the NOLA Jerk Chicken com-petition, and her *doubles* (curried chickpea stew between two pieces of fluffy flatbread) are perfection, literally—she spent nearly a year refining her recipe for this street food standard, and serves it in a bigger meal-size version than you find in Trinidad. Look for the Coco Bread fish sandwich or seafood *doubles* on special. Get an extra hibiscus tea to go, you'll be craving it later.

4200 D'Hemecourt St. www.queentrinilisa.com. ☏ **504/345-2058.** Everything under $17. Mon–Sat 11am–5pm.

Willie Mae's Scotch House ★★ SOUL FOOD   Since the 1970s, this humble chicken shack in the 6th Ward neighborhood was known mainly to locals, the foodie community, and a few enterprising tourists. In 2005, octogenarian Willie Mae and her secret-recipe fried chicken were designated "America's Classic Restaurant for the Southern Region" by the James Beard Foundation, and the world came knocking. Weeks later, her home and restaurant were 8 feet under water. A remarkable volunteer-driven recovery began quickly (with hands-on help from local restaurateurs—a testament to New Orleans' supportive food community), bringing even more attention. Nowadays, the matriarch's great-granddaughter runs the operation. The chicken is still beautifully spiced and crisped—on a good day (consistency can be an issue). So go on what you hope is a good day, and because it's a cultural icon, definitely get the creamy butterbeans (which don't get *near* the attention the chicken does but should). Plan to wait in line for the fried-to-order bird.

2401 St. Ann St. www.williemaesscotchhouse.com. ☏ **504/822-9503.** Everything under $15. Mon–Sat 11am–5pm.

CENTRAL BUSINESS DISTRICT & WAREHOUSE DISTRICT

Expensive

Annunciation ★★★ CONTEMPORARY CAJUN/CREOLE   It doesn't get near the accolades it should, but Annunciation mines the classic bentwood-chair, white-tablecloth decor and "good time was had by all" tone we love so well in New Orleans. Time-honored recipes prepped by some of the city's best chefs are attentively served. Fried oysters with spinach and brie, and buttery crispy chicken Bonne Femme au jus, two signature dishes, both belong on the table. A salad of abundant crab and a creamy herb dressing is delicious; a stunning soft-shell-crab special we had here was enough for two, but too good to share. Despite the cool brick, jet-black stained floors, and angular black-and-white abstract artwork, there's a warmth to the room that sets the mood on genial, owing largely to Richard Williams, the perpetually bow-tied maître d'. Good moods mean wine and dessert, and while the wine list is the more interesting of the two, the requisite lemon icebox pie will lengthen a lovely night of lingering.

1016 Annunciation St. www.annunciationrestaurant.com. ☏ **504/568-0245.** Entrees $24–$34. Sun–Mon and Wed–Thurs 5–9pm; Fri–Sat 5–10pm (closed Tues).

Chemin à la Mer ★★ STEAK/SEAFOOD/FRENCH   The mighty Mississippi River looms large on the fifth floor of the new Four Seasons Hotel, what with the sweeping views, flourishes of coastal flora and fauna art, and the graceful curve of the marble top bar emulating her famous crescent-shaped flow. Chemin à la Mer ("Pathway to the Sea") marks Donald Link's first time lending his fine-dining chops and celebrity chef cachet to a hotel property, so it makes sense that it's the new five-star place with THE view. Gulf oysters, shrimp, and crab are revered on the seafood- and steak-focused menu, prepared with a classic French precision befitting its elevated setting—though a touch lacking in the soul we've come to expect (and maybe take for granted) at our favorite spots. We found our groove at the grand oyster bar with bergamot negronis and requisite oysters, then digging into the baked feta appetizer with honey, lemon, thyme (and a hint of spice), plus a shared entree alfresco on the terrace, watching the sunset sky turn purple while lingering over a rice pudding cloud topped with brown-sugar braised pineapple. Chemin serves breakfast too, with a perfect east-facing sunrise view.

2 Canal St. www.cheminalamer.com. © **504/434-5898.** Entrees $26–$49 (steaks start at $56). Daily 7–10:30am, 11:30am–2:30pm, and 5–10pm.

Commons Club ★★★ CONTEMPORARY SOUTHERN

Part of the fun of dining at the Commons Club is in visiting the Instagram-ready Virgin Hotels New Orleans—a fun-suffused eyebomb that stops just short of overkill. Each eating and drinking space here has a singular ambiance: One is literally named the "Funny Library," and definitely check out the Shag Room. But when it's time to get serious, Commons Club exec chef Alex Harrell brings a sophisticated hand to inevitably fresh, ingredient-forward, and fully approachable modern Southern cuisine. We're long-time Harrell fans, and without hesitation trust his pastas and seafoods (and pasta with seafood). The crawfish hush puppies are a requisite starter. Cocktails deliver (it's New Orleans), and the wine options in the $60 to $80 range are equally satisfying. We're partial to tables in the anachronistic but delightful "springtime on the verandah" window-lined lane, but with kitchen counter and community picnic table seating, any mood can be met.

550 Baronne St. www.virginhotels.com/new-orleans. © **833/791-7700.** Entrees $13–$27 lunch/brunch, $25–$36 dinner. Mon–Tues 4–10pm; Wed–Thurs 4–11pm; Fri–Sat 9am–2pm and 4–11pm; Sun 9am–2pm and 4–10pm.

Compère Lapin ★★★ CREOLE/AFRO-CARIBBEAN

Top Chef alumnus and St. Lucia native Nina Compton blends Caribbean, French, Italian, and Creole influences into playful, James Beard award–winning dishes of uncompromising quality that are just unusual enough for adventurous diners: the forever-popular curried goat with sweet plantain gnocchi, Hamachi tartar with puréed cauliflower, jerk pineapple, and fried okra; jerk pork belly with plantain crema and tamarind au jus. Don't miss the baked-to-order biscuits with bacon and honey butter (if only to prepare you for the divinity to come). Commune at the bar, watching shimmery, beautifully balanced drinks coming out of one of the city's consistently top bar programs. Stellar lighting, blue highlights, and the dotted bunny logo enliven the room's warehouse-y bones (huge windows, weathered wood, brick), though it suffers on the noise front, thanks to the lively buzz bouncing off all those hard surfaces.

535 Tchoupitoulas St., in Old No. 77 Hotel. www.comperelapin.com. ☎ **504/599-2119.** Entrees $30–$38. Mon–Thurs 5:30–10pm; Fri–Sat 5:30–11pm; Sun 10:30am–2pm and 5:30–10pm.

Emeril's ★★★ CONTEMPORARY SOUTHERN He heads an empire and pioneered New Orleans' modern restaurant scene, but Emeril's flagship restaurant has never flagged. Menu and decor underwent major overhauls during the pandemic shutdown, and it's still exciting high-quality (and high-priced) dining, with a clear commitment to first-rate locally sourced ingredients. Dishes build meaningfully on local traditions with global touches that never overwhelm the finery. The wine list is intelligent and broad; service is helpful and professional but unstuffy; and noise is well managed in the buoyant room. If you're able, go for one of the splendidly composed multi-course tasting menus. A snapper ceviche appetizer benefits from sweet satsuma, bright ponzu, and plantain crisps; grilled pork chops, done perfectly despite their girth, are artfully glazed with tamarind and tomatillo mole sauces. Get the banana cream pie, too, a new deconstructed version that might top the original version of this legendary menu staple. *Tip:* The open-kitchen bar seating is perfect for single diners.

800 Tchoupitoulas St. www.emerils.com. ☎ **504/528-9393.** 5-course tasting menu $165–$185; 3-course $95; a la carte entrees $24–$65. Tues–Thurs 5–9pm; Fri–Sat 5–10pm. No shorts, flip-flops, or T-shirts; men must wear collared shirts, jackets recommended. No children 8 and under.

Herbsaint ★★★ FRENCH/SOUTHERN Donald Link may not be a national television star like Emeril, but he's right up there in terms of modern New Orleans restaurant royalty (and dominance). This is his sweet, window-lined flagship bistro, rooted in French, rustic Italian, and Southern traditions; usually packed and always lacking elbow room, but never rushed. Herbsaint dishes superb gumbos, including, occasionally, a meatless, herb-based gumbo z'herbes version we crave. The winning signature starter of house-made spaghetti with a creamy guanciale-spiked sauce is topped with a batter-fried poached egg (yes, you can—and should—double it as an entree); Herbsaint's version of ceviche has a Creole spice kick and crunchy pepitas, a refreshing cup of summer. Trust that whatever sounds good on special is a must. Desserts here are terrific—lean towards whatever they put in a tart shell.

701 St. Charles Ave. www.herbsaint.com. ☎ **504/524-4114.** Entrees $21–$42. Mon–Thurs 11:30am–9pm; Fri 11:30am–10pm; Sat 5–10pm. Reservations essential.

Josephine Estelle ★★ ITALIAN Though it's located in the vampy Ace Hotel, this sprawling, high-ceilinged space is full-on tropical chic, thanks to leafy-green velvet and leather booths, Corinthian columns, gold globe lights, and the circa 1940s palmetto murals salvaged from the New Orleans Opera House. The food delivers on the lushness (so do the drinks). Breakfast highlights include a smoked preserved tomato toast with ricotta and eggs and seasonal beignets (like dried cherry custard). For lunch or dinner, start with a generous order of meatballs, and then work your way through the pasta selection—the entrees pale in comparison to, say, thin *tajarin* with crab, asparagus, butter, and basil; or the very tasty, very traditional *mafalde* "with maw maw's gravy," aka marinara sauce. You could also make a meal of the tasty veggie sides. Save room for the delectable peanut butter *budino*. The Quick Fixe lunch of one of two classic pastas (*cacio e pepe* or rigatoni with gravy) and a tender green salad is a great deal for $20 (weekdays, closed Tues)—plus a cookie to boot.

600 Carondelet St. www.josephineestelle.com. ✆ **504/930-3070.** Entrees $10–$28 breakfast/brunch/lunch, $21–$42 dinner. Mon–Fri 7am–10:30am, 11am–3pm, and 5–10pm; Sat–Sun 8am–3pm and 5–10pm.

La Boca ★★★ STEAK   One might not think of New Orleans as a steak town, but it's yet another tradition that runs deep here—this is the city that gave us Ruth's Chris, after all. You choose your cut and your knife at this Argentinean steakhouse in a commodious loft-like room where aged brick mingles with contemporary fixtures—and regardless of what else you order, you should get the transcendent 3-day fries. For the best-flavored beefiness, we suggest the *entraña fina* skirt steak (which can also be had skin-on, interesting but unnecessary) or the *centro de entraña* hanger steak. Temperatures are proper; a trio of chimichurri sauces adds zip. Servers know their meats and are helpful about the (accordingly Argentinian) wines but aren't particularly sociable.

870 Tchoupitoulas St. www.labocasteakhouse.com. ✆ **504/525-8205.** Entrees $31–$54. Tues–Sat 5:30–10pm.

Le Chat Noir ★★★ SEAFOOD   Newly opened in 2021, Le Chat Noir adopted the namesake of its former iteration as a cabaret theatre. Now the stage is an open kitchen, its orchestra the wood fire. Breakout stars are rotating roasted vegetable sides and an already-legendary "Brick" chicken (we've heard it referred to it as "fowl magic"), but really, you cannot order wrong; most everything exceeds expectations. Louisiana native chef Seth Temple is focused on sustainability, sourcing 70% of ingredients locally through direct-to-farmer relationships. Oysters at the stand-up shucking bar are served clean and cold, and so are the martinis. We recommend sliding into happy hour at the bar before dinner to share a dozen shucker's choice oysters chased with the happy-hour-only Miller High Life pony and a shot of amaro for $6—it's called a "pick-me-up" for a reason. Don't skip dessert (here, or anywhere in New Orleans, actually).

715 St. Charles Ave. www.lechatnoirnola.com. ✆ **504/381-0045.** Entrees $15–$28 lunch, $25–$40 dinner. Mon–Thurs 5–9:30pm; Fri–Sat 11:30am–3pm and 5–10pm; Wed–Sat happy hour 3–5pm.

Miss River ★★★ CONTEMPORARY SOUTHERN   The latest from Israeli-born, New Orleans–made chef Alon Shaya (see **Saba**, p. 144) lands him in the swanky new Four Seasons Hotel. Miss River's decor walks the line comfortably between shiny glitz and hotel diner, and when it comes to the food, subtle details and flavorings amp up Louisiana classics and comfort foods—dishes commonly found on New Orleans tables are next-level here. Sure, the red beans are thrice the price of the nearby diner, but there's a creaminess, a hint of lemongrass, and some *je ne sais quoi* (the recipe is Emily Shaya's, chef's wife). Ingredients convey careful curation and scratch-made attention (there's even an in-house butchery). Buttermilk fried chicken is presented whole—crisped and juicy beyond belief—then carved nearby for all to gape (and envy); and the clay pot dirty rice with creamy liver pate has a bold country-meets-city spirit. Weekend jazz brunch features a Bloody Mary garnish bar (pickled quail eggs! praline bacon!) and a prix fixe family-style for the table that starts with a spread of primo shared sides (hot-from-the-oven sweet potato brioche among them) plus one entree per person—the more in your party, the better the odds of tasting the whole menu (plus butter-fried beignets for dessert). If chef Shaya is greeting diners, as he does often, do engage with him; his telling of the Miss River story would be a highlight of a meal here.

2 Canal St. www.missrivernola.com. ℂ **504/434-5100.** Entrees $32–$70. Mon–Fri 11am–3pm and 5:30–10pm; Sat–Sun 10:30am–3pm and 5:30–10pm.

Pêche ★★★ SEAFOOD   Probably already on your list as a popular tourist spot, this uber-popular, mega-award winner features contemporary and rustic wood-fired seafood dishes, and there's nary a dud on the menu. The raucous room works best for plate-sharing parties, not dates or deep convos. Ordering something off all sections of the menu is the way to go. Start with beer-battered fish sticks (really), then sample from the raw bar (steak tartare included). Get that whole grilled fish for the table. Balance with some vegetable sides (the roasted squash with shitake and miso is a winner). Terrific craft beers, Eurocentric wines, and cocktails deliver. Reserve well in advance for a table, though you can likely snag a single or double spot at the bar if you hover.

800 Magazine St. www.pecherestaurant.com. ℂ **504/522-1744.** Small plates $10–$18, entrees $26–$37, whole grilled fish $45–$69. Daily 11am–10pm.

Restaurant August ★★★ CONTEMPORARY CREOLE/FRENCH   The fine-dining flagship of the restaurant empire started by award-winning TV food star John Besh (who stepped down after a #MeToo-era exposé), August remains a marvel of Frenchified Creole creativity. There is a rare misfire when a boundary-pushing dish goes one ingredient beyond, but on the whole, your experience will be decorous, cultured, stunningly plated—and memorable. Foie gras here is unfailingly off the charts, salads are perfectly composed. Soft luscious gnocchi done with sweet blue crab and slabs of earthy truffles melt on the palate. The signature breaded trout Pontchartrain, in its envelope of paper-thin white bread, with shrimp, crab, and local mushrooms, is Gulf finery. Slowly roasted lamb spiked with andouille produces an orchestra of earthy, rich flavor. Sweets are urbane yet playful, like a golden milk *mille feuille* with banana whipped ganache. Service is utterly professional and unhurried. Tables are well-spaced in the sedate main dining room; chandeliers glint off tall windows, gilded mirrors on brick walls, and the dark hardwood floors. Like we said, memorable.

301 Tchoupitoulas St. www.restaurantaugust.com. ✆ **504/299-9777.** Entrees $36–$55; tasting menu $150 ($220 with wine). Daily 5–10pm. Reservations recommended.

Moderate

Cochon ★★ CONTEMPORARY CAJUN   This inspired and authentic Cajun restaurant with a serious moonshine list pays homage to all things swine. It's also the spot in restaurateur demigod chef Donald Link's local empire that runs closest to his rural Louisiana roots. All visits to Cajun Country should kick off with some cracklins and a good local beer, like the Parish Canebrake. Follow with boudin balls—crunchy outside, savory and porky inside—with a side of creamy burnished mac 'n' cheese. For a break from hog, briny wood-fired oysters bathed in chili garlic butter, or hog's head cheese with house mustard are both astoundingly good (in truth, we like the starters here the most). Some skillet-seared and wood-burning oven–fired entrees are staples (rabbit and dumplings, beef short rib), but we recommend sticking to the small plates, which keep this in the moderate price range. Ambrosia cake is a potluck-perfect finish—a creamy, fruity, happy ending.

930 Tchoupitoulas St. www.cochonrestaurant.com. ✆ **504/588-2123.** Small plates $10–$24, entrees $28–$39. Daily 11am–10pm. Reservations strongly recommended.

Domenica ★★ ITALIAN   Bittersweet chocolate walls, soaring ceilings, great art, glossy surfaces, small bar, large crowd. All sets the scene for perfectly bubble-edged Neapolitan pizzas, one of the best salumi in the city, and a kitchen that knows its way around a vegetable. We rarely make it to the *secondi* here because it's such a pleasure to load up on antipasti, *primi,* and a pizza or two. Buttery sautéed chanterelle mushrooms are flavored with marrow and cut through with parsley—decadently rich. A roasted whole cauliflower with whipped feta makes a delicious addition to the table. Fresh tagliatelle is sauced with rabbit and porcini mushrooms, hearty and divine (we love that pastas come in two sizes). End with a satiny chocolate hazelnut *budino.* Domenica's superb daily happy hour, with half-price pizzas from 2 to 5pm, helps explain why it's often cacophonous. The bar pours well-priced boutique Italian wines and homemade limoncellos. Service is inconsistent, ranging from prompt and knowledgeable to perfunctory. Still, it's worth it. Also consider the casual Uptown and Mid-City **Pizza Domenica** ★★ outposts (www.pizzadomenica.com).

123 Baronne St., in the Roosevelt Hotel. www.domenicarestaurant.com. ✆ **504/648-6020.** Pizza $17–$23, entrees $19–$35. Daily 11am–10pm. Reservations recommended.

Drago's ★ SEAFOOD   The booming Hilton lobby has all the atmosphere of a casino without the flashy thrill of slot machines and card tables (though there are TVs). But that's not relevant when you're here for one thing and one thing only: Drago's buttery, garlicky, Parmesan-y charbroiled oysters. Not much else matters. Other places do them, but Drago's is the original (though their original location is out in Metairie, at 3232 N. Arnoult Rd., ✆ **504/888-9254**).

However many you think you want to order, double it. Sports-minded folks can sit at the bar, order oysters, and watch what's on (though there are no beers on tap—wassup with that?).

2 Poydras St., in the Hilton Riverside. www.dragosrestaurant.com. © **504/584-3911.** Raw oysters $21/dozen, charbroiled $29. Daily 11:30am–10pm.

Gianna ★★ ITALIAN The Link Restaurant Group's first foray into Italian cuisine is, no surprise, a solid hit. Comfort, atmosphere, and noise levels all land firmly in the winner column (well, the wood chairs could be a stitch more cush; try for a booth, or a seat at the generous bar)—even before the Southern-Italy-meets-Southern-U.S. dishes show up. (Lower the meatball appetizer, tortellini in brodo, and crisped saltimbocca, please.) The rigatoni dish is always on point (though we still miss the walnut pesto version). Flavors are deeply steeped and not overly complex; sauces are light (like the white-on-cream decor), yet each fresh local ingredient is clearly evident. Portions are on the small side, which allows room for ricotta cheesecake and lemon mousse. Service is on point as expected, given Link's well-oiled machine.

700 Magazine St. www.giannarestaurant.com. © **504/399-0816.** Entrees $17–$32. Daily 11am–10pm. Reservations suggested.

Maypop ★★★ SOUTHERN/ASIAN/ITALIAN Possibly our all-around favorite nouveau spot in the city; hands-down our favorite spot for lively Asian, Italian, Indian, Southern-American cuisine (sometimes all in one dish). The inventive, flavor-packed cooking surprises rather than stuns, satisfying both the serious foodie and the food-shy (especially at the more affordable brunch). Don't skip the standard-sounding bibb lettuce salad, or underestimate the sometimes uproarious combinations (like smoked rabbit, glazed turnips, collard greens, and coconut in a dumpling). You'll do well with any handmade pasta. Servings aren't huge; thus, everyone should get the seasonal crepe, cheesecake, or crisp. It's all beautifully plated, in keeping with the room's high style. Make sure to check out the lenticular mural from both sides.

611 O'Keefe Ave. www.maypoprestaurant.com. © **504/518-6345.** Entrees $16–$26. Mon–Fri 4–9pm (Fri until 10pm); Sat–Sun 11am–3pm and 5–10pm (Sun closes 9pm).

Meril ★★ CONTEMPORARY SOUTHERN Meril is the famed Emeril Lagasse's casual, spacious, and lower-priced concept restaurant, and it's bustling. The large, popular horseshoe-shaped bar centers on cocktails with local ingredients and fresh herbs; it opens onto an expansive dining room with floor-to-ceiling windows. The menu is large, but most plates are small, featuring inventive cross-cultural takes influenced by the docu-series *Eat the World with Emeril Lagasse.* Yet it's not too adventurous—meat-and-potato types will find plenty to enjoy. House-made meatballs have lemon-whipped ricotta, pomodoro, and toasted breadcrumbs; crispy turkey necks are spiked with local Crystal hot sauce. A good variety of salads, sides, and flatbreads makes this a crowd pleaser.

424 Girod St. www.emerilsrestaurants.com/meril. © **504/526-3745.** Entrees $18–$28, flatbreads/salads $15–$20. Mon–Thurs 5–9pm; Fri–Sat 11:30am–2pm and 5-10pm; Sun 11:30am–2pm and 5–9pm.

Vyoone's ★★ FRENCH/CREOLE   Enter through the narrow hallway, discreetly tucked into one of the CBD's busiest blocks for destination restaurants, and you'll find an incredibly charming French Quarter–style courtyard spot serving up French Creole fine-dining favorites like *crevettes et gruau* (shrimp and grits topped with smoked gouda) and *duck a l'orange* (with mushroom bread pudding). Fourth-generation New Orleanian Ms. Vyonne herself will likely greet you (unless it's a Saints game day—she'll be at the Superdome), a classically-trained musician and former pediatric geneticist, motivated by cultural preservation to become a restaurateur and share the dishes she grew up with. (Don't hesitate on the French onion soup.)

412 Girod St. www.vyoone.com. ℭ **504/518-6007.** Entrees $19–$40, brunch to $27. Wed–Sat 5–10pm, happy hour 3–5pm; Sun 10:30am–2:30pm.

Inexpensive

Bearcat ★★★ CAFE   You know those places where people wait an hour for breakfast, and you think, *why?* Bearcat is why. It's that good. Also, because you can get excellent coffees or juices while you're waiting. And because servings are huge. And because there's something for everyone to love here—starting with the menu concept: a "good cat" section for relatively healthy dishes and a "bad cat" section for indulgences. There's a robust variety of breakfast burritos, topped biscuits (the "daddy" biscuits are personal faves), and other carb-laden options, as all good breakfast spots must serve. But vegans, ketos, paleos, and other dietary preferences are gladly accommodated; a mushroom scramble oozing with boursin will please all. We're so enamored of the breakfasts here that we forget the lunch, but it deserves your attention too, for all the reasons we've enumerated—plus the crab dip and bison burger. The loft-like interior and sprawling patio are jumping most hours, but servers are kind and efficient here and at the smaller Uptown location. No reservations.

845 Carondelet St. www.bearcatcafe.com. ℭ **504/766-7399.** Most items under $20. Tues–Fri 8am–2pm; Sat–Sun 8am–3pm. Also Uptown at 2521 Jena St., ℭ **504/309-9011.**

Cochon Butcher ★★★ CONTEMPORARY CAJUN   As the name attests, meat is butchered and cured on-site, turning house-smoked meaty goodness into small plates and world-rocking sandwiches. The boudin sausage is one of the best east of Acadiana (Louisiana's Cajun Country); the muffuletta may surpass Central Grocery's (p. 114); pork belly with cucumber and mint is wondrous. Get the vinegary Brussels sprouts, some potato chips, and dreamy mac 'n' cheese or rue your decision. Don't hold back on starting with a fresh sausage plate if you're with a group. It's counter service only—and super popular with visitors and conventioneers—but the casual high-top tables rotate quickly, spilling onto the street via garage-style doors, and good local beers are offered at the full bar. Bonus points for the mad *Star Wars* diorama/table.

930 Tchoupitoulas St. www.cochonbutcher.com. ℭ **504/588-7675.** Sandwiches $12–$16, small plates $7–$10. Daily 11am–10pm.

Most visitors anticipate beignets; po' boys; the traditional Creole, Cajun, and French-inflected cuisine for which Louisiana is known; and their modernized chef- and ingredient-driven varietals. But some of the most exciting—and award-winning—local restaurants are spotlighting diverse threads of the cultural fabric that makes New Orleans a world-renowned food destination. Consider these for a richer, deeper, more unique New Orleans dining experience:

- **14 Parishes** Bright, friendly family-owned Uptown spot for authentic Jamaican classics. 8227 Oak St.; www.14parishes.com; ℰ 504/420-7433.
- **Addis NOLA** Ethiopian fare in a stunning space on Bayou Road (p. 119).
- **Bésame** Come for the ceviche, empanadas, shrimp mofongo, and excellent mezcal and rum drinks—come back again for the all-Latin drag brunch or salsa nights. 110 S Rampart St.; www.besamenola.com; ℰ 504/308-0880.
- **Budsi's Authentic Thai** Street-food inspired, sit-down Thai food (p. 116).
- **Cleo's** Far better than average Mediterranean fare in the back of a convenience store, open 24/7. 940 Canal St.; www.facebook.com/cleosnola; ℰ 504/522-4504. Also at 117 Decatur St.
- **Dakar NOLA** A "Best of" choice (p. 138).
- **Dian Xin** Superb traditional dim sum with some localized nods, such as crab and crawfish bao, in the French Quarter. 1218 Decatur St.; www.dianxinnola.com; ℰ 504/266-2828. Also at 620 Conti St.
- **Fritai** Haitian food in an art-filled dining room (p. 120).

- **Green Room Kukhnya** Popular "Slavic soul food" like tasty, affordable perogies, kielbasa, blinis, and oh that beet burger. 1300 St. Bernard Ave.; www.greenroomnola.com; ℰ 504/766-1613.
- **Lengua Madre** Traditional Mexican tasting menu (p. 139).
- **LUVI** About as far Uptown as you can go, itty-bitty Shanghai-meets-sushi hybrid turning out ultra-fresh, tastebud-tantalizing dishes. Reservations a must. 5236 Tchoupitoulas St.; www.luvirestaurant.com; ℰ 504/605-3340.
- **Mais Arepas** Consistently delicious house-made Colombian specialties. 1200 Carondelet St.; www.facebook.com/maisarepas; ℰ 504/523-6247.
- **Maypop** A "Best of" choice (p. 131).
- **Pho Tau Bay** Scrumptious Vietnamese food, and unlike many of its compatriots, it's right in town. 1565 Tulane Ave.; www.photaubayrestaurant.com; ℰ 504/368-9846.
- **Queen Trini Lisa** Trinidad/Tobagonian island soul food (p. 124).
- **Saffron** Sophisticated Indian gourmet food (p. 144).
- **Tava** A former pop-up in a festive and friendly permanent spot with fresh takes on Indian street food. 611 O'Keefe Ave.; www.tavanola.com; ℰ 504/766-9612.
- **Wishing Town Bakery Café** Metairie's favorite dim sum, now served in a sweet little house Uptown, with a sprawling deck under the shade of a live oak tree (get cake to go). 802 Nashville Ave.; www.wishingtown.com; ℰ 504/533-9166.

Mother's ★ CREOLE/CASUAL   Similar to the balcony bead-throwing barter for chest-bearing on Bourbon Street, legendary Mother's is a self-perpetuating tourist trap: Locals don't do it, visitors do. We're here because someone will tell you to go. If there are more than four or five parties ahead of you, our advice is to go elsewhere. But if you can waltz right in, the combo platter ($23) makes a decent intro to Creole cuisine. Follow the line rules lest you get some hostess lip: 1) no table-saving; 2) get steam-table items and order po' boys and plates; 3) order and receive drinks; 4) pay; 5) then and only then, find a table—don't send a scout to save one; 6) a server delivers the rest of your food.

401 Poydras St. www.mothersrestaurant.net. ✆ **504/523-9656.** Sandwiches $10–$23, entrees $13–$38. Daily 7am–10pm.

UPTOWN/THE GARDEN DISTRICT/CENTRAL CITY
Expensive

Avo ★★★ ITALIAN   Bet someone $5 that you'll witness a marriage proposal tonight—then book a table on the ultra-romantic, candle-lit patio at Avo. Even if you don't witness a Big Moment, you're a winner when you dine at this Uptown beauty, considering chef-owner Nick Lama's indisputable qualifications: deep Sicilian roots, experience in some of the city's best kitchens, and his family's decades-long immersion in New Orleans' food scene. When his talents met this tantalizing locale, lightning—and love—struck. We fell for the perfectly charred, tender octopus, and a bucatini *cacio e pepe* with jumbo lump crab. The delicious meatballs and lasagna don't stray far from tradition (both are simultaneously hearty and delicate), and Gulf fish piccata is a delightful, light version. Though it's not as inventive as it once was, it's consistently seasoned Just Right. Skip the cocktail standards and go straight to the winning, almost all-Italian wine list.

5908 Magazine St. www.restaurantavo.com. ✆ **504/509-6550.** Pastas and entrees $21–$37. Tues–Sat 5–9pm. Reservations recommended.

Brigtsen's ★★★ CONTEMPORARY CAJUN/CREOLE   Brigtsen's was one of the early modern Creole revolutionaries, and one of the first to convert a beautiful 19th-century house into an upscale neighborhood restaurant, way back in 1986. This perennial locals' favorite still maintains a warm, romantic intimacy, with a hostess circulating amiably through sweet little memorabilia- and mural-decorated rooms. The service and cuisine—which shows homey, Cajun-country roots—have been polished to consistent excellence. The famously grand "Shell Beach Diet" seafood platter changes seasonally but includes five or six sauced, baked, or otherwise unfried seafood items—an impressive extravagance for sharing or for a one very hungry diner ($45). Chef Brigtsen has a special touch with game, seafood, and pecans. His crispy, moist roast duck and pan-fried flounder with roasted pecans are known far

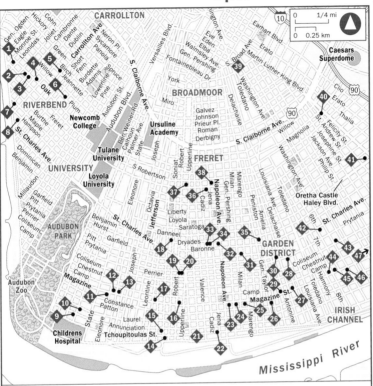

Avenue Pub **47**
Avo **11**
Bearcat **38**
Boucherie **5**
The Bower **47**
Breads on Oak **1**
Brigtsen's **7**
Café Reconcile **41**
Cajun Seafood **39**
Camellia Grill **8**
Casamento's **23**
Charlie's **34**
The Chloe **31**
Clancy's **9**
Commander's Palace **43**
Coquette **46**
Creole Creamery **20**
Cure **37**

Dakar NOLA **26**
Delachaise **28**
Domilise's **15**
14 Parishes **4**
French Truck Coffee **33, 45**
Gautreau's **18**
Gracious Bakery **19, 42**
Gris Gris **47**
Guy's Po'Boys **17**
Hansen's Sno-Bliz **21**
Heard Dat Kitchen **40**
High Hat **36**
Imperial Woodpecker **27**
Jacques-Imo's **3**
Joey K's **44**
La Petite Grocery **24**
Lengua Madre **47**
Lilette **29**
LUVI **14**

Mister Mao **22**
Molly's Rise and Shine **47**
Mosquito Supper Club **35**
Parish Ice Cream
 Parlor **47**
Pascal's Manale **32**
Patois **10**
Pizza Domenica **16**
Plum Street Snoball **6**
Saba **13**
Saffron **25**
San Lorenzo **47**
Seafood Sally's **2**
Surrey's **47**
Turkey and the Wolf **47**
Wakin' Bakin' **30**
Wishing Town Bakery
 Café **12**

and wide; his pecan pie with its perfect, copious crust is also justifiably revered. The online menu is almost never current; all the better to be in the moment. Reserve well in advance during peak periods; expect a comfortable, relaxed, thoroughly enjoyable adult evening.

723 Dante St. www.brigtsens.com. ℭ **504/861-7610.** Entrees $26–$38. Tues–Sat 5–8:30pm. Reservations essential.

Charlie's ★★★ STEAK   There are fancier steak houses in town. All of them, actually. But none with the literal sizzle of Charlie's, which doesn't even have a menu, just a recitation. Start with a heap of onion rings, follow with a massive wedge salad (save some rings to crunch onto the wedge). There are five cuts, seared tuna for those who must, and various sides (we get 'shrooms and asparagus; if there is such a thing as overkill in New Orleans, it's the rich crabmeat au gratin. But you do you.). Ending with a scoop of Angelo Brocato's ice cream is de rigueur. Steaks arrive plattered, buttered, sizzling (as we said)—and perfectly cooked. Tucked away in an unassuming neighborhood, it's all friendly and efficient, and the ageless dining room, packed with locals, is just as it should be.

4510 Dryades St. www.charliessteakhousenola.com. ℭ **504/895-9323.** Steaks $45–$65. Tues–Sat 5–8:30pm.

Clancy's ★★★ CONTEMPORARY CREOLE   Clancy's epitomizes the New Orleans tradition of fine neighborhood dining, where white tablecloths meet good ole boys. Thing is, everyone's a good ole boy here—it's been that way for 70 years. It's got the look: tuxedoes on the waiters, linen on the laps, bead board on the walls. It's got the attitude: It's fun fine dining, aspirational for some, a weekly ritual for others. It's got a handwritten menu full of new Creole classics, superbly done: flash-fried oysters topped with brie; creamy, succulent shrimp and grits; a colossal smoked duck leg that stands on its own with the simplest of sides. When soft-shell crab is in season, it's de rigueur on every menu in town, but Clancy's' is smoked—and it's a wonder (so are the salads). We love the (un-published) availability of half-portions on the most popular menu items, but if we were going all-in, we'd order several of the pricey starters—the mussels with andouille in tomato broth and crawfish vol au vent, to name two. Alas, the ample wine list is short on lower-end options, but pours are generous. Once you give in to the kind of splendid evening to be had, you'll invariably end up communing over conversation and cognac. (Consider lunch too—the atmosphere still permeates.)

6100 Annunciation St. www.clancysneworleans.com. ℭ **504/895-1111.** Entrees $26–$35 lunch, $27–$47 dinner. Tues–Wed and Sat 5–10pm; Thurs–Fri 11:30am–2pm and 5–10pm. Reservations advised.

Commander's Palace ★★★ CONTEMPORARY CREOLE   The Commander's Palace miracle: It has an uncanny ability to serve up just the amount of formality your mood requires (and a room to match). An elegant "event" evening? Got it. Rollicking (civilized) good time? They're on it. Party-dressed kids being introduced to fine dining? They'll get the royal treatment, and maybe a rubber duckie garnish. Late, great matriarch Ella Brennan understood that service reigns supreme and for the ultimate New Orleans experience, stately needn't be stuffy, formal can still be fun, and tradition is often best honored through innovation. Her philosophy still reigns through Brennan family co-proprietors Lally and Ti, who rotate as the "Brennan on Duty" to warmly greet guests as they dine. They also mentor and foster the city's culinary scene: A who's who of New Orleans restaurateurs resembles a Commander's family tree. Yet regardless of how many "Best of" lists and awards Commander's racks up, it never rests on its laurels. And now, for the first time in its history, a woman chef is at the helm. Chef Meg Bickford's influence on the continually changing "New Haute Creole" menu embraces her Cajun roots and digs deeper into the region's culturally diverse influences—best experienced in the seven-course "Chef's Playground" menu. The a la carte menu mixes its classics—spicy-sweet shrimp and *tasso henican*; consistently perfect pecan-crusted Gulf fish—with seasonal newbies. It can be hard to choose between the gumbo, turtle soup, or the soup du jour, which is why we appreciate the 1-1-1 demitasse tasting of all three. For enders, the famed bread pudding soufflé is a puff of gladness with whiskey sauce (and must be ordered ahead). The wine list is one of the finest in this or any city, with a good selection offered by the glass in half or full pours. Everyone should dine at Commander's, and everyone can. Its unintimidating finery—plus multi-course lunch and happy-hour deals (did we mention 25¢ martinis at lunch?)—starts at around $23 at lunch, $42 at dinner. So worth it.

1403 Washington Ave. www.commanderspalace.com. © **504/899-8221.** Entrees $29–$49; 3-course dinner $42–$48; 2-course lunch $23–$25; dinner tasting menu $125 ($166 w/wine pairing). Mon–Wed 5:30–9:30pm; Thurs–Fri 11:30am–2pm and 6–9:30pm; Sat 11am–2pm and 6–9:30pm; Sun 10am–2pm and 6–9:30pm. No shorts or T-shirts; collared shirts for men; jackets preferred for men. Reserve well in advance.

Coquette ★★★ CONTEMPORARY SOUTHERN   It feels like Coquette has occupied this tin-ceilinged, chandeliered, bistro-chic space forever. We mean this in the best way—because it's altogether contented in its skin, even if that skin changes daily. Chef Michael Stoltzfus and his team are wells of culinary creativity, absolutely smart, polished, and dedicated to perfect ingredients. With top talent heading the bar and pastry programs as well, Coquette lands firmly in the upper echelon of New Orleans' restaurants and it's one of our perennial favorites. Whatever we suggest will be long gone by the time you dine. If possible, spring for the five-course blind tasting menu (occasional special menu nights turn up too; check the website). Crawfish agnolotti with bits of sweet corn and country ham was beautifully bright, and a mélange of asparagus, burrata, and crab was just right on a humid afternoon. Finishes are light and often herb-driven and servings aren't enormous—you won't leave here uncomfortably overfull. If any version of cheesecake is on the menu, make that your choice.

2800 Magazine St. www.coquettenola.com. © **504/265-0421.** Small plates $10–$18, large plates $28–$40; 5-course tasting menu $85 ($125 w/wine pairing). Sun–Thurs 5:30–9pm; Fri–Sat 5:30–9:30pm. Reservations highly recommended.

Dakar NOLA ★★★ SENEGALESE/SEAFOOD Dakar offers one seating per evening, a seven-course tasting menu that explores the deep cultural connection between Senegambia and New Orleans—and it's a profound (and delicious) experience, exquisitely joyful and engaging. Classically trained Chef Serigne Mbaye draws on childhood memories of cooking with his mother, in Senegal, West Africa, and Harlem NYC, to define modern Senegalese cuisine, using local seafood and produce. In this understated and comfortably refurbished house Uptown, the food righteously takes center stage (though the soundtrack is kicking, too). The entire staff, led by co-owner Effie Richardson, knows they are part of something bigger here, and everything is done with intention, from welcoming guests with a tableside handwashing bowl (a traditional practice in Senegalese homes) to Chef Mbaye introducing the menu. There's a story behind everything: "The Last Meal," for example, a savory black-eyed pea, crab, crispy rice, and palm oil soup, references the palm oil and black-eyed peas fed to enslaved West African ancestors departing on a ship to New Orleans, as well as Africans from Haiti who worked in the kitchens of New Orleans, influencing Creole cuisine as it was developed. It may sound heavy, but this is a shared space of celebration, possibility, and breaking down barriers through incredible food. Chef Mbaye says he and his team cook "to nurture the soul," and indeed we leave full in every way: mind, heart, belly, and soul, with memories of a meal and a 3-hour evening that whizzed by, and one we can't stop talking about.

3814 Magazine St. www.dakarnola.com. No phone. 7-course menu (Thurs–Sat) $150; 3-course menu (Wed) $65. Thurs–Sat 7pm seating; Wed 5–7:30pm. Prepaid advance (non-refundable) reservations required.

Gautreau's ★★ CONTEMPORARY SOUTHERN Uptown in a residential neighborhood, with no signage to speak of, there's this reclusive spot that most every major food magazine and organization has managed to find and lavish with praise and awards. The finery of its food hews close to classic French treatments, but steps forward by virtue of modernity, ingredient perfection (particularly seafood), and artisanal everything. A starter of seared scallops and kabocha squash over arugula is married with a bright pomegranate beurre blanc; a dewy foie gras torchon adds a reduction of stone fruit and huckleberries, with bits of macadamia for crunch. The grown-up wine list matches the low-ceilinged room, with its trompe l'oeil linen walls and warm lighting. Service is flawless.

1728 Soniat St. www.gautreausrestaurant.com. ☏ **504/899-7397.** Entrees $30–$42 ($60 filet mignon). Tues–Sat 5:30–9:30pm. Business casual, no shorts or flip-flops. Reservations advised.

La Petite Grocery ★★★ CONTEMPORARY FRENCH/CREOLE Among the many bistros along Magazine Street, this way-Uptown standard-bearer is more traditionally French than some in terms of decor and wine selections. Ambience-wise, there's a comfortable welcoming groove here. Food is a distinctive mélange of Creole creativity, local ingredients, classic technique, and the adroit palate of chef/owner/*Top Chef* contestant Justin Devillier. We believe deeply in the steak tartare (which comes and goes from the menu) and require the blue crab beignets as well as ricotta dumplings with lobster and fresh peas. The chefs are also soup geniuses, making preliminary courses a tough choice. For entrees, smoky shrimp and grits with roasted mushrooms is one of the better treatments we've tried; the kitchen also delivers a perfect cheeseburger with perfect fries. Desserts crush it: Butterscotch pudding with flecks of crispy ham (!) changed our view of pudding completely. The bar can get pretty lively. (Also see sister restaurant **Justine,** p. 105.)

4238 Magazine St. www.lapetitegrocery.com. ✆ **504/891-3377.** Entrees $22–$42, brunch $14–$30. Mon–Wed 5–9:30pm; Thurs 11:30am–2:30pm and 5–9:30pm; Fri–Sat 11:30am–2:30pm and 5–10:30pm; Sun 10:30am–2:30pm and 5–9:30pm.

Lengua Madre ★★★ MEXICAN   Though overused, the "hidden gem" moniker applies wholeheartedly to chef Ana Castro's speakeasy-like space on a residential corner in the Lower Garden District; figuring out which door to enter through is part of the allure. Once inside the intimate and dimly lit space (after your selfie in the fluorescent-pink-lit hallway) you are in for something special. Castro takes pleasure in creation: Her affordable five-course tasting menu changes every 5–6 weeks, and though you never know exactly what to expect (the menu is not shared in advance), you can count on a reframe of how you think about Mexican cuisine. Rooted most deeply in traditional techniques (Lengua Madre translates to "Mother Tongue"), there will be beans, masa, rice, Gulf seafood, local produce, tequila, mezcal, and a reverence for the artisans and sustainable farmers who have guided it all here. Their presence will be made known, their stories told. The Caldito starter is the only constant: a warm shot of shrimp broth inspired by Castro's favorite seafood spot in Mexico City, where she grew up in her grandmother's home. Even the dishes are special, made by Oaxacan master potter Maestro Francisco Martínez.

1245 Constance St. www.lenguamadrenola.com. ✆ **504/655-1338.** Tasting menu $80; $120 with wine. Wed–Sat 5–10pm; Sun 5–9pm. Reservations required. Special diets can mostly be accommodated with advance reservation and notice.

Lilette ★★★ CONTEMPORARY FRENCH   Lilette's pedigreed chef-owner John Harris trained in some of New Orleans' finest kitchens and at Michelin-starred restaurants in France, resulting in an artistic, serious approach. The NOLA classic space—high-ceilinged, columned, tiles—is made East Village–ready with tobacco-toned walls. Lunch is thick with businesspeople and ladies who lunch; dinner sees a mixed crowd of tourists, neighbors, and young hipsters, all here for the chef's tasteful, clean lines. Start with truffled Parmigiano toast with wild mushrooms, marrow, and veal glace (you may end with it, too; it's divine) or chunky crab claws doused in slightly sweet passion-fruit butter, rich yet restrained (if you stop now, you've done well). Both the grilled hanger steak with marrowed bordelaise fries and the roast chicken breast with Brussels sprouts and balsamic-glazed onions are flawless simplicity. Desserts are worth the indulgence. Opt here if your wine enthusiasm influences your dining decision.

3637 Magazine St. www.liletterestaurant.com. ℭ **504/895-1636.** Entrees $24–$39. Mon 5:30–9:30pm; Tues–Thurs 11:30am–9:30pm; Fri–Sat 11:30am–10:30pm.

Mosquito Supper Club ★★★ CAJUN In this residential double-shotgun home in Central City, Mosquito Supper Club set the bar for the intimate communal, multi-course dinner that's now seen as an essential New Orleans culinary experience. The original 12-strangers-at-a-table meal is still available, but more options (like private party reservations and a bar open to walk-ins) have been added to meet the demand. What hasn't changed is the magic of owner/host/chef (and award-winning cookbook author) Melissa Martin's creations. Hearty, rustic suppers star Gulf seafood, seasonal vegetables, and flavors passed down for generations in Martin's hometown on the bayou in Chauvin, Louisiana. The menu pays homage to Martin's native land and its waters, her ancestors, the cultures of shrimpers, farmers, and Cajuns, conveying her passion for the issues they (and we) face. Woven through are understated lessons around sustainability, climate change, and the viability of a lifestyle. There are no dry lectures, just dialogue and deliciousness—and in the process, knowledge, friends, and memories are gained.

3824 Dryades St. www.mosquitosupperclub.com. No phone. $125–$150 per person; alcohol additional. Thurs–Sun 1 seating at 7:30pm (private party seating 5:30pm; small plates at bar 5:30–9:30pm). Prepaid advance (non-refundable) reservations required for dinner.

Patois ★★★ CONTEMPORARY CREOLE This tucked-away, near-perfect bistro is chic and inviting, the locally sourced ingredients pop with freshness, and service is practiced. Its refined, modern Southern Creole menu is shot through with French influences and an occasional dash of something else, like curried cauliflower or furikake-seasoned deviled eggs. Servings are generous, and like the grilled hanger steak in a rich red-wine bone-marrow reduction, deeply flavored. Desserts bring a sense of whimsy—a fanciful bread pudding has strawberries and white chocolate sauce. You can even buy a round of drinks for the hard-working kitchen staff for $11. We love sitting at the bar with neighborhood folks.

6078 Laurel St. www.patoisnola.com. ℭ **504/895-9441.** Entrees $29–$43 dinner, $18–$32 brunch. Wed–Sat 5–9pm; Sun 10:30am–2pm. Reservations advised, well in advance.

San Lorenzo ★★★ ITALIAN We're smitten with the cool Italian-disco vibe of the newly renovated Hotel Saint Vincent (p. 88), the latest iteration of this historic brick-and-wrought-iron balconied former orphanage. San Lorenzo, the most upscale of its three on-site eateries, leans more toward comfy and calm than cool. Which is a-okay with us (actually the cushy banquettes might be a bit too serene—you'll sink in a good 3 inches below your date across the table in a chair). But cool is in the details, and they're here—those light fixtures, those checker-tiled floors! The menu is coastal Italian, with its best items coming from the sea. All things raw are worth ordering.

The arugula frisee salad, tossed in balsamic sherry vinegar and truffle oil, is impeccably bright and simple; the fish perfectly tender, delicately and sensually sauced. We dream of the impossibly pillowy *gnudi*—a ricotta cheese–based version of gnocchi—in a mushroom sauce topped with fresh peas and shoots. Service is friendly and will guide your way. Terrific selection of wines by the glass, albeit a bit pricey (ditto for breakfast).

1507 Magazine St. www.saintvincentnola.com/dining. ✆ **504/350-2450.** Entrees $22–$48 (lobster/steak $51–$125), $18–$31 breakfast/brunch. Mon–Fri 8–10:30am, 11am–3pm, and 5–10pm; Sat–Sun 8am–3pm and 5–10pm. Reservations recommended.

Moderate

Boucherie ★★★ CONTEMPORARY CAJUN When Boucherie first opened, we wrestled with the selfish tell-or-don't-tell moral dilemma. That didn't last. Word got out, and it's been popular ever since. The food retains its original sense of playfulness, and prices remain solidly affordable for what chef/owner (and *Chopped* alum) Nathaniel Zimet calls "fine dining for the people." The menu is limited, but most everything has Cajun-inflected, meaty goodness, with dashes of global influences. At dinner, a deeply savory brisket is piled with crispy, Parmesan-sprinkled fries (too good to share; get an extra side); we wouldn't ignore the blackened shrimp and grit cake, either. At happy hour (5–6:30pm) you can rock a house-ground burger, fries, *and* a Caesar salad for under $25. They'll happily accommodate herbivores with something special too. *Tip:* Around the corner, spinoff **Bourrée** (1510 S. Carrolton Ave.; www.bourreenola.com; ✆ **504/510-4040**) is crushing it as an amped-up wing, barbecue, and daiquiri shack.

8115 Jeannette St. www.boucherie-neworleans.com. ✆ **504/862-5514.** Small plates $8–$20, large plates $30–$42. Wed–Sat 5–9:30pm.

The Bower ★★★ CONTEMPORARY SOUTHERN In a city with so much historical ambiance, we confess an aversion to trendy new architectural construction. Why dine in a warehouse space you could find anywhere when you're in New Orleans? Well, the Bower is why, and its farm-centric menu, lush green interior, and Storyville Mai Tai (with edible maple glitter) have won us over completely. Chef Marcus Woodman's small and large plates of house-made pastas, charcuterie, heritage meats, and Gulf seafood receive constant new flourishes of flavors driven by whatever local partner Sugar Roots Farms harvests this week; like the already-scrumptious whipped feta starter with turmeric-pickled watermelon radish one night, or the beef carpaccio in an herbed caper and fresh cantaloupe vinaigrette another. The perfectly al dente pappardelle pork and beef Bolognese is topped with a scoop of truffle cultured cream so oozy that it brings a flush to our cheeks. Did we mention how all these shareables make a great date night? The on-point service can read the table, offering up seasonal house-made 'cello liqueurs to make the feeling last *just* a little bit longer. Get the cheesecake too, you won't regret it.

1320 Magazine St. www.thebowernola.com. ✆ **504/582-9738.** Entrees $23–$31. Mon–Thurs 4–9pm; Fri–Sat 4–10pm; happy hour Mon–Sat 4–6pm.

The Chloe ★★ CONTEMPORARY SOUTHERN Whether on the charming front porch and yard, noshing under a canopy of oaks with the clackety clack sound of the passing St. Charles Avenue streetcar, or out back in the lush garden around the pool, the Chloe delivers an enchanting way to pass an afternoon (even your flighty servers can't dampen the loveliness). The Chloe salad, flavorful pork belly lettuce cups, and sandwiches (hello, shrimp roll) satisfy for lunch and brunch. The bartender's crafty concoctions stay delectably consistent right through the golden hour, when sultriness sets in and the entrees come out. Go with a juicy burger if that's your mood, though the roasted pork loin and sausage could set a new one. Either way, there's a couch or a velvet-booth corner table in the dimly lit lobby designed to savor the feeling.

4125 St. Charles Ave. www.thechloenola.com/restaurant. ✆ **504/541-5500.** Entrees $15–$35 lunch/brunch, $18–$38 dinner. Hours vary, but generally Mon–Thurs 11am–10pm; Fri 11am–11pm; Sat 10am–11pm; Sun 10am–9pm.

Delachaise ★★ FRENCH Sitting on its own little island on St. Charles Avenue, this bistro feels so distinctly Parisian that you might crave a Gauloise. It's a worthy hangout for the stellar wine selection (French-leaning and fairly priced; booze and beer options are also plentiful); for the atmosphere (sidewalk bistro tables and a long, narrow tin-ceilinged interior); and for the small but excellent bar-food menu. The best options are the logical ones: pate; frog legs; moules frites; steak frites. Okay FINE, just get the frites. We always end with chocolate souffle and a tawny port. Servers with attitude and air-conditioning set to frigid don't seem to dissuade a youthful crowd that populates the tables for hours on end. Bring a wrap. Open late.

3442 St. Charles Ave. www.thedelachaise.com. ✆ **504/895-0858.** Entrees $10–$18 (steak $33). Mon–Thurs 4pm–1am; Fri–Sat noon–2am; Sun noon–1am.

Gris Gris ★★★ CONTEMPORARY SOUTHERN Gris Gris's entertaining, wrap-around chef's kitchen counter is a great place for fans of cooking shows, communal conversation, or hearty Southern cooking (you can order based on what appeals as it's prepared and plated before your eyes, but be warned—it looks and tastes universally great). Start with the rare indulgence of chicken gizzards, smothered in caramelized peppers and onions, and a cup of gumbo (one of the better versions around). Whole branzino, seared, encircling a rustic ratatouille, is a visual and taste TKO; the wow-factor pork chop will be enjoyed for at least two meals (while still managing to stay moist). Mom's chicken and dumplings is irresistible on a chilly day. Dessert should be pie (if they're not too busy, ask about the pie man). Upstairs in the bar, outside on the sidewalk, or on the casual balcony, you'll miss the show—but get a charming Magazine Street view. Oh, and brunch is served *every day* (did you say *cochon de lait* Benedict?).

1800 Magazine St. www.grisgrisnola.com. ✆ **504/272-0241.** Entrees $12–$28. Sun–Mon and Wed–Thurs 11am–9pm; Fri–Sat 11am–10pm. Reservations recommended.

Jacques-Imo's ★ CAJUN The gator-painted pickup in front of Jacques-Imo's actually has a table set up in its bed, where some lucky couple can dine (they'll have way more space than in the crowded dining room). This funky, colorful spot with the long line (longer in proportion to who's playing next door at the **Maple Leaf;** see p. 221) is hugely popular for all that jacked-up fun, not to mention giant portions and heavily Cajun soul-food stylings. Fortunately, the drinks are well made, and as soon as you're seated you'll be appeased with righteous cornbread muffins. The signature shrimp and alligator-sausage "cheesecake" (more like a quiche) has fans and detractors (we're on board); the diamond-hard crunchy fried chicken and less-complicated specialties fare best.

8324 Oak St. www.jacques-imos.com. ✆ **504/861-0886.** Entrees $27–$39. Wed–Fri 5–10pm; Sat 4–10pm. Reservations required for 5 or more.

Mister Mao ★★ GLOBAL   The decor is a "tell": You're in for a little mischievousness, a lot of quirk, a fair amount of spice, and a ton of fun. Abandon all culinary rules and expectations, you shall be rewarded. Owner/wife Sophina (who heads the kitchen) and owner/husband "Wildcat" (who runs the bar) deliberately eschew all boxes, committing only to their "tropical roadhouse" vibe. Bits of Southeast Asia, Latin America, the Caribbean, and other globe-hopping flavors zing off the teal tiger mural, zebra rugs, and grandmotherly tableware in bewildering, refreshing, and sometimes riotous ways. It's a drinking place for sure, so get in the mood with a yummy, rummy Billion Dollar Betsy, accompanied by *sikil pak* (addictive habanero and pumpkin seed dip) and the now-signature escargot Wellington, horseradish-laden flavor bombs encircled in puff pastry. A section of the menu lists items at the far end of the Scoville scale—steer clear if heat is not your thing. (*Fair warning:* Some of those in other sections aren't exactly benign, and Wildcat doesn't have milk on the bar menu.) Try the Indian street-food-inspired *pani puri,* crispy lentil popper cups filled with potato masala, marinated blueberries, and mint water. The menu changes often, but octopus and scallop preparations are consistent. Save room for chocolate garlic tart (for real). Servers are kindly, cognizant guides through the menu and equally eclectic wine list. Consider it if you're heading to **Tipitina's** (p. 223) for the night, it's a few steps away. Brunch is on fire, too.

4501 Tchoupitoulas St. www.mistermaonola.com. ✆ **504/345-2056.** Plates $13–$28. Mon 5–9pm; Thurs–Sat 5–10pm; Sun 11am–2pm and 5–9pm.

Pascal's Manale ★★★ ITALIAN/SEAFOOD   We adore the old-school neon and the everybody-knows-your-name feel at this vintage neighborhood joint founded by Sicilian immigrants in 1913. Starting a meal at the oyster bar is compulsory: The bivalves might be frigid, but if celebrity shucker Thomas "Uptown T" Steward is present, his repartee is hot. Ask him anything, and your party is officially started. The buttery bowl of barbecued shrimp (heads on, eaten with your hands while wearing a bib) made Manale (mu-*nah*-lee) famous. In 2023, when news spread that the landmark had changed hands a second time in less than 4 years, the city breathed a sigh of relief to hear that

Dickie Brennan was taking over. We love our institutions, and since the Brennans are one, we expect the classics to stay the same or get even better.

1838 Napoleon Ave. www.pascalsmanale.com. © **504/895-4877.** Entrees $22–$28 (steak $44). Wed–Fri 11am–9pm; Tues and Sat 4–9pm. Closed Sun–Mon. Reservations advised.

Saba ★★★ MIDDLE EASTERN   Soon after chef Alon Shaya left the eponymous, mega-award-winning restaurant he helped originate (we'll spare you the breakup details), he roared back by opening Saba. The fresh, modern Middle Eastern flavorings are intact, with a bit more localism woven through. That's evident in the blue crab topping velvety hummus, and the rich duck broth in the matzo-ball soup. The Middle Eastern herbs and spices are as subtle as the textures are supple, and the menu encourages a table full of shared plates—tiny, small, medium, and major. Start with some pretty plates of salatim, like *ikra* (smoked trout roe with herbs) or Bulgarian *lutenitsa* (oven-fired peppers, tomatoes, and eggplant pureed and seasoned to pure perfection). Order as many plates as your table can fit—that way your server will keep bringing the glorious steam-puffed pita bread, piping-fresh from the oven. The harissa-roasted whole chicken is moist and perfect, and the astute wine list is stocked with a contingent of beautifully complementary rosés. Close with the divine labneh cheesecake. Or, do all the dips for brunch, and swap out dessert for latkes, lemon butter pancakes, and egg-centric entrees.

5757 Magazine St. www.eatwithsaba.com. © **504/324-7770.** Small plates $8–$24, family-style entrees $20–$32. Mon and Wed–Thurs 4–9pm; Fri 11am–2pm and 4:30–10pm; Sat 10am–2:30pm and 4:30–10pm; Sun 10am–2:30pm and 4:30–9pm.

Saffron ★★★ INDIAN   Who comes to New Orleans and eats Indian food? Smart people who appreciate the stellar, unpretentious service and sophisticated, delicately seasoned food served by the Vikhu family in this comfortable, elegantly contemporary setting. Share a few *sathi,* small bowls served with crisp roti flatbread for dipping or spooning: an excellent *daal* (lentil stew) or saag paneer. And/or the chargrilled oysters, a NOLA staple done here with curry leaf. Standout entrees include the goat masala, subtle and unctuous, and a spice-crusted Gulf fish—another perfect melding of the two cuisines. Cocktails mirror the menu, with crafty hints of tamarind or cardamom; beer and wine are thoughtfully paired. If Indian desserts aren't your jam, the ethereal "Curry is My Jam" ginger cake will change that (literally).

4128 Magazine St. www.saffronnola.com. © **504/323-2626.** Small and large plates $14–$35. Tues–Thurs 5–9pm; Fri–Sat 5–9:45pm. Reservations recommended.

Seafood Sally's ★★ SEAFOOD   Sally's is a straightforward, approachable seafood spot in a delightful converted-house setting that draws neighbors and visitors (Oak St. is outside the typical tourist zones, but a fun stroll). The outside space is especially welcoming, with small and large picnic tables and perhaps a few kids playing between them. If, on the way to your table, you notice something tasty on someone else's plate, you'd feel comfortable stopping to ask them about it, and they'll offer an opinion and a taste. Sharing a

BLACK bayou ROAD

The oldest road in New Orleans is a vibrant hub for African and Afro-Caribbean culture, community, and (of course) cuisine. Opt for an Ethiopian dish in **Addis NOLA**'s stunning space (p. 119), or duck into the bright-and-tiny **CoCo Hut** (2515 Bayou Rd.; www.instagram.com/coco_hut_nola; ℭ **504/945-8788**) for a Jamaican jerk plate (or salad or wrap). **McHardy's Chicken and Fixin'** (p. 124) fries up some of the best chicken in town for a takeout picnic; and **Froot Orleans'** "fruit parlor" (2438 Bell St.; www.frootorleans.com;

ℭ **504/233-3346**) cools down varying degrees of heat with fresh-cut fruit, juices, and smoothies. Or, jumpstart a day of shopping da' road (p. 235) with a breakfast taco at worker-owned co-op **Pagoda Café** (1430 N Dorgenois St.; www.pagodacafe.net; ℭ **504/644-4178**) or take a load off at speakeasy-like **Whiskey & Sticks** (2513 Bayou Rd.; www.whiskeyandsticks.com; ℭ **504/259-2025**) for premium pours, cigars, and people-watching (also occasional food pop-ups, trivia and DJ nights).

platter of the super-fresh seasonal selections, boiled or fried, is good fun; we can also attest to either of the crab claw starters and the Buffalo fried oyster sandwich (fried oysters + bleu cheese = yes). If you're uncertain about how to eat all these local seafood standards (whole crabs, head-on shrimp, raw oysters), it's an affordable place to practice and the sociable servers will help (so might some of the folks at the neighboring tables). *Tip:* Good pre-show option for the **Maple Leaf** (p. 221).

8400 Oak St. www.seafoodsallys.com. ℭ **504/766-8735.** Entrees $15–$28. Mon and Wed–Fri 3–9pm; Sat–Sun 11am–9pm.

Inexpensive

Camellia Grill ★★ DINER   Even though it's only been a part of the city's food culture since 1946, the white-columned Camellia Grill seems to have always been here. We go for luncheonette-style counter service with white linens, Southern hospitality, witty banter dished out by white-jacketed servers, and a classic grill-top burger. The omelets manage to be simultaneously hefty and fluffy and come in the standard varieties. Late-night hours make it a popular after-club spot, but any time is good for the chocolate pecan pie (heated on the grill and a la mode, please). Good prices, true character.

626 S. Carrollton Ave. www.facebook.com/thecamelliagrill. ℭ **504/309-2679.** All items under $15. Mon–Thurs 8am–7pm; Fri–Sun 8am–8pm.

Casamento's ★★★ SEAFOOD   Probably the best "erster" joint in the city, Casamento's takes its oysters so seriously that it simply closes down when they're not peak season (well, Gulf oysters are always in season nowadays, but everyone needs a vacation). The subway-tiled restaurant has been family-owned since 1919. The oysters are scrubbed clean and well selected; the shucker is a hoot (if you dare him, he'll shoot a bivalve into your mouth from across the room). You should absolutely take the plunge and order oyster loaf: a whole loaf of bread fried in butter, filled with oysters (or shrimp), and fried again to seal it. Seriously.

4330 Magazine St. www.casamentosrestaurant.com. ✆ **504/895-9761.** Entrees $9–$26; some items, including oysters, market price. No credit cards. Thurs–Sat 11am–2pm and 5:30–9pm; Sun 4:30–8:30pm. Closed June–Aug.

Domilise's Po' Boys & Bar ★★ CASUAL   Under "Classic Neighborhood Joint," reference materials list a picture of Domilise's (or could). At this century-old, cluttered, lowdown poor-boy shop hidden away Uptown, your hands-down order is the wet-dry, battered-and-fried-to-order shrimp, piled onto puffy poor-boy loaves by friendly fry-counter ladies. Peak lunchtime can move slowly along (take a number), and tables are scant. Don't ever change, Domilise's.

5240 Annunciation St. www.domilisespoboys.com. ✆ **504/899-9126.** Po' boys $8.50–$25. Mon–Wed 11am–3pm; Thurs 11am–5pm; Fri–Sat 11am–7pm.

Heard Dat Kitchen ★★ SOUL FOOD   The food from chef Jeff Heard is worth the trip outside the tourist zones for those interested in "The Real New Orleans." It's a casual, no-frills place where you order at the window and eat outside at a picnic table (to-go orders and delivery available, too). His soulful, homecooked dishes are laden with 'dat crawfish, 'dat cream, and 'dem puns. The "Superdome," a dome of mashed potatoes atop a crispy catfish filet, topped with wafer-thin onion rings and surrounded by crab and crawfish creamed corn, is pretty much all you need to eat this week—and so worth it. But get the stuffed bell pepper if it's available, and anything covered in the famous CrawDat sauce.

2520 Felicity St. www.hearddatkitchen.com. ✆ **504/510-4248.** Entrees $10–$20. Mon–Sat 11am–8pm.

High Hat ★★★ CONTEMPORARY SOUTHERN   Located on Uptown's now-popular (and post-Katrina gentrified) Freret Street, this casual neighborhood spot once had nothing to go on but an idea and original tile floors. It's become one of the city's go-to beacons for unfussy, reasonable brunches, lunches, and dinners made with obvious care. We come for the always interesting drinks. We come for graceful oyster fennel soup, and Mississippi Delta and Louisiana comfort foods, like a mound of fork-tender slow-roasted pork with sublime braised greens and addictive mac 'n' cheese. But mostly we come for the dark gumbo and the plateful of fried awesomeness that is the catfish: crispy, light, piled high (that is, if we can resist the daily specials). Then we get whatever oven-fresh pie is available. Everything here is chef-made on-site, even the condiments. Be prepared for a wait with a party; solo diners can usually slip into a bar seat.

4500 Freret St. www.highhatcafe.com. ✆ **504/754-1336.** Most entrees under $20. Fri–Sat 11am–9pm; Sun–Tues 11:30am–8pm. No reservations.

Joey K's ★ CREOLE   This corner hangout gets locals and a few visitors who know that the trout Tchoupitoulas—a rocking pan-fried trout topped with grilled veggies and shrimp—is worth a stop if you're out for a shop. Service is beyond friendly, and the menu is a solid mix of local dishes. Daily blackboard specials such as brisket, lamb shank, and white beans with pork chops are tasty—and convenient—we are often on this stretch of Magazine when hunger strikes.

3001 Magazine St. www.joeyksrestaurant.com. © **504/891-0997.** Most entrees under $20. Mon–Sat 11am–9pm.

Surrey's ★★★ CAFE   No embellishment needed, just a straightforward, unfancy breakfast-and-lunch cafe with a Latin-influenced menu and fresh organic juice bar, where most everything is homemade and really good. Corned-beef andouille hash is outstanding; huevos rancheros with mole sauce a delight. OMG award goes to the felonious sugar- and rum-drenched French toast stuffed with bananas Foster. The creamy shrimp and grits aren't far behind. No wonder there's always a line of locals willing to wait too.

1418 Magazine St. www.surreysnola.com. © **504/524-3827.** Everything under $20. Thurs–Mon 8am–3pm. No reservations.

Turkey and the Wolf ★★★ CASUAL   In 2017, *Bon Appetit* magazine named this Irish Channel hideaway the best new restaurant in the country. *In the country.* For a counter-service sandwich shop. The goodness stems from comfort, creativity, '90s nostalgia, stoner cravings, and pure talent. Thick-cut fried custom-made bologna, kettle chips, and gooey American cheese are stuffed between fat white bread slabs. Slow-stewed, heat-spiked collard greens make their way into a sandwich, oozing with cheese and Russian dressing. Homemade vanilla soft serve comes with rainbow sprinkles (okay) or tahini and date molasses (whoa). *Bonus:* Drinks are equally creative and carefully wrought. *Double-bonus:* Chef /owner Mason Hereford regularly welcomes

road trip **EATS**

You can snag plenty of good eats in the city's nearby suburbs and parishes. These local favorites are well worth the 15- to 45-minute drives:

o **Dong Phuong** ★★★   New Orleans has a huge, vibrant Vietnamese population and the restaurant scene reflects it. Head east for the best *banh mi* (on legendary French bread) and baked goods, as a 2018 James Beard Award corroborated. 14207 Chef Menteur Hwy., N.O. East; © **504/882-9878;** $3–$12; daily 8am–5pm except Tues.

o **Middendorf's** ★★★   This classic joint near the Manchac swamp fries

up the crispiest, thinnest, freshest catfish imaginable. 30160 Hwy. 51 South, Akers; © **985/386-6666;** $16–$24; Wed–Sun 10:30am–9pm.

o **Mosca's** ★★★   Generations of New Orleanians have made the 25-minute drive to this roadside joint in the middle of nowhere to devour old-school Sicilian immigrant classics served family style—prepared by the same family who founded it in 1946. 4137 U.S. 90, Westwego; www.moscasrestaurant.com; © **504/436-8950;** $12–$40, no credit cards; Wed–Thurs 5–8pm, Fri–Sat 5–8:30pm.

one-time-only chef collabs, check Instagram to see what's coming. Sister spot **Molly's Rise & Shine** (2368 Magazine St.; www.mollysriseandshine.com; © **504/302-1896**) follows the tasty wacky retro excess pattern for breakfasts.

739 Jackson Ave. www.turkeyandthewolf.com. © **504/218-7428.** Everything under $13. Wed–Mon 11am–4pm.

BAKERIES & DESSERT

For other sweet treats, see **"Candies, Pralines & Pastries"** in chapter 9, p. 241; also **Bakery Bar** (p. 227); **Bywater Bakery** (p. 117).

Angelo Brocato Ice Cream & Confectionery ★★★ ICE CREAM/ BAKERY This sweet old-school ice-cream parlor celebrated its 100th birthday under 5 feet of flood water from Katrina—and celebrated its 118th as a national James Beard finalist for Outstanding Bakery. The Sicilian Brocato family (who have run this since 1905) make rich Italian ice cream and ices, cookies, and pastries amid a beloved throwback atmosphere (anchored by a portrait of Angelo himself, and a stunning copper-and-brass espresso machine). Italian flavors like *tracciatella* (chocolate chip) and panna cotta are capital-P Perfect; hard-to-find specialties like spumoni and cassata are spot-on; and the fresh lemon ice is legendary (don't try to decide between that and seasonal fresh fruit ices, blood orange or passion fruit; just get both). After that we get freshly filled cannoli to take home. We tell them it's for a party.

214 N. Carrollton Ave. www.angelobrocatoicecream.com. © **504/486-1465.** Everything under $10. Tues–Sat 10am–10pm; Sun 10am–9pm.

Café du Monde ★★★ CAFE/BAKERY Since 1862, iconic Café du Monde has been selling *café au lait* and beignets (and nothing but) on the edge of Jackson Square. A New Orleans landmark, it's a must-stop for fried goodness, people-watching, and live music (tip the street musicians). Beignets are served steaming-hot and covered in powdered sugar. At three to an order for under $4, they're a hell of a deal. Wash them down with chicory *café au lait* or really good hot chocolate. *Tip #1:* Don't wait for a clean table. Just sit (the servers will clear them when they take your order). *Tip #2:* The takeout line is around the back. If that line is long, be advised that the line for a table generally moves faster. *Tip #3:* Consider a special visit to the one in the midst of glorious oak-filled City Park (p. 183). *Tip #4:* Don't wear black. *Tip #5:* Don't breathe in when you bite.

800 Decatur St. www.cafedumonde.com. © **504/587-0833.** 3 beignets $3.85. No credit cards. Sun–Thurs 7:15am–11pm; Fri–Sat 7:15am–midnight. Also in the City Park Casino Bldg., Riverwalk Mall, and Louis Armstrong International Airport. All closed Christmas Eve and Day.

Creole Creamery ★★★ ICE CREAM Shakes and malts and scoops, oh my! Thick, luscious, truly fabulous ice cream and sorbets with a rotating list of signature, seasonal, and unusual flavors, from brown butter pecan and bananas Foster to red velvet cake and nectar sherbet. Fortunately, they offer a sampler of four or six mini-scoops. Refreshing, maybe even mandatory in summer, and open late enough for a scoop on the way to or from an Uptown club or bar.

4924 Prytania St. (look for the old McKenzie's sign). www.creolecreamery.com. *C* **504/894-8680.** Most items under $10. No credit cards. Sun–Thurs noon–10pm; Fri–Sat noon–11pm.

Croissant D'Or Patisserie ★★ CAFE/BAKERY A quiet and calm place with the same snacks you might find in a cosmopolitan coffeehouse, and you can almost always find an open table inside or in the pretty courtyard. Are the pastries and croissants made of gold? The prices feel like it sometimes, but they are credibly, crustily French. Quiches, omelets, soups, and light sandwiches as well.

617 Ursulines Ave. www.croissantdorpatisserie.com. *C* **504/524-4663.** Everything under $12. Mon and Wed–Fri 7am–1pm; Sat–Sun 7am–3pm.

Gracious Bakery ★★ BAKERY Two Uptown locations of this independent bakery helmed by pastry chef Megan Forman serve fresh baked bagels, donuts, cakes, pies, cookies, and terrific sandwiches (house-cured salmon bagel and tarragon chicken salad are faves).

4930 Prytania St. www.graciousbakery.com. No phone. Everything under $12. Mon–Fri 7am–6pm; Sat–Sun 7am–4pm. Also in Garden District at 2854 St. Charles Ave. (daily 7am–3pm).

Loretta's Authentic Pralines ★★ DESSERT "Praline Queen" Loretta Harrison was the first Black woman in New Orleans to successfully own and operate her own praline company, which she did for over 35 years before her untimely passing in 2022. She was famous for her loving spirit, big personality, and pralines (using her great-great grandmother's recipe), but also her beignets: sweet praline and savory crabmeat-stuffed. Her sons and niece continue her legacy, now the sixth-generation keepers of the family recipe. *Tip:*

bean FREAKS

Single-source, third-wave, cold-pressed, pour-over-only people might be satisfied at one of these spots. *Might.* All offer some variation on pastries and light savory fare.

- **Backatown** ★★ (Tremé): 301 Basin St. (www.backatownnola.com; *C* **504/372-4442**).
- **Coffee Science** ★★★ (Mid-City): 410 S. Broad St. (www.coffee sciencenola.com; *C* **504/814-0878**).
- **French Truck** ★★★: www. frenchtruckcoffee.com. **French Quarter:** 217 Chartres St.; **Lower** **Garden District:** 1200 Magazine St.; **Uptown:** 4536 Dryades St.; **CBD:** 640 Poydras St.
- **Mammoth Espresso** ★★ (Warehouse District): 821 Baronne St. (www.mammothespresso.com; *C* **504/475-4344**).
- **Old Road Coffee** ★★★ (Tremé): 2024 Bayou Rd. (www.oldroad coffee.com; *C* **504/354-8814**).
- **Orange Couch** ★★★ (Marigny): 2339 Royal St. (www.theorange couchcoffee.com; *C* **504/267-7327**).

A snoball's CHANCE

Shaved-ice clone? Let us assure you: It's no such thing. These mouthwatering concoctions are made with custom machines that shave the ice so fine that skiers envy the powder. The better proprietors make their own flavored syrups, and the far-reaching flavors—such as wedding cake (almond, mostly), nectar (think cream soda, only much better), and orchid cream vanilla (bright purple that must be seen to be believed)—are absolutely delectable. Order them with condensed or evaporated milk if you prefer your refreshing drinks on the decadently creamy side, or go further— some shops spike them with booze. At any time on a hot day, lines can be out the door, and like so many other local specialties, loyalties are fierce. You should stop in at any snoball stand you see, but the following are worth seeking out. Hours vary, so call ahead; most open midday until 7 or 8pm, and many close for winter. Get plenty of napkins.

The snoballs at **Hansen's Sno-Bliz ★★★** (4801 Tchoupitoulas St.; www.snobliz.com; ℂ 504/891-9788) are a revered city tradition, still served with a smile by third-generation owner Ashley

Hansen, who officially took over after her grandparents died in the months following Katrina (and won the 2014 James Beard "American Classic" award). Those grandparents invented the shaved-ice machine in use here and elsewhere and concocted their own proprietary syrups. Snoballs come in a souvenir cup. Try the bubble-gum-flavored Sno-bliz.

Plum St. Snoballs ★★★ (1300 Burdette St.; www.plumstreetsnoball.com; ℂ **504/866-7996**) has been cooling New Orleanians for more than 70 years, serving favorites in Chinese food containers. Fans of **Pandora's ★★★** (901 S. Carrollton Ave.; ℂ **504/289-0765**) say its ice is the softest anywhere, and the flavor list is so long it's taking over the neighborhood. You'll have to fight the hordes of school kids in line, even, it often seems, during school hours. **Imperial Woodpecker ★★** (3511 Magazine St.; www.iwsnoballs.com; ℂ **251/366-7777**) has the edge on contemporary flavors, like black sesame, cardamom, and cereal cream, while **NOLA Sips** (2633 St. Claude Ave.; www.nolasips. com; ℂ **504/314-1192**) covers the boozy and over-the-top snoball market.

Fried seafood platters, gumbo, and more served at the Rampart St. Café location.

N. Rampart Café at 2101 N. Rampart St. www.lorettaspralines.com. ℂ **504/944-7068.** $4–$8 (lunch $10–$15). Thurs–Sat 9am–4pm. Also in the French Market at 1100 N. Peters St. #9 (Wed–Sun 9am–5pm, Mon until 4pm).

Parish Ice Cream Parlor ★★ ICE CREAM   Luscious small-batch homemade ice creams, sorbets, and custards are the draw here with their creamy fruit-and-ganache combos (strawberry with white chocolate ganache; coconut with dark chocolate ganache), but rotating seasonal flavors keep us coming back.

1912 Magazine St. www.parishparlor.com. ℂ **504/302-2244.** $4–$8. Sun–Thurs noon–9pm; Fri–Sat noon–10pm.

EXPLORING NEW ORLEANS

By Lavinia Spalding

W e've made no secret of our favorite New Orleans activities: walking, eating, people-watching, listening to music, dancing, and eating again. But between those activities, there's much to see, do, and experience. New Orleans is a vibrant, visual, utterly authentic city with a rich history and gobs of culture worthy of your time.

Though the French Quarter is certainly a seductive place, visiting New Orleans and never leaving the Quarter is like standing in Times Square and believing you've seen New York. Stroll the lush Garden District, marvel at the live oaks in City Park, ride the St. Charles Avenue streetcar and admire the gorgeous homes, or go visit some gators on a swamp tour. Take a walk along Bayou St. John, tour the remarkable Tremé neighborhood, or ride a bike through the Bywater. We'll guide you to some of the city's amazing museums, diverse neighborhoods, and prettiest parks, with suggestions for action-lovers and armchair adventurers, history buffs, and partiers. *One note:* If you have questions about a business, it's best to check social media sites (or send a DM, email, or call), since, frankly, keeping websites updated isn't on the list of things New Orleans does best.

THE FRENCH QUARTER

Those who have been to Disneyland might be forgiven if they experience some déjà vu upon first seeing the French Quarter. The same might be said for those who have visited Paris. It's more worn than Disneyland, of course, and more compact than Paris, on which it was based. But despite the fact that Walt actually did replicate a French Quarter street in Disneyland's New Orleans Square, there ain't nothing like the real thing, baby—and there's certainly no other square mile in the U.S. that resembles the French Quarter. This one turned 300 years old in 2018 and is one of the most interesting neighborhoods in America. The endless eyefuls of florid architecture, the copious cultural oddities, and the stories that emanate from the very streets make it easy to look beyond the ubiquitous souvenir shops and bars. We make the *very* occasional foray to Bourbon Street in all its tacky, outlandish, odoriferous glory, and

New Orleans Attractions

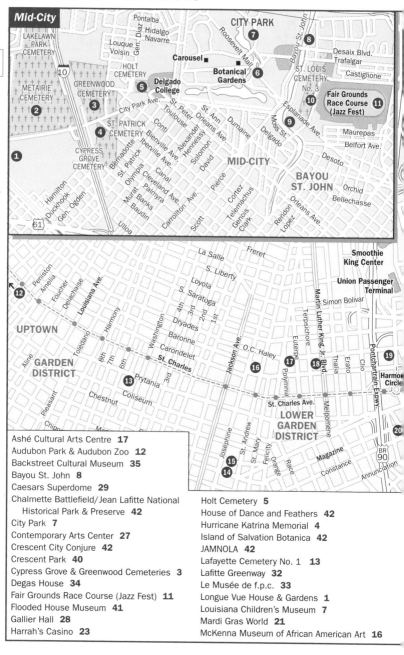

Mid-City

Pontalba
Hidalgo
Navarre
LAKELAWN
PARK
CEMETERY
Louque
Voisin
HOLT
CEMETERY
GREENWOOD
CEMETERY
METAIRIE
CEMETERY
Carousel
Botanical
Gardens
Delgado
College
ST. PATRICK
CEMETERY
CYPRESS
GROVE
CEMETERY
City Park Ave.
Toulouse
St. Peter
St. Ann
Orleans Ave.
Conti
Bienville Ave.
Iberville Ave.
Alexander
Hennessy
Solomon
David
Bernadotte
St. Patrick
Canal
Cleveland Ave.
Olympia
Murat
Banks
Baudin
Palmyra
Carrollton Ave.
Scott
Pierce
Cortez
Telemachus
Genois
Clark
Rendon
Lopez
Orleans Ave.
Hamilton
Duckhook
Gen. Ogden
Ulloa

CITY PARK
Roosevelt Mall
Desaix Blvd.
Trafalgar
ST. LOUIS
CEMETERY
No. 3
Castiglione
Fair Grounds
Race Course
(Jazz Fest)
Esplanade Ave.
Dumaine
Moss St.
Delgado
Maurepas
Belfort Ave.
Desoto
MID-CITY
BAYOU
ST. JOHN
Orchid
Bellechasse

La Salle
Freret
Smoothie
King Center
Peniston
Amelia
Foucher
Delachaise
Louisiana Ave.
Harmony
S. Liberty
Loyola
S. Saratoga
4th
3rd
2nd
1st
Simon Bolivar
Martin Luther King Jr. Blvd.
Terpsichore
Union Passenger
Terminal
UPTOWN
Toledano
8th
7th
6th
Washington
Dryades
Baronne
Carondelet
St. Charles
Prytania
Coliseum
Chestnut
Jackson Ave.
O.C. Haley
Euterpe
Polymnia
Thalia
Erato
Clio
Pontchartrain Expwy.
Aline
GARDEN
DISTRICT
Pleasant
Chip
Mar
3rd
St. Charles Ave.
Melpomene
LOWER
GARDEN
DISTRICT
Josephine
St. Andrew
St. Mary
Felicity
Orange
Race
Constance
Magazine
Annunciation
Harmony
Circle
BR
90

Metairie (Lake Lawn) Cemetery **2**

Museum of the Southern Jewish Experience **19**

Music Box Village **42**

National World War II Museum **20**

New Orleans African American Museum **37**

New Orleans Museum of Art **6**

Ogden Museum of Southern Art **26**

Pitot House **9**

Sazerac House **24**

Southern Food and Beverage Museum/
  Museum of the American Cocktail **18**

St. Alphonsus Art and Cultural Center **14**

St. Augustine Church **38**

St. Louis Cemetery No. 1 **30**

St. Louis Cemetery No. 2 **31**

St. Louis Cemetery No. 3 **10**

St. Mary's Assumption **15**

St. Patrick's Church **25**

St. Roch Cemetery and the Campo Santo **42**

Studio BE **42**

TEP Center **42**

Treme's Petit Jazz Museum **36**

Voodoo Spiritual Temple **39**

Vue Orleans **22**

we believe there's an argument for experiencing it (at least once). But the operative word is "occasional." (You also have our blessing to skip it *entirely* and spend your time and money elsewhere.) The key to this city is fully exploring it. Still: It's New Orleans, so as the Rebirth Brass Band song goes: "Do Whatcha Wanna." (Within reason, of course.)

A French engineer named Adrien de Pauger designed the Quarter in 1718. Almost all the buildings burned in the fires of 1788 and 1794, though, and were rebuilt while the city was under Spanish ownership, so in truth, the architecture is mostly Spanish, not French. But much French culture remains, and today the Vieux Carré ("Old Square") is a great anomaly in America, where many other cities have torn down or gutted their historic centers. Thanks to a strict local preservation policy, the area looks much as it has since the late 18th century, and it's still the heart of town.

Jackson Square bustles with musicians, artists, fortune-tellers, jugglers, and those mesmerizing "living statue" performance artists who entertain for change (we try to always carry some $1 bills to throw in the hat of those who catch our eye or ear). Pay attention to that seemingly ad hoc jazz band playing right in front of the Cabildo—these talented musicians might be in jeans now but may very well be in tie and tux later, playing high-end clubs. **Royal Street,** our favorite for strolling, is home to stellar street musicians, numerous antique shops, and world-class galleries. You'll also encounter interesting businesses on **Chartres** and **Decatur Streets** and the cross streets between.

The closer you get to **Esplanade Avenue** and toward **Rampart Street,** the more residential the Quarter becomes (in the business sections, the ground floors are commercial and the stories above are often apartments). Peep in through any open gate, where surprises await in the form of graceful brick- and flagstone-lined courtyards filled with foliage and bubbling fountains. At the same time, be mindful that throughout the Quarter, you are walking by people's homes. Please be courteous, quiet, and clean, folks.

The Vieux Carré Commission is ever vigilant about balancing contemporary economic interests in the Quarter with historical preservation. There are few chain stores or restaurants, and no traffic lights in the whole interior of the French Quarter (they're relegated to fringe streets); streetlamps are the old gas-light style. Large city buses are banned, and during part of each day, Royal and Bourbon streets are pedestrian malls. No vehicles are *ever* allowed around Jackson Square. The Quarter streets are laid out in an almost perfect rectangular grid, so they're easily navigable. They're also well-traveled and thus relatively safe. Again, as you near the fringes and as night falls, you should exercise caution; stay in the busy, well-lit parts, walk briskly, and try not to walk alone.

The French Quarter **walking tour** in chapter 10 will give you the best overview of the historic structures in the area and its history. Many other attractions that aren't in the walking tour are listed in this chapter (and mapped on p. 155), so make sure to cross-reference as you go along.

As mentioned elsewhere, driving in the French Quarter isn't ideal. But if you must, and you're planning a full day of sightseeing in the Quarter, check out our parking tips on p. 294.

French Quarter Attractions

Audubon Aquarium and Audubon Insectarium **28**

Beauregard-Keyes House **23**

The Cabildo **13**

Café du Monde **18**

Congo Square **1**

The 1850 House **16**

The French Market **25**

Gallier House Museum **22**

Germaine Wells Mardi Gras Museum **5**

Hermann-Grima House **6**

Historic New Orleans Collection **10**

Jean Lafitte's Old Absinthe House **7**

Madame John's Legacy **20**

Museum of Death **4**

New Orleans Historical Pharmacy Museum **9**

New Orleans Historic Voodoo Museum **21**

New Orleans Jazz Museum at the Old U.S. Mint **26**

Old Ursuline Convent **24**

Our Lady of Guadalupe Chapel – International Shrine of St. Jude **3**

Pontalba Buildings **12, 17**

The Presbytère **15**

Preservation Hall **11**

St. Louis Cathedral **14**

St. Louis Cemetery No. 1 **2**

Voodoo Authentica **19**

Williams Research Center **8**

Woldenberg Riverfront Park **27**

Major Attractions in the French Quarter

Audubon Aquarium and Insectarium ★★★ AQUARIUM It's hard to imagine this vaunted institution—included on most "Best Aquariums in the U.S." lists—getting any better, but guess what: It's even better, after wrapping up a whopping $41-million renovation. Exhibits, which focus on the Mississippi and Gulf of Mexico, are highly entertaining and painlessly educational for kids and grown-ups. We love the huge interior Amazon rainforest, an immersive experience complete with birds, piranhas, and a sloth. Also unmissable: a fine exhibit on seahorses, a rare leucistic (white, blue-eyed) gator, a 13,000-gallon shark and ray touch pool, and the adorable penguins in a newly redesigned home. Perhaps most exciting, the renovation includes the addition of the **Audubon Insectarium,** formerly on Canal Street, adding 17,000 square feet of new immersive exhibits dedicated to all things bug and arachnid. (Though located inside the aquarium, the insectarium still charges a separate admission.) Many favorites from the insectarium's previous location made the move, including the "Bug Appetite Café" where you can treat yourself to snacks that include, yep, insects. (Dare ya!) And the new butterfly pavilion is a breathtaking and peaceful departure from the hustle outside, with 500 to 700 butterflies flying through a lush garden that overlooks the Mississippi River. The outdoor splash fountain is also irresistible on a warm day. Right on the edge of the Quarter, the aquarium is a handy refuge from the heat or rain. *Tip*: If you plan to visit more than one of the Audubon attractions, combo packages to the aquarium, insectarium, and zoo provide savings. Best (but not required) to purchase tickets online, in advance.

1 Canal St., at the river. www.auduboninstitute.org. ℂ **800/774-7394** or 504/861-2537. Prices change from day to day, but generally aquarium $30–$35 adults, $25–$30 seniors and children 2–12; insectarium $30–$35 adults, $25–$30 seniors and children 2–12. Daily 10am–5pm.

The French Market ★★ MARKET The site of the French Market was originally used as a bartering market by Indigenous peoples, including the Chitimacha, Choctaw, Ishak, Tunica, and Natchez nations. What's known today as the French Market is said to have been founded by the Oumas people, who sold goods to travelers (including Bienville, "founder" of New Orleans). It grew into an official market in 1812. From around 1840 to 1870, it was part of Gallatin Street, a rough area full of bars, drunken sailors, and criminals. Today it's a mixed bag and not nearly as dynamic as its past, but still a fun, historic amble. The foodstuffs, from produce and seafood to more tourist-oriented items like hot sauces and Cajun spice mixes, are pricier than at local supermarkets—but here they'll pack it for air travel or ship it home. Snacks like gator on a stick will amuse the kids, while the oyster bar and food vendors will satisfy grown-ups. **Meals from the Heart** (p. 122), a standout cafe, will appease any vegetarians in the group, and **Loretta's Authentic Pralines** (p. 149) are stellar. The shops and eateries are open every day (10am–5pm), and on some days things are even enlivened by some entertainment (music, cooking demos), which harkens back to what it was once like here. The famed

flea market section (daily 10am–5pm) is kind of junky, but sprinkled among the T-shirts, caps, and cheap sunglasses are a few original art vendors (some original art here is tax-free). It's convenient for souvenir shopping and trinkets, especially inexpensive silver jewelry and all manner of fleur de lis. If you've outshopped your luggage, you can pick up a duffle bag, a gorgeous West African basket, or a small suitcase. There are (all-important) clean public bathrooms here.

1235 N. Peters St. (from Jackson Sq. to Barracks St.). www.frenchmarket.org. ☏ **504/ 522-2621.** Shop hours vary but generally 10am–5pm.

St. Louis Cathedral ★ CHURCH   St. Louis Cathedral is the oldest continuously active site of a cathedral in the U.S. The stately, iconic building is certainly pretty, but the rather staid interior barely gives a nod to the grand cathedrals of Europe. Still, history and spirituality seep from within, so venture in—if you're lucky, you may catch a choir practice. Volunteer docents, available most weekdays, are full of fun facts about the windows and murals and how the building nearly collapsed once from water-table sinkage. Note the sloping floor: Clever architectural design somehow keeps the building upright even as it continues to sink. Outside, a statue and plaque mark a 1987 visit by Pope John Paul II.

The cathedral formed the center of the original settlement and remains the French Quarter's central landmark. This is the third building to stand on this spot. A hurricane destroyed the first in 1722. On Good Friday 1788, the bells of the second cathedral structure were kept silent for religious reasons (or wind, some say) rather than ringing out the alarm for a fire—which eventually burned down that cathedral and 850 other buildings. It was rebuilt in 1794 and remodeled and enlarged between 1845 and 1851. The structure's bricks were taken from the original town cemetery and covered with stucco to protect the mortar from dampness. That issue arose again during Katrina, which caused a leaky roof to ruin the $1-million organ (it's been rebuilt).

Outside in back, you can see where two magnificent ancient live oaks fell, narrowly missing a statue of Jesus. A forefinger and thumb were amputated, however, and Archbishop Emeritus Hughes, in his first post-Katrina sermon in the cathedral, vowed not to replace them until all of New Orleans was healed. The statue was repaired in 2015. (Current Archbishop Aymond acknowledged that there was still work to be done, but he wanted to celebrate and focus on a symbol of hope as the city moved forward.) The dramatically lit statue makes a resplendent, if somewhat eerie, nighttime silhouette. Well, we think so; others call it "Touchdown Jesus"—do make a point to walk by at night to see why.

615 Pere Antoine Alley. www.stlouiscathedral.org. ☏ **504/525-9585.** Free admission. Self-guided-tour brochure available ($1 donation); formal tours by advance reservation. Daily 9am–4pm; Mass Mon–Fri at 12:05pm, Sun 9 and 11am.

Woldenberg Riverfront Park ★★ PARK   This 16-acre linear park along the river serves as promenade and public art gallery, with numerous works by popular local and internationally known artists amid green lawns and hundreds of trees. Seek out the kinetic Holocaust memorial sculpture by noted Israeli sculptor Yaacov Agam and make a slow circle around it to get the full impact of its changing perspectives, which use a rainbow to unexpected symbolic effect. At the upriver end, you're rewarded with a splash fountain for a soggy cool-down (an excellent incentive to get kids to take a scenic walk).

It connects to the nearby **Moonwalk ★★★**, a paved pedestrian thoroughfare along the river near Jackson Square. It's a wonderful walk on a pretty New Orleans day, or in fact for any weather other than pouring rain. Newly renovated steps allow you to get right down to Old Muddy—on foggy nights, you feel as if you are floating above the water. There are many benches from which to view the city's busy port—perhaps while enjoying sugar-dusted beignets to a street musician's song, or watching the moon rise over the river. To your right is the Crescent City Connection bridge; the former World Trade Center of New Orleans skyscraper, now a super-swanky Four Seasons Hotel (p. 76); and the Toulouse Street wharf, the departure point for excursion steamboats. There are plans to potentially connect the downriver section of the French Quarter's riverfront walkway with **Crescent Park** (p. 184) at the Faubourg Marigny border. For now, make a short jog along N. Peters St. (beside the French Market) to reach the Mandeville Crossing (a pedestrian bridge and elevators) into Crescent Park.

Along the Mississippi River from the Moonwalk to the Aquarium of the Americas at Canal St. ⓒ **504/581-4629.** Daily 6am–10pm.

Historic Buildings in the French Quarter

Beauregard-Keyes House ★ HISTORIC HOME This "raised cottage," with its Doric columns and handsome twin staircases, was built as a residence for a wealthy New Orleans auctioneer, Joseph LeCarpentier, in 1826. It's named for two other past residents: Confederate General P. G. T. Beauregard, who lived here from 1865 to 1867, and novelist Frances Parkinson Keyes (pronounced *Kize*), who resided here from 1944 until 1970. Her most famous book, *Dinner at Antoine's,* was penned here, as was *Madame Castel's Lodger,* concerning General Beauregard's stay in this house. Mrs. Keyes left her home to a foundation. The house, gardens, and her collections of dolls and porcelain *veilleuse* teapots are open to the public. Hourly tours are available, with renewed emphasis on telling the stories of the enslaved and free people of color who lived in and contributed to the building.

1113 Chartres St., at Ursuline St. www.bkhouse.org. ⓒ **504/523-7257.** $10 adults; $9 seniors and students; $4 children 6–12; $7.50 military; free for children 5 and under. Mon–Sat 10am–3pm. Tours on the hour. Closed holidays.

The 1850 House ★★ HISTORIC HOME James Gallier, Sr., and his son designed the historic Pontalba Buildings, which include the 1850 House, for the Baroness Micaela Almonester de Pontalba (see box, p. 159). She had these rows of town houses on either side of Jackson Square built in 1849 to combat the deterioration of the older part of the city; at the time, they were the country's largest private buildings. Legend has it that the baroness, miffed that her friend Andrew Jackson wouldn't tip his hat to her, had his statue erected in the square, where to this day he continues to doff his chapeau toward her top-floor apartment. It's probably not true, but we never stand in the way of a good story.

The 1850 House, a branch of the Louisiana State Museum, demonstrates life in 1850, when the buildings opened for residential use. The self-guided tour uses a fact-filled sheet explaining the history of the interior, and a "soundscape" feature lets you "earwitness" sounds and conversations in the house that you might have heard in 1850. Period furnishings vividly illustrate the difference between the upstairs portion of the house, where the upper-middle-class family lived in comfort (and the children, largely confined to a nursery, were raised by enslaved people and indentured servants), and the downstairs, where servants and enslaved toiled in considerable drudgery to make the family comfortable. It's an insightful look at life in the good, and not so good, old days.

Lower Pontalba Bldg., 523 St. Ann St., Jackson Sq. www.louisianastatemuseum.org. ⓒ **800/568-6968** or 504/524-9118. $5 adults; $4 students, seniors, military; free for kids 6 and under. Tues–Sun 9:30am–3:30pm (free museum tour if you take the **Friends of the Cabildo** French Quarter walking tour, p. 195, which starts here). Closed Mon and all state holidays.

Jean Lafitte's Old Absinthe House ★ HISTORIC SITE   The drink for which this 1806 building was named was once outlawed in this country (unsanitary production and chemical additives, not the wormwood flavoring, caused blindness and madness). Now you can legally sip the infamous libation here and feel at one with the famous types who came before you, listed on a plaque outside: William Thackeray, Oscar Wilde, Sarah Bernhardt, and Walt Whitman—and of course, the unlikely team of Andrew Jackson and the

lady bountiful: BARONESS DE PONTALBA

New Orleans owes a great debt to Baroness Micaela Almonester de Pontalba and her family. Without them, Jackson Square might still be a soggy mess. Her father, Don Almonester, used his money and influence to have St. Louis Cathedral, the Cabildo, and the Presbytère built. The baroness was responsible for the two long brick apartment buildings that flank Jackson Square and for the renovation that turned the center of the Quarter into what it is today.

Born in 1795 into the most influential family in New Orleans, the baroness married her cousin, who subsequently stole her inheritance. When she wanted a

separation, at a time when such things were unheard of, her father-in-law shot her several times and then shot himself. She survived, though some of her fingers did not (nor did he). In subsequent portraits, she would hide the wounded hand in her dress. In the end, she got her money back—she used it for those French Quarter improvements—and also ended up caring for her slightly mad husband for the rest of his life. She died in Paris in 1874; her home there is now the American ambassador's residence. The book *Intimate Enemies*, by Christina Vella (Louisiana State University Press, 1997), details this remarkable woman's life.

Lafitte brothers, who plotted their desperate but successful defense of New Orleans here in the War of 1812. It became a speakeasy during Prohibition; before it was raided by federal officers in 1924, the antique bar and absinthe fountain mysteriously disappeared (just as mysteriously, they later reappeared in a warehouse down the street, safe from the raiders' axes). The historic venue is now split into two sections in the evening: a divey front, wallpapered with business cards (and day drinkers); and a classy speakeasy-style back room, where the atmosphere is more old-timey. This back room is also where the original bar and marble absinthe fountain now reside. Visitors often confuse this one with Lafitte's Blacksmith Shop (p. 225), the oldest U.S. *building* that currently houses a bar. The Absinthe House, as locals call it, was never a blacksmith shop, so it seems more likely to be, as the bartenders claim, the oldest continuously operating bar in New Orleans. Either way, it's a genuinely fun, friendly hangout—stop by for an absinthe and pin your business card to the wall. Just don't be surprised if we call you someday.

240 Bourbon St. www.ruebourbon.com/old-absinthe-house. ✆ **504/523-3181.** Mon–Wed 9am–2am; Thurs and Sun 9am–3am; Fri–Sat 9am–4am. No credit cards (but there's an ATM).

Old Ursuline Convent ★★ RELIGIOUS SITE   Forget tales of America being founded by brawny, brave tough guys in buckskin and beards. The real pioneers—at least, in Louisiana—were well-educated Frenchwomen clad in 40 pounds of black wool robes. That's right; you don't know tough until you know the Ursuline nuns, and this city would have been a very different place without them. The Sisters of Ursula came to the mudhole that was New Orleans in 1727 after a journey that nearly saw them lost at sea or succumbing to pirates or disease. Here, they provided the first decent medical care (saving countless lives) and later founded the first local school and orphanage for girls. They also helped raise girls shipped over from France as marriage material for local men, providing exacting lessons in languages and etiquette, laying the foundation of many local families.

The convent dates from 1752 (the sisters themselves moved uptown in 1824, where they remain to this day), making it the oldest building in the Mississippi River Valley and the only surviving building from the French colonial period in the United States. It also houses Catholic archives dating back to 1718. **Tours** of the first floor of the convent show rooms typical of the era, as well as religious and artistic icons. It includes access to St. Mary's Church, original site of the Ursuline convent and a former archbishop's residence. Tours take an hour or less.

1100 Chartres St., at Ursuline St. www.stlouiscathedral.org/convent-museum. ✆ **504/529-3040.** $8 adults; $7 seniors; $6 students and military. Tours on Thurs, Fri, Sat, and Mon at 10 and 11am and 1 pm.

Our Lady of Guadalupe Chapel—International Shrine of St. Jude ★★ CHURCH   This "funeral chapel" was erected in 1826 conveniently near St. Louis Cemetery No. 1, specifically for funeral services, so as not to spread disease through the Quarter. We like it for three reasons: the catacomb-like devotional chapel with plaques thanking the Virgin Mary for favors granted; the gift shop full of religious medals, including a number of obscure saints; and the statue of St. Expedité. The saint got his name, according to legend, when his unidentified crate arrived, stamped EXPEDITE. Now he's the "saint" you pray to when you want things in a hurry (for real). Sunday 9:30 and 11:30am Masses are backed by a jazz-tinged band and choir.

411 N. Rampart St. at Conti St. www.judeshrine.com. ✆ **504/525-1551.** Gift shop Mon–Sat 9am–5pm, Sun 7am–6pm. Mass Mon–Sat starting at 7am, Sun from 7:30am.

French Quarter Museums

In addition to the destinations listed here, you might be interested in the **Germaine Wells Mardi Gras Museum** at 813 Bienville St., on the second floor of **Arnaud's** restaurant (p. 98; www.arnaudsrestaurant.com/about/mardi-gras-museum; ✆ **504/523-5433**). It has a collection of dazzling gowns worn by Wells, who reigned as queen of more than 22 Mardi Gras balls from 1937 to 1968. Admission is free, and the museum is open daily during restaurant hours.

The Cabildo ★★ MUSEUM   One of two fine museums flanking St. Louis Cathedral in the heart of the French Quarter, the Cabildo houses the premier collection of New Orleans and Louisiana historical artifacts. It starts with the earliest explorers and covers slavery, post–Civil War reconstruction, and statehood. It is well qualified to do so: The Cabildo is where the Louisiana Purchase transfer was officially signed (this 1795 building was the seat of government at the time; at other times it served as a courthouse and a prison). The detailed history is covered from a multicultural perspective and touches on topics like pre–Civil War music, mourning and burial customs (a big deal during yellow fever epidemics), immigration and assimilation, and the role of the Southern woman. The **Napoleon Room** houses the crown jewel: Napoleon's death mask. The item and its story (it almost ended up in a trash dump) are quite fascinating.

701 Chartres St. www.louisianastatemuseum.org/museum/cabildo. ✆ **800/568-6968** or 504/568-6968. $10 adults; $8 students, seniors, and military; free for children 6 and under. Discounts if visiting multiple Louisiana State Museums. Tues–Sun 9am–4pm (last ticket sale 3:30pm); closed Mon and state holidays.

Gallier House Museum ★★ MUSEUM   James Gallier, Jr. (it's pronounced *Gaul*-ee-er, by the way—he was Irish, not French), and his father were the leading architects in New Orleans in the mid-1800s. They designed the French Opera House, Municipality Hall (now Gallier Hall), and the Pontalba Buildings (see 1850 House, p. 158). This was Junior's personal home, now meticulously restored, with the fancy furnishings appearing much as they would have when the family resided there (some claim Gallier's ghost still does). The home displays some of his innovations—such as early indoor plumbing—and a decided lack thereof in the slave quarters. It's made even more gorgeous for holiday season, with period decor; check the website for other special programs. Discounted combination tickets with the Hermann-Grima House (below) are available.

1132 Royal St., btw. Gov. Nicholls and Ursuline sts. www.hgghh.org. ☏ **504/274-0748.** $16 adults; $13 military, seniors, students, and children 8–18; free for children 7 and under. Wed–Mon 9:30am–3:30pm; guided tours 9:30 and 10:30am, and 12:30, 1:30, and 2:30pm; advance booking recommended. Closed most holidays; fewer tours in summer, call to confirm times.

Hermann-Grima House ★★ HISTORIC HOME

This symmetrical Federal-style building (perhaps the first in the Quarter) is very different from its French-style neighbors. The house, which stretches from St. Louis Street to Conti Street, passed through two different families before becoming a boardinghouse for women in the 1920s. It has been meticulously restored and researched, and a tour of the house is one of the city's more historically accurate offerings. Significant efforts are made to tell the stories of the enslaved who lived in the house (including a tour called "Urban Enslavement in New Orleans"). Knowledgeable docents make this a satisfactory stop at any time, but keep an eye out for occasional special tours. At Halloween, the house is draped in typical 1800s mourning cloth, as docents explain mourning customs. Cooking demos, using methods of the era, take place in the authentic 1830s kitchen twice a month on weekends from November to April. The house also contains the Quarter's last surviving stable, complete with stalls. A small but excellent gift shop carries women-made, local, artisanal treasures. (We love the El Guapo cocktail syrups and Blackbird Letterpress notebooks.) Discounted combo tickets with the Gallier House (above) are available.

820 St. Louis St. www.hgghh.org. ☏ **504/274-0750.** $16 adults; $13 seniors, students, military, and children 8–18; free for children 7 and under. Wed–Mon 9:30am–3:30pm; guided tours 10 and 11am and 1, 2, and 3pm; advance booking recommended but not required.

Historic New Orleans Collection ★★★ MUSEUM

Nine of the 10 buildings in this treasured complex have a centuries-old tale to tell; one newly built stunner is just starting to create memories. The HNOC was already chock-full of wonderful artworks, maps, and documents, but with the 2019 completion of a mega-million, tech-forward upgrade, it has vaulted into the pantheon of New Orleans' museums. (And it's free!) The new galleries at 520 Royal St. feature one permanent exhibition called the French Quarter Galleries, excellent interactive displays, and the captivating "French Quarter at Night" film with quad-projected imagery covering 300 years. You can enjoy something savory or sweet from **Café Cour.** Don't overlook exhibits at the Williams Research Center (410 Chartres St.), a grandly restored, Beaux Arts–style building that houses historical archives for serious researchers and inquisitive visitors.

520 Royal St. and 410 Chartres St. www.thnoc.org. ☏ **504/523-4662.** Free admission. Both locations Tues–Sat 9:30am–4:30pm; Royal St. location also open Sun 10:30am–4:30pm.

Madame John's Legacy ★ HISTORIC HOME

This is the second-oldest building (well, parts of it) in the Mississippi Valley, after the Ursuline

Convent (p. 160), and a rare example of French Colonial architecture that miraculously survived the 1794 fire. Built around 1788 on the foundations of an earlier home destroyed in the fire of *that* year, the house has had a number of owners and renters (including the son of Governor Claiborne), none of them named John—or even Madame! It acquired its moniker courtesy of author George Washington Cable, who used the house as a setting for his short story *'Tite Poulette.* The protagonist was a quadroon, Madame John, who took the name of her lover who left this house to her in his will. Now a Louisiana State Museum, it's been undergoing extensive (and contentious) renovations for years. It should reopen . . . someday. For now, you can check out the exterior.

632 Dumaine St. www.louisianastatemuseum.org. ℂ **800/568-6968** or 504/568-6968.

Museum of Death ★ ATTRACTION   If vampire tours are too banal and you need more death in your death, here's all the gore you could ask for. It's graphic, no-holds-barred gruesome, for the thick-skinned only (the lobby rocking chairs are for companions who opt out; those touring the collection are advised to "sit on one of the coffins if you feel faint"). It's an outpost of a similar museum in Hollywood, one man's lurid collection of crime, accident, and autopsy photos (gunshot victims, dismemberments); serial killers' correspondence, diaries, and doodles (John Wayne Gacy's clown drawings; love letters to Jeffrey Dahmer); videos of a cannibal discussing his act; and much more. There's a lengthy movie to watch, and, perhaps the most thought-provoking item, a rare Thanotron, Dr. Kevorkian's suicide machine. Pick up a serial-killer "tarot card" T-shirt on the way out. No photos allowed, due to "respect for the dead." Not entirely sure how respectful the place is, but true-crime fans will likely dig it.

227 Dauphine St. www.museumofdeath.net/nola. ℂ **504/593-3968.** $17. Wed–Mon 10am–6pm.

New Orleans Historical Pharmacy Museum ★★★ MUSEUM Leeches. LEEEEECHES. Yeah, they're here. So are many other icky things, and fascinating potions, and instruments-of-torture-looking artifacts (antique surgical devices, in actuality). The first licensed pharmacist in the United States, Louis J. Dufilho, Jr., opened an apothecary shop in this Creole-style town house in 1823. This bizarre and beguiling museum, opened in 1950, displays old apothecary bottles, Voodoo potions, opium products of every ilk, suppository molds, and all variants of snake oil, in exquisite wood and glass cases. Also interesting are old makeup and perfume paraphernalia, which were brewed up by pharmacists back in the day. You'll never appreciate a modern doctor's appointment more. Check the website for occasional guided tours; if there's one going on while you're in town, join it—they're insightful, shocking, and so worth it. Otherwise, just stop in and poke around.

514 Chartres St., at St. Louis St. www.pharmacymuseum.org. ℂ **504/565-8027.** $10 adults; $7 students, seniors, and military; free for kids 6 and under. Tues–Sat 10am–5pm. Closes early for private events some Sat; check website calendar.

New Orleans Historic Voodoo Museum ★ MUSEUM   This small museum is packed with dusty displays of Voodoo objects from around the world and right here in New Orleans, including some that allegedly belonged to the legendary Voodoo queen Marie Laveau. While serious practitioners might scoff at the tourist orientation of this place, it offers a good introduction to the truth behind the myths of this much-maligned practice. You'll get the most out of your visit if you engage with whoever is manning the front desk, usually someone involved in Voodoo, who can answer inquiries, arrange a reading, or hook you up with a custom gris-gris bag or Voodoo doll.

724 Dumaine St., at Bourbon St. www.voodoomuseum.com. ℗ **504/680-0128.** $10 adults; $8 students, seniors, military, and kids 12 and under. Daily 10am–6pm.

New Orleans Jazz Museum at the Old U.S. Mint ★★ MUSEUM Dedicated to an original American art form, this museum near Frenchmen Street features stellar art and collectibles. You might see Louis Armstrong's first cornet, Fats Domino's upended (from Katrina) piano, Sidney Bechet's soprano saxophone, or Edward "Kid" Ory's trombone. A "Drumsville" exhibit launched in 2018 includes equipment and instruments from legendary and contemporary New Orleans drummers. Rotating exhibits come from an archive of irreplaceable treasures ranging from costumes, photos, manuscripts, and historic recordings to rare film footage. Best of all, there are **free concerts** (in the lovely third-floor performance space or sometimes, during warm months, on an outside stage— check schedule). The building, the only mint that was both a U.S. *and* a Confederate mint, also has exhibits of interest to numisma-tists (O-minted coins, struck right here!) and other curious folk. *Fun fact:* Ghost hunters believe William Mumford, who met the noose here in 1862, still hangs around.

400 Esplanade Ave. www.louisianastatemuseum.org and www.nolajazzmuseum.org. ℗ **800/568-6968** and 504/568-6993. $8 adults; $6 students, seniors, military; free for children 6 and under. Discounts for visiting multiple Louisiana State Museums. Tues–Sun 9am–4pm; last ticket sale 3:30pm. Closed Mon and state holidays.

The Presbytère ★★★ MUSEUM   The Presbytère, which flanks St. Louis Cathedral to the right, was originally built to house the clergy serving in the cathedral. That never came to pass, and the clergy's loss is our gain. It's now a museum with two excellent permanent exhibits. Upstairs, the Mardi Gras exhibit walks visitors through the holiday's history—which is so much more (and so much more interesting) than cwazy kids doing cwazy kid stuff. It shows ornate Mardi Gras Indian costumes and antique Mardi Gras Queen jewels, and there's even a replica float so you can toss mock beads at mock crowds. (To see the real thing, visit Blaine Kern's **Mardi Gras World,** p. 169.) On the first floor, the multimedia exhibit "Living with Hurricanes: Katrina and Beyond" is an in-depth look at the human drama of hurricanes. First-person audio, video, and interactive displays create an educational but wholly accessible experience, and an emotionally evocative one at that (but with enough optimism, humor, and science to keep it from being too down-beat). One man's IN CASE OF EMERGENCY memo hangs on a wall: his jeans, scrawled with his name, blood type, and next of kin. A reproduction of a small attic with a rough hole chopped through its ceiling—and the very axe one woman used to commit a similar act—accompany her voiceover describing the incident. It's powerful stuff.

751 Chartres St., Jackson Sq. www.louisianastatemuseum.org. (℘) **800/568-6968** or 504/568-6968. $7 adults; $6 seniors, students, military; free for kids 6 and under. Discounts if visiting multiple Louisiana State Museums. Tues–Sun 9am–4pm (last ticket sale 3:30pm).

BEYOND THE FRENCH QUARTER

Exploring Uptown & the Garden District

If you can see just one thing outside the French Quarter, make it the **Garden District ★★★**. This area epitomizes what first springs to mind when one hears the words "New Orleans"—no significant historic buildings or important museums, just gorgeous homes standing quietly amid lush foliage, elegant but ever so slightly (or more) decayed. It's simply beautiful, and authors as diverse as Truman Capote and Anne Rice have become enchanted by its spell. You can see why this is the setting for so many novels; it's hard to imagine that anything real actually happens here.

But it does. Like the Quarter, this is a residential neighborhood, so please be courteous as you wander about. To see the sights, you need only mosey around and admire the exteriors and gardens of beautiful houses. We've mapped out a comprehensive **walking tour** (p. 261) to help guide you to the Garden District's treasures and explain a little of its history. Naturally, it starts with a ride on the **St. Charles Avenue streetcar.** You might also check out the listings starting on p. 236 to find the best shops, galleries, and bookstores on **Magazine Street,** the eclectic shopping strip that bounds the Garden District.

Meanwhile, a little background: Across Canal Street from the Quarter, "American" New Orleans begins. After the Louisiana Purchase of 1803, an essentially French-Creole city came under the auspices of a government determined to develop it as an American city. Tensions between Creole society and American newcomers began to increase. Some historians lay this tension at the feet of Creole snobbery; others blame the naive and uncultured Americans. In any case, Creole society succeeded in maintaining a relatively distinct social world, deflecting American settlement upriver of Canal Street (Uptown). The Americans in turn came to outpace the population with sheer numbers of immigrants. Newcomers bought up land in what had been the old Gravier Plantation (now the Uptown area) and began to build a parallel city. Very soon, Americans came to dominate the local business scene, centered along Canal Street. In 1833, the American enclave now known as the Garden District was incorporated as Lafayette City, and—thanks in large part to the New Orleans–Carrollton Railroad, which ran the route of today's St. Charles Avenue streetcar—the Americans kept right on expanding until they reached the tiny "resort town" of Carrollton, a few miles away. It wasn't until 1852 that the various sections came together officially as a united New Orleans.

Exploring Bayou St. John, Esplanade & Lake Pontchartrain

7 **Bayou St. John** ★★★ is one of the key reasons New Orleans exists. This body of water originally extended from the outskirts of New Orleans to Lake Pontchartrain. Indigenous people, including the Chapitoulas and Choctaw, lived along the bayou, or Bayouk Choupic (mudfish). In 1699, they showed the waterway to French explorers Pierre Le Moyne Sieur d'Iberville and Jean-Baptiste Le Moyne, Sieur de Bienville. Soon after, Bienville was commissioned to establish a settlement in Louisiana that would both make money and protect French holdings in the New World from British expansion. Bienville chose the spot where New Orleans now sits because he recognized the strategic importance of Bayou St. John's "back-door" access to Lake Pontchartrain, and ultimately to the Gulf of Mexico. The French renamed it Bayou St. John. Boats could enter the lake from the Gulf, then follow the bayou to its end. From there, they were within easy portage distance of the mouth of the Mississippi River. The mellow waterway provided some protection from detection and attack, while avoiding the trickier river waters.

The early path from the city to the bayou is today's Bayou Road, an extension of Governor Nicholls Street in the French Quarter. Modern-day Gentilly Boulevard, which crosses the bayou, was another trail used by Indigenous people—it led around the lake and on to settlements as far as Florida.

As New Orleans grew and prospered, the bayou became a suburb as planters moved outward along its shores. In the early 1800s, a canal was dug to connect the waterway with the city, reaching a basin at the edge of Congo Square (which begat today's Basin St.). The Bayou became a popular recreation area, lined with fine restaurants and dance halls (and meeting places for Voodoo practitioners, who held secret ceremonies along its shores). Gradually, New Orleans reached beyond the French Quarter and enveloped the whole area—overtaking farmland, plantation homes, and resorts.

The canal was filled in long ago, and the bayou is a meek re-creation of itself (though its ecosystem has been brought a bit closer to its original state by reopening nearby floodgates—allowing more natural ebb and flow from Lake Pontchartrain—dredging a channel through a sand bar that had closed it off from the lake, and planting wetland in the bayou). It is no longer navigable (even if it were, bridges were built too low to permit the passage of watercraft other than kayaks), but residents still prize their waterfront sites, and kayaks, rowboats, and paddleboards make use of the bayou's smooth surface. This is one of the prettiest areas of New Orleans—full of the old houses tourists love to marvel at without the hustle, bustle, and confusion of more high-profile locations. A stroll along the banks and through the nearby neighborhoods is one of our favorite things to do on a nice afternoon. To gain a more comprehensive understanding of the city's most beloved waterway, read Cassie Pruyn's excellent *Bayou St. John: A Brief History.*

The simplest way to reach Bayou St. John from the French Quarter is to drive or ride straight up **Esplanade Avenue** about 20 blocks, or hop on a bus that says ESPLANADE at any bus stop along the avenue. Right before you reach the Bayou, you'll pass **St. Louis Cemetery No. 3** (just past Leda St.). It's open to the public (unlike St. Louis No. 1 and Lafayette No. 1) and is the final resting place of many prominent New Orleanians, among them Father Adrien Rouquette, who lived and worked among the Choctaw; Storyville photographer E. J. Bellocq; and Thomy Lafon, the Black philanthropist who bought the old Orleans Ballroom as an orphanage for African-American children and put an end to its infamous "quadroon balls" (p. 21). Walking just past the cemetery, turn left onto Moss Street, which runs along the banks of Bayou St. John. To see an example of an 18th-century West Indies–style plantation house, jog left at Moss Street and stop at the **Pitot House,** 1440 Moss St. (p. 173). For a more detailed exploration of this area, see our walking tour on p. 267.

Esplanade leads into **City Park** (p. 183) at Wisner Boulevard. Turn left on Wisner for about 3 miles as it hugs the border of City Park. It'll jog right into Beauregard Avenue; then turn right on Cloverleaf and look for water—and Lakeshore Drive. Turn left. You've reached **Lake Pontchartrain,** which you've probably figured out. Meander along Lakeshore Drive for a couple of miles until you reach a marina (the road will curve and become W. End Blvd.). It's hard to believe this area (known as the **Lakefront**), home to commercial fishing since the late 1800s, was devastated by the 17th Street Canal breach after Hurricane Katrina. The storm piled boats atop each other, smashed buildings into rubble, and destroyed a lighthouse. Now, there's a thriving restaurant hub and shopping along Harrison Avenue, and the nearby **Lakeview** residential neighborhood boasts some of the highest property values around. That canal is just ahead of you, as is the fishing-oriented **Bucktown** neighborhood. Park at the Bucktown Marsh Boardwalk and take a sunset walk on Lake Pontchartrain. After, turn back—or hit up **Deanie's** for old-school seafood just like a local.

Lake Pontchartrain, technically an estuary connected to the Gulf of Mexico, is some 40 miles long and 25 miles wide, and is bisected by the 24-mile **Pontchartrain Causeway,** the world's longest continuous over-water bridge.

Museums & Galleries
CBD/WAREHOUSE DISTRICT/LOWER GARDEN DISTRICT
Contemporary Arts Center ★★ MUSEUM/CULTURAL CENTER
The CAC's two stories of airy galleries (about 10,000 sq. ft.) anchor the city's thriving arts district. (The third and fourth stories are a co-working space.) The center shows influential work by regional, national, and international artists in various media, and often presents theater, performance art, dance, or concerts. It's worth a walk-by to check out whatever provocative, large-scale installation is showing in the street-level windows—and often worth checking

black CULTURAL HERITAGE

New Orleans' Black history is rich with important milestones, from the birth of jazz (and, well, all American music, really) to the horrors of the slave trade to crucial civil rights achievements. The ways in which Black people contributed to the creation of the city's culture, cuisine, politics, and literature are endless, and their influence is incalculable. In this majority-Black city, many businesses we list are Black-owned, and almost all museums you visit will cover some aspect of Black heritage.

If you have only a little time to explore, here's a short list to get you started. Begin in the **historic Tremé neighborhood** (America's oldest Black neighborhood), which has a number of significant sights (p. 175), including **Congo Square** inside Louis Armstrong Park (p. 191); the **Backstreet Cultural Museum** (p. 175), which highlights street culture and Black Masking Indian (aka Mardi Gras Indian) traditions; the nearby **Tomb of the Unknown Slave** (in the yard of **St. Augustine Church;** p. 178); the **New Orleans African American Museum** (p. 175); and **Treme's Petit Jazz Museum** (p. 176). In the Upper Tremé, **Le Musée de f.p.c.** (p. 175), dedicated to sharing the story of free people of color, is an edifying visit. In the **9th Ward, the new TEP Center** (p. 176) houses exhibits formerly on display at the popular Lower Ninth Ward Living Museum and is an essential step toward learning the history of Civil Rights. (It was created by three of the women who famously de-segregated the south when they were 6 years old.) The newly reopened **House of Dance and Feathers** (p. 175) is at the top of our list. The **McKenna Museum of African American Art** (p. 175) in the Lower Garden District is also worth your time. And if you're genuinely interested in Black culture and the area's history, please do

not miss **Studio BE** (p. 174) or a day trip out to **The Whitney Plantation** (p. 280).

Definitely visit the shops on **Bayou Road** (p. 235), many of which are Black-owned, especially **Community Book Center** (p. 240), and treat yourself to a meal at Ethiopian-food hotspot **Addis** (p. 119). The *Essence* Festival is a *huge* draw (p. 33), of course, and among the city's Black-owned restaurants, **Dooky Chase** (p. 119) is a classic, and **Compère Lapin** (p. 126) another highlight. We'll also steer you to **Dakar NOLA** (p. 138), a new and amazing Senegalese eatery. (The $150 tasting menu is 100% worth it.) The statewide **African American Heritage Trail,** a network of cultural and historic points, is also a good source (information and maps are available at www.astorylikenoother.com).

Wonderful **Know NOLA Tours** (p. 195) specializes in African-American heritage tours; **All Bout Dat** (p. 193) is another tour company we highly recommend. **Hidden History Tours** (www.hiddenhistory.us; ☎ 504/432-9901) gives brilliant walking tours. **Tours by Judy** (toursbyjudy.com; ☎ 504/416-6666) offers a number of excellent tours, including one that educates about free people of color and one dedicated to the Civil Rights Movement. All are guided by a former history teacher. Finally, check out **Our Sacred Stories** (oursacredstories.com; ☎ 504/452-9237) for tours with Denise, a 7th-generation Creole storyteller who will deepen your understanding and appreciation of the city's complex and nuanced narrative.

One final lagniappe: Bookworms and latte lovers, hit up **Baldwin & Co.** (p. 240) in the Marigny for great books, tasty coffee and pastries, and some eminently Instagrammable artwork. If you're lucky, you might even be in town for one of the bookstore's fab, free community events.

out in deeper detail. Also, inside the CAC Atrium is **Mr. Wolf Espresso and Books,** an artsy place to get your coffee, lit, and art fix.

900 Camp St. cacno.org. ✆ **504/528-3805.** $10 adults; $8 seniors and students; free for K–12 students. Performances may have additional charge. Wed–Mon 11am–5pm.

Mardi Gras World ★★ ATTRACTION   The Kerns, the first family of float-making, design and build some 75% of the floats used by the Mardi Gras krewes during Carnival season. You'll see massive floats from previous years and those in the works for next season and meet Pixie, the robot that helps build the props. The tour starts with a 15-minute video about Mardi Gras. Sketches, sculptures (and sculptors at work), engineers' drawings, and king cake are all included on the tour of the warehouse. It's pretty nifty to see the handiwork up close, and if you can't come for Mardi Gras, at least you can get a taste here—and a better understanding of what goes into it. (*Pro tip*: Look for a Groupon to defray the cost of entry, and call for a free shuttle to avoid paying the $20 parking fee!)

1380 Port of New Orleans Place. www.mardigrasworld.com. ✆ **504/361-7821.** $22 adults; $17 students, seniors, and military; $14 children 2–12. Daily 9am–5:30pm. Last tour 4:30pm. Closed Mardi Gras, Easter, Thanksgiving, Christmas. Free shuttle from Canal St.

Museum of the Southern Jewish Experience ★ MUSEUM   Shalom, y'all! This new 9,000-square-foot museum offers a thorough history of the Jewish experience across the South. It houses some 4,000 artifacts, including an original Steinmart cash register, antique housewares, letters, photos, an 1800s-era quilt, even a prosthetic leg. Moving stories are shared by Holocaust survivors via videos. You can learn some Yiddish, and your own creativity can become part of the collection when you digitally design a corner of a community "crazy quilt"—sure to be a hit with any tech-y teens or old-school crafters in your entourage.

818 Howard Ave. www.msje.org. ✆ **504/384-2480.** $15 adults; $13 seniors; $10 children; free for kids 5 and under. Wed–Mon 10am–5pm.

National World War II Museum ★★★ MUSEUM   This must-see, world-class facility boasts a collection of artifacts that is beyond abundant. The exhibits include stellar videos and advanced digital techniques, but still manage to emphasize the personal side of war. Descriptions don't do justice to the incredibly moving, interactive experiences.

Founded by the late historian and best-selling author Stephen Ambrose, with support from actor Tom Hanks (Ambrose wrote *Band of Brothers* and consulted on the film *Saving Private Ryan,* both of which starred Hanks), the museum now spans 6 acres and five buildings. Visitors are given the dog tag of a soldier whose story unfolds when the tag is scanned at stations along the route. In the **Road to Berlin** and **Road to Tokyo** exhibits, atmospheric floor-to-ceiling decor re-creates battle locations—right down to the temperature and scent. In the U.S. Freedom Pavilion, seven original warplanes hang from a 10-story ceiling. From the ground up, it's an imposing sight; from eye level, it's an almost intimate perspective. Other exhibits of note are the "What Would You Do?" kiosks, which pose thoughtful moral and technical questions; a short, shocking film about the atomic bomb (not for kids)—appropriately silent except for a few excerpts of classical music; a copy of Eisenhower's backup speech apologizing to the nation in the event that D-Day failed; and the amazing story of the B-17 known as **My Gal Sal**—its desolate downing, the daring rescue, and its comeback decades later. The newest permanent exhibit, on level 2 of the Louisiana Memorial Pavilion, **"The Arsenal of Democracy,"** highlights America's industrial efforts during World War II.

Showing in the **Solomon Victory Theater,** *Beyond All Boundaries* is a short film with "4D" multisensory effects—shaking seats, flashing lights, falling snow—which may be moderately successful at interesting older kids in war history ($7). Time is better spent on **Final Mission: USS** *Tang,* which enlists visitors into "silent service" inside a realistic mock submarine as it undergoes its harrowing final sea battle ($7—and worth it). Perhaps most affecting are the intimate stories told through the artifacts and personal items of former soldiers and their loved ones. Take every opportunity to hear these first-person audio stories at the listening stations.

War veterans and civilians who were involved in the war effort often volunteer at the museum. Say thanks and talk with them. We met Jim Weller, who told us how he lied about his age to enlist; he showed us his photo at the Battle of the Bulge and said of the woman and baby next to us: "That's why I won the war—for the babies." That's about the best possible museum experience one can have.

Allow for at least 3 hours, though you won't be able to absorb everything in that time. You could easily spend days here—and if that's your plan, get a second-day pass for $7.

The museum's restaurant, **The American Sector,** isn't bad (though you could also walk 4 minutes to excellent Pêche, p. 129; Cochon, p. 130; or Cochon Butcher, p. 132). Also on site, **BB's Stage Door Canteen** presents live, 1940s-era USO-style shows that are good, swinging fun for a dinner or brunch show ($45–$65 with modest discounts for kids 11 and under; $20–$30 show only). The museum has also added an outdoor evening program, **Expressions of America,** a short stage production followed by an immersive sound-and-light spectacle with videos projected onto buildings. Across the street, the spiffy museum-owned, 1940s-themed **Higgins Hotel** (www.higginshotelnola.com)—named for local boat builder Andrew Jackson Higgins, whose boats helped win the war—is a fun place to grab a drink and food and enjoy the skyline view from **Rosie's on the Roof**—especially during happy hour (4–6 pm daily).

945 Magazine St. www.nationalww2museum.org. ℂ **504/528-1944.** $31 adults; $26 seniors; $19 children K–12, college students, and military with ID. Free for WWII veterans and their companions, and children age 4 and under. Second-day pass $7. Daily 9am–5pm. Closed Mardi Gras day, Thanksgiving Day, Christmas Eve, and Christmas Day.

The Ogden Museum of Southern Art ★★★ MUSEUM If NOMA is the crown jewel, this is the crown, the premier collection of Southern art in the United States. The artists' works are impressive, and the graphics are informative and even clever. We particularly like the permanent exhibit of self-taught and outsider art, including some from the local area. Though the building itself is quite dazzling, anchored around a sky-high atrium, one can't help wondering if that soaring space could be put to better use if it were hung with even more fine Southern art (we do appreciate the Ogden-installed rotating sculptures along Poydras St.). If you're visiting on a Thursday, you can combine your art gazing with drop-in meditation at 12:30pm. We're also keen on the well-curated gift shop, which has consistently covetable souvenirs with a local spin.

925 Camp St. www.ogdenmuseum.org. ℂ **504/539-9650.** $14 adults; $11 seniors, students, and military; $7 children 5–17; free for kids 4 and under. Daily 10am–5pm; adjusted hours during Mardi Gras season.

Sazerac House ★ ATTRACTION We're guessing this gleaming new distillery exhibit/tasting room/interactive museum looks nothing like the original Sazerac House, once located 350 feet away, where (so the much-debated story goes) the Sazerac, the first branded cocktail, was invented in the mid–19th century. It's now the city's official cocktail, and the Sazerac Company produces 22 brands, displayed here in a three-story glass case. That, and much more, will impress even teetotalers at this all-ages attraction. The gloriously restored 1860s building, complete with a working rye-producing still, offers self-guided tours covering the history of distilled spirits in New Orleans, and now there's a new historical guided tour, "Tropical Cocktails" (Fri at 1pm), that explores the impact of rum and the sugarcane industry on New Orleans and American history. There's a small bottling operation, merch, and yes, samples (for 21+, natch). We especially dig the virtual bartenders who "prepare" an adult beverage based on your preferences and text you the recipe.

101 Magazine St. www.sazerachouse.com. ℂ **504/910-0100.** Free admission. Tues–Sun 11am–6pm; last tour begins 4:20pm. Reservations required.

Vue Orleans ★★ OBSERVATION DECK This is NOLA's version of the Empire State Building, with indoor and outdoor observation decks high above the city. It's not *quite* as tall, at 34 floors, but it's by far the best view you'll find of the Crescent City—and the only 360-degree vista. There are also state-of-the-art exhibits offering touchless, interactive cultural experiences and introducing historical figures who helped create the New Orleans we know and love today. (Best paired with brunch, lunch, or dinner at **Miss River,** p. 128).

2 Canal St., atop the Four Seasons Hotel (p. 76). www.vueorleans.com. ℂ **504/285-3600.** $25 adults; $20 seniors; $15 children 3–12, students, military, hotel guests, and groups of 10+. Daily 10am–6pm.

MID-CITY/ESPLANADE/GENTILLY

Degas House ★ HISTORIC HOME Legendary French Impressionist Edgar Degas had a tender spot in his heart for New Orleans. His mother and grandmother were born here, and he spent several months in 1872-73 visiting his brother René and sister-in-law Estelle Musson at this house, built in 1854. (Estelle and her children reclaimed her maiden name, Musson, so it's formally known as the Musson home). A number of paintings resulted, and historians say this is the place that led Degas to Impressionism. This is the only residence or studio associated with Degas anywhere in the world that is open to the public. One of the artist's paintings showed the garden of a neighboring house. His brother liked that view, too: He later ran off with the wife of the judge who lived there. Over the years the house has been sliced in two, redone in an Italianate manner, and restored as a B&B and events space; it was recently inducted into the prestigious *Maisons des Illustres* network of homes of noted Frenchmen (only the second such home in the U.S.). It's open for tours, which can be combined with a Creole breakfast.

2306 Esplanade Ave., near N. Broad Ave. www.degashouse.com. ✆ **504/821-5009.** Guided tours $29/person; senior, student, military discounts available. Breakfast only $25, tour plus breakfast $50. Breakfast 9am; tours daily 10:30am and 1:45pm. Reservations required for both breakfast and tours.

Flooded House Museum and Levee Exhibit Hall ★ MUSEUM   Peer through the windows of this average brick house for an eerie appreciation of the ways in which the floods that followed Hurricane Katrina in 2005 (p. 12) turned suburban normalcy into upended nightmare. Through sights like a decrepit, waterlogged teddy bear, this mild but effective artist's rendition shows what the homes in this area, abutting the London Avenue canal breach, may have experienced. Next door the extremely informative **Levee Exhibit Hall** display is capped by a simple tribute of two empty rocking chairs.

5000 Warrington Dr. www.levees.org/flooded-house-museum. ✆ **504/722-8172.** Free admission, donations accepted. Go during daylight hours (visitors observe from outside the house; there is no entry).

New Orleans Museum of Art ★★★ MUSEUM   The crown jewel of City Park, and of New Orleans art, NOMA houses a 40,000-piece collection of 16th- through 20th-century European paintings, drawings, sculptures, and prints; early American art, Asian art, pre-Columbian and Indigenous ethnographic art, and a vast collection of photography, African works, and decorative glass. Not everything is on display, of course, and this very manageable museum does not take hours to visit. From the front, the original 1911 neoclassical building is an imposing sight among the greenery of City Park. The contemporary rear portion is all angles and curves, steel and glass; and the handsome interior galleries are well lit and organized. It all works to the visitor's advantage. (Well, Lichtenstein's *Five Brushstrokes* sculpture, prominently installed at the front entrance in late 2013, met with comparisons to streaky bacon. But what's art without controversy?) The curation is unfailingly impressive.

Next door, the already superb **Besthoff Sculpture Garden ★★★** doubled in size in 2019, bringing this truly world-class attraction to nearly 100 large-scale works set in 11 serene, lushly landscaped acres winding around reflecting lagoons. Works by noted 20th- and 21st-century artists George Segal, Henry Moore, Louise Bourgoise, Frank Gehry, Lin Emery, Hank Willis Thomas, Fred Wilson, Maya Lin, and Frank Stella are here, as well as a version of Robert Indiana's famous pop-art *LOVE* sculpture and the Canal Link Bridge, an unusual walkway that puts visitors at lagoon level (watch your fingers, thar be turtles). The Sculpture Garden's a gorgeous place to bring kids for an open-air art walk—they'll definitely dig Jeppe Hein's Mirror Labyrinth (as will you). It's a cultural highlight, and admission is free. Early risers: Register in advance for $10 yoga classes on Saturday mornings (BYO mat). **Ralph Brennan's Cafe NOMA** inside the museum has light lunch fare and wine during museum hours. Dessert? Beignet it up at City Park's nearby branch of **Café du Monde** (p. 148).

1 Collins Diboll Circle, at City Park and Esplanade. www.noma.org. ✆ **504/658-4100.** $15 adults; $10 seniors and active military; $8 students; free for ages 19 and under. Museum Tues–Sun 10am–5pm; sculpture garden daily 10am–5pm. Closed major holidays.

Pitot House ★★ HISTORIC HOME   Set along pretty Bayou St. John, the Pitot House is a typical West Indies–style plantation home, restored and furnished with early-19th-century Louisiana and American antiques. Dating from 1799, it originally stood where a nearby Catholic school now stands. In 1810 it became the home of James Pitot, the first mayor of incorporated New Orleans (he served 1804–05). Tours, given by knowledgeable docents or architecture students, are surprisingly interesting and informative. A combined tour of St Louis Cemetery No. 3 and Pitot House is available through Save Our Cemeteries (p. 199).

1440 Moss St., near Esplanade Ave. www.pitothouse.org. ✆ **504/482-0312.** $10 adults; $7 seniors and students; free for kids 6 and under. Wed–Fri 10am–3pm by appt. only (last tour 2:15pm).

CENTRAL CITY

See also the **McKenna Museum of African American Art** (p. 175).

Ashé Cultural Arts Center ★★ ARTS CENTER   This multi-use facility in the historic Central City neighborhood emphasizes the contributions of people of African descent through programs and creative works. With 10,000 square feet of gallery space and 20,000 square feet of performance space, there's always something moving to see and experience here, through fine art and folk art exhibitions, dance performances, concerts, conversations, and film screenings.

1712 Oretha Castle Haley Blvd. www.ashenola.org. ✆ **504/569-9070.** Tues–Sat 10am–5:30pm.

Southern Food & Beverage Museum & Museum of the American Cocktail ★★ MUSEUM   Located in a historic but off-the-tourist-beat part of town, the South's first food-and-beverage museum features clusters of alimental artifacts from each Southern state. It's a jumbled, informative assemblage, showcasing farms, tables, and everything in between, and illustrating how different ethnic groups, geography, and time have contributed to the regional cuisines of the American South. Creole-Cajun cooking classes in the gorgeous demo kitchen run $100 (includes museum admission and private tour). Interesting events and rotating exhibits detail obscure but fascinating topics from absinthe drips to Appalachian soups.

Along one side of the single-room facility, the **Museum of the American Cocktail** (MoTAC) presents 200 years of cocktail history and New Orleans' vital role in the same; exhibits come largely from founder Dale "King Cocktail" Degroff and curator Ted "Dr. Cocktail" Haigh's mind-blowing collection, offering a lively glimpse into the history of everyone's favorite poison (including, of course, absinthe). The booze-obsessed will lose it over the extensive historical artifacts here, including defunct product packaging, glassware, and Prohibition-era photos. (We love the branded bottles of liquor flavorings used to make homemade rotgut palatable.)

1504 Oretha Castle Haley Blvd. www.southernfood.org and www.museumofthe americancocktail.org. © **504/569-0405.** $10.50 adults; $5.25 seniors, active military, and students; free for kids 11 and under with adult. Thurs–Mon 11am–5pm.

FAUBOURG MARIGNY/BYWATER

JAMNOLA ★ ATTRACTION   If you're a fan of local art, tactilely pleasing interactive exhibits, wacky Instagrammable photo ops (bathtub selfie with giant crawfish, 5-foot-tall bust of Big Freedia), optional costuming, and a quick culture/history primer, this'll be your jam. (Kids and teens will also be highly entertained.) The 17 immersive exhibits are designed by 30+ local artists whose work is largely upcycled, including a wall of vinyl records melted and sculpted into flowers, and floors inlaid with 22,000 Mardi Gras beads. Knowledgeable storytellers guide you through 12 rooms. Look online for a coupon, and visit the gift shop; the groovy "NOLA roots run deep" T-shirts make fab gifts (and support a terrific organization that brings musical education to local low-income kids).

2832 Royal St. www.jamnola.com. © **504/233-9152.** Mon and Thurs–Fri $29 adults, $25 seniors and students, $20 kids 3–12; Sat–Sun add $3 to ticket prices. Free for kids 2 and under. Mon 11am–4pm; Thurs 2–7pm; Fri noon–8pm; Sat 10am–8pm; Sun 10am–6pm. Timed tickets must be bought in advance (non-refundable). No cash accepted.

Studio BE ★★★ GALLERY   This one is a must-visit *and* a must-return-often. The power of artist, activist, and educator Brandan "bmike" Odums' astounding work is evident on first glimpse of the exterior murals covering this 35,000-square-foot gallery/museum/warehouse/shop. Inside, large-format spray-painted and sculptural works portray iconic figures important to civil rights; they're reflective, instructive, inspiring, and jaw-dropping. We love the group exhibition "Radical Freedom Dream," a collaboration with local artists aged 8–18.

2941 Royal St. studiobenola.com. © **504/252-0463.** $15 adults; $10 students, veterans, first responders, seniors, and educators; $5 children 5–12; free for ages 5 and under. Wed–Sat 2–8pm; Sun 2–6pm.

TREMÉ

Backstreet Cultural Museum ★★★ MUSEUM   This small cultural gem in the heart of the Faubourg Tremé is dedicated to certain wholly unique New Orleans cultural traditions, mostly of the African-American community. Social aid and pleasure clubs, second-line parades, brass bands, jazz funerals, and especially Mardi Gras Indians are all well documented and recollected here. We guarantee that the Mardi Gras Indians' ornate beaded costumes are like nothing you've ever seen, and they're best appreciated up close. But the suits are just an entree into the community's intriguing folk traditions. The museum's founder Sylvester Francis, who curated the collection, passed away in 2020, but his daughter Dominique has kept it going. In 2021, Hurricane Ida severely damaged the building, but the beloved collection has found a new home on North Villere Street, right behind the New Orleans African American Museum (see below).

1531 St. Philip St. www.backstreetmuseum.org. ✆ **504/657-6700.** $20 adults; $15 locals, seniors, and veterans; $10 children 12 and under. Daily 10am–4 pm.

Le Musée de f.p.c. ★★★ MUSEUM   Louisiana's shameful history of slavery is well-known. In this elegant 1859 Greek Revival house, the lesser-known chronicle of the **free people of color (f.p.c.)** is told through a one-of-a-kind personal collection of artworks and priceless original documents, and a 1-hour tour that's in turns sobering and inspiring. These wealthy, highly educated, sophisticated, and industrious men and women of French, African, and Caribbean origin populated New Orleans since the early 1700s, and they had a massive cultural and commercial impact on the city. Exhibited works range from gallant formal portraits of finely attired men and women to copies of the Dred Scott decision and Civil War–era activist newspapers. The **McKenna Museum of African American Art,** a sister museum in Central City, also houses a terrific collection (www.mckennamuseum.com; ✆ **504/323-5074;** by appt. only).

2336 Esplanade Ave. www.lemuseedefpc.com. ✆ **504/323-5074.** $25 adults; $18 K–12 students. Tours by reservation only. Fri 1pm, Sat 11am. Call ahead; museum sometimes closes for private events.

New Orleans African American Museum ★★ MUSEUM   The Tremé had to live without this museum for 6 years after it shuttered—a criminal omission considering its location in the oldest African-American neighborhood in the U.S. Finally reopened in 2019, it's currently just a few rooms in a beautifully converted house, displaying collections that tease at what's in store once it returns to its rightful and former glory in the buildings across the street. We love to support it; the artworks and documents shown are a vital telling of the African-American experience in New Orleans and in the U.S. To learn even more, book a half- or full-day "Tremé Experience" tour through the museum.

1418 Governor Nicholls St. www.noaam.org. ✆ **504/218-8254.** Self-guided tours $20 adults, $10 students and children 11 and under. Guided tours $35 adults, $10 students and children. Discounts for Louisiana residents. Thurs–Sun 11am–4pm.

Tremé's Petit Jazz Museum ★ MUSEUM   The smallest museums sometimes deliver the richest experiences, because your chance of connecting with the curators is so much higher—and this one delivers. The only jazz museum located in the birthplace of jazz (the Tremé), it's a must-schedule for both aficionados and beginners. Al Jackson, a lifelong resident, shares his collection of instruments and artifacts, including original recording contracts for Ray Charles and Fats Domino, and a 1954 performing contract signed by Louis Armstrong. But the real treasures in the room are Jackson himself and his musical knowledge and passion.

1500 Governor Nicholls St. ✆ **504/715-0332.** $15 adults. Free for children 9 and under. Wed–Sat 10:30am–4pm.

NINTH WARD

The House of Dance and Feathers ★★ MUSEUM   This is a classic New Orleans "If you know, you know." In 2002, a man named Ronald Lewis opened up his backyard shed so visitors could peruse his incredible collection of memorabilia dedicated to the culture of the Ninth Ward and African-American parading. Lewis, one of the city's most beloved culture bearers, passed away in 2020. The museum was closed for years, but thanks to his wife, Charlotte "Minnie" Lewis, and a team of donors, volunteers, and students, it has recently reopened. Call the number here (not the numbers you see online, most are outdated) after 10am to ask Ms. Minnie if you can stop by to view this unique treasure trove. If the answer is yes, head over for a deep dive into the culture of Mardi Gras, social aid and pleasure clubs, Black masking Indians, Skull & Bones gangs, and Baby Dolls.

1317 Tupelo Street. ✆ **504/905-6006.** Donation requested.

TEP Center ★★★ HISTORIC SITE   This center—formerly the Lower Ninth Ward Living Museum—has long held a world of insight, telling the full story of the area—not just of the levee failure and its devastation, but of the centuries leading up to it—and why all are so deeply intertwined. It's illuminating, thought-provoking, and even more relevant now that it's relocated to the Lower 9th Ward School, closed for 15 years since Hurricane Katrina. In this same school building, "The McDonogh Three"—6-year-old Leona Tate, Gail Etienne, and Tessie Prevost—famously desegregated classrooms in 1960. After a $14-million renovation, the center, opened in May 2022, was reimagined by Tate and her nonprofit Leona Tate Foundation for Change. The new TEP Center (named for Tate, Etienne, and Prevost) is designed to educate the community about New Orleans civil rights history and to help visitors engage in honest conversations about racism. The installation of the Desegregation Exhibit is still being completed, but the center offers tours of the building and exhibits that were relocated from the Living Museum.

5909 St. Claude Ave. www.leonatatefoundation.org. ✆ **504/273-9709** or email tours@tepcenter.org. Admission $10. Tours Mon–Fri 10am–2pm, by appt. only.

anne rice IN NEW ORLEANS

Long before Sookie, Angel, Cassidy, Buffy, any Originals, or even those wacky What We Do in the Shadows roomies, before anyone cared whether you were Team Edward or Team Jacob, there was Lestat—and the originator of the modern vampire era, the late author Anne Rice. Love her or loathe her, the New Orleans native was one of her hometown's biggest boosters. After Interview with the Vampire exploded in the 1980s, hordes of fans descended on her Garden District home, hanging out for days on end, communing with each other and whatever spirits they could conjure. For years Rice famously egged on the whole spectacle, inviting fans into her home, throwing elaborate Halloween bashes, even making appearances in a coffin. Eventually she moved to California, where she died in late 2021, but visitors still come here to honor the doyenne of fang fiction, including obsessed Twihards mining the eerie ore.

Rice's seductive descriptions of her hometown and actual locales are often quite accurate—minus the undead, of course. You can find her books in the shop where she always began her book tours, **Garden District Book Shop**, 2727 Prytania St. (p. 241). The following landmarks play a role in her books, movies, and inspirations.

FRENCH QUARTER SITES

In Rice's books, the romance of the French Quarter seems to attract vampires, who found easy pickings in its dark corners in the days before electricity. In the Vampire Chronicles books, a tomb (empty, of course) with Louis the vampire's name is located in **St. Louis Cemetery No. 1** (p. 188), where Louis occasionally sits and broods. Exteriors for the Interview with the Vampire movie were filmed at **700-900 Royal St.**—though set decorators had to labor long to erase all traces of the 20th century,

covering the streets in mud. (What fun for the present-day residents.) Also in the Interview with the Vampire movie, caskets are carried from **Madame John's Legacy** (p. 162) as Brad Pitt's voiceover describes Lestat and the little vampire Claudia's night out: "An infant prodigy with a lust for killing that matched his own. Together, they finished off whole families." Yum. **Hotel Monteleone** (p. 67), 214 Royal St., was Aaron Lightner's home in The Witching Hour. Rice's characters spent time dining well at **Café du Monde** (p. 148), 800 Decatur St.; **Court of Two Sisters** (p. 102), 613 Royal St.; and **Galatoire's** (p. 102), 209 Bourbon St.

If all this talk of fables and fangs gets you in the mood, head to **Boutique du Vampyre** (709 St. Ann St.; boutique-du-vampyre.myshopify.com; ✆ **504/561-8267**) for themed tours, custom fangs, coffin-shaped backpacks . . . you know, the usual. More on vampire tours on p. 199.

GARDEN DISTRICT & LOWER GARDEN DISTRICT SITES

Rice's books also feature many locales in and around the Garden District where she and her family lived and owned properties. **Lafayette Cemetery No. 1** (p. 188) is a frequent setting, especially as a roaming ground for Lestat and Claudia in Interview with the Vampire and as the graveyard for the Mayfairs in The Witching Hour. The upscale **Pontchartrain Hotel** (p. 88), 2031 St. Charles St., appears in The Witching Hour. At **Nolé,** 2001 St. Charles Ave., the vampire Lestat disappeared from this world through an image of himself in the front window (it was then an abandoned car dealership; now it's a special events venue and hotel). Rice readers will also recognize **Commander's Palace** (p. 136), 1403 Washington Ave., as a favorite of the Mayfair family.

Historic New Orleans Churches

Church and religion aren't likely the first things that jump to mind in a city known for debauchery. But New Orleans remains a pious, mostly Catholic city—don't forget Mardi Gras is a pre-Lenten celebration. Religion of one form or another directed much of the city's early history and molded its culture in countless ways. (For a detailed review of **St. Louis Cathedral,** see p. 157.)

St. Alphonsus Art and Cultural Center ★★ CHURCH   The Irish community built St. Alphonsus in 1855, in what is now the Lower Garden District, because they wanted to establish their own church, rather than worship at nearby St. Mary's (see below) with their German-speaking neighbors. The church hasn't held Mass since the late 1970s—ironically, after St. Mary's was restored, St. Alphonsus closed and the congregation moved there. Hopes for similar restoration here are high, but it's no small undertaking. Katrina caused half a million dollars in damage, and the downriver belltower was blown dramatically across the street. Though it was completely rebuilt, in 2021 Hurricane Ida blew a hole in the roof and damaged two stained-glass windows, and until the church is restored (an expensive proposition), visitors aren't allowed in. It's too bad, because St. Alphonsus' interior is perhaps the most stunning of any church in the city, right up there with some of the lusher Italian splendors.

2025 Constance St., at St. Andrew St. www.friendsofstalphonsus.org. ✆ **504/482-0008.**

St. Augustine Church ★★★ CHURCH   One of the great cultural landmarks of New Orleans' Black history, St. Augustine has been a center of community life in the Tremé neighborhood since the mid-1800s. Homer Plessy, Sidney Bechet, and Big Chief Tootie Montana all called this their home church. The church was founded by free people of color, who also purchased pews to be used exclusively by enslaved people (to the dismay of their white masters)—a first in the history of slavery in the U.S. In the modern era, under the direction of its visionary former pastor, the charismatic Father Jerome LeDoux, St. Augustine integrated traditional African and New Orleans elements into its services. In late 2005, the archdiocese decided to close St. Augustine because of dwindling membership, but a major public outcry bought a reprieve. It's been going strong since. We're quite enamored of the jazzy 10am **Sunday Mass,** especially when it features a soul-stirring guest performer like James Andrews or John Boutté. The deeply moving **Tomb of the Unknown Slave** (outside on the right side) makes this worth a stop anytime (call ahead to make sure it's open). Don't forget to leave a donation to help keep St. Aug going. (It was hit hard by Hurricane Ida and can use the help.)

1210 Governor Nicholls St. staugchurch.org. ✆ **504/525-5934.** Mass Sun 10am, Wed 5pm.

St. Mary's Assumption ★ CHURCH   Built in 1860 by German Catholics, this is an even more baroque and grand church than its Irish neighbor across the street, St. Alphonsus (see above). These two Lower Garden District

REAL gospel, NO BRUNCH

You could do the slick "Gospel Brunch" at the House of Blues. But if you're someone who prefers to experience the real thing in a real place of worship, there are wonderful options. Don't expect fancy robes or masses of choir members, just rooms full of spirit and a seriously joyful noise. Try **St. Peter Claver Catholic Church** (1923 St. Philip St.; 𝄐 **504/822-8059**), where the voices are beautiful and the congregation welcoming; show some respect when the collection plate comes 'round. Sunday services are at 7:30 and 10am. **Our Lady Star of the Sea Catholic Church** (1835 St. Roch Ave.; 𝄐 **504/944-0166**) also has a gospel Mass on Sundays at 10am, with a fantastic choir. **Franklin Avenue Baptist Church** (8282 I-10 Service Road S; 𝄐 **504/488-8488**) is a bit of a drive— and it's a huge congregation—but they have superb rotating gospel choirs on Sundays at 9am. Every second Sunday of the month at 6:30pm, the glorious

Gospel Soul Children raise their extraordinary voices in praise at **St. James Methodist Church** (1925 Ursulines Ave.; 𝄐 **504/822-8138**). The city's oldest active community choir, the GSPP appears on Jon Batiste's album *We Are*, which was nominated for a whopping 11 Grammys and won five, including Album of the Year.

At the other end of the spectacle spectrum, Bishop (and Internet star) Lester Love incorporates his smooth soul vocals into powerful sermons, adding an R&B backing band and singers at his mini-mega, full-gospel **City of Love Church,** 8601 Palmetto St. in the Gert Town neighborhood (www.thecityoflove.com; 𝄐 **504/895-5410**; Sun 9:30am). Inspiration is practically preordained. If you're attending the jazzy Sunday Mass at **St. Augustine's** (p. 178), join the throngs walking to brunch afterward at nearby **Lil Dizzy's** (p. 123).

churches make an interesting contrast to one another. Along with dozens of life-size saints' statues, St. Mary's houses the national shrine to the hero of the 1867 yellow fever epidemic, Blessed Father Francis Xavier Seelos, who was beatified (one step away from sainthood) in 2000. See his original coffin, a display containing recently discovered locks of his hair, and the centerpiece of the shrine, a reliquary containing his bodily remains. Should Father Seelos become a saint, expect this shrine to be a big deal and place of pilgrimage. Before visiting the shrine, check in at the adjacent welcome center and the interesting **Walk of Life Museum** in the Seelos Shrine Welcome Center at 919 Josephine St.

923 Josephine St. www.stalphonsusno.com. 𝄐 **504/522-6748.** Mass Sun 10:30am, vigil Sat 4pm. Mass at St. Mary's Chapel (1516 Jackson Ave.) Sun 9am, Mon–Fri 7:30 am.

St. Patrick's Church ★★ CHURCH   The original St. Patrick's was a tiny wooden building founded to serve the spiritual needs of Irish Catholics—a far cry from this elaborate structure. Begun in 1838, it was built around the old one, which was then dismantled. Distinguished architect James Gallier, Sr., designed much of the interior, including the altar. It opened in 1840, proudly proclaiming itself as the "American" Catholics' answer to St. Louis Cathedral in the French Quarter (where, according to the Americans, God spoke only in French).

724 Camp St., at Girod St. www.oldstpatricks.org. ℂ **504/525-4413.** Mass Mon–Fri 7:15am (Latin), 11:30am, noon; Sat 5:30pm; Sun 8am, 9:15am (Latin), 11am, 5:30pm.

St. Roch (Campo Santo) ★★ CHURCH   A local priest prayed to Saint Roch, patron saint of plague victims, to keep his flock safe during the 1867 yellow fever epidemic. When they survived, he made good on his promise to build Saint Roch a chapel. The Gothic result is fine enough, but what is better yet is the small room just off the altar, where successful supplicants to Saint Roch leave *ex voto* gifts in the form of plaster anatomical parts or medical supplies as thanks for their healed affliction. The resulting collection of bizarre artifacts (everything from eyeballs to false limbs) is either deeply moving or a great, creepy spontaneous folk-art installation. While there, do check out the magnificent mural inside **Our Lady Star of the Sea** church, next door. This area of the Bywater district isn't great, so be aware. The chapel, located on the cemetery grounds, has been under restoration but is due to reopen; check ahead.

1725 St. Roch Ave., at N. Derbigny St. nolacatholiccemeteries.org/st-roch-cemetery-1. ℂ **504/482-5065.** Chapel visitation: 1st Friday of the month, 11am–noon. (Monthly healing Masses 1st Friday at 10 am).

A Few More Interesting New Orleans Buildings

The Caesar's Superdome ★ SPORTS COMPLEX   Completed in 1975, the Superdome is a physical and emotional landmark that took on a new worldwide image when it was used as shelter during Katrina. The structure was intended as an evacuation locale of last resort, but quickly turned into hell on earth when tens of thousands of refugees ended up here in a scene of suffering and despair. People were trapped without sufficient food, water, medical care, or, it seemed, hope.

Just months later, the New Orleans Saints reopened the Superdome in 2006 to much hoopla for their first home game (and a halftime show featuring U2) and went on to the playoffs. Three years later they won their first Super Bowl ever (in Miami), to rejoicing far beyond the city boundaries. Atop the team's gleaming success and the Dome's $118-million renovation, the entire building was then "reskinned" in glittery gold tone, a shining beacon of what can arise from the darkest days. Two years later it hosted the 2014 Super Bowl, a huge symbolic comeback. In 2021, the stadium was rebranded as Caesars Superdome and is in the process of a $450-million, multi-year renovation (set for completion in 2024, in time to host the Super Bowl in 2025). You can't tour the Superdome (once upon a time, very occasional tours were given), so if you want to see it, your best bet is to attend a game. Not exactly a hardship. Seriously: If you're in town during a home game, GO. Either way, join the locals in a chant of "WHO DAT?!"

The stats: It's the largest fixed-dome structure in the world (680 ft. in diameter, covering 13 acres), a 27-story windowless building with a seating capacity of 76,000. Inside, there are no view-obstructing posts. The flying-saucer-like building also hosts conventions, balls, and concerts, as does its sister **Smoothie King Center** next door. **Champions Square,** its adjoining outdoor plaza, has become pre- and post-game central and home to many a festival and special event.

1500 block of Poydras St., at LaSalle St. www.mbsuperdome.com. ℂ **504/587-3663.**

Gallier Hall ★ HISTORIC SITE   This impressive Greek Revival building in the Central Business District was the inspiration of James Gallier, Sr. Now an events hall, it was erected between 1845 and 1853, served as City Hall for over a century, and has been the site of many key events in the city's history—especially during the Reconstruction and Huey Long eras. Several important figures in Louisiana history lay in state in Gallier Hall, including Jefferson Davis and General Beauregard. Of late, local music legends Ernie K-Doe and Earl King were so honored, as was Blaine Kern ("Mr. Mardi Gras"), founder of the float-building empire (p. 169). Five thousand mourners paid respects to K-Doe, who was laid out in a white costume with a silver crown and scepter. A $10-million exterior renovation was completed in 2017, followed by an interior spiff. Peek inside if you can, it's a stunner.

545 St. Charles Ave. www.nola.gov/gallier-hall. ℂ **504/658-3627.** Not open to the public.

---

floating ACROSS THE RIVER TO ALGIERS POINT

Algiers, established in 1719 and annexed by New Orleans in 1870, is about a quarter-mile across the Mississippi River from the city. The second oldest neighborhood in New Orleans after the French Quarter, it's generally ignored because of its location, but it became a sort of God's country after the hurricane because it did not flood at all; many services, such as mail delivery, were restored quite quickly. It still has the feel of an undisturbed turn-of-the-20th-century suburb, and strolling around here is a delightfully low-key way to spend an hour or two (daytime only). There's a good bit of jazz history in Algiers, the neighborhood that 1920s musicians called "over da river." There's even a Jazz Walk of Fame at the ferry terminal. Though our friends at the **House of the Rising Sun Bed and Breakfast** were closed at press time (with hopes of reopening), there's still a great walking tour on their website (www.risingsunbnb.com). Before heading to Algiers. make a point of calling ahead (ℂ **504/261-6231**) to schedule a visit to **Folk Art Zone** (folkartzone.org), a small and wonderful museum of self-taught artists. If Charles Gillam, artist and museum founder, is around, chances are good you'll be treated to a memorable conversation. Algiers is easily accessible via the ferry that runs from the foot of Canal Street. This working ferry, in continuous operation since 1827, is a great (and cheap, at $4 round-trip) way to get out onto the river and see the skyline (and at 30 min., it's perfectly timed for kids' attention spans). See schedule and fares on p. 297.

PARKS, GARDENS & A ZOO

New Orleans' verdant vegetation and expansive tree canopy is one of its many charms, with greenery bursting from small condo courtyards, lavish mansion landscaping, abundantly overflowing terrace pots—and wonderful public parks and gardens. Glorious live oaks are a city hallmark, spreading across streets and over roofs everywhere (an amazing 320 million trees were lost or damaged due to Hurricane Katrina, including many old oaks; thankfully, plenty survived). The city's parks and gardens can be an inviting respite from pounding the sightseeing pavement.

Audubon Park ★★ PARK Across from Loyola and Tulane universities, Audubon Park and the adjacent Audubon Zoo (see below) sprawl over 340 acres, extending all the way from St. Charles Avenue to the Mississippi River. This tract once belonged to city founder Jean-Baptiste Le Moyne and later was part of the Etienne de Boré plantation, where sugar was first granulated in 1794. Although John James Audubon, the country's best-known ornithologist, lived only briefly in New Orleans (at what is now the **Audubon Cottages** hotel; p. 67), the city has honored him by naming the park, zoo, and even a golf course after him.

The huge trees with black bark are live oaks; some are centuries old. More than 200 live oaks were planted to replace the many that didn't survive Hurricane Katrina. The park is a very pretty, wide-open place to stroll or enjoy a shaded picnic among statuary, fountains, and gazebos. There's a lovely 1.75-mile paved walking, running, skating, and biking path that loops around the lagoon (and Bird Island rookery) and golf course (overlooked by a lovely cafe). Along the track are 18 exercise stations. You'll also find tennis courts, baseball diamonds, horseback-riding facilities, and three playgrounds (the one on Walnut St., donated by former Saints quarterback Drew Brees, is great and accessible and has ziplines and bathrooms). Audubon Zoo is toward the back of the park across Magazine Street. Behind the zoo, a popular green space on the riverbank, called Riverview but nicknamed **the Fly,** has pleasant views of Frisbee players and the Mississippi. While you're there, don't miss the **Tree of Life** (p. 46).

6500 Magazine St. audubonnatureinstitute.org/audubon-park. ⊘ **504/861-2537.** Daily 5am–10pm.

Audubon Zoo ★★★ ZOO A place of justifiable civic pride, this zoo delights even non–zoo fans—small enough to be manageable, but big enough to cover all important bases, including elephant, orangutan, giraffe, and lion exhibits, with bonuses, like Malayan sun bears, gorgeous free-ranging peacocks and loads of tropical birds in the new immersive **Wings of the World** exhibit. Some 15,000 animals (including rare and endangered species) live in natural habitats of subtropical plants, waterfalls, lagoons, and a Louisiana swamp replica complete with rare white gators. For restless kiddos, there's also a playground, a carousel (although at press time, the carousel had been removed for repairs from Hurricane Ida damage), and some great hot-day diversions for the little ones, including **Monkey Hill**—one of the city's tallest points, complete with a grassy hill for rolling down and a wading stream with a mini-waterfall—and the **Cool Zoo** splash park (open seasonally; check website) with its Gator Run lazy river for inner-tube floating. So, bring swimsuits and towels if the weather warrants. There are misters and shady oaks for humans of all ages, plus refreshment stands. For maximum animal action, avoid midday, when the animals are sleeping off the heat. (Bonus track: Crank the Meters' "They All Ask'd for You" before or after you visit. How many zoos have their own hit song?) We like taking the historic St. Charles Avenue streetcar to Audubon Park, then walking through the park to reach the zoo.

6500 Magazine St. www.auduboninstitute.org. ✆ **504/861-2537.** Prices change day by day, but generally $30 adults, $25 seniors and children 2–12 (book tickets ahead to lock in best price). Cool Zoo $10 (open May–Sept.). Mar–Aug daily 10am–5pm; Sept–Feb Wed–Mon 10am–5pm. Closed Mardi Gras day, Thanksgiving, and Christmas.

Chalmette Battlefield/Jean Lafitte National Historical Park & Preserve ★ BATTLEFIELD These are the grounds where the bloody **Battle of New Orleans** was won on January 8, 1815. Ironically, it should never have been fought: A treaty signed 2 weeks before in Ghent, Belgium, had ended the War of 1812. But word had not yet reached Congress, the commander of the British forces, or Andrew Jackson, who stood with American forces to defend New Orleans and the mouth of the Mississippi River. The battle also succeeded in finally uniting Americans and Creoles. Markers on the battlefield allow you to follow the course of the fighting (or you can just watch the film in the visitor center). Inside the park is a national cemetery, established in 1864. It holds only two American veterans from the Battle of New Orleans, but also some 14,000 Union soldiers who fell in the Civil War. For a terrific view of the Mississippi River, climb the levee in back of the Beauregard House. It's about 6 miles from the French Quarter.

1 Battlefield Road, Chalmette. www.nps.gov/jela. ✆ **504/281-0510.** Free admission. Daily 9am–4:30pm. Visitor center closed Mardi Gras and federal holidays (open Veterans and Memorial days).

City Park ★★★ PARK Once part of the Louis Allard plantation and named one of America's "Coolest Parks," City Park's 1,300 beautifully landscaped acres provide a charming spot for jogging, birding, or just gazing at the moss-dripping live oaks (the largest collection in the world). It's also a trove of culture and activity, with botanical gardens, a conservatory, picnic areas, lagoons for boating and fishing, **swan boats** (p. 204), and bike paths and **rentals** (p. 204). Then there are tennis courts; two golf courses; two New Orleans–themed **miniature golf** courses (p. 205), a bandstand with summertime concerts, two stadiums, playing fields, playgrounds, and a miniature train you can ride in. That's just a start. **Carousel Gardens** is a kids' amusement area with rides; **Children's Storyland,** inside Carousel Gardens, has fairytale figures for little kids to scamper on and over and an exquisite antique carousel (p. 204). In 60-acre **Couturie Forest,** you can wander, hike, and reach New Orleans' highest point of elevation, **Laborde Mountain,** which is

27 whole feet above sea level. (Birders, bring your binoculars: It's the best spot in town!) At Christmastime, the mighty oaks are strung with more than a million lights—quite a magical sight.

You'll also find the **New Orleans Museum of Art** (p. 172) at Collins Diboll Circle, on Lelong Avenue, in a building that is itself a work of art. Flanking it to the left is the wonderful **Besthoff Sculpture Garden** (p. 172); to the right is the **Louisiana Children's Museum** (p. 205). Tucked away inside the **Botanical Gardens** is one of the oddest and most charming attractions in this odd and charming city, the **Train Garden.** Imagine a massive train set located in Dr. Seuss's basement, if Dr. Seuss were obsessed with both New Orleans and organic materials. Along 1,300 feet of track are exact $\frac{1}{22}$-scale replicas of 1890s streetcars and ornately detailed representations of actual New Orleans neighborhoods and landmarks—all made from plant matter! The Botanical Gardens are open year-round from Wednesday to Sunday 10am to 4:30pm (they close at 4pm Fri–Sat); check website for Wednesday evening concerts in the fall. Trains operate Saturday and Sunday from March through November (weather permitting).

1 Palm Dr. www.neworleanscitypark.com. ✆ **504/482-4888.** Park free. Botanical Gardens $12 adults; $6 kids 3–12; free for kids 2 and under (includes Train Garden). For hours and rates of other attractions, see separate listings. Park daily sunrise–sunset. Admissions and hours may vary seasonally, so check website or call.

Crescent Park ★★ PARK   This newish, river-hugging 1.4-mile green space paralleling the Marigny and Bywater neighborhoods is ideal for a picnic, run, dog walk, or stroll, or just to get a different, thoroughly modern perspective on New Orleans. That starts as you cross the enormous rust-colored steel arc, the Piety Street Bridge (aka the Rusty Rainbow), to reach the park. Or access it via the less dramatic, wheelchair-accessible Mandeville Crossing closer to the French Quarter. From the park's landscaped and paved paths, the Quarter is a mysterious, distant vision; from its expansive waterfront stage set amid decayed wharves, the area's industrial legacy is ever-present. Watch for concerts and other events at this substantial welcoming space. For free workout classes, see p. 299.

Enter from bridges near 2300 N. Peters St. at Elysian Fields (accessible); 3360 Chartres St. near Piety St. (stairs only); 3900 Chartres St. near Bartholomew St. (accessible). crescentparknola.org. ✆ **504/636-6400.** Free admission. Daily 6am–7:30pm (may close earlier in winter).

Lafitte Greenway ★★ PARK   This 2.6-mile walking trail and bikeway on a former railbed is a post-Katrina success story that now connects neighbors and neighborhoods: It starts just above the French Quarter and traverses the Tremé, Bayou St. John, and Mid-City. There's a FitLot, a playground, basketball courts, and baseball and soccer fields. If you're renting a bike (p. 296), the greenway will facilitate your explorations with nary a pothole in sight. (*Bonus:* It passes several adjacent eat- and drinkeries.) It's well lit, but use caution after dark. Check the website for free workouts, occasional events, and info about the very important history of this area and the Greenway's storm-water management techniques.

Trailhead begins at Basin and St. Louis sts. just outside the French Quarter (near St. Louis Cemetery No. 1); look for signage. Other access points intersect its route. www. lafittegreenway.org. ℂ **504/462-0645.** Open 24 hr.

Longue Vue House & Gardens ★★ HISTORIC HOME   Longue Vue mansion is a little pocket of the unexpected. Just 20 minutes from the city center, near the interesting end of suburban Metairie, it's a unique expression of Greek Revival architecture set on an 8-acre estate, constructed 1939–42 and listed on the National Register of Historic Places. It's like stumbling across a British country-house estate—and though it was never a plantation, it may satisfy Tara-esque cravings, if you can't get out to River Road (p. 273) or are plantation-averse.

The mansion was designed to foster a close rapport between indoors and outdoors, with vistas of formal terraces and pastoral woods. The charming gardens were partly inspired by the Generalife, the former summerhouse of the sultans in Granada, Spain; look also for fountains and a colonnaded loggia. Unlike at some attractions for garden enthusiasts, kids can actually have fun here in the delightful **Discovery Garden,** with clever and amusing exhibits where they can play (and maybe even learn). All in all, it's a nice place to ramble on a pretty day. Also on occasional offer are twilight or lunchtime garden concerts, volunteering opportunities, yoga, and tai chi.

7 Bamboo Rd., near Metairie. www.longuevue.com. ℂ **504/488-5488.** Mon–Sat 9:30am–5pm. Admission to gardens (self-guided) $10; guided house tour $25; guided tour of house and gardens $30. Tours on the hour until 4pm. Closed most major holidays.

NEW ORLEANS CEMETERIES

Along with Spanish moss and lacy cast-iron balconies, the cities of the dead are indelibly associated with New Orleans. Known the world over for their elaborate and beautiful aboveground tombs, their inscrutable ghostly presence enthralls visitors. There are more than 45 cemeteries in New Orleans—33 are considered historic, and 5 are officially listed in the National Register of Historic Places. Iconic tourist attractions as much as Jackson Square or Bourbon Street, the cemeteries have a fascinating backstory—one that has become twisted over time by mythology. But the truth is so fascinating that it needs little embellishment.

Sometimes called "Cities of the Dead" for their resemblance to urban centers, the cemeteries have, of course, been a part of New Orleans nearly since its founding. For the earliest settlers, dying wasn't that big of a deal; everyone was doing it, and the dead were buried in common graves or along the riverbanks (except the hoitiest of the toity, who were buried at St. Louis Cathedral). But when the river rose or a major rain caused flooding, that didn't work out too well. Old Uncle Etienne had an unpleasant habit of bobbing back to the surface, doubtless no longer looking his best. This practice gave rise to some good stories (though experts debate their veracity) of coffins floating downriver, bodies weighted down with rocks, and holes drilled in caskets to let the water through and keep them from popping up from the ground like deathly balloons.

Add to that cholera and yellow fever epidemics, which helped increase the number of bodies and also the possibility of infection. Given that the cemetery of the time was *inside* the Vieux Carré, it's all pretty disgusting to think about.

Around the late 1780s, death was getting to be a bigger deal. Not only was death more *prevalent,* what with fires and epidemics and such, *honoring* death and the dead was also becoming more ceremonial. When new cemeteries became necessary, they were plotted on the outskirts of town where illness and odor were less likely to be troublesome. The first, St. Peter, was begun in 1725 by the Catholic diocese, and rests where a Superdome parking lot now sits. Bodies were buried in the soil there. When St. Peter was full, the famed St. Louis No. 1 came about, in 1789, on what is now Rampart Street. The first major city of the dead, with fancy tombs and a parklike setting, it provided a more fitting tribute to departed loved ones. When it filled up, others soon followed, improving on the haphazard layout of St. Louis No. 1 to form designated "streets" in a grid pattern.

Following Old-World Style

It's true that the high water table and muddy soil here influenced the popularity of the aboveground "condo crypt" look—the dead are placed in vaults that resemble miniature buildings. But such tombs are actually customary in France and Spain (and elsewhere); it was just another tradition that the colonists brought with them to New Orleans. Some say St. Louis No. 1 was inspired by the famous Père Lachaise cemetery in Paris. Perhaps it's just because they are both such impressive, prestigious sights.

The aboveground vaults are also often adorned with stunning works of sculptural art, decorations that represent the family name, occupation, or religion (which was invariably Catholic; the first Jewish cemetery was not founded until 1828). Some tombs were not owned by families, but by a group, like the firefighters, police, or a benevolent society. These were decorated accordingly: Witness the enormous elk visible from the corner of Canal Street and City Park Avenue. Group tombs were helpful for families who could not afford a family tomb. The cemeteries may also have fancy ironwork in the gates and fences—and on the whole are well worth a visit.

Hi Honey, I'm Home

So . . . all that tomb for one dead guy? Not so much. The tombs indeed host multiple bodies. The methodology is actually fairly clever. Inside the tomb are long chambers, one above the other, separated by shelves. When a casket goes in, it rests on the top shelf, and the vault is resealed with simple brick and mortar. Heat and humidity act like a slow form of cremation. After a year and a day (by custom and rule—to accommodate the traditional year-long mourning period), another family member may be buried here. Whatever's left of the first one is moved to the bottom level, and the casket bits are removed. In some tombs, that shelf has a gap toward the back, and the remnants just get pushed back, where they fall through the gap to the vault below. Everyone eventually lies jumbled together to continue their quest for a dusty family reunion. And so room is made for a new casket, and the exterior is closed up once again. The result is sometimes dozens of names, going back generations, on a single spot. It's an efficient, space-saving system that gives new meaning to the phrase "all in the family." If a family loses two people within the year, one of them rests in a temporary holding vault until that year-and-a-day period has passed.

Upkeep Issues

By law, families must maintain their tombs. Traditionally, All Saints' Day (November 1) is when families gather to honor their dead, and in the days leading up to it, you will see some people busily tidying up and washing down the sun-bleached, whitewashed brick buildings. Some are treated with lime, leaving a yellow or green tint. Flowers, candles, photos, and memorabilia are left on and around the tombs of loved ones. To this day, if you go to a cemetery on November 1—which we recommend—you may see a tender graveside party atmosphere. The Krewe de Mayahuel (facebook.com/krewedemayahuel) also puts on a Day of the Dead cemetery procession to honor loved ones who have passed.

But many graves have fallen into disrepair, when family members are no longer willing, able, or around to do the maintenance. There are laws that allow the city to take over and transfer a neglected tomb, but these are largely unenforced (and there's the creepy factor). Other laws and customs around these centuries-old tombs are murky, and responsibility for the expensive upkeep gets shifted or shunted off. So sadly, many cemeteries today face moderate to severe dishevelment. For years, crypts lay open, exposing their pitiful contents—if they weren't robbed of them—bricks, shattered marble tablets, even bones, lay strewn around. Several of the worst eyesores have been cleaned up; others still remain in deplorable shape. Concerns were high for the fate of the iconic cemeteries during the Katrina disaster days, but in large part, "the system worked." The tombs survived unscathed, except for some high-water marks much like those borne by any other flooded structure.

Restoration and cleanup efforts have been spearheaded by the nonprofit **Save Our Cemeteries** (www.saveourcemeteries.org; ✆ **504/525-3377**). Consider throwing a few, um, bones their way, or even volunteering. The website accepts online donations. Save Our Cemeteries also offers tours and occasional lectures.

For more information, we highly recommend Robert Florence's *New Orleans Cemeteries: Life in the Cities of the Dead.* It's full of photos, facts, and human-interest stories for those with a deeper interest in this fascinating aspect of New Orleans culture and is available at bookstores throughout the city.

If you've read through this section, or if you're a human being, we hope you have some respect for the historic nature of these cemeteries and their cultural significance. If nothing else, we trust that you recognize these are sacred burial places. Thus, we can't even believe we need to implore you to refrain from marking these tombs in any way or removing anything from cemeteries, ever. Due to their age, it's best not to even touch the tombs. If you've heard leaving offerings or scrawling "XXX" on graves brings good luck or calls up the ancestors, that's bogus. In actuality, it's just defacing someone's hallowed resting place (and it's illegal, and the reason many cemeteries are currently closed to the public). Take your photos of these beautiful, sanctified spaces. But otherwise, leave them and their inhabitants in peace.

Cemeteries You Should (or Must) See with a Tour

A number of the tour companies listed on p. 193 provide cemetery tours. Several of the city's most impressive and historically important cemeteries are now closed to the public. Check www.nolacatholiccemeteries.org (or be content to peek through locked gates).

Lafayette Cemetery No. 1 ★★★ CEMETERY   Right across the street from Commander's Palace restaurant, this lush uptown cemetery was once in horrible condition, but it's been mostly restored. It's also been closed for *years,* sadly. Anne Rice's Mayfair witches have their family tomb here (p. 177).

1400 block of Washington Ave.

St. Louis Cemetery No. 1 ★★★ CEMETERY   The oldest extant cemetery (1789) is also the most iconic. It's part of the **African American Heritage Trail.** Here lie Marie Laveau (p. 192), Bernard Marigny, and (eventually) Nicolas Cage, in the pyramid he had inscribed *"Omnia Ab Uno"* (Everything From One). It's also recognizable for the acid-dropping scene from *Easy Rider* shot here. You can see this cemetery *only* by booking a tour through **Cemetery Tours NOLA** (cemeterytourneworleans.com).

Basin St. btw. Conti and St. Louis sts.

St. Louis Cemetery No. 2 ★ CEMETERY   Established in 1823, it's the city's next-oldest cemetery. Although the neighborhood is much improved, its old rough reputation has kept most tours away, so it's less trafficked (and more rundown). **Save Our Cemeteries** (p. 199) and **Historic New Orleans Tours** (p. 194) offer tours (but it was also closed at press time, with tours suspended, so call ahead to check if it has re-opened). Emperor of the Universe, R&B legend Ernie K-Doe, was laid to rest here in 2001; his widow, Empress Antoinette, joined him in 2009. Claude Tremé, founder of the historic neighborhood that bears his name (p. 40), also rests here.

N. Claiborne Ave. btw. Iberville and St. Louis sts.

Cemeteries You Can See on Your Own

This Mid-City cluster of cemeteries on or near City Park Avenue is an easy streetcar ride up Canal Street from the Quarter. Just take the streetcar called—can you guess?—"Cemeteries." Most of these cemeteries (such as St. Louis No. 3 and Metairie) have offices that can provide maps or direct you to a grave location. All have sort-of-regular hours—anytime from 9am to 4pm is a safe bet. Cemeteries are often secluded spaces, and once were known for thieves preying on tourists. That's no longer common, but going in pairs or groups and being alert is always a good idea.

Cypress Grove and Greenwood Cemeteries ★★ CEMETERY Located across the street from each other, both were founded in the mid-1800s by the Firemen's Charitable and Benevolent Association. Each has some highly original tombs; keep your eyes open for those made entirely of iron.

120 City Park Ave., at Canal Blvd. www.greenwoodnola.com. ✆ **504/482-8983.** By car, take Canal Blvd. north to City Park Ave. Greenwood is across City Park Ave. to the right; Cypress Grove is on your left. Daily 8am–4pm.

Holt Cemetery ★★★ CEMETERY This one is not so easy to find, but it's worth seeking out. Dating to the mid-1800s, this former burial ground for indigents is the rare New Orleans cemetery with nearly all in-ground graves. They are maintained by the families—or not maintained at all, in many cases—which results in its particular folk-art appeal, with hand-drawn markers and family memorabilia scattered about. It's incredibly picturesque and poignant in its own way. Jazz pioneer Charles "Buddy" Bolden is buried here, in an unmarked grave.

635 City Park Ave. (turn down tiny Buddy Bolden Pl., across City Park Ave. from the Burger King and next to Delgado College). Mon–Fri 8am–2:30pm; Sat 8am–noon.

Hurricane Katrina Memorial ★ CEMETERY On the former site of Charity Hospital's paupers' field, this affecting circle of tombs holds the bodies of 85 unclaimed victims of the 2005 levee failures and the names of others who perished. It's a dignified place that's easily missed (look for a discreet black-iron gate), the better for contemplative solitude. Surrounded by a storm-shaped series of pathways, the memorial does its duty in giving one substantial pause.

5056 Canal St. Take the Canal St. streetcar to City Park Ave. Mon–Fri 8am–2pm.

Metairie (Lake Lawn) Cemetery ★★ CEMETERY Don't be fooled by the slightly more modern look—some of the most amazing tombs in New Orleans are here. Don't miss the pyramid-and-sphinx Brunswig mausoleum, the "ruined castle" Egan family tomb, and the former resting place of Storyville madam Josie Arlington. Her mortified family had the madam's body moved when her crypt became a tourist attraction (her move may have also resulted from the complaints of blue-blood families, themselves mortified at Josie's proximity). But the tomb remains exactly the same, including the statue of a young woman knocking on the door. Legend has it that the young woman is Josie herself being turned away from her father's house, or a virgin being denied entrance to Josie's brothel—she claimed never to despoil anyone. The reality is that it's just a copy of a statue Josie liked. Other famous residents include jazz greats Louis Prima and Al Hirt, Saints owner Tom Benson, and *Vampire Chronicles* author Anne Rice. Foodies wishing to pay last compliments to the chef will find Ruth Fertel of Ruth's Chris Steakhouse (in a marble edifice that oddly resembles one of her famous pieces of beef) along with the founding owners of Antoine's, Galatoire's, Brennan's, and Arnaud's. You'll have to drive or taxi, but you can also drive the lanes through the cemetery, a good option for a rainy day.

5100 Pontchartrain Blvd. ℂ **504/486-6331.** Daily 8:30am–5pm. By car, take Canal St. to City Park Ave.; turn left until it becomes Metairie Ave., turn right onto Pontchartrain Blvd. (signs for I-10), then make a quick left under highway; stay on Pontchartrain to the stop sign, cross traffic into the entrance on your left.

St. Louis Cemetery No. 3 ★★★ CEMETERY   Conveniently located next to the Fair Grounds racetrack (home of Jazz Fest), St. Louis No. 3 was built atop a former graveyard for lepers. Storyville photographer E. J. Bellocq lies here, as do architect James Gallier and iconic chefs Paul Prudhomme and Leah Chase. It's a scenic cemetery near Bayou St. John, accessible via Esplanade Avenue.

3421 Esplanade Ave. ℂ **504/482-5065.** Daily 8am–4:30pm (Sun and holidays closes 4pm).

VOODOO

Voodoo's mystical presence is one of the most common New Orleans motifs—though it is mostly reduced to a tourist gimmick. With kitschy dolls for sale and exaggerated mythology surrounding Voodoo queen Marie Laveau, a very real, culturally important religion with a serious past gets lost amid all that camp.

Voodoo's roots can be traced in part back to the religion of West Africa's **Yoruba** people, which incorporates the worship of several different spiritual forces that include a supreme being, a pantheon of deities, and the spirits of ancestors. When Africans were kidnapped, enslaved, and brought to Brazil, Haiti, and, ultimately, Louisiana, they brought their religion with them.

Later, other African religions met and melded, and when enslaved people were forced to convert to Catholicism, they found it easy to merge and practice both religions and rituals. Rites involved dancing and singing to intricate drum rhythms. Some participants might even fall into a trancelike state, during which a *lwa* (or *loa*), a spirit and/or lower-level deity intermediary between humans and gods, would take possession of them.

Voodoo was banned in Louisiana until the Louisiana Purchase in 1803. The next year, enslaved Haitians overthrew their government, and new immigrants came from there to New Orleans. By 1809, more than 10,000 Haitians arrived, doubling the city's population. They brought along a fresh infusion of Voodoo (or more accurately, Vodou, the Haitian spelling you'll often see in New Orleans).

Napoleonic law (which still holds sway in Louisiana) and the Code Noir (p. 18) gave the enslaved Sundays off, and in 1817, a city ordinance restricted gatherings of enslaved people to one place: what is now known as **Congo Square** on Rampart Street, part of Louis Armstrong Park. African worship there, including dancing and drumming rituals, gave enslaved people a way to have their own community and a small amount of freedom. These gatherings naturally attracted white onlookers, as did the rituals held (often by free people of African descent) along **Bayou St. John.** The local papers of the 1800s are full of lurid accounts of Voodoo "orgies" and of spirits possessing both white and Black people. In Congo Square, Voodoo blended with the dominant religion, Catholicism, and gatherings became more like performance pieces than religious rituals. Legend has it that nearby madams would come down to the Sunday gatherings and hire some of the performers to entertain at their houses.

During the 1800s, the famous Voodoo priestesses came to some prominence. Mostly free women of color, they were devout religious practitioners and very good businesswomen with a steady clientele of whites who secretly came to them for help in love or money matters. During the 1900s, Voodoo largely went back underground, but by the end of the century, it was viewed as entertainment and commercialized for tourism.

It is estimated that today as much as 15% of the population of New Orleans practices Voodoo, though the public perception—casting spells or sticking pins in Voodoo dolls—is largely Hollywood nonsense.

Most of the stores and places in New Orleans that advertise Voodoo are set up strictly for tourism. This is not to say that some facts can't be found there or that you shouldn't buy a mass-produced souvenir. For an introduction to Voodoo, check out the **New Orleans Historic Voodoo Museum** earlier in this chapter (p. 164) or the shop **Voodoo Authentica** (p. 249). For true Voodoo, however, seek out real Voodoo temples or practitioners. You can find them at the temples listed below or by calling **Ava Kay Jones** (yorubapriestess.tripod. com; ✆ **504/484-6499**), who creates custom gris-gris bags (packets of meaning-infused herbs, stones, and other such bits), potions, candles, and dolls by appointment only. If you happen into one of these temples and find no one about, come back or wait quietly; they may be conducting a reading in a side room. And be sure to check out Robert Tallant's book *Voodoo in New Orleans* (Pelican Pocket, 1983).

Voodoo Temples & Spiritual Practitioners

The city has several authentic Voodoo temples and *botanicas* selling everything you might need for potions, spells, and ritual implements for altars. The public is welcome, and employees are happy to educate the honestly inquisitive. (See a few more on p. 249 in the Shopping chapter).

The venerable **Island of Salvation Botanica** in the New Orleans Healing Center, 2372 St. Claude Ave. #100 (islandofsalvationbotanica.com; ✆ **504 /948-9961**), is run by Vodou priestess **Sallie Ann Glassman.** The *botanica* is open Monday to Saturday 10am to 5pm and Sunday 11am to 5pm, but call first to make sure they are not closed for readings (or to schedule a reading). Start with a visit here, or a stroll down **Rosalie Alley** to see beautiful Voodoo imagery (in the Bywater, off Rampart between Piety and Desire sts.).

Priestess Miriam, who has practiced for decades at the **Voodoo Spiritual Temple,** 1428 N. Rampart St. (www.voodoospiritualtemple.org; ℂ **504/943-9795**), is the real McCoy, a serene spirit and practitioner in the traditions of the West African ancestors. No pins in dolls here, folks, but healings, prayers, blessings, spiritual consultations, and training are available. The temple is just off Esplanade Avenue, easily accessed from the French Quarter or via the Rampart streetcar. Interested, respectful tourists are welcome. Call for an appointment.

The vibe feels right at **Crescent City Conjure** (www.crescentcityconjure.us; ℂ **504/421-3189**), a pretty little Marigny shop with supplies and expertise for root, herb, and oil work, along with various other items for practicing hoodoo and witchcraft. Authenticity and education are the watchwords; owner Sen Elias is welcoming of experienced practitioners and patient with the genuinely curious. Readings start at $35 for 15 minutes. For related shops, see p. 249.

ORGANIZED TOURS

The free, self-guided walking tours we've developed for you (see chapter 10) are pretty great, if we do say so ourselves. But there are also great advantages to taking organized tours. Though they're touristy by definition, someone else does the planning, and it's an easy way to get to outlying areas. A good tour

VISITING marie laveau

The most famous New Orleans Voodoo queen, Marie Laveau was a real woman, although her life has been so mythologized that it is nearly impossible to separate fact from fiction. But who really wants to?

She was born a free woman of color in 1794. A hairdresser by trade, Marie became known for her psychic abilities and powerful gris-gris. Then again, her day job allowed her into the best houses, where she heard all the good gossip and could apply it to her other clientele. In one famous story, a young woman about to be forced into a marriage with a much older, wealthy man approached Marie. She wanted to marry her young lover instead. Marie counseled patience. The marriage went forward, and the happy groom died from a heart attack while dancing with his bride at the reception. After a respectable time, the now-wealthy widow was free to marry her lover.

Marie wholeheartedly believed in Voodoo—and business. Her home at

what is now 1020 St. Ann St. was purportedly a gift from a grateful client. A devout Catholic, Marie attended daily Mass and was well known for her charity work. Her death in 1881 was even noted by the *Times-Picayune.*

Her look-alike daughter, Marie II, took over her work, leading some to believe (mistakenly) that Marie I lived a very long time, looking quite well indeed—which only added to her legend. But Marie II allegedly worked more for the darker side than her mother. Her eventual reward, the story goes, was death by poison (delivered by whom is unknown). Visitors have long brought Marie tokens (candles, beads, change) and asked her for favors—she's buried in **St. Louis Cemetery No. 1.** Because misguided or outright disrespectful people marred her tomb with X's, the cemetery was long closed to tourists. It has recently reopened; to visit, you must book a tour through **Cemetery Tours New Orleans** (cemeterytourneworleans.com).

guide can entertain, enlighten, and even inspire. We lean toward some of the smaller companies, in hopes that they may have fewer people than the allowable 28 per group. We like to hang close to the guide in case we have questions; they'll often continue to share knowledge while on the way to the next point of interest—and we find that these kinds of serendipitous personal interactions are easier to come by when fewer people are being herded along. It's reassuring that New Orleans tour guides must be licensed, which involves actual study and testing. So not just anyone can load you on a bus and take you for a (literal or figurative) ride.

Tours almost always run rain-or-shine (no refunds), but in some instances you're allowed to move your reservation to another day. Walking tours and large bus tours have a designated meeting point; smaller van tours usually provide hotel pickup. Before booking, check for deals on tickets—they pop up regularly on **Groupon** (www.groupon.com), **Yelp** (www.yelp.com), and elsewhere.

Be aware: It's fairly common practice for hotel concierges and storefront tour offices to **earn commission on the tours they sell or recommend** (ditto restaurants). Some may have honest opinions about the merits of one over another, and those may be perfectly good options, but often they're selling you what they get paid to sell. If you're looking for a tour, do the research yourself and cut out the middleman; and no matter how you learned about it, pay the fee directly to the company, not to your concierge or a street-corner booth.

And about those "free tours" you may run across: Keep in mind that they're not really free (and they're always packed to the gills). They usually come with a heavy-hitting request for tips, and by the time you tip the guide, you're not far from the cost of tours from established providers. We don't love the business model, and then when we found large chunks of our published walking tours lifted wholesale and republished on their website—without copyright permission or attribution—well, draw your own conclusions about the authenticity of their tours.

While you're on the lookout: Hawking tours on the street, including in front of cemeteries, is illegal (although not well enforced). If your guide does that, it's just not a good sign from the get-go about what you're in for.

Tour Companies

We're supportive of legitimate businesses that legitimately support the city we love so much. The following companies offer multiple tours (and may offer discounts if you commit to more than one). Most have walking tours of the **French Quarter,** the **Garden District,** and the **cemeteries,** as well as city van tours and tours to the **plantations** and **swamps** (they provide transportation and tickets to an associated swamp or airboat tour). Other specialty tours are noted, but if you have a particular interest you don't see, contact these companies—customized tours can often be arranged.

All Bout Dat Tours ★★★   This woman-owned, Black-owned tour company is known—and loved—for telling the whole truth, nothing but the truth. Singer and storyteller Mikhala offers a handful of tours, including a moving, powerful "Singing is Praying" walking tour of Tremé, Armstrong Park, and Congo Square. On her 2½-hour Black Heritage and Jazz tour, you'll be driven around to visit historical sites, learn about Voodoo and Creole architecture, and meet local shop owners, artists, and elders.

www.allboutdat.com. ℰ **504/457-9439.** Singing is Praying Walking Tour $35; Black Heritage and Jazz Tour $60. Check website for other tours and full schedule.

Beyond the Bayou ★★★

We're all thumbs-up for this locally owned company. For starters, it's *legitimately* eco-conscious, and one of very few travel companies that's 100% carbon neutral. Groups are small; guides are friendly, fun, factual, and flexible. Tour options are ever-evolving but include an all-day Cajun Country excursion (swamp tour, unique music experiences, and two meals can be included), and a sustainable swamp tour in the Atchafalaya Basin (breakfast and lunch included, plus a visit to the Whitney Plantation).

www.beyondthebayoutours.com. ℰ **504/708-5161.** Tours start at $49.

Cajun Encounters ★

This is a large company, but it's been around for 25+ years, and it is locally owned—a point of pride and also a bit of a hallmark, as they like to hire local guides. Tours are on a 33-seat bus. The City & Cemetery bus tour takes you through the French Quarter, St. Louis No. 3 Cemetery, Warehouse and Central Business districts, City Park, and Garden District, with cemetery walk-around opportunities. The company also offers swamp and plantation day tours (see chapter 11).

941 Decatur St. www.cajunencounters.com. ℰ **866/928-6877** or 504/834-1770. City + Cemetery Tour $55 adults; $38 children. Swamp tour (with hotel pickup) $60 adults; $39 children. Check website for other tours, schedules, and discount offers.

Gray Line ★

This well-known, well-established (since 1926) nationwide company runs coach and walking tours of the city, swamps, and plantations—in pretty much every combination (including tour/cruise combos with sister companies **Steamboat *NATCHEZ*** and ***City of New Orleans* riverboat**; see p. 198). River cruises offer fab views and nostalgic fun. As the big kahuna of tour companies, Gray Line offers large groups, full-size buses, and a slicker, more scripted presentation—but also a glitch-free operation, from the call center to the deep bench of backup guides to the heavy tour schedule, so one call can set you up.

Toulouse St. at the Mississippi River. www.graylineneworleans.com. ℰ **800/233-2628.** Walking tours start at $27 adults, $15 children; bus tours start at $54 adults, $25 children. Check website for itineraries, prices, and full schedule.

Historic New Orleans Tours ★★★

This is one of our favorite midsize tour companies, mostly because the guides are terrific. Quite often they have advanced degrees in history or other related disciplines, and they're free to bring their own perspectives and interests to the tour, thereby keeping things fresh versus a noticeably routine script. The company emphasizes authenticity over sensationalism and is particularly expert in cemeteries. Guides lead walking tours of the French Quarter, Garden District, and cemeteries, plus a fun adults-only "Scandalous Cocktail" tour, which strings together local bars and drinks with tales of historic brothels, organized crime, and even the JFK assassination. The colorful bartenders, when not too busy, also tell their own tales (do pace your drinking, though!). Other special-interest tours (available by advance arrangement, some private) focus on music, literature, film, and the Tremé.

www.tourneworleans.com. © **504/947-2120.** Most tours $25 adults; $18 students, seniors, and military; $7 children 6–12; free for kids 5 and under. Tours available in French, Spanish, and German.

Walking Tours

The nonprofit volunteer group **Friends of the Cabildo ★★** (523 St. Ann St.; www.friendsofthecabildo.org; © **504/523-3939** or 504/524-9118) offers an excellent 2-hour introductory walking tour of the Quarter, starting from the 1850 House on Jackson Square (p. 158), daily at 10:30am and 1:30pm. Tour guides are licensed, and often Quarter residents, so they know whereof they speak. Tours cost $25 adults; $20 seniors, students, and military; ages 12 and under free. Purchase tickets online or on-site and arrive 15 minutes early.

One of the more established **walking tours of the Tremé ★★★**, focusing on African-American history and the incredible cultural and musical legacy of this historic neighborhood, is offered by **French Quarter Phantoms** (www. frenchquarterphantoms.com; © **504/666-8300**). It leaves from 718 N. Rampart St. Saturday through Monday at 10:30am. Reservations are required; it's $22 ($5 for kids 7 and under) when booked online. **Know NOLA Tours ★★★** (www.knownolatours.com; © **504/264-2483**) also offers, among other tours, a phenomenal African heritage walking tour of the Tremé and the French Quarter. Owner/guide Malik is from this culture, and his personal connection to the history and cultural traditions you'll learn about (such as the Mardi Gras Indians and social aid and pleasure clubs) are an enormous added value to his depth of knowledge. Advance reservations are required; times vary. It costs $25 for adults and $15 for kids 12 and under; free for children 4 and under.

Two Chicks Walking Tours ★★ (www.twochickswalkingtours.com; © **504/ 975-4386**) adds a dollop of sass to its informative, entertaining tours. In the adults-only Bordellos and Ladies of the Night tour, for example, perky guide Christine, adorned in a rainbow tutu, knows her stuff and weaves plenty of standard history through this soft-focus lens, bringing it new interest. Each tour stop has some relation to the oldest profession, from the Ursuline Convent to Storyville. It's a bit bawdy but not at all frivolous (even with the soundtrack of hooker-related tunes played between stops—think "Roxanne" and "House of the Rising Sun"). Our group had men and women of all ages and a mature teen with her parents, and all were equally engaged. The guide went well off-script answering questions, which personalized the tour even if causing it to run a bit over the 2 hours. Most of their tours cost around $30; reservations are required.

For something more high-end and personal, try **Soul of New Orleans Tours** (www.neworleansprivatetours.net; © **504/905-4999**). The delightful, intrepid Cassandra arranges a custom walking or van tour for your small group, however straightforward or unusual. Prices start at $225 for up to four people (additional people $30 each, up to 12 people total for private tours).

Swamp Tours

Depending on weather, area, and operator, a **swamp tour** can be serene and reverent, eerie and mysterious, or a thrill and a hoot. There's no dearth of tour options, but because of how delicate the ecosystem is, we favor those that take measures to preserve the natural environment. The truth is, you'll be hard pressed to find guides who don't throw marshmallows to gators and raccoons, a surefire means of attracting the critters, but one we find cringeworthy (especially since feeding wild animals trains them to view humans as a food source, which can be, um . . . hazardous). Airboat rides are wildly popular, but we haven't listed them; they might be hella fun, but they're hella invasive, too. We've made efforts to include tours that are ethical and eco-conscious, along with a few of the more mainstream, old-school, locally owned operations. On the following tours, you're likely to see waterfowl such as egrets, owls, herons, bald eagles, and ospreys. Less frequently, you may spot a feral hog, otter, beaver, frog, turtle, raccoon, deer, or nutria. As for alligators, in warm months they're generally plentiful; in cooler months, they sleep, so you probably won't see them. (*One note:* Regardless of season, keep your hands inside the boat—to a gator, they can look like dinner.) Even during winter hibernation,

EXPLORING THE mighty mississippi

New Orleans has always had a complicated and crucial inter-relationship with water. If you're with a group of six or more and want to understand it better, we highly recommend **The Great Delta Tours ★★** (www.thegreatdeltatours.com; © **888/316-1338**), which brings groups out on tours to explore the Mississippi Delta's cultural, economic, and environmental impact on the area.

On **The Delta Discover Tour,** founder/guide/master naturalist Barbara weaves it all together while her van covers a lot of literal and informative ground on this whole-day or half-day eco-tour: from the wetlands to the rivers to canals; from preservation to restoration; and from the shrimpers and fishermen whose families have plied these waters for generations (you'll meet some of them) to the petrochemical industry's effects on them. You'll visit areas that were under 15+ feet of water after the 2005 levee breaches, and areas that will likely be underwater in the very near future. You'll visit the Isleño and Vietnamese communities (lunching at acclaimed Dong Phuong bakery [see p. 147] or a popular local seafood restaurant), who've thrived in the Mississippi Delta region for centuries and decades, respectively—with large and largely overlooked impact.

These tours offer a rare opportunity to delve into important topics, and you'll leave wanting to further explore these fascinating regions and issues. Tours are customized to meet the interests of the group. Private whole-day tours cost $250 per person (minimum 6 guests; per-person price decreases as group size increases). Half-day tours of Bayou Bienvenue are also available ($175 per person, minimum of 12 people). Tours are open to adults and kids over age 12. Departure locations vary (hotel pick-ups available).

a morning spent floating on the bayou is pleasant, and learning about how this unique ecosystem contributes to the local culture and economy is quite interesting. Plus, the swamps are simply beautiful.

Most tour operators listed earlier in this chapter under "Tour Companies" (p. 193) provide swamp tours, but they really just coordinate your transportation, narrate the drive, and deliver you to one of the following knowledgeable swamp-tour folks. You can drive on your own to one of these tours or contact the operators directly to arrange your transportation from the city.

Dr. Wagner's Honey Island Swamp Tours ★, 41490 Crawford Landing Rd. in Slidell, about 30 miles outside of New Orleans (www.honeyisland swamp.com; ✆ **985/641-1769** or 504/242-5877), takes you into the interior of Honey Island Swamp to view wildlife with native professional naturalist guides, all of whom grew up plying these waters. The guides provide a solid educational experience to go with the pure swamp excitement. They do throw food (again, most do), so you'll likely see all manner of close-up critters, from gators to raccoons to feral hogs. Small flat-bottom boats—both covered and uncovered—ease through the swamp for about 2 hours. Prices are $29 adults, $19 children 12 and under if you drive to the launch site yourself; or $58 adults and $36 children with hotel pickup in New Orleans.

It's a little farther out (a little over an hour's drive southwest of New Orleans), and you'll need to provide your own transportation, but we'd be remiss if we didn't add **Annie Miller's Son's Swamp and Marsh Tours** ★, 3718 Southdown Mandalay Rd., Houma (www.annie-miller.com; ✆ **985/868-4758**). Mark, grandson of the legendary Alligator Annie, is carrying on her down-home tradition (including, yes, feeding the critters). Swamp water runs through this family's veins, and they know every inch of this bayou. Reservations required; call for schedules. Prices are $40 adults, $25 children 11 and under; tours run 2 to 2½ hours.

Kayak Tours

One of our favorites, **Honey Island Swamp Kayak Tours** ★★★ (www.honeyislandkayaktours.com; ✆ **504/517-3066**) is owned by friendly, easygoing, eco-conscious Jessica, who knows this swamp like it's her back yard—because it *is her back yard*. Jessica grew up here and takes paddlers into one of the nation's most undisturbed swamps to see ancient cypress trees (one dates from 1803). We love that she walks her eco-talk: She's organized annual river cleanups since 2012 and even grinds into sand the glass bottles she finds in the water. She educates about ecology and wetlands loss and never baits or feeds wildlife. Beginners, kids 6 and over, and pets are welcome, and guests can swim in certain areas. Also, the launch site is a bar, so if you're hungry or thirsty after the workout, you're set. Tours last 2½ hours and cost $59 for adults, $35 for kids 6–12. You'll need your own transportation to get to the launch site.

Kayak-iti-Yat ★★★ (www.kayakitiyat.com; ✆ **985/778-5034** or 512/964-9499, or text 504/909-4049) explains city lore from the unique perspective of a kayak along Bayou St. John. When the weather's right, it's a sublime way to explore some historic neighborhoods. Tours range from 2 to 4 hours, with increasing intensity of upper-body workouts (the better to justify last night's indulgent dinner). It's not difficult even for the inexperienced. Tours run daily; times vary, and advance reservations are required. Two-hour tours are $49; 4-hour tours are $100. There's a two-person minimum. All equipment is provided, but there's no bathroom stop, so plan ahead.

If you're adventuresome and can commit to the better part of a day, **Lost Lands Tours** ★★★ (www.lostlandstours.org; ✆ **504/858-7575**) takes kayakers to the Maurepas Wildlife Management Area, 45 minutes outside of New Orleans, on a 3- to 4-hour tailored paddle (weather permitting) through the elegant, mysterious blackwater swamps, returning to the city around 3 to 4pm. A pre-trip talk by experts, often including a Pulitzer prize–winning writer, highlights the environmental history and challenges of coastal Louisiana. The focus is on the issues surrounding these vital, rapidly disappearing wetlands. It's beautiful and illuminating. Sometimes a courtesy ride is available between the meeting place and boat launch (four people maximum); tours are $100 each if four people sign up (otherwise, per-person rates are $130 each for three or $200 each for two people).

FULL steam AHEAD

C'mon, you know you want to. It's a paddle-wheeler on the Mississippi, fer the love of Mark Twain. A river cruise is cheesy, refreshing fun, and gives everyone an excuse to bust out their best "Proud Mary."

The steamboat **NATCHEZ** (www.steamboatnatchez.com; ✆ **800/233-2628** or 504/569-1401), a marvelous three-deck steam-powered sternwheeler, re-creates the 19th-century version that held the record for fastest steamship till the *Robert E. Lee* famously whipped it in 1870—although the current boat has never lost a race! At press time the *NATCHEZ* was in dry dock for repairs, so check the website to see if it's rolling down the river again. Meanwhile, its spiffy newer and newly renovated sister steamboat, the **City of New Orleans,** which launched in 2019, offers leisurely jazz cruises from 7 to 9pm nightly with the Grammy-nominated Dukes of Dixieland providing the tunes; there's narration for a little history and an option to add dinner. There's also a daytime cruise at 11:30am daily, with a lunch option available and music by the Steamboat Stompers. Tickets range from $39 to $95 for adults, $16 to $44 for kids ages 6–12.

Another company operates the smaller **Creole Queen** (www.creolequeen.com; ✆ **800/445-4109** or 504/529-4567), which has a 7pm jazz cruise ($52 adults, $26 kids 6–12, free for ages 5 and under; with buffet dinner $95, $40, and $15 respectively) and a 2½-hour daytime Historical River Cruise, which stops downriver at Chalmette Battlefield (p. 183), site of the Battle of New Orleans ($39 adults, $15 kids 6–12, free for ages 5 and under; additional charge for buffet lunch). It's docked at the end of Poydras Street, next to the Outlets at Riverwalk.

All ships have outside decks and inside lounges with air-conditioning or heat as needed, and cocktail bars, of course. Times vary seasonally, so call ahead. Arrive at least a half-hour early to board. **Tip 1:** Check the online coupon sites for discounts. **Tip 2:** There's better food on land. Just sayin'.

Cemetery, Mystical & Mysterious Tours

Interest in the ghostly, supernatural side of New Orleans has always been part of its appeal. It has also resulted in some rather humorous infighting as rival tour operators steal each other's guides, shtick, and customers. We enjoy a good nighttime ghost tour of the Quarter as much as anyone, but we also have to admit that what's available is really hit-or-miss in presentation (it depends on who conducts your particular tour) and more miss than hit with regard to facts. Go for the entertainment value, not for the education, and you won't be disappointed. All the tours stop outside locations where horrifying things supposedly (or actually) happened, or inexplicable sights have been observed. Allegedly. Just be aware that this isn't a haunted-house tour (you don't enter any buildings other than a bar for a mid-tour break), and no ghouls jump out from dark corners. If you do see any spectral action, it'll most likely be due to that bar stop.

We can send you with a clear conscience on the **Tremé/Storyville/Cemetery and Voodoo Tour** offered by **Historic New Orleans Tours ★★★** (p. 194), which is consistently fact-based and not sensation-based, though still entertaining. (Some guides are even descendants of people discussed on tours.) At press time, guides were holding court from the gates of both St. Louis Cemeteries Nos. 1 and 2. The tour also takes you to Congo Square, the Tomb of the Unknown Slave, and the site of Marie Laveau's home. It leaves daily at 10:30am and 1pm from the courtyard at Backatown Coffee, 301 Basin St. Rates are $25 adults; $18 students, seniors, and active military; $7 children 6 to 12; free for ages 5 and under. The company also offers a nighttime **Haunted French Quarter Tour,** 'cause thrills and chills deserve darkness. The tour departs nightly at 7:30pm from 823 Decatur St. (Reserve in advance online.)

A nonprofit organization dedicated to cemetery maintenance, education, tomb restoration, and authentic tours, **Save Our Cemeteries ★★★** (www. saveourcemeteries.org; ℭ **504/525-3377**) offers tours of the Lake Lawn Metairie cemetery (Sun 10am) and St. Louis Cemetery No. 3 (Mon and Sat 10am). Tours cost $25, kids 5 and under free. Advance reservations required.

New Orleans Secrets Tours ★★ offers, among other experiences (food, cocktails, LGBTQ, ghosts), a Voodoo tour led by guides committed to teaching the truths of Voodoo. Tours are small (nine people or fewer) and focus on the actual religion—in history and today—in relationship to slavery and to the City of New Orleans, in myth and reality. The tour visits significant Voodoo locations in and around the French Quarter, including an authentic altar. It costs $39; departure dates and times vary. The tour departs from 1012 N. Rampart St. Book at www.nosecrettours.com or call ℭ **504/517-5397.**

As for those vampire tours . . . sorry to burst your bubble, friends, but vampires are not real. Personally, we prefer our history with a bit of, well, history—but if tales of bloodsuckery and high drama are what you seek, the current reigning kings are at **French Quarter Phantoms** (p. 195). Costumes, fake blood, Dickensian delivery—the whole megillah (but not all the guides do it). Tours cost $25 ($22 when booked online); it's free for kids 7 and under, but do check ahead with tour guides to see if the tour is appropriate for your child's age and excitability. Tours leave from the Voodoo Lounge, 718 N. Rampart St., nightly at 6 and 8pm. A baby step down on the drama ladder, the 1½-hour New Orleans Vampire tour given by **Haunted History Tours** ★ (www.hauntedhistorytours.com; ✆ **504/861-2727**) departs nightly at 8:30pm from outside St. Louis Cathedral and costs $30 adults, $25 students and seniors, $20 ages 3 to 12, free for kids 2 and under. (Again, check ahead whether it's appropriate for your kid.) Haunted History also offers nighttime French Quarter ghost tours. Advance bookings only via the website.

Tip: Most of these tours usually go out with large groups. Try to stay near the front, so you can see and hear your guide—even the ones with the most booming voices have to regulate their delivery out of respect for French Quarter residents.

Food & Beverage Tours & Classes

Ain't no cuisine in the world like New Orleans cuisine. True dat. Consider taking this fact one tasty step further with a food and beverage tour or class.

Cooking class instructors, just like tour guides, can make or break the experience. **Destination Kitchen Food Tours** ★★ (www.destination-kitchen.com; ✆ **855/353-6634**) delivers a sprightly and cosmopolitan approach to epicurious Big Easy, showcasing culinary and cocktail offerings of the French Quarter, with or without a cooking experience. Commentary is offered in English, French, or Spanish, the three languages that New Orleans has spoken for centuries. Food and beverage tours range from $70 to $108. Some include transportation. History and music tours are also available.

Doctor Gumbo ★★★ (www.doctorgumbo.com; ✆ **504/473-4823**) offers three tours, including a 4-hour food and cocktail "gastronomic odyssey" to seven establishments, where you're pretty much guaranteed a fun, flavorful, and enormously filling experience. Reservations are required; tours cost from $75 to $140 per person.

Drink and Learn ★★★ (www.drinkandlearn.com; ✆ **504/578-8280**) is the aptly named company run by Elizabeth Pearce, noted cocktail impresario and the author of *Drink Dat New Orleans.* Pearce punctuates her walking tours with stops at cocktail-oriented sites, where participants partake of pre-poured smart beverages. Pearce's lively delivery, depth of knowledge, and visual aids transport guests through centuries of New Orleans' storied cocktail history. Daytime and nighttime Cocktail Tours meet at Vacherie Restaurant in the Hotel St. Marie (p. 73), 827 Toulouse St., and cost $60 per person (21 and over only). Book in advance; the small groups fill up fast.

NOLA Brewing Brewery Tour ★★ (3001 Tchoupitoulas St.; www.nolabrewing.com; ✆ **504/896-9996**) isn't a walking tour, but an actual tour through one of the largest and oldest local craft breweries in Louisiana. (For more on local breweries, see p. 229.) The 35-minute, brewmaster-led look behind the scenes is wildly popular (read: crowded) not only for the free samples, but also because it's informative. Kickass New York–style **Nola Pizza Co.** is on-site; those pies go down well with the taproom's brews. Plus, there's pinball and live music on weekends. The taproom is open Sunday to Thursday 11am to 9pm and Friday and Saturday 11am to 10pm; tours are led on Fridays and Saturdays from 2 to 3pm.

One expert mixologist. Up to 10 mixology neophytes. Four drinks. One hour (or thereabouts). Things move snappily along during **The Maison's Mixology Class ★★** (508 Frenchmen St.; www.maisonfrenchmen.com/mixology; ✆ **504/371-5543**), with an instructor doling out cocktail history and how-tos, prepping the next round, and fielding questions—all with aplomb (while occasionally shouting over the band playing downstairs). Perched on stools around the nightclub's small upstairs bar, you get to mix, stir, and schmooze. It's not meant as a drunk-fest, but simple logistics dictate that there will be buzzing. You'll leave with recipes, a few new friends, some new skills, and the aforementioned buzz. Class is in session Friday and Saturday at 5pm (book in advance through the website) and costs $50. Participants must be 21 or over.

Also see the **Confederacy of Cruisers Culinary Bike Tour** (below) and cooking classes at the Southern Food and Beverage Museum (p. 173).

Bicycle & Other Wheeled Tours

A bike tour is a terrific way to explore some lesser-seen parts of this flat city up close and in depth. Our suggested tours go at an outright leisurely pace, so you needn't be a serious rider, but bike familiarity and a healthy dose of pluck will help you handle potholes and traffic (including stretches along some busy avenues). Do opt-in to the optional helmet; bring sunscreen, a hat, rain poncho, and water (though most tours provide a small starter bottle) as conditions dictate. While a restroom stop is included, you'd be wise to take care of that before departure, too. For regular old bike rentals, see p. 296.

Confederacy of Cruisers (www.confederacyofcruisers.com; ✆ **504/400-5468**) offers a history and culture bike tour with an itinerary that hits parts of the Marigny, Bywater, 7th Ward, and Tremé on comfortable, well-maintained single-gear cruisers with baskets. The minimum two-person, maximum six-person, guide-led group pulls over at such diverse stops as the New Orleans Center for Creative Arts (NOCCA), St. Roch Cemetery (p. 180), and the *Plessy v. Ferguson* landmark (Homer Plessy Way at Royal St.), where guides offer up well-informed cultural and architectural insights. The 3-hour tours are $49 and depart twice daily. Its **culinary bike tour** takes different itineraries, but all go to killer, off-the-beaten-track eateries favored by locals. The "tastes" are copious, and the guides' laidback deliveries bely a serious depth of food knowledge (and history and architecture), which they impart between bites. It's $89 all-inclusive, and worth it. A **cocktail tour** is $10 more. (We're not sure riding these streets after four or five drinks is a great idea—then again, it's New Orleans; our great ideas are not everyone's great ideas.) Reservations by email are a must. Most tours depart from 634 Elysian Fields Ave.

Flambeaux Tours (www.flambeauxtours.com; ✆ **504/321-1505**) has thrice-daily bike tours ($50) of either the French Quarter, Marigny, and Tremé; the Garden District and Uptown; or Mid-City. They can customize your itinerary;

book ahead online. They also have weekend nighttime social rides on bikes tricked out with wheel lights—you'll get the looks (10 riders minimum, $350). Bikes are comfy and well-maintained (also available for rental), and if you can get on one of Eric's tours, he's from New Orleans and particularly good with the cultural quips.

Or, try **Get Up N Ride** (www.getupnride.com), with hip locals on organized social rides around town most Tuesday nights. Bring your own bike (with a light and lock), or for $25, rent one (with basket, cup holder, and wheel lights).

Corny it may seem, but a **horse-drawn carriage tour** of the Quarter or beyond has eternal romantic allure. The "horses" are actually mules (they handle the city heat and humidity better), often bedecked with ribbons, flowers, and even hats. Drivers seem to be in a fierce competition to win the "most entertaining" award. They share history and anecdotes (some of dubious authenticity) and can customize itineraries on request. Carriages wait on Decatur Street in front of Jackson Square from 8am to midnight (except in heavy rain). We like minority-owned, family-owned **Mid-City Carriages** (www.mid-citycarriages.com; ✆ 504/581-4415) or just show up in Jackson Square and look for the green carriages. Join a waiting carriage (you may be sharing with other tourists). French Quarter tours are $25 per person per ½ hour. Creole Neighborhood or Tremé tours run $50 for 1 hour. Private tours (up to four people) are $125 for 30 minutes.

We also like family-owned **Royal Carriages** (www.neworleanscarriages. com; ✆ 504/943-8820), in business for 80 years, making it the oldest sightseeing carriage company in the U.S. Look for the red umbrellas at the foot of Jackson Square to join a 1-hour tour, or book in advance online. There are French Quarter or ghost-themed 1-hour group tours for $60 per person or $40 for kids 5 to 12. Private carriages run about $300 for 1 hour, for up to four people. Call for custom tours and hotel pickups. (*Note:* Royal Carriages doesn't operate on Wed.)

ESPECIALLY FOR KIDS

Despite its reputation as a playground for grown-ups, the Big Easy is a terrific family destination, with oodles of only-in-New-Orleans activities to entertain them (and you). **Mardi Gras** (p. 50) and **Jazz Fest** (p. 61) are both doable and enjoyable with kids, as are many of the organized tours listed above. *Tip:* Those above spooking age love to tour the cemeteries (no touching!) and haunted places, but long walking tours of historic homes and landmarks may be best left to the adults.

The **French Quarter** in and of itself is cool for kids 6 and over. You can while away a pleasant morning on a Quarter walkabout, seeing the architecture and peeking into shops, checking out street performers, with a rest stop for powder-sugary beignets at **Café du Monde** (p. 148). If you have kids of museum-going age, the Mardi Gras exhibit at the **Presbytère** (p. 164) or the hurricane exhibit at the **Cabildo** (p. 161) will hold their attention for a while.

You can probably talk them into a riverfront walk along scenic Woldenberg Park in warm weather, ending at a great splash fountain in front of **Audubon Aquarium** (p. 156).

Even self-conscious tweens fall for a **carriage ride** around the Quarter (see "Bicycle & Other Wheeled Tours," above), and it works for all ages when it's hot and nap time is closing in—it might even rock the little ones to sleep. The **Canal Street Ferry** (p. 297) crosses the Mississippi River and ends just pre-boredom (and makes a great intro to reading *Huckleberry Finn* together). Add a clackety-clacking **streetcar ride** (p. 296), and you've hit the trifecta of fascinating transportation options.

If it's just a matter of needing to run, jump, swing, and blow off some energy, head for **Cabrini Playground** (1219 Dauphine St.) in the residential northeast corner of the French Quarter at Barracks and Dauphine streets. (It's also a dog park, so plenty of pooches to pet.) We also love the **New Orleans Boulder Lounge** in the Faubourg Marigny at 2360 St. Claude Ave. (www.climbnobl.com) for getting kids climbing on a bad-weather day, followed by lunch at the nearby **St. Roch Market** (p. 116).

A number of the city's top attractions are obviously family-friendly, including the wonderful **Audubon Aquarium of the Americas** (p. 156). The St. Charles Streetcar will deliver you to **Audubon Park** (p. 182), home to three great playgrounds. Our top pick is the **Walnut Street Playground** (built by Drew Brees, the Saints' recently retired quarterback, who has occasionally been spotted there with his own kids)—it's inclusive, offering features (including two ziplines) to kids of all abilities, plus plenty of trees to climb and turtles to look at just across the jogging path. And right there at the park, the highly regarded **Audubon Zoo** (p. 182), complete with a seasonal splash park for the pool-deprived, is both lovely and a great diversion.

For more animal action, a **swamp tour** (p. 196) is a sure-fire winner. While you're not guaranteed to see gators, it's a pretty good bet (in warm months), and even so, hey, you're on a boat in a swamp.

Older kids may get a kick out of **Escape My Room** ★ at its new location (1152 Camp St.; www.escapemyroom.com; ✆ 504/475-7580), a New Orleans version of the popular escape room craze. Participants are "locked" in one of four heavily decorated rooms (our fave is the tough Inventor's Attic) themed around an actual local family. They must answer clues to solve a mystery and thereby "escape." It works best when clue hunters' backgrounds and ages are diverse ($34–$53 per person, advance reservations required, two people minimum; small groups are more expensive per person). It's not for young kids, and those ages 16 and under must be accompanied by adults. Bring your reading glasses!

Kidding Around in City Park

And then there is the wonder that is **City Park.** We've already mentioned some of its all-ages features (p. 183), and with the stunning **Louisiana Children's Museum** located there (see details below), you could just make it your base. In December, more than a million holiday lights turn the City Park

A Kid-Oriented Tour

Run by a former schoolteacher (and excellent kid-wrangler), **French Quarter Kids Tour** ★★ (www.french quartourkids.com; ⓒ **504/975-5355**) offers six different 1½-hour walking tours that cover all age groups, including pirate treasure hunts, spooky tours, and music tours. The company's founder conducts the tours in costume and keeps the enthusiasm level high; her spiels make it all relatable, bringing attention to what life was like for kids in the olden days. History is definitely conveyed as sites are explored, but the lessons use props (which she totes around in a colorful wheeled cart), storytelling, play-acting, and enough gory details to hold most kids' focus. Emphasis on "most." Ask about seasonally themed tours. Tours cost $24 to $27 per person (there must be at least one adult). Tour times vary, but are generally between 9:30am and 5pm daily. Reservations are required.

landscape into fairy-tale scenery for the **Celebration in the Oaks** (p. 34). Here are just a few the park's offerings for kids and parents to love:

Big Lake Boating and Biking ★★ RECREATION   Big Lake in City Park is a pretty spot for a boat ride, and the kids can scour the shoreline for turtles. Canoes, kayaks, and glam **swan boats** (LED-lit at night) can be rented from **Wheel Fun,** which also rents **bicycles, tandems,** and **surreys** for use inside City Park. All that pedaling action can be a workout, which means you can justify a visit to nearby **Angelo Brocato's** ice-cream parlor afterward (p. 148). Life jackets (provided) required. Check website and www.groupon. com for discounts.

Wheel Fun Rentals, Big Lake Trail. www.wheelfunrentals.com. ⓒ **504/252-5655.** Swan boat $30/hr. adults, $6 kids (holds 4–5); kayak $16–$23/hr.; surrey $28–$38/hr.; bikes and tandems $9–$21/hr. (in-park use only). Check website for various rental hours.

Carousel Gardens and Children's Storyland ★★★ PLAYGROUND
The under-7 set will be delighted with this recently updated playground (rated one of the country's 10 best by *Child* magazine), its charming decor inspired by well-known children's stories and rhymes. It offers plenty of characters to slide down and climb on and just generally get the juvenile ya-yas out. Kids and adults will enjoy the carousel, Ferris wheels, bumper cars, miniature train, Tilt-a-Whirl, ladybug-shaped roller coaster, and other rides at the **Carousel Gardens** amusement park, just next door. Delighting local families since 1906, the gorgeous carousel (or "da flying horses," as real locals call it) is one of only 100 all-wood merry-go-rounds in the country, and the only one in the state.

Victory Ave. www.neworleanscitypark.com/in-the-park/carousel-gardens. ⓒ **504/483-9402.** Storyland admission $6; Storyland and Carousel Gardens unlimited rides $25. Free for kids under 36" tall. Chaperones $15; seniors $13. Storyland Wed–Thurs and Sun 10am–4:30pm; Fri–Sat 10am–3:30pm. Carousel Gardens mid-Mar to mid-Nov Sat–Sun 11am–6pm, longer hours June–July.

City Putt Miniature Golf ★★ MINIGOLF   We love the design of these two 18-hole miniature golf courses: On one course, each hole is designed around a New Orleans neighborhood, with iconic statues and signage and stuff; the other course keys off of statewide themes (learning is fun!).

33 Dreyfous Dr., across from Storyland. www.neworleanscitypark.com/in-the-park/city-putt. ✆ **504/483-9385.** $10 adults; $8 children 4–12; free for kids 3 and under. Wed–Fri 3–10pm; Sat–Sun 10am–10pm; last rental 1 hr. before closing. Hours may vary during Celebration in the Oaks.

Louisiana Children's Museum ★★ MUSEUM   This gleaming new museum is really a playground in disguise. Set amidst 8 gorgeous acres of nature, it subtly "teaches" sustainability and stewardship of our world and its waters in wonderful, hands-on ways. Geared toward kids 8 and under and their parents and caregivers (but fine for older kids, too), it's a dazzling gem that makes a visit to already-jam-packed City Park de rigueur for families. A few outdoor and lobby exhibits are free; beyond that, five interactive themed galleries focus on "play and learning in equal parts." "Follow That Food" goes from fields and waters to ports, markets, and tables; "Make Your Mark" immerses young'uns in the fun of New Orleans' music, art, and architecture. Other highlights include a kid-powered barge pedaled across a lake to an island made of recycled plastic; a "make-your-own-music" garden; and "All About Bubbles," whose perspective is from inside a bubble. While the adults are learning about learning (and gathering ample take-home ideas), kids have plenty of space to roam, crawl, explore, and play, including the darling "kindows" (kid-size pop-out window cubbies). The excellent, eco-friendly on-site **Acorn Café** (a Brennan's restaurant) satisfies all bellies.

15 Henry Thomas Drive. www.lcm.org. ✆ **504/523-1357.** $16 adults and kids 1 and up; seniors, active military $13. Wed–Sat 9:30am–4:30pm; Sun 11:30am–4:30pm. Admission by timed-entry tickets, available online.

SPECTATOR SPORTS

Big Easy Roller Derby ★ SPORTS   Okay, it's a total goof, but a hoot of a goof. By definition, roller derby is going to be a bit wild (though the athleticism can't be denied). Mix in New Orleans, and the resulting outcome is pure wackiness. The all-gender Big Easy league plays it up for all it's worth, and the crowd action is equally rowdy. More of a hipster scene but with a smattering of families, it's all in fun, and worth the modest ticket price just to check out the cheerleaders, halftime entertainment, outfits, and food trucks. Season runs March through August.

The BERD Warehouse, 3632 Desire Pkwy. www.facebook.com/bigeasyrollergirls. No phone. Suggested donation $10 at door; kids $5; free for ages 6 and under.

New Orleans Pelicans ★★ SPORTS   What to say about the NBA Pelicans? They're up, they're down, they're up again. Who knows where they'll be next? During a glorious stretch when Chris Paul and Anthony Davis led the team to playoffs and higher heights, tickets were pricey and hard to acquire;

GET THE KIDS jazzed

In such a musical town, there aren't as many music options for the younger set as we'd like. Blame it on booze—most music venues serve alcohol and are legally prohibited from allowing anyone younger than 21 to enter. Breweries (p. 229) are generally family-friendly, though, and some offer live music and arcade or lawn games. Otherwise, the street performers along **Royal Street** and in **Jackson Square** work well (as do the city's many festivals), and fear not, we've got a few other interesting ideas.

o **Preservation Hall** The historic, inimitable traditional jazz venue is open to all ages. The earliest show starts at 5pm nightly; get there early so the young ones can sit far enough in front to see (if they're really young, sit by the door in case a quick exit is required). See p. 216.

o **Frenchmen Street Clubs** Yes—you can make the Frenchmen Street scene with kids in tow. The **Maison** (p. 216) and **Three Muses** (p. 220) allow kids for the early shows,

which usually start around 4 or 5pm (parents must be in attendance). Grab a table, order snacks, and let the little ones shake their miniature groove thangs. They may be asked to leave when the tables break down and the drinking crowd moves in, around 9 or 10pm.

o **Music Box Village** Kids (like adults) may or may not "get" the performances here—the eclectic music made in this "sonic village" isn't exactly mainstream. But curious minds of all ages will find the musical-instrument structures fascinating. During the hands-on public hours, visitors can explore them and create their own eclectic tunes. It's a great way to spend a few hours outdoors. See p. 233.

o **New Orleans Jazz Museum at the Old U.S. Mint** This museum has some form of free music nearly every day, and all ages are welcome. See p. 164.

they're generally more affordable now (as in, $6 plus tax) and easily procured. These days, much depends on phenom Zion Williamson—the number one draft pick in 2019—who's been on and off the court since his 2021 foot surgery and 2023 hamstring injury. (When he's on, though, boy is he on.) Nevertheless, the Pelicans put on a fun b-ball show, and it's worth the price of admission to see the celebrity mascots, which *USA Today* decreed the two creepiest mascots in sports: Pierre the Pelican, who was revamped after scaring too many kids, and King Cake Baby, whom tourists find terrifying and locals find hilariously, perfectly, weirdly New Orleans.

Smoothie King Center, 1501 Girod St. www.nba.com/pelicans. © **504/525-4667.** Tickets start at $6 and go way up.

New Orleans Saints ★★★ SPORTS Who dat won the Super Bowl? The Saints' incredible Super Bowl XLIV victory in 2010 was the culmination of the city's 43-year collective dream (to say nothing of the end of 43 years of frustration), in which the beloved 'Aints finally won the big one, becoming a metaphor for the city's post-Katrina comeback and a source of frenzied pride. A scandal here and there hasn't come close to dampening the enthusiasm for this team (2019's missed call actually increased it). Whether you're a football fan or not, try to get yourself inside the Superdome (p. 180) for a Saints game—there's really nothing like it. Your best bet is the **NFL Ticket Exchange** (www.ticketexchangebyticketmaster.com). Otherwise, the pregame party at **Champions Square** outside the Superdome is an excellent place to start your game day. Another option: Watching the game in a local bar is a cheap cultural experience—not only will you get to know the city, you'll often find free food.

Caesars Superdome, 1500 block of Poydras St. Saints home office: 5800 Airline Dr., Metairie. www.neworleanssaints.com. ℂ 504/733-0255. Ticket info: ℂ 504/731-1700. Tickets around $45–astronomical, depending on the game.

NOLA Gold Rugby ★★ SPORTS   When Major League Rugby came to the United States in 2018, NOLA Gold was one of the inaugural teams. The Gold plays in a 10,000-seat stadium in Metairie where even cheap-seat views are surprisingly good. Games are rowdy, bone-bashing, and boozy, but also family-oriented and affordable—and at 80 minutes, they whip by. We appreciate the commentator who explains the game in real time so we're not entirely lost. There's a customized theme for each home game tailored to the times (think Jazz Fest theme, St. Patrick's Day theme, and so on, and before each home game, kids aged 6–12 can sign up online to practice with players on the field).

The Gold Mine at the Shrine on Airline, 6000 Airline Dr., Metairie. www.nolagoldrugby.com. ℂ 504/507-8429. Tickets $18 and up; season pass $135.

BET YOU CAN FIND places to gamble

The history of the **Fair Grounds Race Course** (1751 Gentilly Blvd.; www.fairgroundsracecourse.com; ℂ 504/944-5515) is *deep*. Founded in 1872, it's the third oldest in the country; General Custer ran his horses here, and it was, until recently, the longest homestretch in North America. The horse-racing season kicks off on Thanksgiving, a tradition for many local families who don their finest attire and silliest hats for the occasion. Horses run through March; simulcasts and OTB continue on and a large slots casino is open year-round (Mon–Sat 9am–midnight, Sun 10am–midnight).

Bordering the French Quarter, **Harrah's Casino** (which will become **Caesar's Casino** in 2024), 229 Poydras St., (www.caesars.com/harrahs-new-orleans; ℂ 504/533-6000), is quite like a Vegas casino: 115,000 sq. ft., 1,700 slot machines, more than 100 tables, sports betting, a steakhouse restaurant, a dedicated poker room, a food hall with eateries helmed by celeb chefs (including local fave Nina Compton), and the Masquerade Lounge. When the $325-million renovation is complete, the transformation to Caesars will even include a Nobu hotel (a "hotel inside a hotel") and restaurant. *Tip:* The voluminous buffet can satisfy the most serious munchies for not-so-serious cash.

A classic riverboat-style casino, **Treasure Chest Casino** (www.treasurechest.com; ℂ 504/443-8000) is docked on Lake Pontchartrain not far from the New Orleans airport.

Slot machines can be found in every imaginable locale in the city, from bars to laundromats, separated (by law) from the main room by a door or curtain.

NEW ORLEANS NIGHTLIFE

By Tami Fairweather

New Orleans works her wily charms most effectively after dark, when the cocktail slingers and jazz bands ply their magic. It is impossible to imagine this city without its non-stop melodious soundtrack. After all, this is the town where a loved one's remains are escorted to the grave with a brass band and mourners dance back from the cemetery in celebration of a life well lived—and everyone's invited to join in. Here, some of the world's greatest musicians—no exaggeration—can be seen and heard with relative ease in remarkably intimate surroundings. And when the clubs get too full, no matter: The crowd spills into the street, where the talking, drinking, and dancing continue.

In this chapter, we'll help you wend your way through all the theater, club, and bar awesomeness. (Here, that's "Daylife" as well as "Nightlife.") But keep in mind that tomorrow beckons, with more of the city's enchantments to explore. First, a few things to know:

- **Club-hopping is easy.** The city is compact, so most clubs are within easy walking or a car ride distance from your hotel or dinner locale. On Bourbon and Frenchmen streets they're closely clustered so you can hop from one to another.
- **Showtimes vary.** Posted start times range from strict to strictly a suggestion (and sometimes indicate door times, not showtimes). Shows often start later than promised—except when they start on time (more likely in a seated venue). We'd say call first, but phone answering is rare; better to check on social.
- **Show proof.** IDs are requested everywhere. A few places allow kids to early shows when accompanied by a parent (p. 206). Mostly (definitely, if there's no food), it's 21+ and expect to be carded. Even you, grandpa. It's da law.
- **Cover charges vary widely.** During big events and for big acts, they can be much higher than cited here. Crowd sizes also vary accordingly.

- **Early shows rock.** Shows starting from 2ish to 7pm often are no- or low-cover, have mellower music, and are a great way to avoid the crowds and the crazy. Some allow kids.
- **No cover doesn't mean free.** It means buy beverages (boozy or not) and tip the band generously, with love. And/or buy their vinyl, CDs, merch, whatever.
- **Music is everywhere.** A blurry line separates "clubs" from bars, restaurants, hotel lounges, streets, parks, front porches, and stoops. All can showcase excellent music, so don't overlook them.
- **Smoking is nowhere.** All clubs, bars, and restaurants are nonsmoking. Take it to the streets, if you must (or courtyards, where allowed).
- **Drinking is optional.** Despite its preeminent reputation, non-drinkers can and do enjoy New Orleans. Fun is fun. You be you.
- **Roll with it.** You can legally stroll the streets with alcohol as long as it's in a plastic "go cup." (Sturdier logoed cups reduce waste and make nice souvenirs.)
- **But easy does it.** The ubiquitous "Be Nice or Leave" signs are sincere. Niceness gets you far, but keep your cool, and your wits—especially as you move between places (and never, *ever* pee on the street).
- **What's going on.** Check **Offbeat.com** and **WWOZ.org/livewire** for performance listings. You can also stream or tune in to WWOZ (90.7 FM): Live, local music lineups are announced at the top of every odd hour.

THE RHYTHMS OF NEW ORLEANS

New Orleans R&B legend Ernie K-Doe was once quoted as saying, "I'm not sure, but I think all music came from New Orleans." That may seem like hyperbole, but ask any musician from here—or who followed the spiritual call to come—and they'll say they don't think, they *know,* because New Orleans *is* music; distinctly considered the birthplace of what we know as American music. The jazz of **Jelly Roll Morton, Kid Ory, Charles "Buddy" Bolden,** and **Louis Armstrong,** yes. But also, the pioneering rock 'n' roll rhythms of **Fats Domino** and the piano blues of **Professor Longhair.** Even modern hip hop is derived from funk, which is derived from the percussive tambourines and call-and-response-chants of New Orleans' own Black Masking Indians (p. 55), whose Afro-Caribbean rhythms descended from the symbiotic connection of Indigenous Houma and Choctaw people joining with enslaved Africans in the birthplace of it all: **Congo Square** (p. 21). This was where—under Spanish colonial rule in the early 19th century—the enslaved were allowed to gather on Sunday afternoons. Here, they danced and drummed—a sacred practice that continued (and was reinforced by post–Haitian revolution immigrants) after the Louisiana Purchase in 1803. Eventually, the gatherings were banned when harsher American slavery practices prevailed; but the sublime, new, and distinctive music that came to define the city itself had already taken root. No less an authority than **Wynton Marsalis—**Grammy award–winning jazz trumpeter, composer, and member of New Orleans music family royalty—put it aptly, saying, "Every strand of American music comes directly from Congo Square."

Brass Bands

In the 19th century, military bands and European marching bands brought brass instruments into popular American culture. In New Orleans, the syncopated African rhythms jumped from drum to horn. Toward the end of the century, social aid and pleasure clubs and benevolent societies were popping up in the Black neighborhoods, and the mobility of brass bands were a natural fit for occasions from baptisms to funeral processions. When jazz formed, around the turn of the 20th century in New Orleans' **Storyville** red-light district (since replaced by Armstrong Park and the Iberville housing development in present-day Tremé, p. 22), brass bands began incorporating jazz style, continuing the evolution.

Today, there's way more to New Orleans brass bands than "When the Saints Go Marching In." Classics like the **Tremé Brass Band** and members of the original **Olympia Brass Band** (in their current incarnations) still hold court, but since a revival in the late 1970s, bands started mixing things up to incorporate popular music of the day. Now, brass is imbued with funk, R&B, reggae, hip hop, and bounce; appearances on the HBO TV show *Tremé* have engendered a new crop of fans.

Today this horn-heavy, booty-moving, New-Orleans-born-and-bred style packs the clubs and the streets. Try to catch the sounds of Louis Armstrong–inspired and reigning king **Kermit Ruffins and his Barbecue Swingers; Hot 8;** or the **Stooges. Dirty Dozen Brass Band** and **Rebirth Brass Band** (their song "Do Whatcha Wanna" is a citywide mantra) are the nouveau classics. Newer-ish arrivals like the blazing **TBC Brass Band,** raging **Brass-A-Holics,** or the pumping street-corner gods **Soul Brass** are sure bets. Did we mention the all-women **Original Pinettes?** Yeah, see them. Also, the **Soul Rebels, New Breed, Young Fellaz, Kings of Brass, Sporty's, Dat Truth,** and the **New Orleans Nightcrawlers.** In short, if you depart without catching a brass band, there must have been something blocking your front door.

Cradle of Jazz

At the turn of the 19th century one of the most popular dance bands in the Black "Backatown" neighborhood of South Rampart and Perdio streets was led by cornet player **Charles "Buddy" Bolden.** "King" Bolden's loud, foot-stomping, Baptist-church- and blues-infused music—totally improvised—had the power to captivate an entire room of dancers into the wee hours of the morning. It was a musical sensation that came to be known as jazz, and Bolden was its king, even after his tragically early death preceded by severe mental illness.

The Storyville red-light district's heyday overlapped Backatown's, and the music lineup at the better brothels included live piano players in the parlor—the immortal ragtime pianist **Jelly Roll Morton** most famous among them, and the first to capture improvisational jazz with arrangement and composition.

By the 1920s, as Storyville was folding, its emerging players took the swinging New Orleans jazz sounds on the road: Morton and **Kid Ory** to California; **King Oliver** and his protégé **Louis Armstrong** to Chicago; **Papa Jack and his Original Dixieland Jazz Band** to New York. Their shows drew hordes and their records sold wildly. After World War II, **Sidney Bechet** and horn set up shop in France, and jazz consumed the continent.

New Orleans is still producing jazz greats and pushing the form forward. Often, it's a family affair. Start with the Marsalis family: the late patriarch **Ellis Marsalis,** father to jazz-playing sons **Branford, Jason, Delfeayo,** and Pulitzer Prize–winning trumpeter **Wynton,** and mentor to countless others including trumpeter, pianist, professor, and film-scorer **Terence Blanchard,** who grew up with them. Multi-award-winning pianist, songwriter, and composer **Jon Batiste** comes from a far-reaching line of local musicians including **Harold, Alvin, Milton, "Uncle" Lionel, Russell Jr.**, and his own father **Michael,** who co-founded the **Batiste Brothers Band** with six of his brothers. "Stretch Music" innovator **Chief Xian aTunde Adjuah (Christian Scott)** is the grandson of **Big Chief Donald Harrison, Sr.,** and nephew of **Donald Harrison, Jr.** (both sax men). Brothers **Troy "Trombone Shorty" Andrews** and **James "Satchmo of the Ghetto" Andrews** and their cousin **Glen David Andrews** blow their horns both at home and to ever-adventurous distances.

Meanwhile, the nouveau traditional jazz movement is mad hot. On any given night in any given club, players from their 20s to their 70s share the bandstand, covering **Jelly Roll, Satchmo (Louis Armstrong),** and **Louis Prima** (also a New Orleanian)—or playing originals straight outta their eras. The **New Orleans Cottonmouth Kings, Smokin' Time Jazz Band, Miss Sophie Lee, Tuba Skinny, Meschiya Lake and the Little Big Horns,** the **Palmetto Bug Stompers,** and **Hot Club of New Orleans** start the long list; the clarinet queen **Doreen Ketchens** tops it (find her on the corner of Royal and St. Peter streets in the Quarter, and tip well).

Cellist **Helen Gillet,** bassist **James Singleton,** percussion madman **Mike Dillon,** and multi-instrumentalist **Aurora Nealand** are among those advancing into newer reaches of the form.

Rhythm & Blues (& Funk & Soul & Bounce, Oh My)

The Delta isn't far, and the blues' gospel and Afro-Caribbean bloodlines took deep root in the Crescent City in the 1950s when rock 'n' roll pioneers **Fats Domino** and his great producer-collaborator **Dave Bartholomew** fused those elements into the seminal hits "Blueberry Hill" and "Walkin' to New Orleans."

Simultaneously, **Professor Longhair** and **"Champion" Jack Dupree** were developing trailblazing piano sounds, contrasting mournful woe with party-time spirit. More piano geniuses followed, from eye-patched eccentric **James**

Booker and his protégé **Harry Connick, Jr.,** to the recently-departed **Dr. John** and love-and-life-affirming golden man **Jon Batiste;** while **Jon Cleary, Josh Paxton, Tom McDermott, Joe Krown, David Torkanowsky,** and many more carry on the city's unparalleled piano tradition around town and the world.

The soulful R&B end of the rock 'n' roll spectrum is well represented by late greats like **Snooks Eaglin, Ernie K-Doe, Jessie Hill,** and **Earl King.** **"Deacon" John Moore** has been on the scene since the 1950s, as a guitarist, banjo player, singer, and bandleader par excellence, and still rips it up (and oh,

CAN'T-MISS NEW ORLEANS MUSICAL
experiences

o A show at **Preservation Hall** (p. 216), where the soul of traditional jazz permeates the hallowed walls. benches, and floorboards. Alternatively, any show featuring a member of Preservation Hall's 60+ musician collective (like **Wendell Brunious, Charlie Gabriel,** or **Leroy Jones**).

o **Kermit Ruffins,** anywhere he and his rowdy trumpet show up: Try Blue Nile (p. 218), Bullet's (p. 220), or his own clubs, the iconic Tremé Mother-in-Law Lounge (p. 221) or Kermit's 9th Ward Juke Joint (www.instagram.com/ruffinsbbq).

o Letting the groove of a brass band sweep you up, like the **TBC Brass Band** at the Maple Leaf (p. 221) on a Tuesday; the **Soul Rebels** on a Thursday at Les Bon Temps Roulé (4801 Magazine St.; www.lbtrnola.com); or **Rebirth Brass Band** at the Rabbit Hole (p. 222)—or anywhere, any day.

o Shedding a tear at the early set of the sublime **John Boutté** at d.b.a. (p. 219).

o Taking a trip to iconic **Tipitina's** (p. 223) and catching a show—even better if it's someone huge (give the 'Fess Head statue an extra rub for your good fortune).

o Piano wizards **Tom McDermott, Josh Paxton,** or **Jon Cleary,** solo or not.

o Trombonist **"Big Sam" Williams.** He grooves and moves, and so will you.

o A full show in the city's premier (and classic) jazz room, **Snug Harbor** (p. 219).

o **DJ Soul Sister,** queen of the rare groove vinyl, who jams the floor monthly at the Hi-Ho Lounge (p. 219) or her other special events (like New Year's Eve or her Prince tribute).

o **The Wild Magnolias.** Or **Cha Wa.** Or any Mardi Gras Indian band (or practice session to go even deeper, if you find it at a local bar). You will be changed.

o Getting serenaded by the Songbird of New Orleans **Robin Barnes** at the divine Peacock Room in Hotel Fontenot (p. 80) or the Polo Club in the Windsor Court (p. 77).

o The rare treasure that is **Little Freddie King** at B.J.'s Lounge (p. 227).

o The Texas-Mexico-Caribbean-inspired roots rock of the **Iguanas** (consisting of musicians who play with everyone in town).

o Breakout national stars **Trombone Shorty, The Revivalists, Tank & the Bangas, Galactic, Big Freedia, PJ Morton,** or **Jon Batiste** if they happen to be back in town on their home turf (Jazz Fest or Christmastime are good bets).

the stories he tells). Velvet-voiced **Irma Thomas** (The "Soul Queen of New Orleans") is not to be missed if you get the chance; or get blessed by a soul-stirring serenade from **Erica Falls, Robin Barnes,** or **Joy Clark.**

Current keepers of the blues flame include axe men **Tab Benoit, Anders Osborne, Sonny Landreth,** and harpist nonpareil **Johnny Sansone.** (We lost the great **Walter "Wolfman" Washington** in late 2022, but we do believe our beloved Delta bluesman **Little Freddie King** will live forever as long as he can play his guitar.)

New Orleans–style "swamp-funk" added deep grooves, synths, and guitars to second-line music, epitomized by **The Wild Tchoupitoulas** 1976 album that brought Mardi Gras Indian songs and chants from the streets in the studio. Produced by **Allen Toussaint,** the album was the first recording of the **Neville Brothers,** and their funky offshoot the **Meters** are going strong in various guises, **George Porter, Jr.,** and **Cyril Neville** chief among them. Modern exemplars of the Mardi Gras Indian funk band sound, like **Cha Wah** and **Flagboy Giz,** have brought jam and hip hop into the mix. Other regal funksters include **Galactic, Dumpstaphunk,** and **Lettuce.**

Bounce is New Orleans' own genre of hip hop, played over a hyper-fast beat, and **Big Freedia** the reigning booty-twerking "Queen Diva." Producer **DJ Mannie Fresh** is the godfather, producing almost all the genre-defining records under the beleaguered Cash Money Records label (founded in 1991) including **Lil Wayne** and **Juvenile** (props for *"Back That Azz Up"*). The "King of Bounce" house-party master **DJ Jubilee** committed the first use of the word "twerk" to a record, while **Cheeky Blakk** and **Mia X** kicked the all-male recording studio doors down. You can still catch all of them performing from time to time, or look for their contemporaries **Choppa** and **HaSizzle the Voice.**

The genre-bending New Orleans music mash-up continues with modern-day breakouts **Tank and the Bangas, PJ Morton, The Revivalists, Hurray for the Riff Raff, Boyfriend,** and **Leyla McCalla.**

Music aficionados aside, it can be hard to keep up with all the names dropped around here (and with such reverence that you question yourself, "Should I know who that is?"). Part of the magic is following along and finding out on your own, which is exceedingly easy to do with so much to choose from. (But if you clap along, just make sure to do it on the 2 and the 4, 'cause that's the beat, baby.)

MUSIC CLUBS

Unless otherwise noted in the listings below, clubs are open 7 days a week.

The French Quarter

The Famous Door ★ Open since 1934, it's the oldest music venue on Bourbon Street, and many luminaries have played here (including a 13-year-old Harry Connick, Jr.). Great historic value, cheap drinks, loud but super-solid cover bands. Drunken dancing might happen. 339 Bourbon St. No phone. No cover.

New Orleans Nightlife

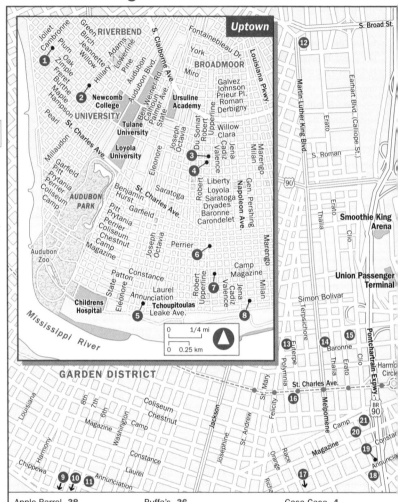

Apple Barrel **38**	Buffa's **36**	Gasa Gasa **4**
Avenue Pub **16**	Bullet's Sports Bar **34**	Hi-Ho Lounge **43**
Bakery Bar **19**	Café Negril **37**	Howlin' Wolf **23**
Bar Marilou **27**	Chickie Wah-Wah **31**	Igor's Checkpoint Charlie's **4**
Bar Redux **44**	Courtyard Brewery **21**	Kajun's Pub **43**
Barrel Proof **20**	Cure **3**	Kermit's Tremé
Bayou Beer Garden **31**	d.b.a **37**	Mother-in-Law Lounge **35**
Bayou Wine Garden **31**	Dos Jefes Uptown Cigar	Kingpin **6**
B.J.'s Lounge **44**	Bar **5**	Le Bon Temps Roulé **7**
Blue Nile **39**	Double Dealer **30**	Manning's **25**
Brieux Carre **41**	The Dream House Lounge **14**	Maple Leaf Bar **1**
The Broadside **32**	Faubourg Brewery **43**	Miel Brewery **9**

ulate's **24**
OLA Brewing Taproom **10**
arleaux Beer Lab **44**
ete's Out in the Cold **11**
he Rabbit Hole **15**
aturn Bar **44**
azerac Bar at the Roosevelt **29**
iberia **43**
nake & Jake's
   Christmas Club Lounge **2**
nug Harbor Jazz Bistro **37**
he Spotted Cat Music Club **38**

The Tell Me Bar **18**
Three Muses **39**
Ticki Tock **42**
Tiptina's **8**
Urban South **17**
Vaughan's **44**
Zony Mash **12**

Gay Nightlife

AllWays Lounge &
   Cabaret **43**
Country Club **44**

**Performing Arts, Theaters &
Concert Halls**
Ashé Cultural Arts Center **13**
Café Istanbul **43**
Civic Theater **28**
Contemporary Arts Center **22**
The Fillmore **26**
Mahalia Jackson Theater
   for the Performing Arts **33**
Marigny Opera House **44**
Music Box Village **44**
Orpheum **30**

Fritzel's European Jazz Pub ★★ From the open street front, this 1831 building looks sketchy, overlookable even. The pushy door folk will aggressively attempt to hustle you to a seat at the cramped picnic tables and rush you to order a drink. Let them: Some of the best traditional jazz is played on the teensy stage here, and the quasi-hofbrau atmosphere breeds community. Music starts midday; good kids and cool cats can come. 733 Bourbon St. www. fritzelsjazz.com. ✆ **504/586-4800.** No cover; 1-drink minimum per set.

House of Blues ★ You can find this chain club elsewhere and you can find authentic (vs. ersatz) folk-art-laden roadhouses within a few miles (hello, Tipitina's). The mainstage no longer has its former booking muscle, but an occasional name comes through and burlesque nights are fun. These days we're more apt to go for a midsize show upstairs in the inviting **Parish Room,** a DJ set in the velvet-and-leather **Foundation Room,** or some free music outdoors in the **Voodoo courtyard.** 225 Decatur St. www.houseofblues.com/ neworleans. ✆ **504/310-4999.** Cover varies.

The Jazz Playhouse ★★ This swank, draperied room in the Royal Sonesta Hotel is a go-to spot for established and on-the-rise local jazz and funk artists (Big Sam, Shannon Powell, Luther Kent, and Brass-a-Holics are sure things). Trixie Minx, queen of the NOLA burlesque scene, holds court Fridays. The well-prepared drinks aren't inexpensive, and service can be a bit snooty; seating (sometimes club-style at small tables, sometimes theater-style) can get crammed at popular shows. But we're still in the "Yes" column for solid talent, good sound, and French Quarter convenience. 300 Bourbon St. in Royal Sonesta Hotel. www.sonesta.com/jazzplayhouse. ✆ **504/553-2299.** Cover $25 and up.

Maison Bourbon ★★ Despite its location and the DEDICATED TO THE PRESERVATION OF JAZZ sign (a solid attempt to confuse tourists into thinking it's Preservation Hall), Maison Bourbon isn't a tourist trap. The music is authentic, often superb Dixieland and traditional jazz, and the brick-lined room is a respite from the mayhem outside. 641 Bourbon St. www.maisonbourbon. com. ✆ **504/522-8818.** No cover; 1-drink minimum per set.

Palm Court Jazz Cafe ★★ This white-linened and mosaic-tiled dinner club is a reliable, mature, and comfortable venue for top-notch classic and traditional jazz Wednesday through Sunday. Table seating (make reservations) with a small back bar for non-diners. 1204 Decatur St. www.palmcourtjazzcafe.com. ✆ **504/525-0200.** Wed–Sun 7–11pm. Cover $10 and up; entrees $25–$43.

Preservation Hall ★★★ The original, timeworn building lends just the right air of consecration to the absolute essential spot for traditional jazz fans and, well, everyone (Robert Plant, Mos Def, and Taylor Swift have sat in with the band here). With simple bench seats and no air-conditioning, drinks, or bathrooms (you are warned), the awesomeness lies in the superb musicianship in such a hallowed, preserved, and intimate space. And awesome it is, truly. There are multiple shows nightly starting at 5pm, plus weekend matinees;

French Quarter Nightlife

American Sports Saloon **36**

Aunt Tiki's **34**

Bar Tonique **25**

Cane & Table **33**

Carousel Bar at the Monteleone Hotel **8**

Crescent City Brewhouse **12**

The Dungeon **16**

Effervescence **26**

Erin Rose **3**

The Famous Door **4**

French 75 Bar at Arnaud's **5**

Fritzel's European Jazz Pub **22**

House of Blues **9**

The Jazz Playhouse **6**

Jewel of the South **2**

Kerry Irish Pub **10**

Lafitte's Blacksmith Shop **28**

Latitude 29 **11**

Maison Bourbon **18**

Manolito **30**

Molly's at the Market **32**

MRB Bar & Kitchen **31**

Napoleon House **13**

Palm Court Jazz Cafe **35**

Pat O'Brien's **20**

Patrick's Bar Vin **7**

Peychaud's **17**

Preservation Hall **19**

Toulouse Theatre **14**

Gay Nightlife

The Bourbon Pub & Parade Disco **23**

Café Lafitte in Exile **27**

Golden Lantern **29**

Good Friends Bar & Queens Head Pub **21**

Oz **24**

Performing Arts, Theaters & Cconcert Halls

Le Petit Théâtre **15**

Saenger Theatre **1**

each lasts 45 minutes. All seats are sold in advance: general admission standing or seated; first row bench costs extra. Purchase early—shows often sell out, though a lucky few might get in at the door. 726 St. Peter St. www.preservationhall. com. ✆ **504/522-2841.** Cover $25 (standing); $40 (bench); $50 (first row). Reserve in advance.

Toulouse Theatre ★★ What was once the game-changing rock club One Eyed Jacks, and the storied Shim Sham Club before that, was originally the Toulouse Theatre. One of the city's most important live performance venues has come full circle, renovated and reborn thanks to a team of culture keepers and talent bookers who saved it from a COVID-induced demise. The vintage boudoir wallpaper has been restored and the sound system (and sightlines) upgraded to host up-and-coming nationally touring rock, jazz, and hip-hop acts; local burlesque; and occasional big-name surprise shows in a space cool and intimate enough to earn you "I saw them one time in New Orleans" bragging rights. *Tip:* The bright bordello-chic lobby bar is open outside of show hours starting at noon most days, with craft cocktails at dive bar prices. 615 Toulouse St. toulousetheatre.com. ✆ **504/571-9771.** Cover $10–$40, occasionally higher.

Frenchmen Street

Apple Barrel ★ Snag a spot in the smallest, diviest, and most low-key bar on Frenchmen and you're guaranteed to leave with a few new friends (who may likely be members of the band, since you're all on top of each other). Seriously, it's the size of a living room with one bathroom stall, bar stools, no couches, and dollar bills all over the wall. Some of the city's best jazz and blues musicians play here nightly, and there's never a cover (you'll be moved to tip generously, regardless). 609 Frenchmen St. www.facebook.com/applebarrelbar. No phone. No cover; 1-drink minimum.

Blue Nile ★ This chill, midsize club has a killer sound system and pretty much zero attitude (or seating, or decor, save some murals), making it a fun hang for the local, reggae, funk, and jam bands they book every night of the week. DJs and brass bands rule the upstairs **Balcony Room** venue (be sure to hit the actual outdoor balcony). Trumpeter and local hero Kermit Ruffins and the Caesar Brothers funksters are both mainstays. 532 Frenchmen St. www.blue nilelive.com. ✆ **504/766-6193.** Cover $10–$25; no cover for early shows; never a cover upstairs.

Café Negril ★ Caribbean and reggae-themed (hence the giant Bob Marley mural) Negril is one of the Frenchmen Street originals, and always a good bet, with local music 363 days a year. Never a cover, but you can guarantee seating for a full set for $10 to $30 per person (plus a 2-drink minimum): Worth it if you want to groove in one spot with room to dance, a good view, and table service (food is so-so). The Sierra Green Show, Bon Bon Vivant, and Higher Heights Reggae get funky, danceable, and down—all sure to rock your world no matter where you are in the room. 606 Frenchmen St. www.cafenegril nola.com. ✆ **504/229-4236.** No cover.

THE ST. CLAUDE scene

The local indie/alternative types have carved out a pulsing metal-punk-bluegrass-hip-hop-comedy-funk-and-burlesque-infused underground-ish arts scene (anything goes, really) along a 2-block stretch of St. Claude Avenue in the Marigny. If this is what you're into (or if you think Frenchmen St. has jumped the shark), check out the sundry bookings at funky **Siberia** (2227 St. Claude Ave.; www.siberianola.com) or at the spacious **Hi-Ho Lounge** (2239 St. Claude Ave.; www.instagram.com/hihonola; *€* **504/945-4446**), where we dig the I Love the '90s tribute band nights and DJ Soul Sister's monthly late-Saturday-night "HUSTLE!" deep cuts. The loose, welcoming, and supportive dance-party vibe of **Kajun's Pub** (2256 St. Claude Ave.; www.kajunpub.com; *€* **504/533-9237**) is hands-down the best karaoke in town; and anything onstage at the queer-centric **AllWays Lounge & Cabaret** (p. 230) is a good bet. Food will happen: Pop-ups slinging tacos, burgers, or what-have-you abound outside the clubs and on the "neutral ground" (what New Orleans calls the median). Be mindful crossing the street—it's a state highway, not Bourbon St. (which we hope is a built-in protection of it ever becoming Bourbon-ized . . .).

d.b.a. ★★ A favorite bar/nightclub for its high-quality local bookings and sound, laid-back vibe, and superb beer and spirits selections. Shows (usually) start on time and feature a wide variety of excellent Louisiana talent like soul-stirring crooner John Boutté, Delta bluesman Little Freddie King, and all the hottest brass bands like Soul, Dirty Dozen, The Soul Rebels, and Glen David Andrews. Mostly standing-room only, and the low stage doesn't help those in the back (maybe that's why they're so dang chatty—don't be them). *Tip:* Hit the early shows—always good, often free. 618 Frenchmen St. www.dbanew orleans.com. *€* **504/942-3731.** Cover free–$20, occasionally higher.

Igor's Checkpoint Charlie's ★ See p. 227.

Snug Harbor Jazz Bistro ★★★ The first music venue on Frenchmen Street and the city's premier showcase for contemporary jazz is precisely the smoky, tiny-cocktail-tables-shoved-together experience you'd imagine (without the smoke of course, thanks to the city ordinance). Two levels provide mostly good viewing (beware the pillars upstairs—try to sit along the rail) for an attentive audience of up to 80. They only book top-tier acts—there's no bad show—but Dr. Michael White, Herlin Riley, Delfeayo Marsalis, Charmaine Neville, Germaine Bazzle, and Stanton Moore's regular gigs are likely bets. Prepare for a full sensory immersion: No phones, photos, video, or talking (except to your cocktail server) allowed during the show. The adjoining restaurant has great burgers (**Port of Call**–style with baked potato side, same owners! p. 113) and more, making for a one-stop date night. Monitors screen the concerts in the low-ceilinged bar—for the budget-minded, the next-best thing to live. Advance ticketing is wise. 626 Frenchmen St. www.snugjazz.com. *€* **504/949-0696.** Cover $20–$40 general admission seated; 2 shows a night; closed Mon–Tue.

The Spotted Cat Music Club ★★★ Our aesthetic leans toward cramped rooms, little amplification, and riveting bands with a fresh take on all kinds of jazz. So, we adore the oft-crowded Cat. The scarce bar stools are hardly comfy, but when it's swinging the 100% reliably fine music is the real deal, as evidenced by the frenetic jitterbuggers squeezed in front of the teeny stage in the window. We love the uncrowded early hours (music starts at 2pm) and the frequent surprise guests, plucked onstage from the audience. Sidewalk seating works for a drink and a footrest (the music doesn't really reach). Cash only, and please tip the band! 623 Frenchmen St. www.spottedcatmusicclub.com. No phone. Cover free–$10; plus 1-drink minimum per set.

Three Muses ★★★ Sophisticated modern lounge meets classic 1920s saloon, and we're all-in. It serves up beautifully balanced, new-timey cocktails and American comfort food with an Asian twist, set to old-timey, piano-driven jazz and blues. The scant tables and stools go fast; reserve in advance for evening shows, or take your chances on a walk-in for early sets. If they're here, don't miss Tom McDermott, Mia Borders, Betty Shirley, or Monty Banks. Tuesday open mic is a special treat. 536 Frenchmen St. www.3musesnola. com. ✆ **504/252-4801.** Daily until 11pm; no food Mon–Tue. $3 music charge.

Elsewhere Around the City

The Broadside ★★ The Broad Theatre was already our favorite place to catch a flick. When communal movie viewing went out the door during the pandemic, so did the Broad. Enter the Broadside, an outdoor live music venue alongside the theater that hit the spot so perfectly, it went full-time. Dress for the weather and join the locals at this laid-back scene for music on the huge stage, or classic films on the outdoor screen (come early to get a chair for movies). Some of our most memorable nights have been dancing under the stars to Afro-Cuban funk artist Cimafunk and Haitian roots band RAM here: it's *that* kind of magic. There's usually a food truck, crawfish boils in season, and nice bathrooms. 600 Broad St. broadsidenola.com. ✆ **504/218-1008.** Tickets free–$25.

Buffa's ★★ "Hey, let's throw some diner-style tables and chairs in our nondescript back room, book some top local jazz-leaning musicians, and create a friendly, laid-back scene." Okay, we're hooked. The bar food is Cajun (and outstanding), the beer's cold, and kids are welcome. Adjacent to Frenchmen Street and on the edge of the Quarter, its name has its own New Orleans–style pronunciation ("BOOF-ah's"), but no one will fault you if you say it wrong. 1001 Esplanade Ave. www.buffasbar.com. ✆ **504/949-0038.** Cover $10. Food served 'til 4am Fri–Sat.

Bullet's Sports Bar ★★ Situated on a residential street named for a civil rights attorney who helped desegregate local schools, this unassuming Seventh Ward neighborhood bar cuts loose when the brass band assembles on the floor near the door, especially on Fridays with Sporty's Brass Band or when trumpeters Shamarr Allen or Kermit Ruffins show up. The show will start late, but a DJ will fill in, and you'll be glad for your table when the band materializes (doesn't take 'em long to set up). The crowd is friendly, bartenders efficient (order a DIY cocktail "setup," it's practically required and part of the fun), and the experience pure booty-shaking NOLA. If the kitchen isn't frying chicken and catfish, there's probably a barbecue outside for eats. It's about a 2-mile car ride from Bourbon Street. Don't wander. 2441 A.P. Tureaud Ave. www.facebook. com/bulletssportsbar. ℂ **504/948-4003.** Cover free–$15; more during special Jazz Fest sets.

Chickie Wah-Wah ★★★ We're ever so fond of this Mid-City club, and especially glad that actual musicians, including regular Meschiya Lake, stepped in to save it from demise after the owner passed away in 2021. Top local roots, rock, jazz, blues, and singer-songwriter acts draw reverent crowds to its clean, midsize, shotgun-style room decorated with cool old tin signs. Food usually pops up in the kitchen or outside. It's a stand-alone off the Canal Street streetcar at N. White Street, just past Broad. Try to catch The Iguanas, Paul Sanchez, Nigel Hall, Joy Clark, Jon Cleary, or The New Orleans Night-crawlers. 2828 Canal St. www.chickiewahwah.com. ℂ **504/541-2050.** Cover $10–$40.

Gasa Gasa ★ Filling the eclectic, indie-rock niche in a single room, Gasa draws a Tulane-to-20-something crowd. Occasional readings, art exhibits, the hopping Freret Street scene, and the mind-blowing exterior mural by Berlin-based street artist MTO augment the allure. 4920 Freret St. www.instagram.com/ gasa_gasa. No phone. Cover $10–$20, occasionally higher.

The Howlin' Wolf ★★ In the Warehouse District, the big (10,000-sq.-ft.) not-at-all-bad Wolf books leading local and occasional mid-level national acts focusing on rock, funk, and jam (Parliament Funkadelic, Of Montreal; local faves like Rebirth Brass Band and Dumpstaphunk). Good sound, good sight lines, good times—especially Sundays, when the Grammy-winning Hot 8 brass band plays the smaller "Den." *Fun fact:* The bar is from Al Capone's Chicago hotel (and cranks out some killer fried pickles from its kitchen at the end). 907 S. Peters St. www.thehowlinwolf.com. ℂ **504/529-5844.** Cover $5–$50.

Kermit's Tremé Mother-in-Law Lounge ★★ All aboard! If you've come to New Orleans to pay homage to its musical past, this brightly muraled shrine to the dearly beloved R&B singer and former owner Ernie K-Doe ("Mother-in-Law" was his 1960s breakout hit) is a requisite touchstone. Decor once included his illustrious mannequin, which Ernie's widow—cul-ture bearer, bar owner, and genius self-promoter Antoinette K-Doe—dressed in his clothes and kept behind the bar until her own passing on Mardi Gras morning 2009 (this is the stuff of legends, truly). If Kermit or brass bands are blowing (Sun, lately) on the outdoor patio, it'll be a night deep in the culture that you won't forget. (Bonus if he's also barbecuing or has cooked up some of his famous red beans and rice.) 1500 S. Claiborne Ave. www.facebook.com/ ruffinsbbq. ℂ **504/975-3955.** Cover $10–$20. Most shows 6pm–midnight.

Maple Leaf Bar ★★★ This classic New Orleans club is a local's bar by day, a poetry hub on Sundays (show starts at 4:20pm) and a medium-size,

cajun & zydeco MUSIC

Cajun and zydeco music don't come from New Orleans at all, despite the soundtrack you hear blaring out of Bourbon Street T-shirt shops. Both genres originated in the bayous of southwest Louisiana in what's called Acadiana (or **Cajun Country,** p. 282), a good 2 to 3 hours away. Their foundations lie in the arrival of two different French-speaking peoples in the swamp country: Acadians (French migrants who were booted out of Nova Scotia by the English in 1755), Louisiana Creoles (originally a class distinction meaning any first-generation person born in the colony, but later meaning mostly French-speaking people of African, Afro-Caribbean, or Indigenous descent). In this relatively isolated area, cultural practices were rich, and locals took to the folksy button accordion, newly introduced from Germany and France, which added a richness and power to their fiddle and guitar music. Later, drums, amplifiers, and steel guitars filled out the sound.

Chickie Wah Wah (p. 221), **d.b.a.** (p. 219), or **Tipitina's** (p. 223) are a few joints here in the big city where you might catch the world-renowned **Beausoleil,** raucous **Pine Leaf Boys,** the king of accordion **Dwayne Dopsie,** the pop-rock of **Sweet Crude,** powerhouse **Amanda Shaw,** the edgy **Lost Bayou Ramblers,** or **Corey Ledet** and **Jeffrey Broussard,** who blend hip hop and other influences du jour with zydeco. **Sunpie Barnes and the Louisiana Sunspots** bring zydeco-flavored Afro-Louisiana accordion and harmonica to **Dos Jefes Uptown Cigar Bar** (yes, it's allowed) on Saturdays (5535 Tchoupitoulas St.; www.dosjefes.com; ✆ **504/891-8500**). Tip's hosts a *Fais do-do* (the charming Cajun term for a dance) with **Bruce Daigrepoint** every Sunday. For folksy all-ages fun, try **Mulate's** (201 Julia St.; www.mulates.com; ✆ **504/522-1492**), a tourist-friendly, conventioneer-laden Cajun dinner-dancehall with so-so food, live music, and patient instructors, open daily except Mondays. (Check first to make sure it's not closed for a private event.)

tin-ceilinged, twinkle-light-strung club at night. Personal space can become a wistful memory when the crowds pack in (usually by 11pm), and the drunk frat crowd can be maddening; seek temporary refuge on the back patio, at the back bar's junky pool table, or on the sidewalk where the overflow party goes. But it's got that magical, transformative vibe you can't manufacture, and when the TBC Brass Band rips it up on Tuesdays it's pretty much a NOLA must-do (if you're only around on Mon, see The George Porter Jr. Trio). 8316 Oak St. www.mapleleafbar.com. ✆ **504/866-9359.** Cover $10–$20.

The Rabbit Hole ★★   On weekend nights, this newish spot on a quiet street in Central City near the CBD is a three-for-one: the early brass band show (some of the city's best, with room to dance!) gives way to sweaty, foggy electronic DJ sets under a giant disco ball just before midnight; while a sprawling outdoor night market comes to life out back with art, food pop-ups, another dance floor, and cozy corners for conversations and make-out sessions. National acts come through often (a recent 420 Funk Mob show here was in the top 10 of our life), and landing the Rebirth Brass Band's legendary Tuesday night residency is bona fide, y'all. Must be that primo sound system, because the small bar can be slow (but kind). There's a row of portable toilets outside:

Use them, it's a long wait for the single one inside (let's hope that changes). 1228 Oretha Castle Hayley Blvd. www.rabbitholnola.com. No phone. Cover free–$25.

Tipitina's ★★★ Dedicated to the late piano master Professor Longhair (that's him in bronze just inside the entrance; rub his head for luck) and named for one of his most enigmatic records, Tip's is, if not *the* New Orleans club, a major musical touchstone and a reliable place for top local and out-of-town hip hop, roots, brass, jam, rock bands, and DJs. If you can catch locals like hometown hero Troy "Trombone Shorty" Andrews, Galactic (who bought the place in 2019), Mardi Gras Indian funk band Cha Wa, the Funky Meters, or any tribute show (that might feature any or all of them), do not waver for a sec. It's nothing fancy: four walls, buncha bars, wraparound balcony (up front reserved for VIPs), and a stage (which, if you're under 6 feet, isn't easy to see from the back on crowded nights). This uptown institution has good (loud) sound and air-conditioning, and there's usually some late-night food truck action. Get advance tix for festival bookings and other big-name acts, and plan on Lyfting. Age 18+ okay. 501 Napoleon Ave. www.tipitinas.com. ✆ **504/895-8477.** Cover $10–$40.

THE BAR SCENE

You won't have any trouble finding a place to drink in New Orleans. Heck, thanks to liberal laws and "go-cups," you won't have to spend a minute *without* a drink in hand. But there's more to this town than bars (much), and more to bars than Bourbon Street (ditto), so as with all things, let moderation preside. There, that's our sermon. Our suggestions include some of the most convivial, quaint, or downright eccentric spots; also keep in mind that many hotels and restaurants have excellent bars; see chapters 5 and 6.

The French Quarter

Bar Tonique ★★ One of the city's first craft cocktail bars may have opened at the edge of the Quarter *waaay* back in 2008, but the glow of candlelight bouncing off its original brick walls around a cozy horseshoe-shaped bar make it feel perpetually stumbled-upon. Crew and clientele are diverse and welcoming (it's a service-industry favorite), the punches are prodigious, and the daily specials are ridiculous ($6 mai tais and daiquiris?!). Early dates start at the bar for happy hour; later-on dates linger in the smoochy booths near the fireplace. 820 N. Rampart St. www.bartonique.com. No phone; no food; no cover.

Cane & Table ★★★ C&T's "sophisticated faded" decor is marked by perfectly distressed plaster and brick walls, sparkly chandeliers, a gleaming white-marble bar top, and a slim, sexy patio. But rum (that's the cane) is the star, mixed with house-made ingredients and squeezed-to-order juice by some of New Orleans' most revered craft cocktail pros. The fruity Hurricane & Table is a solid bet, but don't pass over the seasonal cocktails, where the mixologists flex their creativity. Excellent small and large plates follow the Latin/Caribbean tide: Share the tostones, but bogart the crispy spiced ribs. Love.

There's no sign; it's next to Coop's. 1113 Decatur St. www.caneandtablenola.com. © **504/581-1112.**

Carousel Bar at the Monteleone Hotel ★★   No, you're not drunk (or maybe you are). The bar *is* spinning (one drink per rotation is the purported ratio—don't worry, its slo-o-o-w). There's plenty of soignée sofa seating and fine piano-based entertainment, but the classic experience requires a coveted seat at one of the 25 barstools ringing the Carousel, sipping a Vieux Carré cocktail (rye, cognac, sweet vermouth), invented here some 70 years ago. Be prepared to wait for your (literal) turn. 214 Royal St. www.hotelmonteleone. com/carouselbar. © **504/523-3341.**

Effervescence ★★   What's not to love? This white-on-white-on-crystal bub-pub on a low-key stretch of Rampart Street is ideal for a languid evening or a sparkling Sunday morning. It's low-commitment fancy: dressy or jeans, a flute or a magnum, a date or a chick night. The expansive list of all things bubbly ranges from a $10 glass of prosecco to fun flights to a kir royale. Oysters and small plates (emphasis on the small) provide spot-on accompaniments. 1036 N. Rampart St. www.nolabubbles.com. © **504/509-7644.**

Erin Rose ★★★   Triple threat: friendly unassuming Irish pub, cocktail bar, and Killer PoBoys in the back room (that's the name *and* the bold-but-accurate description of the enterprise). Try the rum-marinated pork-belly po' boy with citrus lime slaw. Killer, indeed (so good they opened another location, **Big Killer PoBoys,** at 219 Dauphine St.). Erin's signature frozen Irish coffee eradicates humidity: It's highly recommended as a mid-afternoon pick-me-up,

Pat O'Brien's & the Hurricane

Pat O'Brien's (718 St. Peter St.; www. patobriens.com; © **504/525-4823**) is world-famous for the hefty, vivid red, definitively New Orleans drink with the big-wind name (see Drink and Learn tours, p. 200). The bar's owners created the Hurricane's rum-heavy formula in the 1940s when whiskey was scarce (supply and manufacturing sources focused on World War II efforts), and rum was plentiful (especially post-Prohibition, though it was regularly smuggled in from the Caribbean the whole time). It's served in hurricane-lamp-style glasses, including a 3-gallon magnum size, taller than many small children and shared through long straws while standing up, at least for the first few sips. Naturally, this attracts drinkers in droves.

The entrance line can get long, and the once-peaceful courtyard can get raucous. In all honesty, the $11.50 pre-mixed drink is kinda sickly sweet (try a fresh one elsewhere for comparison), but it's a rite of passage and the glass is a great souvenir (they'll pack it up for you). Pat O's is still a reliable, rowdy, friendly introduction to New Orleans. The dark dueling-pianos lounge is awfully fun (music starts at 3pm Fri–Sat, 4pm Thurs and Sun)—send up a napkin, a 10-spot, and a prayer with your request and get ready to sing along. Locals populate the main bar up front, but when weather permits, the often-boisterous tropical patio with the flaming fountain is the place to be. Closed Monday–Tuesday.

or even to start the morning (it's only $3.50 on the "Wake Up and Live" special starting at 10am). 811 Conti St. www.erinrosebar.com. ✆ **504/522-3573.**

French 75 Bar at Arnaud's ★★★   A beautiful, intimate bar space in one of the Quarter's most venerable restaurants (p. 98), French 75 has won a James Beard Award for Outstanding Bar Program. It feels like drinking in New Orleans should: classic and classy. Bartenders are adept at vintage mixes (including a perfect Ramos Gin Fizz and the namesake French 75 champagne cocktail) and original concoctions. Order a side of Arnaud's dreamy soufflé potatoes to munch on. Perfection. 813 Bienville St. www.arnaudsrestaurant.com/bars/french-75. ✆ **504/523-5433.**

Jewel of the South ★★★   At this upper-Quarter gem, the "Jewel" reference is not just a nod to a classic Southern cocktail. Truly, everything here is jewel-like, from the exquisitely prepared cocktails (no surprise—owner Chris Hannah is a multi-award-winning stalwart of New Orleans' modern cocktail era) to the demure dining room and come-hither courtyard. While the bar team is intentional, passionate, and proud about their products, they're not precious. Those interested in mixology are willingly indulged; those with an appetite can enjoy finely plated modern tapas and caviar; those who come for fun or flirtation will find their needs fulfilled by the Best Restaurant Bar in America (awarded in 2022). 1026 St. Louis St. www.jewelnola.com. ✆ **504/265-8816.**

Kerry Irish Pub ★   This pub has darts, pool, a proper pint of Guinness, and live Irish music most nights. The Kerry specializes in very-late-night drinking. Nightcap, anyone? 331 Decatur St. www.facebook.com/Kerry-Irish-Pub-163926209622. ✆ **504/527-5954.**

Lafitte's Blacksmith Shop ★★   Even if it wasn't a legendary pirate's lair and the oldest bar (and maybe building) in the Quarter, Lafitte's would merit a visit. It's ancient and ultra-atmospheric, so despite the crowd chatter and blaring jukebox (when much-preferred one-man-piano-band Mike Hood isn't around), sipping an ale in this crumbling, cavern-like, candlelight-only interior is nearly akin to time traveling (that's right, no lights); crowds always spill into the street. Avoid the vaunted Voodoo daiquiri, aka Purple Drank, and stick with beer and ambience instead. 941 Bourbon St. www.lafittesblacksmithshop.com. ✆ **504/593-9761.**

Manolito ★★   This teensy two-story divot just off Decatur Street, helmed by some of the city's shiniest bar luminaries, has exactly two outdoor tables, four bar stools, and a handful of tables throughout. The lucky who find their way to the expansive, reverent menu of Cuban-inspired daiquiris usually stay a while. Whether blended, thrown, or shaken, these are serious, good, seriously good drinks. Get the tortilla Española. 508 Dumaine St. Ave. www.manolitonola.com. ✆ **504/603-2740.**

Molly's at the Market ★   Bohos and literary locals chew over the state of the world and their city in this casual, comfortable hangout, a kind of platonic-ideal locals' bar. It's perpetually popular and populated—including Mr.

Wu, the resident bar cat. Need a late-night pick-me-up? It's open until 3am and the frozen Irish coffee always flows like wine. 1107 Decatur St. www.mollys atthemarket.net. ℂ **504/525-5169.**

Napoleon House ★★★ Set in a landmark 1815 building, the cave-dark barroom and romantically faded courtyard seem almost too perfectly aged. No plastic surgery here: The building, a National Historic Landmark, was owned by the same family for 101 years until a 2015 sale; the new owners would have been exiled had they changed a thing. Even locals come for the toasty muffuletta, subtle classical music, and signature Pimm's Cup—a cucumber-infused glass of summer any time of year. Looking for an atmosphere that'll move you to profess your love? This might work. 500 Chartres St. www.napoleon house.com. ℂ **504/524-9752.**

Patrick's Bar Vin ★★ Half a block and a million miles from Bourbon Street, Patrick Van Voorebeek—self- and aptly described bon vivant and one of the city's premier sommeliers—serves conviviality and an excellent selection of wines (and other spirits) by the glass. The bar feels like your great uncle's decorous but restful library; the sweet courtyard screams for something bubbly. 730 Bienville St., in the Hotel Mazarin. www.patricksbarvin.com. ℂ **504/200-3180.**

Peychaud's ★★★ Joined here are two of the most important people in the city's storied cocktail history . . . separated by about three centuries. Antoine Peychaud, namesake, apothecary, and once-resident of this lovely locale (ca. 1830ish) devised world-renowned Peychaud's Bitters, an essential ingredient of the sublime Sazerac, the city's official cocktail (the nation's first, say some). Around 2009, Neal Bodenheimer opened **Cure** (p. 228), the city's first serious craft cocktail bar, largely credited with reviving the city's fine drinks culture. We'd follow Neal anywhere—his imprint virtually guarantees a good drink—but following him to this classic bar and delightful courtyard is a thorough pleasure. 727 Toulouse St. www.maisondeville.com/peychaud-s. ℂ **504/ 884-4783.** Closed Mon.

GAME on

Pretty much every bar and club in town, no matter how unsporty, becomes a **sports bar** on Saints game days. So, if you're looking for a place to watch the game, try anywhere. We'll single out **Manning's** downtown (519 Fulton St.; www.caesars.com/harrahs-new-orleans; ℂ **504/593-8118**) for its wall-size screen and fully reclining leather lounge chairs, though its luxury is first-come, first-served. Everyone's welcome to cheer and jeer in the amply-screened **American Sports Saloon** (1200 Decatur St.; www.theamericansportssaloon.com; ℂ **504/300-1782**) for mostly any game, match, or team. To hang with the locals, hit the outdoor courtyards and shucked oysters at **MRB Bar & Kitchen** (515 St. Philip St.; www.mrbnola.com; ℂ **504/ 524-2558**) in the Quarter, or taxi to **Bayou Beer Garden's** big, covered backyard deck in Mid-City (p. 228).

dive RIGHT IN

If you'd rather drink with Tom Waits than Tom Cruise, you'll appreciate New Orleans' notorious dive bars—and by notorious, we mean neighborhood holes-in-the-wall with four different locks on the bathroom door (only one working) and regulars who can talk philosophy as much as pop culture. Honestly, they don't care which Tom you're with, or if you're with anyone at all. These are prime spots where only-in-New Orleans memories are made into stories to be told. Uptown, **Snake & Jake's Christmas Club Lounge** (7612 Oak St.; www.snakeandjakes.com; ☏ **504/861-2802**) is illuminated only by dwindling Christmas lights, which doesn't make it easier to find this crowded, sweat-soaked, off-the-beaten-path shack. Also Uptown, at the Elvis-themed **Kingpin** (1307 Lyons St.; ☏ **504/891-2373**), 20-somethings in CBGB T-shirts come for shuffleboard, cheap drink specials, and food pop-ups. Uptown in the Irish Channel, **Pete's Out in the Cold** (701 6th St.; www.instagram.com/petesoutinthecold; ☏ **504/895-8893**) covers every need—friendly service, a funky jukebox, patio seating, a bar cat named Foxy, a Bloody Mary Bar on Sundays, and rotating food pop-ups most nights (plus frozen pizza in a pinch, if you have 45 min.). In the depths of the French Quarter, **Aunt Tiki's** (1207 Decatur St.; ☏ **504/680-8454**) is laden with stickers, Halloween dreck, and affable, slouching degenerates. As if that's not draw enough, drinks are strong and cheap. **The Dungeon** (738 Toulouse St.; www.thedungeonneworleans.com) covers the dark end of the Quarter's dive spectrum with blackness, skulls, metal, and a no-photos-inside policy. The surly bartenders at **Igor's Checkpoint Charlie's** (501 Esplanade Ave.; ☏ **504/281-4847**) have been laying out the 24/7 dive-bar-style welcome mat to the Frenchmen Street scene for going on 30 years with plenty to keep you occupied: pool tables, open mic and karaoke nights, live music—and even a laundromat in the back. Further out (take a car), **Saturn Bar** retains its art-project-meets-*Lost-In-Space* dive vibe with rotating indie, funk, karaoke, trivia, whatever (3067 St. Claude Ave.; www.thesaturnbar.com; ☏ **504/949-7532**). In the Bywater/Upper Ninth Ward lies the scruffy trifecta of **Vaughan's** (4301 Burgundy St.; ☏ **504/947-5562**); **B.J.'s Lounge** (4301 Burgundy St.; www.instagram.com/bjslounge; ☏ **504/945-9256**); and **Bar Redux** (4301 Burgundy St.; www.barredux.com; ☏ **504/592-7083**)—come-as-you-are, all-day neighborhood hangs often with food and live music around (and sometimes even potlucks, movies, or rummage sales).

Elsewhere Around the City

Avenue Pub ★★   This beer-geek heaven, with 40+ options on tap and many more in bottles, is open most hours of the day. A recent change in ownership extended an already-good menu (beef-fat tater tots anyone?) and added a tiny streetcar tracking around inside to emulate the Historic St. Charles Avenue one rolling past outside. Everyone enjoys the upstairs balcony overlooking the Ave., especially during Mardi Gras parade season. 1732 St. Charles Ave. www.theavenuepub.com. ☏ **504/586-9243.** Closed Mon–Tues.

Bakery Bar ★★   There are two important reasons to recommend this comfy, oddly located spot tucked in the shadows of the Pontchartrain Expressway: 1) It is a bar. 2) It is a bakery, featuring the elusive, exceptional Debbie

Does Doberge cakes: moist, multi-layered mouthgasms worth the taxi fare. There's other food, too, and board games. But ultimately, it's a bar. With cake. 1179 Annunciation St. www.bakery.bar. ✆ **504/513-8664.**

Bar Marilou ★★★   In a remarkable transformation from stodgy to stunning, this former law library is arguably the city's most stylish bar. Opened in 2019 as part of the Warehouse District's luxe Maison de la Luz hotel (entryway along the building's left side), it's a feast for the senses. Deep gold tones, kicky animal prints, fringe, and those old bookshelves—now persimmon-red and hiding a private speakeasy for hotel guests—anchor the dramatic high style. The menus and vogue vibe, shaped by a group behind some of Paris's top spots, lean swank and French. 546 Carondelet St. www.barmarilou.com. ✆ **504/814-7711.**

Barrel Proof ★★   As the name implies, whiskey is the leading man at this shadowy, wood and tin-walled room in the Lower Garden District. And beer, for the beer-and-a-shot specials. If you know and love your brown liquor, the substantive selection of 300+ options (primarily American, Japanese, and Scottish), will blow your hair back. If you don't, ask nicely and the bartenders will share their expertise. Customized flights work well for both scenarios. They've invariably got something tasty coming out of their pop-up kitchen. 1201 Magazine St. www.barrelproofnola.com. No phone.

Bayou Beer Garden and Bayou Wine Garden ★★   For visitors looking for the "real" New Orleans, here's a taste. Two, actually. Bayou Beer Garden is a neighborhood bar with a big, covered backyard deck, big screens, and a big beer list. The sister wine bar, connected by a walkway, has a slightly upper-scaler atmosphere and food. Where the Beer Garden serves wings and jalapeño poppers, the Wine Garden goes for charcuterie and crab Rangoon dip. Either is a hang with the locals, for a game or after a visit to nearby City Park. Beer: 326 N. Jefferson Davis Pkwy. bayoubeergarden.com. ✆ **504/302-9357.** Wine: 315 N. Rendon St. bayouwinegarden.com. ✆ **504/826-2925.**

Cure ★★★   This mixologist mecca helped instigate the resurgence of craft cocktails in New Orleans as well as now-booming Freret Street. It's an

---

Mocktail Hour

Spirit-forward in all the ways, the city's top mixologists are playing with zero-proof alcohol with such regularity that you're likely to see a collection of non-alcoholic cocktails on most craft bar menus. **Bar Tonique** (p. 223) calls them "temperance drinks," and we're big fans of the tiki versions at **Latitude 29** (p. 110) and the new **Tiki Tock**

(417 Frenchmen St; www.tiki-tock.com; ✆ **504/688-2900**). The **Dream House Lounge** has aromatic oxygen therapy, "conscious cocktails," and a whole host of wellness and alternative health programming if you're seeking to imbibe your full spirit. (1401 Baronne St.; www.dhlounge.com; ✆ **504/475-7964**).

GETTING crafty: MAKING THE BREWERY SCENE

The reclaimed and converted local brewery spaces in New Orleans are as eclectic as the local programming, food pop-ups, and neighbors they attract. Check Instagram handles to see what's on deck (seasonal crawfish boils and oysters are likely).

- **Courtyard Brewery:** Beer-wise, this funky-dive tasting room with a major outdoor patio in the Lower Garden District offers the best of the local IPA lot. 1160 Camp St.; www.courtyardbrewery.square.site; @courtyardbrew.

- **Parleaux Beer Lab:** Deep in the Bywater, the fruit trees and herbs in the simple backyard beer garden may turn up in their creative brews. Stouts are standouts, as is proximity to the **Joint** barbecue (p. 117) and regular pop-ups. 634 Lesseps St.; www.parleauxbeerlab.com; ✆ **504/702-8433;** @parleauxbeerlab.

- **Urban South:** The social scene is the main attraction at this huge, family-friendly warehouse-style spot, especially on game days. 1645 Tchoupitoulas St.; www.urbansouthbrewery.com; ✆ **504/267-4852;** @urbansouthbeer.

- **Brieux Carre:** They're having fun with beer here in the Marigny, an experimental hop oasis steps from the Frenchmen Street madness. 2115 Decatur St.; www.brieuxcarre.com; ✆ **504/304-4242;** @brieuxcarre.

- **Zony Mash:** Locals flock here for the fun scene, cool space (a converted old movie theater in Mid-City), music venue, sours, and seltzers. 3940 Thalia St.; www.zonymashbeer.com; ✆ **504/766-8868;** @zonymashbeer.

- **Faubourg Brewery:** The brewery formerly known as Dixie now has better brews; great musical entertainment programming; and a huge outdoor space about 15 minutes from the city. Great for large groups and families. 3501 Jourdan Rd.; www.faubourgbrewery.com; ✆ **504/867-4000;** @faubourgbeer.

- **Miel Brewery:** Its Irish Channel warehouse is home to a constant rotation of food trucks and pop-ups. A nice range of small-batch beers are on tap, plus some beer slushies. 405 6th St.; www.mielbrewery.com; ✆ **504/372-4260;** @mielbrewery.

- **Crescent City Brewhouse:** Opened in 1991, it was the first new brewery in New Orleans in more than 70 years. Beers hold up, menu is full, balcony has a great view, and there's live jazz. 527 Decatur St.; www.crescentcitybrewhours.com; ✆ **504/522-0571.**

- **NOLA Brewing:** An original, now with some of the city's best pizza (p. 200).

Uptown oasis of sleek, boasting great small plates and some of the most knowledgeable bar chefs in town, who blend exceptional ingredients with personable chat. Avoid the late crowds and go at happy hour. 4905 Freret St. www.curenola.com. ✆ **504/302-2357.**

Le Bon Temps Roulé ★   Another way-uptown, rundown shack with a cramped bar and decent beer list. So? So, schedule your visit for a Thursday, when the Soul Rebels brass band blows this here roof off. The archetypal local characters are quite welcoming the other 5 nights of the week, too. 4801 Magazine St. www.lbtrnola.com. ✆ **504/895-8117.**

Sazerac Bar at the Roosevelt ★★★ If the New Orleans bar scene were a monarchy, the historic Sazerac Bar in the glamorous Roosevelt Hotel might be queen. Its dark, sinuous wood walls and Deco-era murals have borne witness to movie stars, political scandals, and we don't want to know what else (check the bullet hole in the paneling to the left of the bar). You're here for all that panache as much as for the namesake cocktail (now $20) or an impossibly frothy Ramos Gin Fizz, because they own the recipe. 123 Baronne St. www.therooseveltneworleans.com. ☏ **504/648-1200.**

The Tell Me Bar ★★ Its location on a dead-end street shadowed by the behemoth concrete Expressway only adds to the lure of this new, all-natural wine bar—you have to be intentional to get there. Once inside, its "tropical midcentury Italian" vibe features oodles of candlelight flickering on palm fronds, mirrors, leather couches, and mismatched bistro chairs, setting the stage for intimate conversations over expertly curated natural wines from a rotating menu. There are often DJs, live music, and pop-ups too—like caviar bites, fresh oysters, and tarot readings. The twinkly outdoor courtyard attracts clusters of local creative types. Best to visit with a hot date or a small group of friends. 1235 Saint Thomas St. www.thetellmebar.com. No phone.

GAY NIGHTLIFE

Many queer-friendly bars and clubs owned by and catering to New Orleans' thriving LBGTQ+ community are concentrated near the intersection of Bourbon and St. Ann Streets, historically (and lovingly) called the French Quarter's "fruit loop" circuit. Expect late hours, friendly folk, and colossal crowds, costumes, and color during Southern Decadence (p. 33), plus Pride weekend, Mardi Gras, Halloween, Easter—basically at the drop of any quasi-celebratory hat. Also see **www.ambushmag.com** and the **LGBT Queer History Tour by New Orleans Secrets** (p. 199).

Bars & Clubs

AllWays Lounge & Cabaret ★★★ This longtime anchor of the St. Claude Avenue arts scene (p. 219) is a dive bar with flair, home to avant-garde burlesque shows like "AllMost" naked karaoke and lube wrestling cabaret—plus local musician jams and weekly swing, blues, and line dance nights (with lessons). Reserve-in-advance cocktail tables promise table service and performer close-ups on the main floor; bar stools are usually available for the shyer among us. Plenty of restaurants and street food nearby can make it a night. 2240 St. Claude Ave. www.theallwayslounge.net. No phone. Ticket prices and cover vary.

The Bourbon Pub & Parade Disco ★★ Of the two hyper-popular bars housed in this prime corner spot, the downstairs pub is a bit calmer, even on sing-along and karaoke nights. Upstairs, Parade Disco's high-tech dance setup comes alive on weekend nights, especially pre- and post- the Sunday 8pm (sharp!) glam drag show. 801 Bourbon St. www.bourbonpub.com. ☏ **504/529-2107.**

Café Lafitte in Exile ★ Established in 1933, it's one of the oldest gay bars in the U.S., originally housed in the famed Lafitte's Blacksmith Shop Bar (p. 225) on the other end of the block. After a not-gay-friendly landlord took over that space in 1954, the regulars are said to have walked their drinks—and their barstools—all at once to the new digs, where it remains in exile to this day. Downstairs is more of a cruise bar, upstairs has a friendly pub-like atmosphere. Fun happens on both levels including the famed Sunday night Trash Disco, and superb Hurricanes are made with fresh juice (even Pat O'Brien's doesn't do that). 901 Bourbon St. www.lafittes.com. ✆ **504/522-8397.**

The Country Club ★★ Locals still miss the days when this bar, pool, restaurant, and club was an anything-goes, clothing-optional, mostly gay retreat. But we'll admit that the new dressed-up, mostly not-gay version is quite delightful (and cleaner, with a legit menu and chef). To be fair, this converted Creole cottage in the residential Bywater is a neighborhood *day*cation, but it sure sets up a great night for locals and visitors of all persuasions, with a pretty veranda, airy dining room, pool, and hot tub. The hilarious weekend drag brunch (10am and 1pm Sat–Sun) books up months ahead; reserve online in advance. 634 Louisa St. www.thecountryclubneworleans.com. ✆ **504/945-0742.** Day pass for pool $20; more for events.

Golden Lantern ★ The crowd at the uber-diverse *Cheers* of New Orleans (open 24/7) writes its own bingo card at any given hour—find a drag queen; a disco dancer; a person in a suit or a fancy dress; a dog sitting at the bar; and someone buying a round of Jell-O shots. Free space for the retro neon rainbow "LBGT" (Light Beer, Great Taste) Miller Lite sign on the back wall. Labor Day weekend, it's ground zero for Southern Decadence (p. 33). 1239 Royal St. www.thegoldenlanternneworleans.com. ✆ **504/529-2860.** No cover; no credit cards; stash some dollar bills for the drag show.

Good Friends Bar & Queens Head Pub ★★★ This truly friendly spot, drawing all genders, types, and ages, is a favorite for its unpretentious vibe. We like that the decor maintains some NOLA feel, the music is video pop, and that the local denizens will gladly chat anyone up (could help that happy hour runs up to 8 hours long most days). The upstairs Queens Head Pub has a wraparound balcony for your street viewing pleasure. On a hot day, the boozy, creamy, and frozen Separator concoction goes down easy. Karaoke on Tuesdays. 740 Dauphine St. www.goodfriendsbar.com. ✆ **504/566-7191.**

Grrl Spot ★★ The location of this super-popular lesbian/queer dance party pop-up varies, as does its frequency ("monthlyish" is the aim). Check the website and socials to see what magic is brewing. www.grrlspot.io. No phone. Cover varies.

Oz ★★ This bass-heavy, two-story gay dance club (#1 in the city) is a see-and-be-seen spot for a mostly young crowd. Notwithstanding weekend waves of straight bachelorettes, its disco-ball-and-laser-light show and frenzy of go-go boys atop the bar are world renowned. Programming every night of the week peppers in drag, strip-offs, boylesque, comedy, and karaoke to keep any and all y'alls fully in the moment. 800 Bourbon St. www.ozneworleans.com. No phone. Cover varies.

PERFORMING ARTS, THEATERS & CONCERT HALLS

Theater buffs may also want to see what dramas and musicals are on tap at local universities (**Loyola,** cmm.loyno.edu/theatre/events; **UNO,** www.uno.edu/sota-performances/theater; **Tulane,** www.liberalarts.tulane.edu/departments/theatre-dance/performances)or at **NOCCA,** the region's tuition-free, audition-to-get-in high school for performing artists (www.nocca.com/events).

Ashe Cultural Arts Center ★★   Art exhibits, plus dance and musical performances centered around the African diaspora. See p. 173.

Café Istanbul ★★   We never know what legendary or up-and-coming local talent could be onstage here from one week to the next, and therein lies the beauty. Whether live music, a rap battle, dance, poetry, storytelling ("The Moth" monthly residency is here), comedy, film, burlesque, performance art, a variety show fundraiser, or an anything-goes open mic, the sound is great, the crowd is local, and the everyone-is-welcome vibe is on. Though sometimes understaffed, the bartenders are friendly, and the balcony lets us take in the whole scene. No food on-site at night, so plan accordingly. 2372 St. Claude Ave. www.cafeistanbulnola.com. ☎ **504/975-0286.** Ticket prices vary.

Civic Theatre ★   Before 2013, there was nothing here but an exquisite Deco chandelier and a flock of pigeons. Little was spared in restoring the original 1906 architecture and plasterwork of this triple-tiered midsize theater, the oldest one in the city. If our favorite cult or alt-rock band is on tour (think Neko Case, Built to Spill, or Wilco), this will be their stop. 510 O'Keefe St. www.civicnola.com. ☎ **504/272-0865.** Ticket prices vary.

Contemporary Arts Center (CAC) ★★   Art exhibits; dance and theatre performances. See p. 167.

The Fillmore ★★   Scale the daunting stairway on the Canal Street side of Caesars (formerly Harrah's, and there IS an elevator if needed) and you'll find that the industrial black interior and huge crystal chandeliers in the 2,200-capacity main room ably honor its sister club in San Francisco (with NOLA nods like a brass instrument fixture and Louis Armstrong murals). Sound is LOUD, acts are mid-to-big, and general admission standing is the way to go for a full body rock. If we're feeling extra (or our age), the raised VIP section nearer the stage is worth the extra pop over the tiered seats in the way back. Drinks are a bit pricey; food is surprisingly good. 6 Canal St. www.thefillmorenola.com. ☎ **504/881-1555.** Ticket prices vary.

Le Petit Théâtre ★★   One of the oldest community theaters in the U.S., "The Little Theatre" has occupied this building since 1923, save for a scary 2011 shutdown. Fortunately, the opening of restaurant **Tableau** (p. 107) in the shared building enabled the 350-seat theater to reopen, and patrons can once again enjoy a dinner-and-a-show night out in the heart of the French Quarter just off Jackson Square. 616 St. Peter St. www.lepetittheatre.com. ℂ **504/522-2081.** Tickets $15–$75.

Mahalia Jackson Theater for the Performing Arts ★ This handsome midcentury theater bordering the Quarter in Armstrong Park is spacious but not big, so every seat is decent. Named in honor of New Orleans' own "Queen of Gospel," it hosts local opera and ballet companies plus touring theater productions, dance troupes, comedy shows, rock concerts, and other live acts. 1419 Basin St. www.mahaliajacksontheater.com. ℂ **504/525-1052.** Ticket prices vary.

Marigny Opera House ★★ The outstanding acoustics in the former Holy Trinity Catholic church are indeed opera-worthy, along with the theatrical, ballet, jazz, and classical music performances it regularly hosts. Erected in 1853, deconsecrated in 1997, and saved from blight in 2011, the aptly nicknamed "Church of the Arts" is a gracefully worn shadow of its former opulence, and couldn't be more perfectly romantic. 725 St. Ferdinand St. www.marignyoperahouse.org. ℂ **504/948-9998.** Ticket prices vary.

Music Box Village ★★★ We haven't been *every*where, but we're pretty sure there's nothing like the Music Box Village *any*where else. It's an enchanted collection of artisan-fabricated structures, each at once an edifice, an artwork, and a musical instrument. A performance in, on, and around these magical musical houses is a wholly-new, mesmerizing experience that should not be missed. Dress for outdoor conditions; the floor is the earth and seating is rustic, so come early to snag a bench or a tree stump, or bring a folding chair or blanket. The bar opens and local food vendors pop-up for performances. If there are no shows while you're in town, try to check it out during public hours or for whatever oddball event may be happening here. (Shows sometimes cancel due to rain or inclement weather, so check on social.) 4557 N. Rampart St. www.musicboxvillage.com. Performances $20–$85; suggested donation for visits $5–$15.

Orpheum ★★ It took $15 million, 10 years, and lots of elbow grease to restore this drop-dead-stunning, 1,500-seat Beaux Arts vaudeville theater to its original 1908 glory after it languished in post-Katrina ruin. Those in the know (that's you) can wait out the start of the show sipping cocktails behind velvet curtains in the delightful **Double Dealer** speakeasy below ground (Thurs–Sun). 129 Roosevelt Way. www.orpheumnola.com. ℂ **504/274-4870.** Ticket prices vary.

Saenger Theatre ★★ Following an extensive gajillion-dollar post-Katrina renovation, this 1927-built stunner from the glory movie-house days, inspired by a 15th-century Italian garden, is now on the National Register of Historic places, and technologically state-of-the-art. Go for touring concerts, Broadway road companies, and comedy shows. And look to the sky: stars and moving clouds are projected on the ceiling. 1111 Canal St. www.saengernola.com. ℂ **504/287-0351.** Ticket prices vary.

NEW ORLEANS SHOPPING

By Lavinia Spalding

Shopping in New Orleans is a highly evolved leisure activity, with a shop for every strategy and a fix for every shopaholic—and for every budget. Think of the endless souvenir shops on Bourbon Street and swanky antiques stores on Royal Street as the bookends for all the shopping New Orleans has to offer. There are sweet deals to be had, lavish riches to be spent, artworks to be admired. But as all shoppers know, the fun is in the hunt. And New Orleans has some smashing hunting grounds.

Just one note: In the listings below, we outline stores' hours of business, but (especially in summer) many shops change or reduce hours. Call before you go!

MAJOR HUNTING GROUNDS

ART MARKETS   On the second Saturday of every month, the **Arts Market New Orleans** takes place at **City Park**'s Goldring/Woldenberg Great Lawn (8 Victory Ave.), and on the last Saturday of the month, in **Marsalis Harmony Park** (S. Carrollton and S. Claiborne aves., last stop on the St. Charles streetcar line; www.artsneworleans.org; ✆ **504/523-1465**). From 10am to 4pm you'll find paintings, pottery, glass, mosaics, jewelry, soaps, clothing, and much more from high-quality juried artists (plus music and food). On the first Saturday of each month, the **Freret Street Market** (www.freretmarket.org) has food, art, apothecary, and music. We also love browsing the locally made works at **Zèle** (2481 Magazine St.; zelenola.com).

Evenings are for shopping, too. On Frenchmen Street in the Marigny, there are two great side-by-side open-air night markets. At the **Art Garden** (artgardennola.com; most nights Thurs-Sun), goods are original, local, and affordable. (It's mostly art and jewelry, with the occasional awesome vintage box camera upcycled as a lamp.) Next door, **Frenchmen Art Market** has even more neat stuff, plus friendly, talented artists to chat up (Thurs-Mon).

CANAL PLACE   At the foot of Canal Street (333 Canal St.) near the Mississippi River, this sophisticated shopping mall holds more than 30 shops, including elegant retailers like Louis Vuitton, Tory Burch, Michael Kors, G-Star Raw, Saks Fifth Avenue, and Tiffany & Co. There's a two-story Anthropologie, the **Louisiana Crafts Guild** gallery of locally made goods, and the art gallery **Salon** (Thurs-Sat 2-7 pm, Sun 2-6pm). Canal Place (www. canalplacestyle.com) is open Monday through Saturday from 11am to 7pm, Sunday noon to 6pm.

THE FRENCH MARKET   These historic shops begin in the colonnade along Decatur Street across from Jackson Square. Offerings include candy, housewares, fashion, crafts, and toys. The open-air section—originally an Indigenous peoples' intertribal trading grounds—is the oldest continuously operated open-air market in the country. It begins at Ursulines Avenue and N. Peters Street. There's a stage for occasional live music and cooking demos, and food booths including an oyster bar, a terrific fresh juice bar, top-notch pralines, and tasty-healthy **Meals from the Heart Cafe.** The farmers market and foodstuff stalls—including local seafood, meats, and spices—will pack your purchases for travel or shipping. The flea market section has low-end souvenirs (good buys, if not good quality) and a smattering of actual art and handmade goods. (Some of the best art finds are in nearby **Dutch Alley Artist's Co-op.**) It's always a fun stroll. Open daily 10am to 5pm (www.french market.org). See also p. 156.

JAX BREWERY   Just across from Jackson Square at 600-620 Decatur St., the old brewery building is now a jumble of shops and cafes (and good bathrooms, and great views). It's an easy stop for clothing and souvenirs, particularly the crawfish-logo'd polo shirts and other preppie wear at **Perlis.** Open daily 10am to 7pm (www.thejaxbrewery.com; ✆ **504/566-7601**).

JULIA STREET   Some of the city's best contemporary art galleries (many listed under "Art Galleries," p. 237) line Julia Street from Camp Street to the river (and fork off into surrounding side streets). The quality of talent exhibited here—among both creators and curators—is quite astounding.

SHOPPING ON THE bayou

It's not the busiest shopping stretch (by far), but Bayou Road might be the friendliest—and one of the most historic. In fact, without it, New Orleans probably wouldn't exist: It's the city's oldest road, first used by Indigenous people who later introduced it as a trade route to French settlers. Between Esplanade Avenue and N. Broad Street, a handful of sweet businesses, many of which are Black-owned, includes **Community Book Center** (p. 240), a social hub specializing in African-centered books; **King and Queen Emporium Int'l,** where you can stock up on pomegranate soap, African shea butter, and Orisha incense; and **CupCake Fairies,** where you should treat yourself to the extra-large, double-stuffed cupcake you surely deserve. Some Bayou Road *lagniappes* (bonuses): all the great eats on p. 145.

MAGAZINE STREET   This premier shopping drag is 6 miles (you read that right: *6 miles*) of antiques, boutiques, galleries, salons, and all manner of restaurants in 19th-century brick storefronts and quaint Creole cottages, from Canal Street to Audubon Park. Prime sections are roughly the 1900-2200 blocks; 2800-3100 blocks; 3400-4600 blocks (with the odd block or so of nothing); and 5400-5700 blocks. A car or JazzyPass (p. 298) will help you browse the lengthy, lively avenue (www.magazinestreet.com).

THE OUTLET COLLECTION AT RIVERWALK   Whoa. Coach, Kate Spade, Nordstrom Rack, Le Creuset, and some 70 other outlet stores and restaurants fill this sprawling three-story mall. Bargains are a bonus when you can walk from the French Quarter, shop with a daiquiri in hand, and enjoy the best mall food-court view in existence, with tables overlooking the Mississippi. It's behind the Hilton at 500 Port of New Orleans Place, just steps from the ferry and cruise terminals. Open Monday to Saturday 10am to 7pm, Sunday 10am to 6pm (www.riverwalkneworleans.com; ✆ **504/522-1555**).

RIVERBEND, MAPLE & OAK STREETS   To reach these cute Carrollton-area stores, ride the St. Charles Avenue streetcar to stop no. 212 (S. Carrollton and Maple sts.) and walk down Maple Street, where shops like **Sarah Ott** (cool local designs) and the delectable **Maple Street Patisserie** inhabit renovated Creole cottages and old buildings. Return to Carrollton, walk 4 blocks away from the river to Oak Street, and turn left. Along this happening shopping strip, you can caffeinate at **Rue De La Course,** then browse the excellent reads at **Blue Cypress Books,** high-end knives at **Coutelier,** snazzy decor at **Eclectic Home,** guitars and vintage duds at **Glue,** and folky and funky **Malarky** art gallery. For refreshments, try iconic **Camellia Grill** (p. 145), alligator cheesecake at quirky **Jacques-Imo's** (p. 142), Jamaican fare at **14 Parishes,** vegan **Breads on Oak,** spicy crab and quaffable cocktails at **Seafood Sally's,** or something frosty from **Ale on Oak.** (If you're there in the evening, catch a show (and maybe a crawfish boil) at the **Maple Leaf Bar.** A classic night-owl move is to end at legendary dive bar **Snake and Jake's Christmas Club Lounge** (p. 227).

SHOPPING A TO Z

Antiques & Vintage

Collectible Antiques ★★   One of our favorites of the dusty, jumbled, and eclectic antiques/junk stores on the Esplanade end of Decatur, its stock runs from Art Deco to 1960s collectibles. 1232 Decatur St. collectible-antiques.hub.biz. ✆ **504/766-2343.** Daily noon–6pm.

James H. Cohen & Sons ★   A serious place for serious collectors. The fifth generation of antique-dealing Cohens specializes in antique weapons, coins, and currency from points near and far, dating back to 400 B.C. A locally minted antique coin, a gold doubloon, or a coin from actual sunken treasure makes a fine souvenir. 437 Royal St. www.cohenantiques.com. ✆ **504/522-3305.** Mon–Sat 9:30am–5pm.

Keil's Antiques ★   Established in 1899 and currently run by the family's fourth generation, Keil's has a considerable collection of 18th- and 19th-century French and English furniture, chandeliers, jewelry, and decorative items spanning three crowded floors. Ask a staff member about the doorman who worked his spot here for 78 years and you may coax out some other stories as well. 325 Royal St. www.keilsantiques.com. ✆ **504/522-4552.** Mon–Sat 9am–5pm.

Magazine Antique Mall ★★   Diggers will dig the superb browsing and many good deals found among the 50-ish variegated stalls in this 7,000-square-foot space. 3017 Magazine St. www.magazinestreet.com/merchant/magazine-antique-mall. ✆ **504/896-9994.** Daily noon–5pm.

Merchant House ★   The vintage here—furniture, glassware, clothing, art, knickknacks, and so on—are all sourced by discerning New Orleanians. (Bonus, next door is **Freda** (p. 243), one of our top stops for fashion fun.) 1150 Magazine St. www.merchanthouse.co. ✆ **504/233-2240.** Mon and Wed–Sat 11am–5pm; Sun noon–5pm.

M.S. Rau ★★★   The sheer scale of the inventory makes century-old Rau a required destination for serious buyers. Every opulent item that could possibly be crafted from fine metals, gems, crystal, wood, paint, china, and marble, plus articles made by every name known to the antique and art world, is here for the ogling, filling room after jaw-dropping room across three historic buildings. It recently doubled its size to 40,000 square feet and is now even more museum-like than before. We particularly love the selection of walking canes, fifteenth-century iron floor safes, and orchestrion (self-playing) instruments. Most every item has a story to tell, and the knowledge-able sales reps pleasantly indulge your curiosity. 622 Royal St. www.rauantiques.com. ✆ **888/557-2406.** Mon–Sat 9am–5:15pm.

Art Galleries

Galleries share the **Royal** and **Magazine Street** landscapes with the afore-mentioned antiques shops, while in the Warehouse District, the 300-700 blocks of **Julia Street** (and surrounding streets) house some 20 contemporary fine-arts galleries, anchored by the **Contemporary Arts Center** and **Ogden Museum of Southern Art** (p. 171). Go from 6 to 9pm on the first Saturday of each month for the Arts District Gallery Openings. Along Julia Street, in addition to the galleries listed below, check out **LeMieux, Octavia, Steve Martin,** and fantastic newcomer **Spillman Blackwell.** For the more intrepid, explore the burgeoning lowbrow and outsider art movement around **St. Claude Avenue** (no current collective website, but hit **UNO St. Claude, Good Children,** and **The Front Galleries** at 2429, 4037, and 4100 St. Claude Ave., respectively). Two more we really like: Uptown, stop by **Axiom Fine Art Gallery** (4613 Freret St.), where the work of local artists is showcased; and Downtown, make time for **Stella Jones Gallery** (201 St. Charles Ave. #132), which has been shining a light on the historical importance of Black artists for some 25 years. And finally, whatever else you do, don't miss **Studio BE ★★★**, at 2941 Royal St., home to the astounding works of artist, activist, and educator Brandan "BMike" Odums. For more on Studio BE, see p. 174.

Angela King Gallery ★★★   Opened in 2007 in a show of much-needed post-Katrina solidarity, this is still one of the best contemporary art galleries in the city. King shows works by artists such as Peter Max, Andrew Baird, Richard Currier, Raymond Douillet, Patterson & Barnes, and Michelle Gagliano. 241 Royal St. www.angelakinggallery.com. ✆ **504/524-8211.** Wed–Sat 11am–5pm or by appt.

Antieau Gallery ★★★   We adore artist Chris Roberts-Antieau's whimsical side (sewn works that riff on current events and social mores) and her dark side (macabre snow globes and a dollhouse re-creation of the *In Cold Blood* crime scene). 719 Royal St. www.antieaugallery.com. ✆ **504/304-0849.** Thurs–Mon 11am–5pm.

Arthur Roger Gallery ★★★   Arthur Roger pioneered the Warehouse District and fine-arts scene when he opened in NOLA over 40 years ago, tying the local community to the New York art world. Still blazing trails, the expansive gallery represents Francis X. Pavy, Ida Kohlmeyer, Dawn DeDeaux, Dale Chihuly, Demond Melancon, and the stunning figurative photographs of the late George Dureau. 432-434 Julia St. www.arthurrogergallery.com. ✆ **504/522-1999.** Tues–Sat 10am–5pm.

> ### Tax-Free Art
>
> Many original works of visual art in New Orleans are exempt from sales tax, thanks to a statewide program promoting cultural activity in designated districts. Be sure to ask about sales tax where you buy.

Ashley Longshore ★★   Not for the faint of heart or wallet, Ashley's clever, controversial art riffs on pop culture and wealth-worship in bright hues and high gloss. She slams (or glorifies?) materialism and winks at celebrity on pillows and paintings, but they're flower-strewn and alit with butterflies, so hey, it's all good. We were smitten with a fanciful pair of Crest-white armchairs with lipstick-red metallic auto upholstery, emblazoned with "No F**ks Given." Then, some 14-year-old girl bought them for $6,000/pair. 4Realz. 4537 Magazine St. www.ashleylongshore.com. ✆ **504/333-6951.** Mon–Fri 9am–5pm; Sat 11am–4pm.

Carol Robinson Gallery ★★   The grande dame of the local contemporary Southern arts scene, Robinson shows accessible but surprisingly affordable works, including Sandra Burshell's arresting pastels, Jere Allen's mysterious milky-white figures, James King's haunting oils, and Christina Goodman's exquisite minute tableaus. 840 Napoleon Ave. carolrobinsongallery.net. ✆ **504/895-6130.** Tues, Fri 1–5pm; Sat 11am–3:45pm.

Dr. Bob Art ★★★   In his one-of-a-kind Bywater studio, Dr. Bob turns out his colorful, iconic "be nice or leave" folk art signs, rimmed in bottle caps and other found materials. Available in a variety of sizes, materials, and sentiments. 3027 Chartres St. drbobart.net. © **504/701-7297.** Daily 10am–5pm (summer 10am–4:20pm).

Frank Relle Gallery ★★★ Sometimes spooky, sometimes serene, Relle's nightscapes of the local swamps and architecture are undeniably stunning. 910 Royal St. www.frankrelle.com. © **504/265-8564.** Daily 10am–6pm.

A Gallery for Fine Photography ★★★ This incredibly well-stocked photography gallery emphasizes the historic and contemporary culture of New Orleans and the South. Images include Ernest J. Bellocq's legendary Storyville photos, Herman Leonard's jazz images, the haunting work of Sebastião Salgado, and something from just about every period, style, or noted photographer (including books, if photos aren't in your budget). 241 Chartres St. www.agallery.com. © **504/669-3220.** Open by appt., or sometimes by chance.

Jonathan Ferrara Gallery ★★★ Since 1998, Ferrara has been showing emerging cross-media artists in thought-provoking exhibitions that lean playful and ironic. Skylar Fein's pop-pundit pieces are both hilarious and horrifying in their truth; Paul Villinski's winged sculptures are magical. 400a Julia St. www.jonathanferraragallery.com. © **504/522-5471.** Tues–Sat 10am–5pm or by appt.

Martine Chaisson Gallery ★★ The stark, sweeping space screams for high-impact, highly saturated imagery, and Martine delivers. Hunt Slonem's neo-expressionist bunnies, birds, and butterflies are a bright delight; Katrine Hildebrandt's mesmerizing geometrics are oddly serene. 727 Camp St. www.martinechaissongallery.com. © **504/302-7942.** Wed–Sat 11am–5pm; Mon and Tues by appt.

Michalopoulos ★★★ James Michalopoulos's thickly painted, topsy-turvy renderings of shotgun houses and Creole cottages adorn the walls of many a *real* local house, and his portraits of jazz musicians are stunning (proof: He's done seven Jazz Fest posters, more than any other artist in the festival's history). Originals are an investment, but prints are available and affordable. 617 Bienville St. www.michalopoulos.com. © **504/558-0505.** Mon–Sat 10am–6pm; Sun 11am–6pm.

Modernist Cuisine Gallery ★ Those familiar with his *Modernist Cuisine* cookbooks may recognize Nathan Myhrvold's vibrant food photos. Great as they look on the page, the large-format, resin-coated prints are even yummier up close. 305 Royal St. modernistcuisinegallery.com. © **504/571-5157.** Sun–Wed 10am–6pm; Thurs–Sat 10am–8pm.

New Orleans School of GlassWorks & Printmaking Studio ★★★ This institution, with 35,000 square feet of studio space, houses an 850-pound tank of molten glass, a letterpress, and a printing press. At this sister school to the Louvre Museum of Decorative Arts, glasswork artists, bookbinders, and master printmakers display their work, demonstrate glassblowing, and teach classes. 727 Magazine St. neworleansglassworks.com. © **504/529-7279.** Mon–Sat 10:30am–5pm.

Rodrigue Studio New Orleans ★ The late Cajun artist George Rodrigue's ubiquitous Blue Dog is the Zelig of New Orleans art: The cobalt kitsch canine appears in every imaginable pose and setting and invades your consciousness. Adorable? Obnoxious? You be the judge. The gallery also displays some of Rodrigue's more classical works. 730 Royal St. www.george rodrigue.com. ✆ **504/581-4244.** Mon–Sat 11am–5pm; Sun noon–5pm or by appt.

Terrance Osborne ★★★ If you want your walls to reflect your unending devotion to New Orleans, this is the gallery—and artist—for you. Rich, dynamic paintings (including original Jazz Fest posters) of streetscapes, musicians, cultural icons, parades, and more, from $50 prints to $50,000 originals. 3029 Magazine St. www.terranceosborne.com. ✆ **504/232-7530.** Thurs–Mon 11am–5pm.

Books

Arcadian Books ★★ Bibliophiles will bask in these wondrous, dusty stacks, especially lovers of the classics (in English and Latin); the history inquisitive (local and far beyond); and seekers of French, German, or Russian literature in the original. The personable proprietor, Russell Desmond, is ridiculously knowledgeable and knows every item in this gloriously decrepit grotto. 714 Orleans Ave. ✆ **504/523-4138.** Mon–Sat 9am–5pm.

Baldwin & Company ★★★ This bookshop/cafe named for James Baldwin is an oasis of great books, cozy couches, thoughtful art, and sublime iced lattes, in one of the city's rare Art Deco buildings. It emphasizes community, creativity, and Black literature, and hosts author talks, signings, and conversations. 1030 Elysian Fields Ave. www.baldwinandcobooks.com. ✆ **504/354-1741.** Mon–Sun 7am–6pm.

Beckham's Bookshop ★★ Some 60,000 volumes collected by the store's owners (and one cat) jam the bottom two floors at beloved Beckham's—a pillar of the Quarter's thriving indie bookshop scene since 1967. It has used books for all interests (browse the glass cases for rare gems) and a fine small selection of new, locally focused titles. The third floor is all vintage vinyl. 228 Decatur St. ✆ **504/522-9875.** Daily 10am–4pm.

Community Book Center ★★★ The city's oldest Black-owned bookstore has been a social and cultural hub since 1983; we've stopped by for a quick browse and ended up staying hours, engrossed in conversation with the proprietors. African-centered literature reigns, from new fiction and memoir to classics, poetry, history, cookbooks, plus a sweet selection of kids' books. Also trinkets and textiles (and a lovable cat named Yanni). 2523 Bayou Rd. www.readcbc.com. ✆ **504/948-7323.** Tues–Sat 10am–6pm.

Crescent City Books ★★ This small, friendly shop of mostly used books offers serious literature for the seriously literate, with an emphasis on history, local interest, literary criticism, philosophy, and art. It's also a hub of info about literary events and has a small selection of maps and art prints. 240 Chartres St. www.crescentcitybooks.com. ✆ **504/524-4997.** Daily 11am–7pm.

Faulkner House Books ★★★ Yes, Nobel prize–winner William Faulkner lived here while writing his early works, but that's only one ingredient in this winning recipe for a perfect small bookshop. Shelf after high shelf is occupied by desirable titles, from first editions to Southern authors and current bestsellers. Just one room and a hallway, Faulkner House feels like somebody's private home (it is)—but the gracious advice and judicious selection make manifest the art of bookselling. (And by the time you read this, there should be a cat in residence.) 624 Pirate's Alley. faulknerhousebooks.com. ✆ **504/524-2940.** Daily 10am–5pm.

Garden District Book Shop ★★★ Set in an old (1884) roller-skating rink, this lovely, medium-size shop is stocked with just about every New Orleans- or Louisiana-themed book you can think of, no matter the focus: interiors, exteriors, food, Creoles, fiction, poetry, you name it—including many signed copies. Best-sellers, too, and a cozy kids' area. Lots of fantastic literary events happen here, and at press time, a bar was being added, because books + booze = longstanding NOLA tradition. (No cats, but one sweet shop dog named Pete.) 2727 Prytania St. www.gardendistrictbookshop.com. ✆ **504/895-2266.** Mon–Fri 7am–6pm; Sat–Sun 8am–5pm.

Octavia Books ★★★ If you adore independent bookstores, this spacious Uptown beauty will thrill you. There's much to savor here, in the extensive, well-selected stock, in the vast knowledge of the booksellers and friendly owners, and in the frequent signings and readings. It's a local favorite, currently turning a new page with a massive renovation, doubling its size and connecting it to the adjacent restaurant, **Scrambled,** via a speakeasy-style bookshelf doorway. 513 Octavia St. www.octaviabooks.com. ✆ **504/899-7323.** Mon–Sat 10am–6pm; Sun 10am–5pm.

Candies, Pralines & Pastries

Bittersweet Confections ★ Ideal for fortification after (or before) a tough gallery- or museum-hopping stint, this bakery/cafe is known for its chocolates, but the cupcakes also are hard to resist. Wish it were open later for a little something after a Warehouse District dinner. 725 Magazine St. www.bittersweetconfections.com. ✆ **504/523-2626.** Tues–Sat 7:30am–2pm.

Laura's Candies ★ Charming Laura's is said to be the city's oldest candy store, established in 1913. The pralines are fabulous, but the rich, delectable golf-ball-size truffles are a personal favorite indulgence. 331 Chartres St. www.laurascandies.com. ✆ **504/525-3880.** Daily 10am–6pm. Also at 305 Royal St.

Loretta's Authentic Pralines ★★★ This beloved shop carries on the spirit of the late "praline queen" Loretta Harrison, the city's first African-American woman to run her own successful praline company. The pralines are stupendous, and the beignets (especially those stuffed with seafood) are fluffy and addictive, some of the city's best. French Market: 1100 N. Peters St. Stall #9. www.lorettaspralines.com. ✆ **504/323-8350.** Wed–Sun 9am–5pm; Mon 9am–4pm. Also at 2101 N. Rampart St. Ste 9., ✆ **504/944-7068,** Thurs–Sat 9am–4pm.

Southern Candymakers ★★★ Our top choice for pralines, it offers the usual suspects and some nontraditionals (coconut and sweet potato!), all extra creamylicious and made fresh right in front of you in small batches—if the display doesn't reel you in, the aroma will. We swoon for the pecan-laden *tortues;* the boxed chocolate crawfish and gator pops make fine gifts. 334 Decatur St. www.southerncandymakers.com. ☎ **504/523-5544.** Daily 10am–6pm. Also in the French Market at 1010 Decatur St., ☎ **504/525-6170.**

Costumes & Masks

Costumery is big business and big fun in New Orleans, and not just for Mardi Gras; most households boast a well-stocked year-round costume closet. In addition to these shops, try thrift stores, where outfits can sometimes be found at a fraction of their original cost. (Troll Dauphine St. in the Bywater.)

Carl Mack Presents ★★ Mack, doyen of Mardi Gras entertainment, rents or creates ornate costumes for Fat Tuesday or any day. This is high-production-value stuff—no naughty nurses here. 1010 Conti St. www.carlmack. com. ☎ **504/949-4009.** Thurs–Mon noon–4pm or by appt.

Fifi Mahony's ★★ Wig wackiness, why not? Have the hair you've always wanted (even if just for the day). Worth visiting the French Quarter location to try on wigs of every color and length, and ogle outrageous custom pieces. Makeup services, too. 934 Royal St. fifisbywater.square.site. ☎ **504/525-4343.** Mon–Wed noon–6pm; Thurs–Sat 11am–7pm; Sun noon–6pm.

Southern Costume Company ★★ They rent, they design, they alter, they'll get you dressed. Enormous stock, reasonable prices, and helpful service. 951 Lafayette St. sccnola.com. ☎ **504/523-4333.** Mon–Fri 9am–4pm.

Uptown Costume & Dancewear ★★ This is headquarters for Mardi Gras, Halloween, and whenever the costuming bug happens to bite. (In New Orleans, it bites often!) It's hard to imagine anyone leaving this big, well-stocked shop empty-handed. 4326 Magazine St. facebook.com/uptowncostumeand dancewear. ☎ **504/895-7969.** Mon and Wed–Fri noon–6pm; Sat 11am–6pm.

Fashion, Vintage Clothing, Hats & Accessories

Art and Eyes ★★★ Eyeglass wearers who demand something above average: For a souvenir you'll use daily, consider a pair from this extensive assortment of fabulous frames. Artisan-made, unusual materials, vintage, designer, imported . . . too much gorgeousness to pick just one. The team here is deeply passionate about the inventory and will urge you try on anything you're, um, eyeing. 3708 Magazine St. www.artandeyesneworleansla.com. ☎ **504/891-4494.** Sun–Mon 11am–5pm; Tues–Fri 11am–7pm; Sat 10am–6pm; Sun noon–5pm (closed Sun in Aug).

Century Girl ★★★ High-end curated vintage gems. Just choose your decade, be it a shimmering beaded 1920s gown; a wasp-waisted midcentury cocktail confection a la Midge Maisel; a '70s Gucci butterfly-patterned silk kerchief; or an Oscar de la Renta gown so slinky it might escape the store (straight into your closet). 2023 Magazine St. www.centurygirlvintage.com. *C* **504/875-3105.** Mon–Sat 11am–5:30pm; Sun noon–5:30pm.

Dollz & Dames ★★   If the Frenchmen Street jitterbugging scene has released your inner pin-up gal, this is your store. The vintage-y frocks make for darling datewear, but we'd don them any time. Tops cost $60 to $130, and dresses are under $200. Cute accessories, custom T-strap dance shoes, and helpful help. 216 Decatur St. www.dollzanddames.com. *C* **504/522-5472.** Daily noon–6pm.

Fleur de Paris ★★★   The 1920s and '30s elegance displayed here is positively swoonworthy. Hand-blocked, stylishly trimmed hats are expensive, but works of art; you'll also find luscious stockings and scarves, an ever-changing collection of vintage gowns, and custom design services. 523 Royal St. www.fleurdeparis.shop. *C* **504/525-1899.** Mon and Wed–Sat 10am–6pm; Sun 11am–6pm.

Freda ★★★   This uber-stylish shop is like a cocktail mixer for hip clothes, fun accessories, and locally made goods. It's where the perfect festival hat befriends some shiny gold socks and a long, frilly dress. Where a pair of OOAK overalls cozies up to a black vinyl Batsheva Dirndl top. Over in the corner, the scented oils are networking with the ceramics, and an elegant brass necklace is flirting with body oils. No one's going home alone. 1150 Magazine St. Suite 1A. www.shop-freda.com. Mon and Wed–Sat 11am–5pm; Sun noon–5pm.

Funky Monkey ★★   For 25 years, this place has brought the retro. You'll be the life of any party in glittery boots and a '70s-style mini, or a bulky sweater, or a stunning ball gown, or a beaded mosaic vintage vest. Or just scoop up one of the many awesome graphic T-shirts. 3127 Magazine St. www.funkymonkeynola.com. *C* **504/899-5587.** Mon–Wed 11am–6pm; Thurs–Sat 11am–7pm; Sun noon–6pm.

Luca Falcone ★★   Bespoke suits of Italian fabric and shoes of Spanish leather, all cut to custom perfection by master tailors. If clothes make the man, many a gentleman has been made here (and if you can afford these suits, you can afford to come back for the fitting . . . and you'll have a good excuse to do so). 2049 Magazine St. www.lfsuits.com. *C* **504/309-5929.** Mon–Sat 10am–6pm or by appt.

Meyer the Hatter ★★★   Family-owned for more than 125 years, this haberdashery has one of the South's largest selections of fine hats and caps, with distinguished international labels such as Bailey, Stetson, Kangol, Dobbs, and Biltmore for men (the women's collection is smaller). Let these hat whisperers fuss over you and pick out the proper feather for your new chapeau—they know just how to top every head. 120 St. Charles Ave. www.meyerthehatter.com. *C* **504/525-1048.** Mon–Sat 10am–5:45pm.

Miss Claudia's Vintage Clothing & Costumes ★   Gold sequined short-shorts and pink rhinestoned dresses, bright turquoise wigs to put over our tresses, bedazzled leggings and sparkling blings—these are a few of our favorite things. (Also, floral maxis, leather, Hawaiian shirts, men's vintage . . .) This tiny shop is a good time waiting to happen. 4204 Magazine St. www.facebook.com/missclaudiasvintage. ☏ **504/897-6310.** Mon–Fri 11am–6pm; Sat 10am–6pm; Sun noon–5pm.

No Rules Fashion ★   Glam, costume-y, and adventurous stuff for pirates, fetishists, and everyday nonconformists. Think velvet corsets, spangly bustiers, sequined jumpsuits, two-piece suits in skull or flamingo patterns, or Edwardian and military-inspired jackets. Reasonably priced, no-regrets funwear. 927 Royal St. www.norulesfashion.com. ☏ **504/875-4437.** Mon–Fri 11am–5pm; Sat 11am–6pm; Sun noon–5pm.

odAOMO ★★   Owner/designer Dr. Sophia Aomo Omoro designs dresses, bags, and accessories that are hand-crafted in Kenya by her own small team. The looks are breezy, fashion-forward, and eminently wearable; the real standouts are the statement neckpieces, belts, and bags of leather, beading, and metals. Fair wages and eco-friendly materials are central to the odAOMO philosophy. 839 Chartres St. www.odaomo.com. ☏ **504/460-5730.** Sun–Sat 10am–5pm.

Rubenstein's ★★★   Many a proper young New Orleans man learned the art of attire here. For almost a century this hallowed haberdasher has outfitted gents in custom suits, fine menswear, and perfect prepwear. Their pros will dress you to the nines, with quick-turnaround tailoring to get you Galatoire's-ready. 102 St. Charles Ave. www.rubensteinsneworleans.com. ☏ **504/581-6666.** Mon–Sat 10am–5:30pm.

ShoeBeDo ★★   As much a gallery as a shoe store, it's worth a visit just to gawk. The window display's full of glam, outrageous, I-can't-pull-that-off footwear, but oh, you can. (There are cute flats and sandals, too.) 324 Chartres St. www.shoebedousa.com. ☏ **504/523-7463.** Sun–Thurs 10am–6pm; Fri–Sat 10am–7pm.

SoSuSu ★★★   Upscale, contemporary day-, foot-, and night-out wear that will spark joy. Susu selects labels you'll hear about next year, with a practiced eye for elegance, fine lines, and a minimalist pop of quirk. 3427 Magazine St. www.sosusuboutique.com. ☏ **504/309-5026.** Mon–Sat 10am–5pm.

Trashy Diva ★★★   There's actually nothing trashy about the 1940s and '50s vintage-inspired clothes here. Flirty, curve-flattering numbers in silks and velvets appeal to both Bettys and Goths, as do the shoes and va-va-voom corsets and lingerie. Check sales racks for bargains, and ask to be pointed to the nearby lingerie shop and newly opened vintage market! 537 Royal St. trashydiva.com. ☏ **504/522-4233.** Sun–Thurs noon–6pm; Fri–Sat noon–7pm. Also at 2048 Magazine St., ☏ **504/299-8777.**

West London Boutique ★★★   This gorgeous destination for local and visiting fashionistas offers apparel by emerging female designers from around the world. Think elegant fun: dramatic embroidery and romantic lace, bright flowers and mixed prints, satin and ruffles, softness and sparkle. 3952 Magazine St. www.westlondonboutique.com. ☏ **504/558-4649.** Mon–Sat 11am–5pm; Sun noon–5pm.

Food, Wine & Liquor

Every souvenir shop in town stocks spices, hot sauce, coffee, and beignet mix. The French Market vendors do, too, along with meat and seafood, and they're set up to ship it home or pack it for travel. If you get a hankering from home, try **www.cajungrocer.com**.

Grand Krewe Fine Wine & Spirits ★★   Whatever libations you seek, this warm and friendly local shop will sort you out, with fairly priced international wines, boutique bubbles, and small-batch spirits. Plus, free "Thirsty Thursday" evening tastings and the two cutest shop pugs in the known universe. 2305 Decatur St. www.grandekrewe.com. ✆ **504/309-8309.** Mon–Sat noon–8pm; Sun noon–5pm.

Keife & Co. ★★   If you just can't get out the door, Keife & Co. will deliver a basket with gourmet meats, cheeses, and wine to your Central Business District hotel room. If you *can* get out, grab a bottle on your way to the restaurant or to take home. Great selection; even better service. 801 Howard Ave. www.keifeandco.com. ✆ **504/523-7272.** Mon–Sat 10am–7pm.

Vieux Carré Wine and Spirits ★★   Whether you're a serious wine buyer or looking for a souvenir bottle of Herbsaint, absinthe, or Sazerac rye—or just want a BYOB for tonight's dinner—this densely packed 35-year-old French Quarter shop will fit the bill. 422 Chartres St. www.instagram.com/vcwineandspirits. ✆ **504/568-9463.** Mon–Thurs 10am–6pm; Fri–Sat 10am–7pm.

Gifts, Home Decor & Bath

Bevolo ★★★   Even if you don't intend to take home a handmade copper gaslight lantern as a vacation memento, check out Bevolo because 1) the lanterns are a gorgeous local tradition; 2) master craftsmen fabricate them right in front of you at the on-site workshop (weekdays only); and 3) you might

---

WINE TASTINGS a la carte

Sip, shop, sip, shop. Rinse and repeat! With the Wine Institute of New Orleans' enomatic system, you can taste 1-, 2-, or 4-ounce pours (or a whole bottle's worth) of some 120 wines at **W.I.N.O** (610 Tchoupitoulas St.; www.winoschool.org; ✆ **504/324-8000**). **Faubourg Wines** (2805 St. Claude Ave.; www.faubourg wines.com; ✆ **504/342-2217**) always has a nice selection of $5 to $8 pours and a fab take-home selection (plus, $5 tastings on Wed). Uptown, Black-owned **Second Vine Wine** (4212 Magazine St.; www.secondvinewine.shop;

✆ **504/354-9125**) is a friendly, low-key place to sip and shop for decently priced wines from around the globe, with an emphasis on small businesses, organic practices, and equitable labor practices. Free tastings on Fridays from 6 to 8:30pm. Or make an appointment to taste at the state's first Black-owned, woman-owned winery, **Ole' Orleans** (579 Brooklyn Ave.; www.oleorleans.com; ✆ **504/354-2449**), where all wines are Louisiana-made and NOLA-named, like the Gumbeaux merlot and a white blend called Wards. Reserve online.

change your mind. Or select something more modern from the adjoining Interior Collection. 316 Royal St. www.bevolo.com. ☎ **504/522-9485.** Mon–Sat 9am–5:30pm.

Big Sexy Neon ★   Want a neon fleur de lis for your living room? A "You are beautiful" sign for your bedroom? Or pretty much any other neon decor imaginable? Sure you do! This shop and design studio is, you could say, pretty lit. 1618 Oretha Castle Haley Blvd. www.bigsexyneon.work ☎ **919/395-2759.** Daily 9am–6pm.

The Collective Shop ★★   This newish boutique is a favorite for hand-crafted local gifts at really great prices. We're especially into the Louisiana-themed pop-art paper products with illustrations of Zapps Potato Chips, Sazeracs, crawfish boils, sno-ball syrups, okra, oysters, and Slap Ya Mama hot sauce. 3512 Magazine St. www.statementgoods.com. No phone. Thurs–Sat 11am–6pm; Sun–Mon 11am–4pm.

Derby Pottery ★★   One of Mark Derby's hand-pressed tiles, glazed in gleaming single hues, makes a lovely keepsake (particularly the New Orleans street-name tile reproductions); 100 make a dazzling backsplash or fireplace surround. Ceramic mugs and water-meter clocks are excellent handmade souvenirs. 2029 Magazine St. www.derbypottery.com. ☎ **504/586-9003.** Mon–Sat 10:30am–5pm.

The Good Shop ★★★   Good is how you'll feel supporting this collective where the wares are locally, ethically, and eco-consciously crafted by makers who give back to the community. We adore the mission. We also adore the jasmine candles, "brass fed" onesies, and local, all-natural, ethically sourced Smoke Perfume. 1114 Josephine St. www.thegoodshopnola.com. ☎ **504/784-0900.** Mon and Wed–Sat 11am–6pm; Sun 11am–5pm.

Hazelnut ★   The housewares and gifts here are generally cute, with one dazzling standout: the line of toile items with a customized pattern of iconic New Orleans scenes—the St. Charles streetcar, a live oak tree, St. Louis Cathedral, and such. We want it all: bedding, tote bag, tray, picture frame, even the face mask. Sigh. If you're lucky, co-owner actor Bryan Batt (*Mad Men*) will be in the shop. 5525 Magazine St. www.hazelnutneworleans.com. ☎ **504/891-2424.** Mon–Sat 10am–5pm.

Hové ★★★   The oldest perfumery in the city, Hové features a fabulous selection of all-natural scents for men and women. Original creations ("Kiss in the Dark") and Southern smells such as vetivert and tea olive, available in many forms (bath products, travel candles), make lovely presents—even for yourself. Book buffs will appreciate the copy of *Jitterbug Perfume* signed by author Tom Robbins, confirming the shop in his bestseller was roughly based on Hové. 434 Chartres St. www.hoveparfumeur.com. ☎ **504/525-7827.** Mon–Sat 10am–5pm.

NOLA Boards ★★★ Need a gift or souvenir that's a few (big) steps up from a magnet? We're nuts about all things wooden from this sweet local shop—especially the handcrafted roux paddles, cheese boards, rolling pins, fleur de lis oven pulls, and Louisiana-shaped cutting boards. 4228 Magazine St. www.nolaboards.com. ✆ **504/256-0030.** Mon–Sat 10am–6pm; Sun 11am–6pm.

Simon of New Orleans/Antiques on Jackson ★★ Folk artist Simon, whose brightly painted signs hang in homes and businesses throughout New Orleans, will paint-to-order your own personal sign and ship it to you. The studio also has primitive furniture, antiques, and hodgepodgery. 1028 Jackson Ave. www.facebook.com/simonofneworleans. ✆ **504/524-8201.** Mon–Sat 10am–5pm.

Sunday Shop ★ Entering this boutique is like stepping into a glossy lifestyle magazine—everything just looks, feels, and smells so soothing and refined. Luxe linens, lavender soaps, ostrich feather dusters, the odd vintage objet d'art, oh my. Shopping here is an extravagance, but a divine one. 2025 Magazine St. www.sundayshop.co. ✆ **504/342-2087.** Thurs–Sat 11am–5pm; Mon, Tues, Wed by appt.

Jewelry

Gogo Jewelry ★★ Designer Gogo's colorful silver cuffs, necklaces, earrings, and belt buckles in attention-getting designs like a cartoon-punchy "POW!" burst are fun and fabulous conversation pieces. 2709 Decatur St. www.ilovegogojewelry.com. No phone. Mon–Fri 10am–3pm or by appt.

Marion Cage ★★★ Cage's ultrafine, exquisitely wrought work is popular with Paris and New York collectors, where she worked before opening this gallery in her native New Orleans. Crafted in matte rose and yellow gold, rhodium, leather, and hardwoods, items start around $85; a delicate sterling talon runs $245. 3807 Magazine St. www.marioncage.com. ✆ **504/891-8848.** Thurs–Sat 11am–5pm; Mon–Wed by appt.

Mignon Faget, Ltd. ★★ Faget, a New Orleans native, lends her signature style to New Orleans–specific designs in gold, silver, and bronze d'oré (and housewares, like NOLA-themed glassware)—all superb souvenirs or gifts. 3801 Magazine St. www.mignonfaget.com. ✆ **504/891-2005.** Mon–Sat 10am–6pm; Sun noon–6pm.

Saint Claude Social Club ★★★ This gorgeous boutique stocks *all* the pretty things—flouncy vintage frocks, dreamy feather headpieces—but it's the jewelry, sourced mainly from independent female designers around the world, that keeps us running back to the bright yellow door a block off Magazine Street. We obsess over the store's namesake designs, such as Wonder Woman cuffs, locally inspired alligator rings, gingko earrings, and crawfish-claw necklaces. 1933 Sophie Wright Place. www.saintclaudesocialclub.com. ✆ **504/218-8987.** Wed–Mon 11am–5pm.

Music

Domino Sound Record Shack ★★   A one-room beats shop off the beaten track. Stellar ska, rock steady, and R&B collections; world music from countries you've never heard of; local weirdness; and pretty much everything Sun Ra ever put out. All vinyl except for about 37 cassettes. Bonus points for proximity to McHardy's Chicken (p. 124). 2557 Bayou Rd. www.dominosound records.com. ✆ **504/309-0871.** Wed–Mon noon–6pm ('til 7:30 Fri).

Euclid Records ★★   If you love the smell of vinyl in the morning, or any time, Euclid will fire your pheromones. This younger-than-it-feels Bywater shop (sistah of the iconic St. Louis shop) stocks two floors of platters from every era. 3301 Chartres St. www.euclidrecordsneworleans.com. ✆ **504/947-4348.** Daily 11am–6pm.

Louisiana Music Factory ★★★   *The* place to get yourself stocked up on New Orleans music, with helpful staff and a large selection of regional music—Cajun, zydeco, R&B, jazz, blues, gospel—plus books, posters, original art, and T-shirts. It's especially hopping during Jazz Fest, when it hosts live performances. 421 Frenchmen St. www.louisianamusicfactory.com. ✆ **504/586-1094.** Thurs–Tues 11am–6pm.

Peaches Records ★   Peaches' first store (ca. 1975) was a stop-off for R&B royalty (Stevie Wonder!) and helped launch local hip-hop artists like Juvenile and Lil Wayne. Still family-owned and a hip-hop hub, the spacious store stocks a broad swath of locally focused CDs, vinyl, books, DVDs, tons of super-kitschy gewgaws, and one of the better logo'd T-shirts in town. 4318 Magazine St. www.peachesrecordsandtapes.com. ✆ **504/282-3322.** Daily 10am–5pm.

The Occult

Bottom of the Cup Tearoom ★   Open since 1929, it bills itself as the "oldest tearoom in the United States," so a reading with Otis, its premier psychic, is a pretty classic experience. The psychics can read palms, tarot cards, and tea leaves. Great selection of teas for purchase and various psychic-y goods. 327 Chartres St. www.bottomofthecup.com. ✆ **800/729-7148** or 504/524-1997. Wed–Mon 10am–6pm.

Boutique du Vampyre ★   Of course, New Orleans has a brick-and-mortar vampire shop—are you really surprised? (It's one of only a few in the U.S.) Proprietress Marita Jaeger showcases local artisans, custom-made fangs, coffin-shaped backpacks . . . and for the faint of heart, temporary bite tattoos. 709½ St. Ann St. feelthebite.com. ✆ **504/561-8267.** Daily 10am–9pm.

T-Shirts & More

If crass and mass market suits your style, by all means buy up the Bourbon Street goods. But for garments with local flavor, cleverness, and a decent design aesthetic, there are many better options. Shirts (and hats, hoodies, and

DIVING DEEPER INTO voodoo

What better souvenir to bring back from New Orleans than some genuine Voodoo (or Vodou, if referring to the Haitian religion) paraphernalia? Touristy it may be, but **Marie Laveau's House of Voodoo** ★ (739 Bourbon St.; www.voodoonewworleans.com; ✆ **504/581-3751**) has loads of Voodoo dolls and gris-gris bags that make great souvenirs for the right friends. With two big rooms of paraphernalia, **Voodoo Authentica** ★★ (612 Dumaine St.; www.voodooshop.com; ✆ **504/522-2111**) feels like a regular retail establishment, just one selling locally made Voodoo dolls, potions, spell candles, and daubs that range from cheap to costly; there are simple souvenirs as well as serious works of art—plus readings.

On Saint Claude Avenue, Vodou priestess Sallie Ann Glassman's **Island of Salvation Botanica** (www.islandofsalvationbotanica.com; ✆ **504-948-9961**) in the Healing Center is an authentic place of worship with a comprehensive inventory and a soulful shrine to Marie Laveau. Or venture to the Lower Garden District to **Haus of Hoodoo** ★★ (1716 St. Charles St.; hausofhoodoo.com; ✆ **504/302-2042**), run by Vodou Priestess Jessyka Winston; it offers ritual baths, spiritual waters, oils, candles, herbs, bundles, divinations, books . . . and the opportunity to be liberated from any Voodoo-related misconceptions you might harbor. Also see p. 191 for temples and practitioners (they usually have shops, too).

so forth) in these shops will probably run $5 to $10 more than your average show-me-your-whatever tops, but they're softer. And smarter.

DNO (Defend New Orleans) ★★   Small shops with stylish locally inspired goods, comfy shirts and hoodies, caps, home decor, plus some lesser-known NOLA-related books. 1101 First St. www.dno.la. ✆ **504/941-7010.** Mon–Fri noon–6pm; Sat–Sun 11am–5pm. Also at 600 Carondelet St. ✆ **504/324-7463.**

Dirty Coast ★★   With three locations, Dirty Coast sells utterly witty, eye-catching, original T-shirt designs like the "Crawfish Pi," with the Greek symbol composed of a tasty pile of mudbugs, and "504Ever." 5631 Magazine St. www.dirtycoast.com. ✆ **504/324-3745.** Daily 11am–6pm. Also at 1320 Magazine St., ✆ **504/766-0752.**

Fleurty Girl ★★★   It's hard to leave here without one (or more) of its pithy NOLA-centric T-shirts. Dig the cocktail-related tees, like KEEP CALM AND CARRY A GO-CUP and the Mardi Gras–inspired EVERYWHERE ELSE IT'S JUST TUESDAY. Also excellent jewelry, housewares, and accessories. 617 Chartres St. www.fleurtygirl.net. ✆ **504/304-5529.** Mon–Thurs 10am–6pm; Fri 10am–7pm; Sat 9am–7pm; Sun 9am–6pm. Also at 3137 Magazine St., ✆ **504/301-2557.**

WALKING TOURS OF NEW ORLEANS

By Lavinia Spalding

We've said it before, and we'll keep saying it: This town was made for walking. Even at the height of the humid summer months, when everyone's main motivation is to laze in the shade and sip cool drinks, you can flit between air-conditioned restaurant and air-conditioned museum.

With every step in New Orleans, there's something extraordinary to marvel at and commit to memory, in your mind's eye or on your phone: a gorgeous building more interesting than the last, a mighty oak tree dripping with Mardi Gras beads and Spanish moss, a tuba-lugging musician in formal wear. Granted, the sidewalks and streets are crumbly, but the city is laden with eye candy and void of elevation, save bar stools. Stroll along the city streets or the banks of Bayou St. John, turning when it strikes your fancy. You might have a street to yourself—or share it with a fleeting ghost. Imagine it 100 years ago, without the cars and overhead wires: It wouldn't have looked much different than it does now.

The French Quarter, Garden District, and Bayou St. John—each has its own distinct appearance, fascinating history, and a bit of mystery, and all are easily manageable on foot. So put on some good walking shoes, breathe in that Southern breeze, and mosey.

These self-guided walking tours provide a solid introduction to what is simply one of the most beautiful cities anywhere, and answer some "That looks interesting—what the heck *is* it?" queries. For professional guided tours, including excellent and essential Black history tours, see p. 192.

START:	**The intersection of Royal and Bienville streets.**
FINISH:	**Café du Monde.**
TIME:	**Allow approximately 2½ hours, not including time spent in shops or historic homes.**
BEST TIME:	**Any day between 8am and 10am (the quiet hours).**
WORST TIME:	**At night. Some attractions won't be open, and you won't be able to get a good look at the architecture.**

If you only spend a few hours in New Orleans, do it in the exquisitely pictur-esque French Quarter. In these 80 city blocks, built by the enslaved, the colo-nial empires of France and Spain intersected with the emerging American nation. It's called the Vieux Carré or "Old Square," but somehow it's time-less—venerable yet vibrantly alive, filled with brutal history and joyful his-tory. History as complex and mysterious as the lacy ironwork on the balconies, some of which have secret symbols incorporated by the enslaved artisans who created them. Today's residents and merchants are stewards of a rich tradition of individuality and creativity. This tour (which includes a quick stopover in the Tremé) will introduce French Quarter style, history, and landmarks.

Start at the corner of Royal and Bienville streets, heading into the Quarter (away from Canal St.). That streetcar named Desire rattled along Royal Street until 1948 (then came the bus named Desire. Really.). Imagine how noisy these narrow streets were when the streetcars ran here. Your first stop is:

1 337–343 Royal St., Rillieux-Waldhorn House
Now housing art galleries, shops, and apartments (upstairs), this elegant structure was built between 1795 and 1800 for Vincent Rillieux, the great-grandfather of the French Impressionist artist Edgar Degas. The wrought-iron balconies are an example of excellent Spanish colonial workmanship.

2 334 Royal St., Bank of Louisiana (Police Station)
Across the street, this former bank was erected in 1826, with its columned Greek Revival portico added in the early 1860s. It suffered fires in 1840, 1861, and 1931, and has served as the Louisiana State Capitol, an auction exchange, a criminal court, a juvenile court, and an American Legion social hall. Now a creamy peach color, it houses the Vieux Carré police station (with a good beignet shop next door, if you can't wait for Café du Monde).

Cross Conti Street to:

3 403 Royal St., Latrobe's
Benjamin H. B. Latrobe died of yellow fever shortly after completing designs for the Louisiana State Bank, which opened here in 1821. One of the nation's most eminent architects, he contributed to the design of the U.S. Capitol and the White House. Note the monogram LSB on the Creole-style railing. It's now an elegant banquet hall named for the architect.

10

WALKING TOURS OF NEW ORLEANS

The French Quarter

4 417 Royal St., Brennan's Restaurant

The famed, bright-pink Brennan's opened in this historic building in 1955 and was crowned restaurant royalty almost immediately. Shuttered in 2013 following a sad financial, legal, and family squabble, the restaurant changed hands (but stayed in the family) and was gloriously restored and reopened in 2014. One of 200 buildings destroyed in the 1794 fire and rebuilt (also by Vincent Rillieux) in 1855, it has been home to the Banque de la Louisiane, the world-famous chess champion Paul Charles Morphy, and the parents of Edgar Degas. If it's open, take a gander at the elegant center staircase, the player piano, and pretty courtyard, with the turtle-stocked fountain. And by all means, eat! Find out why on p. 99.

Across the street is:

5 400 Royal St., Louisiana Supreme Court

Built in 1909, this was and still is a courthouse, covering the length of the block. The ostentatious baroque edifice laden with Georgia marble seems out of scale here. Sadly, many original Spanish-era structures were demolished to pave its way. Granted, those original buildings were indeed run down; the new construction was positioned as slum-clearing. But all this was well before the Vieux Carré Commission formed in the early 1930s to protect the historic French Quarter buildings. Ironically, rulings in this very courthouse upheld the preservation regulations fueled by the Vieux Carré Commission.

Across the street again is:

6 437 Royal St., Peychaud's Drug Store

When Masons held lodge meetings here in the early 1800s, proprietor and druggist Antoine A. Peychaud served after-meeting drinks of bitters and cognac to lodge members in small egg cups, called *coquetier*—later Americanized to "cocktails." And so it began (the cocktail and the much-debated legend). Now it's James H. Cohen Antique Store, which has, along with antique weapons and rare coins, an original Peychaud's bottle (p. 226).

Cross St. Louis Street to:

7 519–521 Royal St., Antoine's Wine Cellar

See the little barred window between these buildings? Watch how many people walk right by this hidden marvel. Peer inside to spy the 165-foot-long, wow-factor wine cellar belonging to **Antoine's Restaurant** (p. 97), around the corner. The 25,000-bottle capacity leaves oenophiles envious.

8 533 Royal St., Merieult House

Built for the merchant Jean François Merieult in 1792, this house was the only building in the area left standing after the 1794 fire. Legend has it that Napoleon offered Madame Merieult great riches in exchange for her

Walking Tour 1: The French Quarter

1	Rillieux-Waldhorn House	
2	Bank of Louisiana (Police Station)	
3	Latrobe's	
4	Brennan's Restaurant	
5	Louisiana Supreme Court	
6	Peychaud's Drugstore	
7	Antoine's Wine Cellar	
8	Merieult House	
9	The Court of Two Sisters	
10	Pedesclaux-Lemonnier Mansion	
11	LaBranche House	
12	Pat O'Brien's	
13	Preservation Hall	
14	Bourbon Orleans Hotel	
15	Le Pretre Mansion	
16	Congo Square	
17	Former Site of J&M Studios (The Lost Sock)	
18	Madame John's Legacy	
19	Cornstalk Hotel	
20	Andrew Jackson Hotel	
21	Lafitte's Blacksmith Shop	
22	Lalaurie House	
23	Gallier House Museum	
24	Croissant D'Or	
25	Beauregard-Keyes House	
26	Old Ursuline Convent	
27	New Orleans Jazz Museum at the Old U.S. Mint	
28	The Historic French Market	
29	Jeanne d'Arc Statue	
30	Central Grocery	
31	The Pontalba Buildings	
32	The Presbytère	
33	St. Louis Cathedral	
34	The Cabildo	
35	Faulkner House Books	
36	Tennessee Williams House	
37	Café du Monde	

hair, to create a wig to present to a Turkish sultan (she refused). Nowadays, it serves as the entrance to one of several buildings that make up the excellent **Historic New Orleans Collection** (p. 162). This building is currently closed for renovation, but 520 Royal across the street is open. Admission is free.

Cross Toulouse Street to:

9 613 Royal St., the Court of Two Sisters

This structure was built in 1832 for a local bank president on the site of the 18th-century home of a French governor. The two sisters were Emma and Bertha Camors, whose father owned the building; from 1886 to 1906, they ran a curio store here. Consider a charming courtyard cocktail.

If it's open, pop into M.S. Rau, 622 Royal St. (p. 237), the city's most mind-boggling antiques store.

10 640 Royal St., Pedesclaux-Lemonnier Mansion

No one thought this 1811 building would survive a fourth-floor addition in 1876, creating the city's first "skyscraper." Sadly, it now looks quite neglected, but it's one of the most important buildings from New Orleans' Spanish colonial period. (And thankfully, it's in the midst of a lengthy renovation.) Sieur George, fictional hero of George W. Cable's scandalous *Old Creole Days,* "lived" here. And in the mid-1960s, the building housed Loujon Press, legendary in literary circles for its early embrace of avant-garde writers and Beat poets including Burroughs and Bukowski.

Cross St. Peter Street to:

11 700 Royal St., LaBranche House

The lacy cast-iron grillwork, with its delicate oak-leaf and acorn design, makes this one of the most photographed buildings in the Quarter. This is one of 11 three-story brick row houses built from 1835 to 1840 for the widow of wealthy sugar planter Jean Baptiste LaBranche.

Turn left at St. Peter Street and continue to:

12 718 St. Peter St., Pat O'Brien's

Now the de facto home to the famed Hurricane cocktail (p. 224), this building was completed in 1790. Later, Louis Tabary put on plays here, including, purportedly, the first grand opera in America. The popular courtyard is well worth a look, and maybe even a refreshment.

13 726 St. Peter St., Preservation Hall

The exquisitely decrepit early 1800s building is now best known for its tenant since the 1960s—Preservation Hall. Scores of people descend here nightly for traditional New Orleans jazz (p. 216). You should, too! A daytime stop affords a glimpse, through the ornate iron gate, of a lush tropical courtyard in back. Author Erle Stanley Gardner, of *Perry Mason* fame, lived upstairs.

Continue up St. Peter Street until you reach Bourbon Street, and turn right: Walk 1 block to Orleans Street and **stop at the corner.** The beige, three-story hotel with the wraparound balcony is the:

14 Bourbon Orleans Hotel

Site of the notorious quadroon balls, where wealthy white men were supposedly introduced to potential mistresses: free women (and girls) of color who were one-fourth Black (quadroon) or one-eighth (octoroon). During these balls, the young women's mothers are said to have carefully negotiated *placage* arrangements with the men, often including financial, educational, housing, and child support for the mistresses. Imagine the discussions on those balconies . . . if they indeed happened. (Some historians claim there's no evidence of quadroon balls, that they are just a myth.) The building later became a convent for the Sisters of the Holy Family, the second-oldest order of Black nuns in the country. Their founder, Henriette DeLille, has been presented to the Vatican for consideration for sainthood.

Then look up and down Bourbon Street and try to imagine what it was like in the 1950s and '60s during that particular heyday of jazz and burlesque. A couple blocks to the right, clarinetist Pete Fountain held court over the wild, swinging scene at his French Quarter Inn; a few blocks to your left at the Sho Bar, Blaze Starr stripped her way into the limelight and the hearts of tens of thousands of men.

Turn left on Orleans, heading lakeside, and follow Orleans a block to Dauphine (pronounced Daw-*feen*) Street. On the corner is:

15 716 Dauphine St., Le Pretre Mansion

In 1839, Jean Baptiste Le Pretre bought this 1836 Greek Revival house and added the romantic cast-iron galleries. The house is the subject of an oft-told horror story: In the 19th century, a conspicuously wealthy Turk, supposedly the exiled brother of a sultan, rented the house. He brought an entourage of servants and beautiful young girls—all thought to have been stolen from the sultan—and threw lavish parties. One night, screams came from inside; the next morning, neighbors found the tenant and the young beauties lying dead in a pool of blood. The mystery remains unsolved. Local ghost experts say you can sometimes hear music and piercing shrieks. This oft-debated story is strangely similar to "The Brother of the Sultan," a 1922 fictional tale by Helen Pitkin Schertz. Draw your own conclusions.

Turn left on Dauphine and right on St. Peter, then walk 2 blocks to Rampart Street. Once you cross Rampart, you'll no longer be in the French Quarter; we're taking you on a quick detour to the Tremé, the country's oldest Black neighborhood. Cross Rampart and enter Louis Armstrong Park. The large, paved plaza just inside this entrance is known by another name:

16 Congo Square

You can (and must) learn much more about Congo Square, one of New Orleans' most important and sacred landmarks, on pages 21 and 168, and in many of the books on p. 24. But very briefly: A decree in 1817 restricted enslaved people to gathering in only one place, now known as Congo Square. Here, enslaved people congregated with free people of color on Sundays to worship, dance, drum, sing, and trade. These gatherings birthed jazz, rhythm, and blues (and, according to many historians, *all* American music). This is still (especially on Sundays) a place to gather, worship, play music, celebrate African culture, and honor ancestors.

Wander the park, exiting through the big white arch at St. Ann Street. Cross Rampart Street (carefully, since New Orleanian drivers aren't great at stopping for pedestrians, even at crosswalks). Welcome back to the Quarter! Turn immediately left on Rampart, toward Dumaine Street, passing **Bar Tonique,** 820 N. Rampart St. (where you can hydrate with one of the city's tastiest cocktails). On the corner of Rampart and Dumaine is:

17 840 N. Rampart, Former Site of J&M Studios

Now a laundromat and curiosity shop called **The Lost Sock,** this is the former site of **J&M Studios,** one of the birthplaces of rock 'n' roll. Artists including Fats Domino, Little Richard, Jerry Lee Lewis, and Ray Charles recorded hits here, in Cosimo Matassa's first studio.

Turn right on Dumaine Street. At 1014 Dumaine is **Tennessee Williams**' final NOLA home. Continue 2 blocks on Dumaine Street to Bourbon Street, where on the corner you'll see **Cafe Lafitte in Exile,** the South's oldest LGBTQ bar (p. 231). Cross Bourbon Street and continue past Royal Street to find:

18 632 Dumaine St., Madame John's Legacy

Yes, it's a construction site, and has been for ages; Madame John's Legacy, now part of the Louisiana State Museum complex, has been shuttered for renovations for some years. This historic structure, built in 1726, was once thought to be the oldest building on the Mississippi River. Recent research, however, suggests that only a few parts of the original building survived the great fire of 1788. Still, it survived the *other* fire in 1794, and is one of the French Quarter's oldest buildings, as well as one of the few remaining examples of French colonial architecture. (Most are Spanish colonial.) Its first owner was a ship captain who died in the 1729 Natchez Massacre; upon his death, the house passed to the captain of a Lafitte-era smuggling ship—and then passed on to 21 subsequent owners. The structure is a rare example of the once-prevalent French "raised cottage," with an aboveground basement of brick-between-posts construction (locally made bricks were too soft to be the primary building material). Its name comes from George W. Cable's fictional character who was bequeathed the house in the short story "Tite Poulette" (more on p. 162).

Double back to Royal Street. Turn right.

19 915 Royal St., Cornstalk Hotel

Legend persists that the fence surrounding this sweet Victorian was ordered by the home's owner to ease his wife's homesickness for her native Iowa. Oddly, the same story is told about a house in the Garden District with a similar fence (p. 262). It was forged in Philadelphia, and only one more exists (at the Banning Museum in California, but from New Orleans). In any case, it's awfully pretty, isn't it? Enough so that Bill and Hillary Clinton and Elvis himself have walked the supposedly haunted halls here. (At press time, the hotel was up for sale, for the low, low price of about $6 million.)

20 919 Royal St., Andrew Jackson Hotel (Old Federal Courthouse)

Just after General Andrew Jackson slammed the British in the 1815 Battle of New Orleans, Louis Louaillier, a member of the legislature, criticized the popular general. Jackson responded by jailing Louis, as well as a judge who tried to order Louis' release. When the war ended and the prisoners were freed, the judge hauled Jackson back into a courthouse on this site, citing him for contempt and fining him $1,000. Twenty-nine years later, Congress ordered Jackson to be repaid with interest. The courthouse survived until 1890, when this hotel was built.

Continue down Royal Street for half a block (good gallery browsing here). Turn left on St. Philip. Go 1 block to:

21 941 Bourbon St., Lafitte's Blacksmith Shop

This National Historic Landmark claims to be the oldest bar in the country, and it's officially the oldest building currently in use as a bar (p. 225). Legend is this was the headquarters of Jean Lafitte and his pirates, who posed as blacksmiths and used it to fence goods they'd plundered on the high seas. It still reflects the architectural influence of late-1700s French colonists. It may also be the oldest building in the Mississippi Valley, but that has not been documented. An unfortunate exterior renovation that tried to replicate the original brick and plaster makes it look fake (it's actually not), but the candlelit interior is still an excellent place to imagine 19th-century Quarter life and swill some grog.

Turn right onto Bourbon Street and follow it 2 blocks to Governor Nicholls Street. Turn right and go 1 block to the corner of Royal Street:

22 1140 Royal St., Lalaurie House

Two-time widow Madame Delphine Macarty de Lopez Blanque wed Dr. Louis Lalaurie and moved into this residence in 1832, where the couple seduced the city with extravagant parties. When a fire broke out, neighbors crashed through a locked door to find seven starving enslaved people chained in painful positions. The sight, combined with Delphine's stories of past slaves having "committed suicide" and rumors of hideous live-subject medical experiments conducted within, enraged her neighbors. Madame Lalaurie and her family escaped a mob's wrath and fled to Paris. After her death, it's rumored that her body was secretly returned to New Orleans for burial. Tales of hauntings persist, especially that of a slave child who fell from the roof trying to escape Delphine's cruelties. The building was a Union headquarters during the Civil War, a gambling house, and home to actor Nicolas Cage. Haunted himself by financial difficulties, Cage was forced to return the house to the bank. Delphine and the Lalaurie House inspired the third season of the *American Horror Story* television show.

Turn right on Royal Street and go to:

23 1132 Royal St., Gallier House Museum

James Gallier, Jr., built this house as his residence in 1857. He and his father were two of the city's leading architects. Anne Rice based Lestat and Louis's home in *Interview with the Vampire* on this house. It's now an excellent museum (p. 161).

Continue on Royal Street to Ursulines Avenue and turn left, toward the river.

24 617 Ursulines Ave., Croissant D'Or ☕

For a little rest or sustenance, stop in the popular **Croissant D'Or,** 617 Ursulines Ave. (www.croissantdornola.com; ✆ **504/524-4663; p. 149).** The pastries here are very good, as is the ambience—inside or out.

At the next corner, turn left onto Chartres Street. You'll be in front of:

25 1113 Chartres St., Beauregard-Keyes House

This raised cottage was built as a residence in 1826 by Joseph Le Carpentier, though it has other important claims to fame (detailed on p. 158). Notice the Doric columns and handsome "boy/girl" twin staircases.

Across the street is the imposing:

26 1100 Chartres St., Old Ursuline Convent

Built in 1752, this is officially the oldest building in the Mississippi River Valley. It was home to the hearty French nuns of Ursula, who helped raise young girls into marriageable prospects for the lonely men settling this new territory (more on p. 160). Many locals claim to be direct descendants of those proper young girls—so many, in fact, that the math doesn't add up. But it beats the alternate original settler ancestry of criminals and other heathens.

Continue along Chartres until you get to Esplanade Avenue and turn right. This is one of the city's most picturesque historic thoroughfares, with grand 1800s town houses gracing the tree-lined avenue. Take time to read the illuminating historic markers along the route. At Decatur Street, look left. That's the Marigny neighborhood, and Frenchmen Street (p. 218), the city's musical epicenter. Just past Decatur Street, you'll see:

27 400 Esplanade Ave., New Orleans Jazz Museum at the Old U.S. Mint

This was the site of Fort St. Charles, built to protect New Orleans in 1792. Andrew Jackson reviewed the "troops" here—pirates, ragtag volunteers, and a nucleus of actual trained soldiers—whom he later led in the Battle of New Orleans. It's now a Louisiana State Museum housing the New Orleans Jazz Museum, and a coin and minting collection (p. 164).

The French Quarter

WALKING TOURS OF NEW ORLEANS

Follow Esplanade toward the river and turn right at the corner of North Peters Street. Follow North Peters until it intersects with Barracks Street. This is the back end of:

28 The Historic French Market

This European-style market (p. 235), originally the site of Indigenous intertribal trading grounds, has been here for well over 200 years. Today it has food booths, arty-crafty goods, and flea-market stalls with souvenirs.

When you leave the French Market, exit on the side away from the river onto Decatur Street. Follow Decatur to St. Philip Street and look for four tall flags flying in the middle of the pavement, surrounding the:

29 Jeanne d'Arc Statue

Locally dubbed "Joni on the Pony," this gilded replica of mighty Joan of Arc riding into battle was a 1958 gift from France, recognizing sisterhood between the two countries. It took a circuitous and controversial route to this location, and now serves as rallying point for the magnificent Krewe de Jeanne d'Arc parade each January 6 (Joni's birthday and Twelfth Night).

Across the street, you'll pass 923 and 919 Decatur St., where the **Café de Refugies** and **Hôtel de la Marine** once stood, gathering places in the 1700s and early 1800s for pirates, smugglers, European refugees, and outlaws. Now, it's muffuletta time.

30 923 Decatur St., Central Grocery 🍴

If it's lunchtime, it's muffuletta o'clock. The best is from **Central Grocery** (✆ **504/523-1620;** p. 114); however, the building's roof collapsed during Hurricane Ida in 2021. Construction is afoot, and hopes are high that it'll reopen soon. Until it does, score one of Central Grocery's famed sandwiches next door at Sidney's Wine Cellar. Take the olivey goodness with you and dine alfresco in Jackson Square, near your next stop.

Decatur Street will take you on to Jackson Square. Turn right onto St. Ann Street; the twin four-story, red brick buildings here and on the St. Peter Street side of the square are:

31 The Pontalba Buildings

These highly coveted buildings sport some of the most impressive cast-iron balcony railings in the French Quarter. They also represent early French Quarter urban revitalization—and early girl power. In the mid-1800s, Baroness Micaela Almonester de Pontalba inherited rows of buildings along both sides of the Place d'Armes from her father, the wealthy Spanish nobleman-turned-magnate Don Almonester (who rebuilt St. Louis Cathedral [p. 157], among other developments). In an effort to counteract the emerging American sector across Canal Street, Baroness Pontalba had the structures razed, and under her supervision the Pontalba Buildings were begun in 1849 (you can see her mark today in the entwined initials A.P. in the ironwork, along with interlocking G's, which some historians say are an Adinkra symbol left by the blacksmiths, enslaved West Africans). These high-end apartments were built in the traditional Creole-European style, with commercial space at street level, housing above, and courtyards in the rear. The baroness also had Jackson

Square built, including the cast-iron fence and the equestrian statue of Andrew Jackson. Her scandalous personal story (p. 159) is equally fascinating.

Follow St. Ann to Chartres Street, turn left, and continue around Jackson Square; you will see:

32 751 Chartres St., the Presbytère

This, the Cabildo, and the St. Louis Cathedral—all designed by Gilberto Guillemard—were the first major public buildings in the Louisiana Territory. The Presbytère was originally designed as the cathedral's rectory. Baroness Pontalba's father financed the building's beginnings, but he died in 1798, leaving only the first floor done. It was finally completed in 1813. Never used as a rectory, it became a city courthouse and now houses the excellent **Louisiana State Museum** (p. 164).

Next, you'll come to:

33 St. Louis Cathedral

Although it is the oldest Catholic cathedral in the U.S., this is actually the third building erected on this spot—the first was destroyed by a hurricane in 1722, the second by fire in 1788. The cathedral was rebuilt in 1794; the central tower was later designed by Henry S. Boneval Latrobe, again remodeled and enlarged between 1845 and 1851 under the direction of Baroness Pontalba. The bell and stately clock (note the nonstandard Roman numeral 4) were imported from France (much more on p. 157).

The building on the cathedral's right is:

34 701 Chartres St., the Cabildo

In the 1750s, this was the site of a French police station and guardhouse. Part of that building was incorporated into the Spanish government statehouse (known as the "Very Illustrious Cabildo"). It was still under reconstruction in 1803 when the transfer papers for the Louisiana Purchase were signed in a room on the second floor. Since then, it has served as New Orleans' City Hall, the Louisiana State Supreme Court, and, since 1911, a Louisiana State Museum (p. 161).

Think those old Civil War cannons out front look pitifully obsolete? Think again. In 1921, in a near-deadly prank, one was loaded and fired. That missile traveled across the wide expanse of the Mississippi and landed 6 blocks inland in a house in Algiers, narrowly missing its occupants.

Walk up the narrow alley between the Cabildo and St. Louis Cathedral. You'll come to Pirate's Alley:

35 624 Pirate's Alley, Faulkner House Books

In 1925, William Faulkner lived here. He contributed to the *Times-Picayune* and worked on his first novels, *Mosquitoes* and *Soldiers' Pay*, making this lovely store a requisite stop for literature lovers and book buyers of any persuasion (p. 241).

To the left of the bookstore, a small alley leads to St. Peter Street, which is behind and parallel to Pirate's Alley.

36 632 St. Peter St., Tennessee Williams House

Have a sudden urge to scream "Stella!!!" at that second-story wrought-iron balcony? No wonder. This is where Tennessee Williams wrote *A Streetcar Named Desire,* one of the greatest pieces of American theater. He remarked that he could hear "that rattle-trap streetcar named Desire running along Royal and the one named Cemeteries running along Canal Street and it seemed the perfect metaphor for the human condition."

Backtrack toward Jackson Square. Walk toward the river on St. Peter Street to Decatur Street. Make a left on Decatur and pass the carriages and artists in front of Jackson Square. Cross Decatur at St. Ann to get to:

37 800 Decatur St., Café du Monde ☕

You've finished! At **Café du Monde** (*✆* **504/525-4544;** p. 148), get beignets and *café au lait* (of course). Do climb the adjacent stairs to the landing—a micro-park renamed in the wake of the 2020 social justice uprising for Louisiana lieutenant governor Oscar Dunn (when he took office in 1868, he was the U.S.'s first elected Black lieutenant governor). Enjoy the expansive views of Jackson Square and the Mississippi River, take a selfie, relax on a bench and rest your feet, and watch the river roll.

WALKING TOUR 2: **THE GARDEN DISTRICT**

START:	**Prytania Street and Washington Avenue.**
FINISH:	**Lafayette Cemetery.**
TIME:	**45 minutes to 2 hours.**
BEST TIME:	**Daylight.**
WORST TIME:	**Night, when you won't be able to get a good look at the architecture.**

Walking around the architecturally astounding Garden District, you may get the impression that you've entered an entirely separate city—or time period—from the French Quarter. The Garden District was indeed once a separate city (Lafayette) and established later, after the 1803 Louisiana Purchase. But what most profoundly distinguishes the two is that they were developed by two different groups: The French Quarter was settled by Creoles during the French and Spanish colonial periods, and the Garden District was created by Americans.

Thousands of Americans moved here after the Louisiana Purchase, drawn by a booming local economy fueled by lucrative Mississippi River commerce, the abundant (and abominable) slave trade, and national banks. Friction soon arose between these new residents and the Creoles, sparked by language barriers, religious division, commercial competition, and mutual snobbery. With inferior business experience, education, and organizational skills, the Creoles worried that *les Americains* would drive them out of business, and Americans were barred from the already overcrowded French Quarter. The snubbed Americans moved upriver and created their own residential district of astounding, in-your-face opulence: the Garden District. It is, therefore, a culture clash reflected through architecture, with Americans creating an identity by introducing bold, new styles.

Note: With few exceptions, houses on this tour are private homes and not open to the public. Several are owned by celebrities (names are omitted for privacy). Please be respectful of the residents.

To reach the Garden District, take the St. Charles streetcar to Washington Avenue (stop no. 16) and walk 1 block toward the river to:

1 2727 Prytania St., Garden District Book Shop

A stellar collection of national and regional titles, with many signed editions, makes this bookshop (p. 241) an appropriate kickoff for a Garden District tour. The historic property was built in 1884 as the Crescent City Skating Rink, and subsequently acted as a livery stable, mortuary, grocery, and gas station. Today "the Rink" also offers a cafe, a few gift shops, restrooms, and air-conditioning (appreciated if you're doing this tour in summer).

Across Prytania Street, head to the corner of Fourth St. to find:

2 1448 Fourth St., Colonel Short's Villa

This house was built by architect Henry Howard for Kentucky Colonel Robert Short. The story goes that Short's wife missed the cornfields in her native Iowa, so he bought her the cornstalk fence (for a laugh, see Cornstalk Hotel; p. 256). But a revised explanation has the wife requesting it because it was the most expensive, showy fence in the building catalog. The city's second Civil War occupational governor, Nathaniel Banks, was quartered in this 9,800-square-foot beauty.

Continuing down Prytania, you'll find:

3 2605 Prytania St., Briggs-Staub House

This is the Garden District's only example of Gothic Revival architecture (unpopular among Protestant Americans because it reminded them of their Roman Catholic Creole antagonists). Original owner Charles Briggs built the adjacent servant quarters for his Irish indentured servants, who were also starting to create the nearby Irish Channel neighborhood (across Magazine St. from the Garden District).

4 2523 Prytania St., Our Mother of Perpetual Help

The original owner, Henry Lonsdale, made his fortune selling burlap sacks, and was the first to add chicory to coffee. Once an active Catholic chapel, this site was one of several in the area owned by novelist Anne Rice and the setting for her novel *Violin*. The author's childhood home is down the street at 2301 St. Charles Ave.

5 2504 Prytania St., Women's Opera Guild Home

Some of the Garden District's most memorable homes incorporate more than one style. Designed by William Freret in 1858, this one combines his

Walking Tour 2: The Garden District

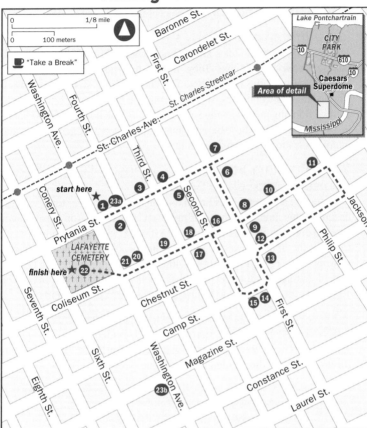

1 The Garden District Book Shop
2 Colonel Short's Villa
3 Briggs-Staub House
4 Our Mother of Perpetual Help
5 Women's Opera Guild Home
6 Toby's Corner
7 Bradish Johnson House &
   Louise S. McGehee School
8 Pritchard-Pigott House
9 Morris-Israel House
10 The Seven Sisters
11 Buckner ("Coven") House
12 Carroll-Crawford House

13 Brevard-Mahat-Rice House
14 Payne-Strachan House
15 Stained Glass House
16 Joseph Merrick Jones House
17 Musson-Bell House
18 Robinson House
19 Koch-Mays House
20 Benjamin Button House
21 Commander's Palace
22 Lafayette Cemetery
23a The Chicory House ☕
23b Coquette ☕

Greek Revival design with Queen Anne–style additions. It's now an events center owned by the Women's Opera Guild. Tours are offered on Mondays from 10am to 3pm. No reservations necessary, $20; ℂ **504/453-7051.**

6 2340 Prytania St., Toby's Corner

The Garden District's oldest known home was built in 1838 for Philadelphia wheelwright Thomas Toby in the then-popular Greek Revival style—by way of the West Indies. The "non-Creole" style still followed Creole building techniques, such as raising the house up on brick piers to combat flooding and encourage air circulation. The house changed hands in 1858 to a family whose descendants still live here, six generations and many renovations and expansions later.

7 2343 Prytania St., Bradish Johnson House & Louise S. McGehee School

Paris-trained architect James Freret (cousin of William; see stop #5 above) designed this French Second Empire–style mansion for sugar factor Bradish Johnson in 1872 at a cost of $100,000 ($2 million plus today). Contrast the house's awesome detail with the stark, classical simplicity of Toby's Corner across the street—illustrating the effect that one generation of outrageous fortune had on Garden District architecture. Since 1929 it has been the private Louise S. McGehee School for girls.

Back track to First Street and turn left (away from St. Charles); it's a short block to:

8 1407 First St., Pritchard-Pigott House

This grand Greek Revival double-galleried town house shows how, as fortunes grew, so did Garden District home sizes.

Note the marble carriage block in front of the house across the street. Past residents used these like a step stool when mounting their horses and carriages.

9 1331 First St., Morris-Israel House

As time passed, the trend toward the formal Greek Revival style took a playful turn. By the 1860s, Italianate was popular, as seen in this (reputedly haunted) double-galleried town house, designed by architect Samuel Jamison. Note the identical ornate cast-iron galleries.

From the Morris-Israel House, turn right onto Coliseum Street. Along this block you'll see:

10 2329–2305 Coliseum St., the Seven Sisters

This row of "shotgun" houses gets its nickname from a (false) story that a 19th-century Garden District resident built these homes as wedding gifts for his seven daughters. Actually, there are eight "Seven Sisters," and they were built on speculation (the eighth looks somewhat different). "Shotgun"-style homes are so named because, theoretically, if one fired a gun through the front door, the bullet would pass unhindered through a series of rooms and out the back. (Or maybe because a West African word for this native African house form sounds like "shotgun.") Common in hot climates, the shotgun style effectively circulates air. The relatively small homes are popular in New Orleans, but rare along the imposing Garden District streets.

Follow Coliseum 1 more block to Jackson St., to:

11 1410 Jackson St., Buckner ("Coven") House

The setting for Miss Robicheaux's Witch Academy from *American Horror Story: Coven*, this stunning 1865 mansion built for a cotton baron has three ballrooms and 48 columns. You can rent them all (and the rest of the house) for a silly sum.

Now turn right on Jackson for 1 block; go right again on Chestnut Street for 2 blocks. At the corner of First and Chestnut, you'll see:

12 1315 First St., Carroll-Crawford House

On the right-hand corner, the Carroll-Crawford House is another of Samuel Jamison's Italianate beauties. An even bigger cousin to the Morris-Israel House down the street, it was built in 1869 for Virginia cotton factor Joseph Carroll.

13 1239 First St., Brevard-Mahat-Rice House

On the left-hand corner, this 1857 Greek Revival town house was later augmented with an Italianate bay, in a fine example of "transitional" architecture. The fence's rosettes begat the house's name, "Rosegate," and its woven diamond pattern is said to be the precursor to the chain-link fence. This was novelist Anne Rice's home and a setting in her *Witching Hour* novels.

One block further up First Street you'll see:

14 1134 First St., Payne-Strachan House

As the stone marker out front notes, Jefferson Davis, president of the Confederate States of America, died in this classic Greek Revival ante-bellum home, that of his friend Judge Charles Fenner. Note the sky-blue ceiling of the gallery, traditionally believed to keep winged insects from nesting there and to ward off evil spirits. (Now that you're aware of this local custom, you'll notice it everywhere.)

Turn right on Camp. At the corner of Camp and Second Street is:

15 1137 Second St., Stained Glass House

This house exemplifies the Victorian architecture popularized in uptown New Orleans toward the end of the 19th century. Many who built such homes were from the Northeast and left New Orleans in the summer; otherwise, it would be odd to see this claustrophobic, "cool climate"–style house. Note the exquisite stained glass and rounded railing on the gallery.

Turn right onto Second Street and go 2 blocks to the corner of Coliseum:

16 2425 Coliseum St., Joseph Merrick Jones House

When previous owner Trent Reznor of the band Nine Inch Nails moved in, new anti-noise ordinances were introduced at city council. His next-door neighbor was Councilwoman Peggy Wilson. Coincidence?

The Garden District

Turn left onto Coliseum Street and go 1 block to Third Street. Turn left to get to:

17 1331 Third St., Musson-Bell House

This is the 1853 home of Michel Musson, one of the few French Creoles then living in the Garden District and the uncle of artist Edgar Degas (who lived with Musson on Esplanade Ave. during a visit to New Orleans; see p. 270 below). On the Coliseum Street side of the house is the foundation of a cistern. Most of these once-common water tanks (Mark Twain commented that it looked as if everybody in the neighborhood had a private brewery) were destroyed at the turn of the 20th century when mosquitoes, which breed in standing water, were found to be carriers of yellow fever. Yellow fever epidemics infamously killed 41,000 New Orleanians between 1817 and 1905.

Turn around and cross Coliseum to see:

18 1415 Third St., Robinson House

This striking Italianate villa was built between 1859 and 1865 by architect Henry Howard for tobacco grower Walter Robinson. Walk past the house to appreciate its scale—the outbuildings, visible from the front, are actually connected to the side of the main house. The entire roof is a large vat that once collected water. Add gravity and water pressure: Thus begat the Garden District's earliest indoor plumbing. The lavish 10,500-square-foot interior features a ballroom, a dining table seating 26 guests, and a grand, curving staircase with 28 stairs, each covered in its own design. Hard to believe that, in sorrier, post-Depression times, it was sold for just $500 . . . especially considering that the seven-bedroom home was put on the market a few years back for $12 million (it eventually sold for a trifling $4 million).

Continue down Coliseum Street to the corner of Fourth Street:

19 2627 Coliseum St., Koch-Mays House

This picturesque chalet-style dollhouse (well, for a large family of dolls) was built in 1876 by noted architect William Freret for James Eustis, a U.S. senator and ambassador to France (perhaps justifying the full-size ballroom). It and four other spec homes he built on the block were referred to as Freret's Folly. No detail was left unfrilled, from the ironwork to the gables and finials.

20 2707 Coliseum St., Benjamin Button House

Half a block further down Coliseum, this 8,000-square-footer is best known as the title character's home in the film *The Curious Case of Benjamin Button.* Ergo Brad Pitt slept here, fictionally (he bought his own French Quarter home soon after filming). The house was owned by the same family from 1870 until its 2009 sale. Thus, when the *Button* location scouts came calling, they dealt with the family's 90-year-old matriarch, who had raised seven kids under this roof. Or *roofs,* since it's actually two houses combined: The original 1832 house has been significantly renovated over the years.

At the corner of Coliseum and Washington Avenue:

21 1403 Washington Ave., Commander's Palace

Established in 1883 by Emile Commander, this turreted Victorian (a bordello in the 1920s) is now the pride of the Brennan family, New Orleans' most respected restaurateurs. Commander's Palace has long reigned as one of the city's—nay, the country's—top restaurants (p. 136).

Across the street, behind the white brick wall, is:

22 1400 Washington Ave., Lafayette Cemetery

Established in 1833, this "city of the dead" is one of New Orleans' oldest cemeteries. It's been closed for years, but a peek through the gates provides a glimpse of the classic aboveground tombs. Typically, they house numerous corpses from an extended family—one here lists 37 entrants; others are designated for members of specific fire departments or fraternal organizations. For more on New Orleans' unique burial customs, see p. 185.

Walk up Washington, past the cemetery, to Prytania St.

23 Wind Down at The Chicory House or Coquette ☕

You're back at your first stop, the Rink, where you can enjoy a cup of coffee, an adult bevvy, and some light lunch or pastries at **The Chicory House.** Or double back and continue south on Washington to Magazine Street, where an early dinner at **Coquette** (p. 137) or any of the many eateries along this street will satisfy most appetites.

WALKING TOUR 3: ESPLANADE RIDGE & BAYOU ST. JOHN

START:	**Esplanade Avenue and Johnson Street.**
FINISH:	**City Park.**
TIME:	**It's a healthy trek, about 3 hours and 3 miles, not including museum, cemetery, and lunch stops. If that's too much, you could do stops 1–9 (1 mile) or 12–21 (2 miles) separately. Or bike or drive!**
BEST TIME:	**Monday through Saturday, early or late morning.**
WORST TIME:	**Sunday, when attractions are closed, or after dark. If you decide to stay in City Park or in the upper Esplanade area until early evening, plan to return on the bus, streetcar, or by taxi or rideshare.**

If you're heading to City Park, the New Orleans Museum of Art, or Jazz Fest, consider some sightseeing in this overlooked region. We particularly enjoy the quiet, meandering stretch along Bayou St. John. Historically, Esplanade Ridge was the site of an ancient Indigenous portage route of trade that linked the Mississippi River to Lake Pontchartrain. In 1807, however, an act of Congress gave the city of New Orleans the title to it. This ridge was Creole society's answer to St. Charles Avenue—another lush boulevard of stately homes and seemingly ancient trees stretching overhead. The lots are not quite as expansive as along St. Charles, so the grand front lawns are not in evidence.

Originally home to the descendants of the earliest settlers, the avenue had its finest days toward the end of the 19th century, and some of the neighborhoods along its path have seen better days. Still, it's closer to the soul of the city than St. Charles Avenue (read: Regular people live here, whereas St. Charles always was and is for the well-heeled). For more interesting facts, look for the bronze historic markers in the median along Esplanade Avenue.

From the French Quarter you can catch a bus on Esplanade Avenue at Rampart Street, headed toward City Park and your chosen starting point. Otherwise, stroll (about 15 min.) up Esplanade Avenue to:

1 2023 Esplanade Ave., Charpentier House

Originally a plantation home, this Greek Revival house was built in 1861 for businessman and railroadman A. B. Charpentier. It's now **Ashton's Bed & Breakfast** (p. 84), which maintains a Charpentier room.

Next door, at the corner of Esplanade and Galvez, is:

2 2033–2035 Esplanade Ave., Widow Castanedo's House

Juan Rodriguez purchased this land in the 1780s, and his granddaughter, Widow Castanedo, lived here until her death in 1861 (when it was a smaller, Spanish colonial–style plantation home). Before Esplanade Avenue extended this far from the river, the house was located in what is now the middle of the street. The widow tried and failed to block the extension of the street. The late-Italianate house was moved to its present site and enlarged sometime around the 1890s. It's been split down the middle and is inhabited today by two sisters.

Walk up Esplanade 1 block to the corner of North Miro Street to:

3 2139 Esplanade Ave.

A great example of the typical Esplanade Ridge style. Note the Ionic columns on the upper level.

After you cross North Miro Street, Esplanade Avenue crosses the diagonal Bayou Road, which was the route to the French-Canadian settlements at Bayou St. John in the late 17th century. Bear left at the fork to stay on Esplanade Avenue and look across the street for:

4 2212, 2216 & 2222 Esplanade Ave.

Originally built as spec town homes in 1883, these three Candy Crush–colored Italianate houses now comprise **Le Belle Esplanade B&B** inn. Although they look like triplets, each has its own architectural identity, and the intricate millwork and detailing surely stood out long before the eye-catching paint job was applied.

Turn around to the triangular plot between Bayou Road and Esplanade:

5 Goddess of History—Genius of Peace Statue

At the top of this grassy triangle, dedicated in 1886 to historian and politician Charles Gayarre, stands this terra cotta monument topped with a

Walking Tour 3: The Esplanade Ridge

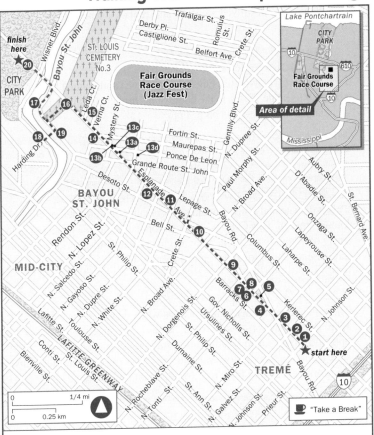

1 Charpentier House (Ashton's)
2 Widow Castanedo's House
3 2139 Esplanade Ave.
4 2212, 2216 & 2222 Esplanade Ave.
5 Goddess of History—
   Genius of Peace Statue
6 Degas House
7 2336 Esplanade Ave. Le Museé de f.p.c.
8 2337 & 2341 Esplanade Ave.
9 2453 Esplanade Ave.
10 2623 Esplanade Ave.
11 2809 Esplanade Ave.
   Cresson House

12 2936 Esplanade Ave.
13a Café Degas
13b Canseco's
13c 1000 Figs
13d Liuzza's by the Track
14 3330 Esplanade Ave.
15 Luling Mansion
16 St. Louis Cemetery No. 3
17 Bayou St. John
18 Magnolia Bridge
19 Pitot House
20 City Park

statue. Originally created for the 1884 New Orleans Exposition in Audubon Park, it was donated to the city by businessman George H. Dunbar. The statue was destroyed in 1938 and replaced with this cement and marble model.

On the corner diagonal from Gayarre Park, find:

6 2306 Esplanade Ave., Degas House

French Impressionist artist Edgar Degas stayed and painted here for several months in the 1870s, in the home of his brother and sister-in-law. The scandalous family story is on p. 171.

As you continue up the block, take a look across the street at nos. 2325, 2327, 2329, and 2331—all interesting examples of Creole cottages. Check out the metal and cinderblock sculptures in the front yard of 2326 Esplanade—the owner, an artist, is a co-founder of the Contemporary Arts Center (p. 167). At the corner of Rocheblave Street is:

7 2336 Esplanade Ave., Le Musée de f.p.c.

This Italianate house now contains a fascinating museum telling the little-known story of New Orleans' historic population of free people of color, many of whom lived in this very neighborhood. If it's a Friday or Saturday, reserve ahead to take a guided tour (p. 175).

On the opposite corner, take a look at:

8 2337 & 2341 Esplanade Ave.

These houses were identical structures when they were built in 1862 for John Budd Slawson, owner of a horse-drawn-streetcar company that operated along Bayou Road. Back then, both were single-story shotgun-style houses (a second story was later added to 2337). Notice the unusual ironwork beneath the front roof overhang on both houses.

Cross North Rocheblave Street and continue up Esplanade to:

9 2453 Esplanade Ave.

This house was one of a matching pair at the corner of Dorgenois Street, built in 1874 by George Dunbar (see stop #5 above) for his two sons. (The other was demolished.) Though its mansard-roofed Second Empire architecture has been greatly altered, it's one of the few buildings in this once-popular style remaining in New Orleans.

If you're just doing the lower portion of this tour, turn left on North Dorgenois Street, head 1 block to Bayou Road (the city's oldest road, p. 235), and you'll find a trove of locals' favorite casual eateries and Black-owned businesses. We especially adore **Community Book Center,** NOLA's oldest Black-owned bookstore (p. 240), **Pagoda** (p. 145), **Leo's Breads,** and **McHardy's Chicken** (p. 124). If you're continuing along the upper portion of this tour, cross North Broad Street to:

10 2623 Esplanade Ave.

Thank booze for this beauty. The Corinthian columns denote the classical revival style of this home, built in 1896 by absinthe and bitters magnate Louis A. Jung. The Jungs donated to the city the adjoining triangle of land at Esplanade Avenue, Crete Street, and DeSoto Street on the condition that it remain public property. The pretty pocket park features a fountain (well, planter) and is graced by an unusual Art Nouveau fence.

On up Esplanade past North White Street, take a look at:

11 2809 Esplanade Ave., Cresson House

This decorative, Queen Anne–style center-hall Victorian, built in 1902, is just one of many pretty houses on Esplanade Ridge. Notice the fleur di lis in the wrought-iron fence in front. Its grandiose mock-Tudor neighbor at 2821 Esplanade was built later, in the 1920s.

Continue 1 block up and across the street to see:

12 2936 Esplanade Ave.

This Gothic villa–style house with its gingerbread-hung eaves is now an ISKCON (Hare Krishna) center (free vegetarian dinners on Sun eves!).

One block further up Esplanade, at the corner of Lopez Street, look down the block to your right for a glimpse of the historic **Fair Grounds Race Course** (p. 207), home to Jazz Fest (p. 61). Then cross Grande Rte. Saint John. Across from triangular Fortier Park, you'll find:

13 a–d Take a Break at Café Degas, Canseco's, 1000 Figs, or Liuzza's by the Track ♨

A cluster of shops and restaurants at this intersection offers some fine lunchtime options. If the weather is nice, the semi-outdoor setting is exceedingly pleasant at **Café Degas** (p. 119). For snacks or picnic food (you're near Bayou St. John and City Park), try **Canseco's,** 3135 Esplanade Ave. (𝒞 **504/322-2594**), or turn down Ponce DeLeon Street, where **1000 Figs** offers great Mediterranean fare (3141 Ponce de Leon St.; 𝒞 **504/301-0848**). A block away, beloved **Liuzza's by the Track** (p. 123) has slammin' barbecue shrimp po' boys, cocktails, and more.

Continue past the park on Esplanade to:

14 3330 Esplanade Ave.

This galleried frame home was built in the Creole-cottage style. Note the orientation of this stretch (and many of the houses along Esplanade Ave.). The lots are on a diagonal, so houses face Esplanade at a slight angle—a remnant either from the original plantation plots or from fortifications built at strategic angles to protect the city from attack.

Continue along Esplanade until Leda Court; turn right for a ½-block detour to:

15 1436 Leda Ct., Luling Mansion

Florence Luling, a German sugar and cotton baron, purchased 80 acres and commissioned famed architect James Gallier, Jr., to design this elaborate, three-story Italianate mansion. Built in 1865 with a full moat and ornate formal gardens that stretched all the way to Esplanade Avenue, it later served as the Louisiana Jockey Club (it abuts the Fair Grounds Race Track). Time, weather, and unfortunate modern adjustments have taken a toll, but its original magnificence is still apparent. It's apartments now, and a film site.

Return to Esplanade Avenue and turn right. On your right is:

16 St. Louis Cemetery No. 3

The public Bayou Cemetery, established in 1835, was purchased and expanded by the St. Louis diocese in 1854. It contains the burial monuments of many of the diocese's priests and religious orders. It might also be called "Restaurateurs' Rest": The tombs for the Galatoire, Tujague, Prudhomme, and Chase families are here. You can comfortably explore this cemetery without a group. As always, be respectful and alert. Open 8am to 4pm daily.

Continue walking on Esplanade Avenue toward City Park. At the bridge, before cross-ing over to **City Park,** turn left on Moss Street to walk along:

17 Bayou St. John

You probably wouldn't be standing here if it weren't for this peaceful, historic waterway, since it's responsible for the city's founding. It's explained on p. 166.

Continue along Moss Street to:

18 Magnolia Bridge (aka Cabrini Bridge)

Originally built in the late 1800s over Esplanade Avenue as a swing bridge to allow boat traffic, it was moved here in 1909 when a new heavier streetcar line put too much weight on its tracks. The Works Project Administration rehabbed it in 1936 (along with other bridges across the Bayou and in City Park). It was converted to pedestrian-only use in 1989, and got its bright blue paint job in 2018, to many neighbors' consternation (for years, the steel had a dark patina; historians claim blue is the original color).

Back-track on Moss Street to find:

19 1440 Moss St., Pitot House

This Creole country house overlooking the historic bayou was home to the city's first mayor. It's open to the public, with docents offering a window onto life when Bayou St. John was the city's main trade route. See p. 173.

Return to Esplanade Avenue, cross the bridge, and walk into:

20 Esplanade & City Park Aves., City Park

Across the traffic circle, white pillars mark the entrance to your final destination: expansive **City Park** (p. 183), with its glorious live oaks, museums, gardens, lakes, and much, much more.

SIDE TRIPS FROM NEW ORLEANS

By Lavinia Spalding

I f you have time (say, 3 days), a sojourn into the countryside outlying New Orleans makes for an interesting cultural and visual contrast to the city. This chapter starts off by following River Road along the banks of the Mississippi, visiting the plantation homes and museums that line it, heading upriver from New Orleans. The second part takes you 150 miles west of New Orleans to the heart of the prairie Cajun Country.

The River Road trip can be done as a day trip, or you could keep rambling north to the St. Francisville area and stay overnight. The Cajun Country trip requires a 1- or 2-night stay, more if you can. A third option is a day trip to a bayou Cajun town. GPS will be your friend for either jaunt.

PLANTATIONS & MUSEUMS ALONG THE GREAT RIVER ROAD

The River Road plantation homes, with their elaborate architecture, opulent decor, and meticulously tended gardens, have long been among Louisiana's top tourist destinations, idealized in books and movies. But the decision of which homes to visit—or whether to visit at all—remains complex. There's simply no getting around the fact that New Orleans was once the center of the U.S. slave trade. It would be unconscionable to downplay the truth: This joyful, exquisite city we love has a brutal, ugly past. And River Road is where much of that brutality occurred.

So, the question is: Should we tour the plantation homes built by the enslaved? In doing so, might we find answers to important questions about the legacy of people of African descent in America—and the roots of systemic racism? Or, by visiting the homes, are we enabling a side of the tourism industry that sugarcoats or ignores slavery? Some argue it's essential to visit so that we never forget the evils of slavery; others say that by touring the homes, we perpetuate the cycle of people profiting from dehumanizing the enslaved.

Here's our humble take: Until recently, most plantation tours were devoid of any authentic discussion concerning the hundreds of thousands of human beings who were captured and carried to Louisiana and forced to build, furnish, clean, maintain, and do every other kind of back-breaking work in and around the homes. But ever-so-slowly, tours are bringing to light these essential stories, and they're important to hear. We've listed a handful of plantation homes near New Orleans where the stories of enslaved people are being brought forward.

Most notable is **The Whitney** (p. 280). In 2014, this former plantation home became one of the nation's first museums dedicated to memorializing the enslaved, and a visit is profoundly edifying and moving. So, if you're conflicted about touring plantations, we recommend the Whitney. And if you're *not* conflicted about touring plantations, we recommend the Whitney.

As for other, more mainstream tours, some persist in focusing solely on "the big house" (the enslaver's extravagant home) and make little or no mention of those who actually built the home. We aren't fans of tours that skirt the topic of slavery. Most do. Near New Orleans, **Laura** (p. 279) has put serious effort into including this history. If a tour glosses over the issue, feel free to ask about it directly. You still may not get an accurate portrayal of the lives and contributions of the enslaved, but requesting the info is at least one small step toward combating racial injustice.

THE EARLY PLANTERS & THE ENSLAVED The early planters of Louisiana were rugged frontier people, most of whom had small plots of land by the river. In 1719, the first two ships carrying 451 captive Africans (rice farmers, mostly) arrived, and over the next 12 years, some 6,000 people were brought to Louisiana and sold into slavery. As the planters spread out along the Mississippi from New Orleans, they relied on the labor of these enslaved Africans, as well as European indentured servants and enslaved Indigenous people, to work their land and to clear vast swamplands, creating waterways for transporting indigo, tobacco, and other crops.

In 1795, enslaved workers successfully granulated cane-sugar crystals, after which sugar replaced indigo as the dominant crop. At this time, there were 19,926 enslaved Africans in Louisiana. Most of them worked on plantations.

By the 1800s, Louisiana planters had introduced large-scale farming and brought more acreage under cultivation. King cotton, rice, and sugarcane were popularized, bringing huge monetary returns, although natural dangers, a hurricane, or a swift change in the course of the capricious Mississippi could wipe out entire plantations and fortunes. In 1808, the importation of enslaved people was banned, ending the transatlantic slave trade. But the domestic slave trade boomed, with Louisiana at its center. By 1812, there were 35,000 enslaved people in Louisiana.

BUILDING PLANTATION HOUSES Generally located near the riverfront, the plantation home was the focal point of a self-sustaining community.

1811 Kid Ory House **2**
B&C Seafood **4**
Butler Greenwood
  Plantation B&B **10**
Destrehan Plantation **1**
Laura: A Creole
  Plantation **5**
Myrtles Plantation **11**
Oak Alley Plantation **6**
Oakley House
  at Audubon State
  Historic Site **13**
Rosedown Plantation **12**
St. Francisville Inn **7**
3V Tourist Court **8**
West Feliciana Parish
  tourism office **9**
Whitney Plantation **3**

Area of detail
LOUISIANA
Baton Rouge
New Orleans

Most were modest, but some had wide, oak-lined avenues leading from their entrance to a wharf. The kitchen was separated from the house because of fire danger. Close by was the overseer's office. Some plantations had pigeon houses or dovecotes—and all had the inevitable cramped slave quarters, lining the lane that led to the crops or set across the fields out of sight.

The first houses were simple "raised cottages," with long, sloping roofs, cement-covered brick walls on the ground floor, and wood-and-brick (brick between posts) construction in the living quarters on the second floor. Influenced by West Indian styles, these colonial structures suited the sultry climate and swampy building sites and made use of native materials. In the 1820s, however, Greek Revival and Georgian influences began to be added, creating a style dubbed Louisiana Classic. As prosperity flourished, homes became more grandiose, many embracing the styles of extravagant Victorian architecture, northern Italian villas, or Gothic lines. Planters and their families brought back ornate furnishings and skilled artisans from their European travels. Glittering crystal chandeliers and *faux marbre* (false marble) mantels appeared. Social lives, families, and egos also grew.

But such enormous wealth still stemmed from an economy based on human servitude. Enslaved people did the grueling work of producing all of the crops. They also raised farm animals, cooked and sewed, cared for their enslavers' children, and served as carpenters, masons, and smiths. They typically worked 10 to 16 hours a day, 6 days a week, from sunrise to beyond sunset. In 1860, just before the Civil War, Louisiana was producing about one-sixth of all cotton grown in the U.S., and almost all of the sugar. By this time, there were 332,000 enslaved people in the state. Nine out of 10 worked on plantations and farms.

The injustice and cruelty of slavery became the seeds of its own demise. After the Civil War, large-scale farming became impossible without that labor base. During Reconstruction, lands were confiscated and turned over to people who proved unable to run them; many were subdivided. Increasing international competition eroded the cotton and sugar markets. The culture represented by the plantation houses you'll see emerged and died in a span of less than 100 years.

PLANTATION HOUSES TODAY Where scores of stately homes once dotted the riverfront, few remain. Several that survived the Civil War fell victim to fires, floods, or industrial development. Others, too costly to be maintained, were left to the ravages of dampness and decay. A few have been preserved and upgraded with electricity and plumbing. Most are private residences; some are B&Bs; a handful are open to visitors, the admission fees supplementing upkeep. Tours are hit-or-miss; much depends on your guide. If you visit a few, you'll begin to hear many of the same facts about plantation life, sometimes as infill for missing or boring history. For far too long, the era has been romanticized. The fact is that these plantations would not exist were it not for unthinkably savage, yet real, human cruelty.

If You Go

The plantation homes shown on the map on p. 275 are within easy driving distance of New Orleans. If you're returning late, the small highways can be a little intimidating after dark. Don't expect broad river views along the Great River Road (the roadway's name on *both* sides of the Mississippi); it's obscured by tall levees. You'll see sugarcane fields and plenty of evidence of Louisiana's petrochemical industry. But spontaneous detours through little, centuries-old towns might result in finding a choice resale shop or good road food.

The **Whitney** and **Laura** are minutes apart, and each offers a different perspective on plantation life and the tourism industry. Both honor stories of the enslaved. The Whitney is unmissable, as it focuses *entirely* on the enslaved perspective. Laura has a low-key but superb presentation. Nearby is Tara-esque **Oak Alley,** which represents the showy Americans and is slicker and glitzier, complete with tour guides in period costumes. While there are reproductions of cabins where the enslaved lived and exhibits dedicated to the enslaved, the tour still focuses primarily on the owners' history, so if you have to choose only one or two plantations, we recommend visiting the Whitney and Laura, and giving Oak Alley a drive-by; the huge, ancient trees are impressive. All three are approximately an hour from New Orleans. There are, of course, more plantation homes than what we have listed, some of which are quite famous and physically beautiful. We've tried to send you only to those that make significant efforts to educate about the unvarnished truth of the abomination of slavery.

Organized Tours

Seeing plantation houses via a bus tour is a comfortable, planning-free option, and you get some bonus narration along the route. Almost every New Orleans tour company operates a tour to one or two plantations; most offer pickup at hotels or a central French Quarter locale. Costs include transportation and admission, and the offerings are always subject to change.

If you're only visiting the Whitney, Black-owned **2nd Line Tours** (2ndlinetours.com) offers round-trip transportation for $69. Also Black-owned, **All Bout Dat Tours** (p. 193) offers a custom combo Swamp and Whitney tour, with transportation and lunch included ($175/person, four people minimum).

The reliable 5- to 7-hour tours (including travel time) given by mainstay **Gray Line** (www.graylineneworleans.com; ✆ **800/233-2628** or 504/569-1401) typically offer a choice of one or two of three plantations: Laura, Oak Alley, or Whitney. Daily tours depart Gray Line's Toulouse Street station (near Jax Brewery in the French Quarter). Times vary, so call ahead (Oak Alley or Whitney tour $79 adults, $39 children 6–12). A double plantation tour is $119 adults, $65 kids 6 to 12. **Cajun Encounters** (p. 194) also offers one- or two-plantation day trips, at a cost of $68 to $96 adults ($51–$71 children 11 and under).

Legendary Tours (www.legendarytoursnola.com; ✆ **504/471-1499**) visits Oak Alley, Laura, or the Whitney for $79 ($45 for kids) including round-trip transportation (one plantation). Some tours are self-guided. For smaller groups, **Tours by Isabelle** (www.toursbyisabelle.com; © **877/665-8687** or 504/398-0365) takes groups of 6 to 13 people in a comfortable van on a half-day or 9-hour expedition to multiple plantations. Check website for details.

Plantations & Museums Between New Orleans & Baton Rouge

The houses and museums below are listed in the order in which they appear on the map, running north along the Mississippi from New Orleans. Tours range from 1½ to 2½ hours; most people do one or two in a day (and may drive past others). Depending on your choices, you may have to cross the Mississippi River by bridge a few times. The winding river makes distances deceiving; give yourself more time than you think you'll need. Several well-known plantation homes are in this area. If you're more interested in learning the deep history of the river parishes (that is, stories of the enslaved), take the 10-mile **1811 Slave Revolt Trail,** which begins at the **1811 Kid Ory House** (see below) and ends at the **Destrehan Plantation** (see below). It commemorates the brutal uprising that some call America's first freedom march.

Destrehan Plantation ★★ HISTORIC HOME   Its proximity (30 min. from New Orleans), in-character docents wearing period clothing, and role in *Interview with the Vampire* and *12 Years a Slave* have made Destrehan Manor a popular plantation to visit. It's the oldest intact plantation home in the lower Mississippi Valley open to the public. Built in 1787 by a free person of color for a wealthy Frenchman, it was modified from its "dated" French colonial style to Greek Revival in the 1830s. One room has been left un-renovated, to show the humble rawness beneath the usual public grandeur. Important history related to the enslaved occurred at Destrehan, and an education center offers exhibits dedicated to these events, including the 1811 uprising. A house display also honors Marguerite, an enslaved cook and laundress, and a tour for groups of 20 or more gives voice to marginalized groups, including Indigenous and enslaved. **Note:** Destrehan is a good choice for those with mobility issues, because unlike most plantation homes, it has ramps and an elevator.

> ### River Road Pit Stop
>
> Restaurants are in short supply along the River Road. The cafe at Oak Alley is the best of the mostly so-so eateries at the plantations. Instead, stop at down-home **B&C Seafood,** just east of Laura Plantation, where you can join the locals digging into steaming trays of boiled seafood and Cajun standards (2155 Hwy. 18, Vacherie; © **225/265-8356;** all items $7–$25; Mon–Sat 11am–3:30pm).

13034 River Rd., La. 48, Destrehan. www.destrehanplantation.org. © **877/453-2095** or 985/764-9315. $26 adults, $24 military and seniors, $15 children 7–17, free for kids 6 and under. Daily 9am–4pm. Closed Jan 1, Mardi Gras, Easter, Thanksgiving, and Dec 24–25.

1811 Kid Ory Historic House ★★ HISTORIC HOME   Also known as the **Bonnet Carre Historical Center,** this is a bit off River Road, on I-61, but it's a worthy detour. This former plantation is now a historical center, research facility, and museum dedicated to studying the area's antebellum, postbellum, land cultivation, and Creole Jazz history. Primary focus is on an important story connected to the property: the 1811 revolt (the largest uprising of enslaved people in the nation's history), which began inside the house. The museum is the starting point of the 10-mile 1811 Slave Revolt Trail. Exhibits also explore the life of Edward "Kid" Ory, jazz pioneer, born in a sharecropper's lodging on the plantation in 1886.

1128 La. 628, Laplace. www.facebook.com/1811KidOry. © **225/937-8792.** Thurs–Sun 10am–3pm. At press time, tours were still being finalized. Check website or call for exact hours and prices.

Laura: A Creole Plantation ★★★ HISTORIC HOME   Laura is simple on the outside but absorbing within. It has no hoop-skirted guides, offering instead a thorough view of daily life on an 18th- and 19th-century sugar plantation, a cultural history of Louisiana's Creole population, and an in-depth examination of one Creole family. Much is known about this house and its residents thanks to extensive records (more than 5,000 documents researched in France), including the detailed memoirs of its namesake, proto-feminist head-of-household Laura Locoul. In 1994, Laura was Louisiana's first plantation to delve into stories of the enslaved. In 2004, many original artifacts were saved by employees in a fire, after which the main house and a slave cabin were accurately restored to the 1805 period. And in 2017, a small on-site museum opened, dedicated to sharing stories of the enslaved and history of the slave trade and resistance. Two more standout facts: The beloved Br'er Rabbit stories were first collected here by a folklorist in the 1870s, and Fats Domino's parents were born on this plantation.

2247 Hwy. 18, Vacherie. www.lauraplantation.com. © **888/799-7690** or 225/265-7690. $30 adults, $23 military, $20 teens 13–17, $12 children 6–12, free for children 5 and under. ($2 discount online for adult tickets.) Tours daily 10am–4pm every 40 min.; last tour 3:20pm. Tours in French available some days; check website. Closed Jan 1, Mardi Gras, Easter, Thanksgiving, and Christmas.

Oak Alley Plantation ★★★ HISTORIC HOME   This is Louisiana's most famous plantation house, probably because it precisely matches Hollywood's depictions. (Proof: Many movies, including *Interview with the Vampire*, were filmed here, as was Beyonce's "Déjà vu" video.) The massive white house, its porch lined with giant columns, is approached by a quarter-mile drive lined with stately oak trees (the 1839 house has 28 fluted Doric columns to match the 28 trees). Oak Alley also has the slickest operation, with golf carts traversing the blacktopped property. It lay disintegrating until 1914; new owners and restorers were responsible for its National Historic Landmark designation. In 2012 a row of re-created slave quarters was added. The well-researched displays do a pretty good job of illuminating the lives of the enslaved and the means by which this plantation survived (though not nearly as well as the Whitney or Laura). Still, we give them passing marks, since big-house tours do make an effort to highlight the stark dichotomy between

St. Francisville doesn't look like much on approach, but history buffs, nature lovers, and ghost hunters will be charmed. This is not Cajun Country—this area has American plantations only and no French history—but if you're interested in plantations from an architectural, historical, or cultural perspective, you'll do well to plant yourself here for an overnighter. (And if you're interested in ghosts, we'll point you straight to a tour or a stay at the **Myrtles Plantation**—www.myrtles plantation.com—billed as "one of American's most haunted homes.") St. Francisville is 30 miles northwest of Baton Rouge and 2 hours by car from New Orleans. Contact the West Feliciana Parish **tourism office** at 11757 Ferdinand St. (www.explorewestfeliciana.com; ⓒ **800/789-4221** or 225/635-4224; Mon–Sun 9am–5pm), located in the Historical Society Museum—stop by here first to get the lay of the land.

Recommended places to stay include the **St. Francisville Inn,** at 5720 Commerce St. (stfrancisvilleinn.com; ⓒ **225/635-6502;** $225–$419), a recently renovated boutique hotel with antiques-laden rooms, fab restaurant **The Saint,** a craft cocktail bar, and pool, all of which welcome guests and locals.

There's also **Butler Greenwood Plantation B&B,** at 8345 U.S. 61 (www.butler greenwood.com; ⓒ **225/635-6312;** double $150–$250), with modest guest cottages, some with Jacuzzis or fireplaces, on oak-laden grounds; and the budget-friendly, hippie-friendly downtown **3V Tourist Court,** at 5687 Commerce St. (www.themagnoliacafe. net/3v-tourist-courts; ⓒ **225/721-7003;** $85–$145), a collection of cute, quirky historic efficiency cabins (hello, fans of tiny houses) built in 1938. (Bonus: Local favorite **Magnolia Café** is on-site.)

Area attractions include:

o **Oakley House at Audubon State Historic Site** ★   John James Audubon received room and board in exchange for giving art lessons

the lives of the owners and those of their forced laborers. A memorial wall and database honor enslaved residents. A sit-down restaurant and casual cafe are on-site, as well as bed-and-breakfast rooms.

3645 La. 18, Vacherie. Plantation: www.oakalleyplantation.org; restaurant and lodge: www.oakalleyplantation.com. ⓒ **800/442-5539** or 225/265-2151. Admission with "Big House" exhibit $28 adults, $9 children 6–17, free for children 5 and under. Discounts for seniors, AAA members, and active military. Admission without "Big House" exhibit $3 less. Grounds open daily 8:30am–5pm, tours every 30 min. 9am–4:30pm. Restaurant open 8:30am–5pm. Closed Jan 1, Thanksgiving, and Christmas.

Whitney Plantation ★★★ HISTORIC HOME   Again, if you see only one plantation, make it the Whitney. Slavery may still get meager mention at other plantations. Here, at the first museum of its kind in the U.S., history comes from the perspective of the enslaved. Visitors receive a name tag with the biography of an enslaved individual, immediately personalizing the experience, and begin the 90-minute guided walking tour with a short film shown in a church. They share the pews with life-size sculptures by artist Woodrow Nash of enslaved children, which are beautiful, spiritual, and heartrending. The tour moves to expansive gardens of somber monuments etched with to the young resident of this 1801 plantation home. After class, he painted 32 of his "Birds of America" series (those lessons helped finance the books' publication). A tour of the just-restored, 17-room colonial is worthwhile; leave time to walk among the gardens and nature trails, part of a 100-acre wildlife sanctuary. There are original slave quarters and occasional special programs highlighting the influence of African Americans on the development of early America. It's at 11788 Hwy. 965, St. Francisville (www.lastateparks.com/historic-sites/audubon-state-historic-site; ℰ **225/635-3739**; $10 adults, $8 seniors, $5 students 6–17, free for kids 3 and under; daily 9am–5pm).

o **Rosedown Plantation ★** Rosedown doesn't have the greatest track record when it comes to telling history's truest truths (in 2019 they finally removed a sign that claimed their slaves were "happy"). Nevertheless, it's among the most visited of the far-flung plantations, with its impressive wide avenue of ancient oaks and dramatic gardens. Tours mostly educate about 19th-century culture and family customs, with some attention given to the lives and contributions of the hundreds of enslaved people who lived and worked there. We appreciate that in February of each year, there's a daily guided "Enslaved Life" tour for Black History month. It's at 12501 Hwy. 10, at La. 10 and U.S. 61, St. Francisville (www.lastateparks.com/historic-sites/rosedown-plantation-state-historic-site; ℰ **888/376-1867** or 225/635-3332; house tour and historic gardens $12 adults, $10 seniors, $6 students 6–17, free for kids 5 and under; daily 9am–5pm; tours begin at 10am; last tour at 4pm).

personal testimonials and 107,000 names; a separate "Field of Angels" remembers enslaved children (40 perished on this very land). These contemplative spaces lay the emotional foundation as the tour moves to sparse cabin homes; the historic kitchen; endless fields; murky creeks that gave cover during escape attempts; and the blacksmith cabin where men toiled over the instruments of their own confinement. Appropriately, scant tour time is spent touring the "big house." Among the most affecting sights is the three-cell jail, a crude iron cage positioned with cruel irony with a full-on view of the big house. Elsewhere, 60 ceramic heads on spikes pay noble, resonant tribute to enslaved persons decapitated during the uprising in 1811. Not everything is original (much was razed), but it's all deeply authentic, haunting, and vital.

5099 Hwy. 18, Edgard. www.whitneyplantation.org. ℰ **225/265-3300.** Self-guided: $25 adults; $23 seniors, students, active military; $11 kids 6–18; free for children 6 and under. Guided: $32 adults; $15 kids 6–18; free for children 6 and under. Wed–Mon 9:30am–4:15pm (last entry 3pm). Guided tours 10:45am, and 12:45 and 2:45pm. Book in advance. Most of tour is outdoors, rain or shine. Paths wheelchair-accessible (some parts rough); 2nd floor of house not wheelchair-accessible. Closed Jan 1, Mardi Gras day, July 4, Thanksgiving, Dec 25.

11 CAJUN COUNTRY

This area, also called Acadiana (though you won't find that on the maps) has a history and culture unique in the U.S. It consists of a rough triangle of Louisiana made up of 22 parishes (counties), from St. Landry at the top of the triangle to the Gulf of Mexico at its base. Lafayette is the unofficial capital of Acadiana.

Meet the Cajuns

The Cajuns' history is a sad one, but it produced a people and a culture well worth knowing. In the early 1600s, French colonists began settling the southeastern coast of Canada in a region of Nova Scotia they named Acadia. They developed a peaceful agricultural society based on the values of a strong Catholic faith, deep love of family, and respect for their relatively small landholdings.

They remained isolated from Europe for nearly 150 years, until Acadia fell under British rule. The king's representatives tried to force the Acadians to pledge allegiance to the British Crown, renounce Catholicism, and embrace the king's Protestantism, but for decades they steadfastly refused. Finally, the British governor sent in troops. Villages were burned and families separated as ships were sent to deport them. A 10-year diaspora began, scattering the Acadians to France, England, America's East Coast, and the West Indies. Terrible shipboard conditions cost hundreds of lives.

In 1765, Bernard Andry brought 231 men, women, and children to establish a permanent home in Louisiana, a natural destination thanks to its strong French background. These industrious settlers worked the swampy, wildlife-teeming lands, building levees, draining fields, and planting many of the farms you still see here.

Cajun Language

Much of this essay was provided by author, historian, and four-time Grammy nominee Ann Allen Savoy, who, along with her husband Marc (an acclaimed accordion maker), are members of the Savoy-Doucet Cajun Band and several other groups. The Savoys are celebrated keepers of the culture, not least for

tuning in TO CAJUN COUNTRY

Our standard soundtrack for the drive from New Orleans to Cajun Country begins with the excellent **WWOZ 90.7 FM** (to which we're assiduously tuned while in the city). After an hour on the road, static takes over, signaling the unwrapping of whatever new music we've recently purchased from **Louisiana Music Factory** (p. 248). After about half an hour, we can usually pull in **KBON 101.1 FM** for some rollickin' classic country, Cajun, and zydeco tunes. At that point we know we've arrived, as much in geography as mood.

Boudin: Get Linked In

Boudin (boo-*dan*) is a Cajun sausage link made of pork, pork liver, rice, onions, and spices, all stuffed inside a casing. If it's done right, it's spicy and sublime. In these parts, you can get this inexpensive (about $7 per pound) snack at just about any grocery store or gas station. Disputes rage about whose reigns supreme (**www.boudinlink.com** has digitized the argument). It's best eaten while leaning against a car, chased with a Barq's root beer. Conducting a comparison test is great fun, but the singular choice in these parts is the **Best Stop** (615 Hwy. 93 N., Scott, exit 97 off the I-10; www. beststopinscott.com; ℰ **337/233-5805**). It's always busy, so the links and crunchy pig-fat cracklins (aka *chicharones*) are always fresh. Did we mention that they ship? Send us some *now*, please. Best Stop is open Monday to Saturday 6am to 8pm, Sunday 6am until 6pm.

having spawned a musical dynasty. All four of their talented children are carrying the cultural torch through their own music and art.

The French influence in Louisiana is one of the things that sets the state apart from the rest of the United States. Although French is spoken by many older Cajuns (ages 60 and up), most middle-aged Louisianans don't speak the language—partially because, from the 1930s on, speaking French became associated with a lack of business success or education. Cajun music was considered hokey; Cajun culture was denigrated and stigmatized.

Today, Cajun culture has experienced a resurgence of respect. Young people emphatically adopt their ancestors' language, music, recipes, and other traditions, and proudly speak with the sharp, bright Cajun accent.

Cajun French is peppered with beautiful old words dating from Louis XIV, unused in France and historically intriguing. It is not a dialect of French; however, many words have been localized (a mosquito can be called a *marougouin* in one area, a *moustique* in another, a *cousin* elsewhere), and "Franglish" is common (*"On va revenir right back"*—We'll be right back).

Additionally, the fascinating Creole language is still spoken by many Black Louisianans. A compilation of French and African dialects, it is quite different from standard French, though Cajuns and Black Creoles can speak and understand both languages.

Cajun Music

It's hard to decide which is more important to a Cajun: food or music. In the early days when instruments were scarce, Cajuns held dances to a cappella voices. With roots probably in medieval France, the strains came in the form of a brisk two-step or a waltz. Traditional groups still play mostly acoustic instruments—fiddle, accordion, triangle, maybe a guitar—and the traditional high, loud vocal wail.

The best place to hear real Cajun music is on someone's back porch, the time-honored spot for eating some gumbo and listening to several generations of players jamming. If you can't wangle an invitation, the local dance halls on any weekend will do just fine. It's quite the social scene, and there are usually willing dance coaches for newbies (don't be shy—everyone will be watching the really good dancers; you should, too). The following 3-day Cajun weekend takes you on a well-rounded musical introduction to this region. For Cajun music clubs in New Orleans, see p. 222.

Planning Your Trip

You'll see and do a lot during this 3-day weekend, which includes options to customize the trip based on your own interests. A bit of adventurous meandering on your own will most definitely reward you with more finds.

It's awfully fun to visit Acadiana during **Cajun Mardi Gras** (p. 60), **Festival International de Louisiane** in April (p. 32), **Festivals Acadiens et Creoles** in October (festivalsacadiens.com), or the **Breaux Bridge Crawfish Festival** in May (bbcrawfest.com)—but any weekend will do. There's plenty of music throughout the year and often a small festival somewhere—if you find one, you simply have to go, as they're almost guaranteed to be a memorable social, cultural, and musical experience.

For tons of good, detailed information, contact the **Lafayette Convention and Visitors Commission** (www.lafayettetravel.com; ✆ **800/346-1958** in the U.S., 800/543-5340 in Canada, or 337/232-3737), and check **Downtown Lafayette** for goings-on (www.downtownlafayette.org; ✆ **337/291-5566**).

Organized Tours

A terrific and oh-so-easy way to explore Cajun Country is with **Gondwana Ecotours** (www.gondwanaecotours.com; ✆ **877-587-8479**), which offers completely customized, all-inclusive 2- to 5-day itineraries including transportation, meals, and lodging. On our 3-day tour, we spent hours chatting with a zydeco legend in his studio; we met a Cajun chef-musician who taught us to cook an unforgettable dinner then played music for us under the stars; we glided through cypress and tupelo trees on a private, eco-friendly swamp tour (and spotted a bald eagle, a red-shouldered hawk, and eight alligators). We bunked in a roomy country-style cottage on the edge of a placid pond, equipped with canoes and life jackets. For all you get—attentive guide, comfy transport, cozy digs, more-than-you-could-ever-eat food at cool local joints, unique experiences, and plenty of sightseeing stops, it's a helluva deal. Call for pricing and availability.

If it's strictly the food you're after (can't blame ya), drive to Lafayette, where **Cajun Food Tours** (www.cajunfoodtours.com; ✆ **337/230-6169**) will shuttle you to five Cajun food stops in a comfy 14-seat bus. They're not all the down-home holes-in-the-walls you might stumble onto yourself, but it's convenient, fairly priced, and you'll get plenty of variety. Tours cost $65 adults; kids 12 and under $39; reservations required). Plan in advance because they may not be offered every day. Each year, **Festival Tours International** (p. 65) offers a stellar music-focused tour of the area during the 3 days between Jazz Fest weekends. Also see "Organized Tours," p. 192.

A CAJUN 3-DAY WEEKEND

The suggested itinerary for a 3-day side trip from New Orleans to Cajun Country is designed to introduce you to this marvelous, singular culture. The drive from New Orleans is about 2½ to 3 hours, mostly via I-10 (140 miles from New Orleans). If you opt to drive back via U.S. 90, it's about 170 miles. You'll be based in Lafayette and going to the smaller towns of Eunice, Mamou, and St. Martinville for a thorough immersion in real Cajun culture. We've provided main highway directions; some form of GPS is recommended to help get you to the in-town destinations.

Friday, Day 1: Lafayette ★★★

Leave New Orleans early in the day and head for the River Road (Hwy. 18) plantations to tour a plantation (p. 273). Or head directly to Lafayette. *Tip 1:* Avoid going through Baton Rouge at afternoon rush hour. *Tip 2:* If you *do* go through Baton Rouge, brake for chargrilled oysters and more at **Parrain's** (parrains.com).

Lafayette is a midsize city of 120,000, with a university (University of Louisiana Lafayette) and plenty of hotel choices. We recommend you opt for an atmospheric B&B. Check in at the 130-year-old (but recently renovated) **T'Frere's Bed & Breakfast** (1905 Verot School Rd., Lafayette; www.tfrereshouse.com; ℂ **800/984-9347** or 337/984-9347; double from $148) or **Mouton Plantation Bed & Breakfast** (338 N. Sterling St., Lafayette; www.moutonplantation.com; ℂ **337/233-7816;** double from $139, suites from $163). For a more freewheeling, downtown experience, **Blue Moon Saloon & Guesthouse** offers en suite rooms or cottage accommodations, with shared kitchen and public areas adjacent to the storied outdoor live music venue (215 E. Convent St., Lafayette; bluemoonpresents.com; ℂ **337/234-2422;** double from $105, bungalow $275). Three-night minimum stay during certain festivals.

Plan to arrive in time for lunch, and if it's a weekday, go directly to **Creole Lunch House** (713 12th St., Lafayette; ℂ **337/232-9929;** Mon–Fri

detour to BREAUX BRIDGE

Though this itinerary doesn't include the town of **Breaux Bridge,** it is close to Lafayette, and antique lovers may want to head here to peruse a handful of worthy stores, especially 17,000-square-foot **Lagniappe Antique Mall** (breauxbridge antiques.com), where we could personally spend about a month. If all the browsing leaves you famished, head to **Café Sydnie Mae** (cafesydniemae.com)

for delicious food and live music. In **Arnaudville,** only minutes from Breaux Bridge, there are two superb (but very different) culinary options: divey **Myran's Maison de Manger** (1023 Neblett St; ℂ **337/754-5064**), especially for crawfish and onion rings, and **The Little Big Cup** (thelittlebigcup.com) for incredible brunch (if you like cats, sit outside here; they reign over the decks).

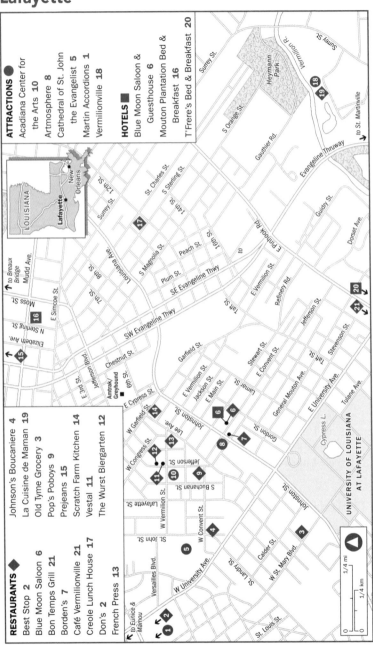

ATTRACTIONS ●

Acadiana Center for the Arts **10**
Artmosphere **8**
Cathedral of St. John the Evangelist **5**
Martin Accordions **1**
Vermilionville **18**

HOTELS ■

Blue Moon Saloon & Guesthouse **6**
Mouton Plantation Bed & Breakfast **16**
T'Frere's Bed & Breakfast **20**

RESTAURANTS ◆

Best Stop **2**
Blue Moon Saloon **6**
Bon Temps Grill **21**
Borden's **7**
Café Vermilionville **21**
Creole Lunch House **17**
Don's **2**
French Press **13**
Johnson's Boucaniere **4**
La Cuisine de Maman **19**
Old Tyme Grocery **3**
Pop's Poboys **9**
Prejeans **15**
Scratch Farm Kitchen **14**
Vestal **11**
The Wurst Biergarten **12**

11am–2pm). Get a couple of stuffed breads and whatever's been smothered that day (chicken thighs, pork chop, shoe, it's all gonna be ridiculously good home cooking). We'll toss out three other casual, worthy eatin' options to bookmark during your Lafayette stay: **Johnson's Boucaniere** for sublime pulled pork (1111 St. John St.; www.johnsons boucaniere.com; ℂ **337/269-8878;** Wed–Fri 10am–3pm, Sat 8am–3pm, Sun 10am–2pm); **Olde Tyme Grocery** for po' boys (218 W. St. Mary Blvd.; www.oldetymegrocery.com; ℂ **337/235-8165;** Mon–Fri 8am–10pm, Sat 9am–7pm); and relative newcomer **Pop's Poboys** (740 Jefferson St.; www.popspoboys.com; ℂ **337/534-0621;** Mon–Wed 10:30am–2pm, Thurs–Sat 10:30am–9pm), whose menu includes great salads—a rare find in these parts—and some of the state's best po' boys (with creative twists and the best names, like the "Cardiac Cajun.")

Relax or stroll the shops and galleries downtown. Take in the exhibits at the **Acadiana Center for the Arts** (101 W. Vermilion St., Lafayette; acadianacenterforthearts.org; ℂ **337/233-7060;** daily 9am–5pm). Or visit the **Church of St. John the Evangelist** (914 St. John St., Lafayette; www. saintjohncathedral.org; ℂ **337/232-1322**), a splendid Dutch Romanesque edifice done in red and white brick, with fine stained glass dating to 1916. Then hop in the car and drive 10 minutes to **Martin Accordions** (2143 Willow St., Scott; www.martinaccordions.com; ℂ **337/232-4001**), a friendly family-owned business for 30-plus years, to lay eyes on their dazzling handmade instruments. Tours and demonstrations are available by appointment, or sometimes by request. (We popped over unannounced when they were hard at work and wound up staying an hour, learning about how accordions are made and hearing incredible music.)

For a great Cajun dinner, it's worth standing in line for a table at **Prejeans** (3480 NE Evangeline Thruway, Lafayette; prejeans.com; ℂ **337/896-3247**), especially during crawfish season. For something a bit swankier (or for a cocktail), reserve at **Vestal** (555 Jefferson St., Lafayette; www.vestalrestaurant.com; ℂ **337/534-0682**), a sleek new bar and restaurant that feels more L.A. than LA. The elegant Southern-meets-French menu focuses on food sourced from local vendors and artisans, cooked over "live fire" on hot hardwood coals. If you have room, flip back the time-travel clock and squeeze in a sundae from **Borden's** (1103 Jefferson St., Lafayette; www.bordensicecreamshoppe.com; ℂ **337/235-9291**), the last retail Borden's shop in the world, and hardly changed since it scooped its first cone of creamy goodness back in 1940. It's just across the street from the **Blue Moon Saloon** (215 E. Convent St., Lafayette; www.bluemoonpresents.com; ℂ **337/234-2422**), so if you've made it this far, beer and dancing are in the stars. This is the city's premier live-music venue for Cajun, zydeco, and all forms of modern alternative roots music, and it's the perfect way to end this, and any, night. Finally, head back and hit your cushy bed—Saturday is a full day.

Grab a quick B from your B&B before heading out to supplement it. If you haven't already stopped for boudin, now's a good time, because 1) pork sausage for breakfast = yes, always; 2) you might want to stop here again tomorrow; and 3) you'll instantly become more welcome at your next stop. Choose the **Best Stop** (see box, p. 283), or if you require a little egg or biscuit action with your sausage, head across Highway 10 to **Don's** (730 I-10 S. Frontage Rd., Scott; www.donsspecialtymeats.com; ℭ **337/234-2528**). A half-link per person is a minimal sampling of boudin; get a few more links to take to the **Savoy Music Center,** 3 miles east of downtown Eunice (about a 35-min. drive; 4413 U.S. Hwy. 190 E.; www.savoymusiccenter.com; ℭ **337/457-9563;** Tues–Fri 9am–5pm, closed for lunch noon–1:30pm; Sat jam 9am–noon). On weekdays this working music store sells instruments, equipment, and Marc Savoy's exquisite, world-renowned handcrafted accordions (check out the folk-art aphorisms scrawled on his workshop cabinets, if you can). At the Saturday-morning jam sessions, this nondescript faded-green building becomes the spiritual center of Cajun music. Local and visiting musicians young and old gather to savor this unpretentious, unparalleled music and culture. It's probably the closest thing to that back-porch experience you'll find.

Stay and savor this utter authenticity, or cut out to head for the alternate universe known as **Fred's Lounge** in Mamou, about 20 minutes north (west on U.S. 190, then right on La. 13; 420 6th St.; ℭ **337/468-5411;** Sat 8am–1pm; music starts at 9am). This is the other end of the Cajun music spectrum: a small-town bar that for half a century has hosted Saturday daytime dances starting in the early morn. Couples waltz and two-step around the mid-floor bandstand. It's pure dance-hall stuff (leaning toward the country-western side of Cajun, but much of it in French), where hardworking locals let loose. And we do mean loose (remember, they started with Coors while you were still on coffee).

Back in Eunice, lunch awaits. If it's the weekend, **Allison's BBQ Pitt** (501 W. Laurel Ave.; ℭ **337/457-9218**) is your ticket to meaty nirvana. Some judge it the best barbecue in southern Louisiana. It's open Saturday and Sunday from 10am until 2pm for takeout lunch; you might have to stand in line (it's popular), but you can call ahead. Best to just arrive early. Either way, you gotta sink your teeth into those smoky ribs, chicken, pork, or brisket with homemade sauce. (Thank us later.) Or for a lowkey lunch, try **Ruby's Café** (221 W. Walnut St.; ℭ **337/550-7665**). Service is consistently warm and the daily-changing menu consistently comforting (think fried chicken, crawfish étouffée, smothered okra).

Head to two side-by-side museums: the **Depot Museum** (220 S. C.C. Duson St.; cajuntravel.com/things/eunice-depot-museum; ℭ **337/457-6540**), in the old train depot, with its sweet collection of memorabilia, toys, and tools (and free admission), and the **Cajun Music Hall of Fame & Museum** (240 S. C.C. Duson St.; cajunfrenchmusic.org/hall-of-fame; ✆ **337/457-6534**), where you can become an expert on the incredible music you've been surrounding yourself with. And speaking of music, just a few blocks away is **KBON** radio station (schedule a tour by calling ✆ **337/546-0007**). More music can be found on weekends from February until late November at **Lakeview Park & Beach** (1717 Veteran Memorial Hwy.; www.lvpark.com), which usually hosts fantastic performers in its barn ($10 admission if you're not staying there), plus a motley array of other fun events, from candy bar bingo to karaoke contests and beef tongue cookoffs. (It also has cute cottages, tent sites, and RV hookups in case you want to spend the night.)

Your dinner bell is probably ringing loudly. Stay in Eunice and head to **Nick's on 2nd** (123 S. 2nd St.; www.facebook.com/Nicks-on-2nd-379231635896583; ✆ **337/466-3433**). Open since 1931, Nick's offers sweet courtyard ambiance and delicious home-style dinners Wednesday through Saturday. Or head back to Lafayette, to **Bon Temps Grill** (1211 W. Pinhook Rd; bontempsgrill.com, ✆ **337/706-8850**), for excellent service, live music, and unfussy Cajun food in a fun family-friendly atmosphere. (Do *not* skip the Fried Catfish Mon Dieu, if it's available.)

Still up for more? Option 1: Cozy, funky **Artmosphere** has an outdoor deck and yes, more live music! Often, it's local Cajun or indie bands or singer/songwriters—and it stays open late (902 Johnston St., Lafayette; check www.facebook.com/Artmosphere1 for updated listings; Tues–Sat 4pm–2am). Option 2: Find a favorite among the wide selection of beers, ciders, and more in a lovely open-air space at **The Wurst Biergarten** (537 Jefferson St., Lafayette; wurstbiergarten.com; ✆ **337/534-4612**).

Sunday, Day 3: Lafayette & St. Martinville ★★

Rise and shine! You're in for a treat: friendly and yummy **Scratch Farm Kitchen** (406 Garfield St., Lafayette; www.instagram.com/scratch_this; ✆ **337/295-4769**) will not disappoint for breakfast, particularly if you need something healthy in your gut to counteract all the fried foods you've consumed lately. Then, visit the reconstructed Cajun-Creole settlement of **Vermilionville ★★** (300 Fisher Rd., off Surrey St.; www.vermilionville.org; ✆ **337/233-4077;** $10 adults, $8 seniors, $6 students, free for kids 5 and under; Tues–Sun 10am–4pm; admission desk closes 3pm). Here, costumed staff and craftspeople demonstrate activities of 18th- to 19th-century daily life. It may sound like a kitschy "Cajunland" theme park, but it's actually quite a good introduction to the culture and a thorough education about the region's Indigenous peoples, European settlers, and people of African descent. Our favorite part was meeting Sitting Bear, a retired chief and current tribal council member of the Avogel Tribe, who shared his vast knowledge. (He's there Tues–Fri until 2pm.) Live music is offered regularly; check the website for schedule.

The food in the on-site restaurant, **La Cuisine de Maman,** is surprisingly good, but for something more upscale, reserve at nearby **Café Vermilionville** ★★ in an historic inn (1304 W. Pinhook Ave.; cafev.com; ✆ 337/237-0100).

Or take an eco-conscious wildlife tour with **Atchafalaya Experience** (www.theatchafalayaexperience.com; ✆ 337/766-1829; $50 ages 13 and up, $25 kids 12 and under; daily 10am), an outstanding 3-hour swamp excursion led by virtuoso naturalists who were raised on these bayous. If you have not yet taken to the waters of the Louisiana swamps, seeing this vital, stunning, primeval ecosystem is a must-do, and these guides are as good as it gets. Bring a hat, sunscreen, water, insect repellent, camera, and binoculars if you have them. Photography and private tours also available.

Another great choice is **Cajun Country Swamp Tours** (www.cajun countryswamptours.com; **337/319-0010;** $25 per seat), for a serene, 2-hour eco-conscious tour of Lake Martin in Breaux Bridge with a knowledgeable guide on an open boat. (Pack a hat and sunscreen!)

Lunch returns you to downtown Lafayette, to the **French Press** (214 E. Vermilion St.; www.thefrenchpresslafayette.com; ✆ 337/233-9449; Mon and Wed–Fri 7am–2pm, Sat–Sun 9am–2pm), a casual but refined spot on the higher end of the hipness scale. The biscuit sliders with boudin balls and sugarcane syrup are to die for; the chicken and waffles aren't far behind. If you want lighter fare, the winning shrimp salad boasts a kicking remoulade.

To further experience the history, legend, and romance of this region, take a leisurely drive to the lovely historic burg of **St. Martinville.** Get there by taking U.S. 90 East heading south out of Lafayette, to the Louisiana 182 exit. Turn left onto East Main Street, and left again onto La. 96 East for 7⅓ miles to reach the peaceful town square. St. Martinville dates from 1765, when it was a military station. It was once known as "La Petite Paris" for the many French aristocrats who settled here after fleeing the French Revolution.

The town centers around **St. Martin du Tours Church,** constructed in 1836—the fourth-oldest Roman Catholic church in Louisiana—and poetry. Besides its natural and historic charm, the town is the home of Evangeline Emmeline, the (debatably) fictional heroine of Longfellow's tragic poem. A statue of her next to the church was donated to the town in 1929 by a movie company that shot the film version here; star Dolores del Rio supposedly posed for the sculptor. At Port Street and Bayou Teche is the ancient **Evangeline Oak** and commemorative mural, where self-proclaimed descendants claim Emmeline's boat landed after her arduous journey from Nova Scotia.

From St. Martinville, make your way to I-10 again to return to New Orleans, or alternately take U.S. 90 for a different view. It's slightly longer and moderately more interesting.

A Cajun Experience Day Trip

If you're not ready to delve deep—or you have only a day to spare—an alternative Cajun experience can be had in **Bayou/Lafourche Parish** (www.lacajun bayou.com), an hour west of New Orleans via U.S. 90 West. There is a loose delineation between "prairie" Cajuns (those residing in the area of our 3-day tour) and those of the coast and bayous, including this swath of South Louisiana, known for its celebration of Cajun culture, extensive outdoor activities, and seafood-based fare.

Start with the **Acadian Wetlands Cultural Center** (314 St. Mary St., Thibodaux; www.nps.gov; ℂ **985/448-1375**), one of six entries into Jean Lafitte National Park, which celebrates Cajun culture. The free museum also offers a free walking tour of the town of **Thibodaux** at 10am every Wednesday and Thursday, plus the kid-friendly outside concert (BYO chair) **Music on the Bayou** at 6pm on Tuesdays. On Fridays and Saturdays there are boat tours of **Bayou Lafourche** for just $15.

Restaurants in this area mostly feature seafood—and it's what you should get. Try **Spahr's** (601 W. 4th St., Thibodaux; www.spahrsseafood.com; ℂ **985/448-0487;** Mon–Thurs 6am–9pm, Fri 6am–10pm, Sat 7am–10pm, Sun 7am–9pm) for catfish, gumbo, and Bloody Marys.

PLANNING YOUR TRIP

By Tami Fairweather

No matter what your idea of the perfect New Orleans trip is, this chapter will give you the information to make informed plans about getting here, getting around, and the essentials for an easy Big Easy vacation. We'll also point you toward additional resources, so you can let the *bons temps* begin even before you arrive.

GETTING THERE

By Plane

Most major domestic airlines serve the city's **Louis Armstrong New Orleans International Airport** (**MSY;** flymsy.com), along with several smaller regional lines. British Airways offers a direct flight from London. The dazzling new-ish Cesar Pelli–designed airport is 15 miles west of downtown. Information booths are in the main terminal and in baggage claim. Private planes often use Lakefront Airport, 9 miles from downtown.

GETTING INTO TOWN FROM THE AIRPORT

Depending on the traffic and your mode of transport, it takes approximately 30 to 45 minutes to get from the airport to the French Quarter or the Central Business District.

For **taxis** and **rideshares,** follow signs to the stands outside the baggage claim area. A taxi from the airport to most hotels downtown costs $36 (up to two people; $15 per person for three or more; credit cards accepted). **Uber** and **Lyft** rates run about $35 to $40 plus tip; beware of surge pricing, and compare apps. If you're going downtown, the flat-rate taxi is often a better deal. Limo service can be arranged via locally-owned **T&A Private Transportation** (www.taprivatetransportation.com; ✆ **877/665-2327** or 504/516-1812). Airport transfers in a luxury sedan start at $120, including tax, gratuity, a meet-and-greet inside the airport, plus help with luggage (a deal if you want to roll VIP like the celebrities and diplomats). In-town hourly rates start at $100 (including tax and gratuity).

Most major **rental car** companies operate out of a unified facility accessed by a free 24/7 shuttle bus. Follow the signs outside baggage claim.

The cheapest option is by **public bus.** The New Orleans Regional Transit Authority (NORTA) **Airport Express No. 202** runs directly from the airport to two different Central Business District stops on Loyola Avenue (Howard Ave. and Poydras St.) several times daily between 4:50am and 9:35pm for $1.25. Another option is the Jefferson Transit (JET) **public bus No. E1** for $2, which runs daily into the city, starting at City Park Avenue and continuing down Canal Street to Tulane Avenue and Loyola Avenue in the CBD, stopping at major intersections along the way. Riders can transfer to Regional Transit Authority lines for an additional $1.25. Buses run from 5am to 8:18pm weekdays (7am-8:30pm Sat–Sun; check schedule for return times). Follow signs outside baggage claim upstairs to the NORTA and RTA public bus stop, located on the outer curb outside departures (level 3). For more information, call **Jefferson Transit** (www.jeffersontransit.org) or the **Regional Transit Authority** (www.norta.com), both at ℂ **504/248-3900.**

Sadly, there's no longer an airport shuttle bus for individual travelers, but the airport offers **group shuttle service** (www.airportshuttlenerworleans.com; ℂ **866/596-2699** or 504/522-3500) for groups of 10 or more with advance reservation.

By Car

You can drive to New Orleans via **I-10, I-55, U.S. 90, U.S. 61,** or across the Lake Pontchartrain Causeway (**U.S. 190**). If possible, drive in during daylight to allow time to enjoy the distinctive swampy scenery. U.S. 61 or the Causeway offer the best views, but the larger roads are considerably faster. Approximate drive time to New Orleans from Atlanta is almost 7 hours; from Houston it's over 5 hours; Chicago, 14 hours; Baton Rouge is an hour and a half away. For info on driving while you're in the city, see "Getting Around," p. 294.

By Bus

Greyhound buses serve New Orleans from **Union Passenger Terminal** (UPT) at 1001 Loyola Ave. (www.greyhound.com; ℂ 800/231-2222), as do **Megabus** (us.megabus.com; ℂ 877/462-6342) and **Flixbus** (www.flixbus. com; ℂ 855/626-8585), both of which have cheap fares to/from select Southern cities where they connect to many others.

By Train

Passenger rail lines pass through some beautiful scenery. **Amtrak** (www. amtrak.com; ℂ 800/872-7245) trains serve the city's **Union Passenger Terminal** (UPT) at 1001 Loyola Ave. in the Central Business District. Once in New Orleans, the RTA Streetcar No. 49 runs all the way through downtown to the riverfront and into the French Quarter from 6am until 11pm, 7 days a week. (Transfer to other bus and streetcar lines to different parts of the city can be made at the Canal/Rampart stop.) Alternately (or after hours), call a taxi or rideshare. Hotels in the French Quarter and the CBD are a short ride or a healthy walk away.

By Ship

Cruise passenger traffic to or from the Port of New Orleans is substantial, largely because passengers can add a Crescent City visit before or after their voyage. Cruise lines include **Carnival Cruises** (www.carnival.com; ✆ 800/764-7419), **Disney Cruise Line** (www.disneycruise.com; ✆ 800/951-3532), **Norwegian Cruise Line** (www.ncl.com; ✆ 866/234-7350), and **Royal Caribbean** (www.royalcaribbean.com; ✆ 866/562-7625). You can also explore the Mississippi River on **American Cruise Lines** (www.americancruiselines.com; ✆ 800/460-4518), **American Queen Voyages** (www.aqvoyages.com; ✆ 888/522-1166), or **Viking Cruises** (www.vikingrivercruises.com; ✆ 800/304-9616). Public transportation to the cruise terminal isn't convenient, but rideshares and taxis are: Fares to most hotels run about $15 to $20. Luggage can be stored with porters at the terminal prior to a cruise; luggage transfer to the airport can also be arranged upon disembarkment. Parking at the terminal is about $22 per day. Disabled U.S. veterans are eligible for free parking up to 7 days.

GETTING AROUND
By Car

Unless you're planning to explore outside the major tourist zones (and, okay, this book does recommend a few outlying destinations), you really don't need to rent a car during your stay in New Orleans. The town is flat, ultra-picturesque, and made for daytime walking (nighttime, not so much). Taxis are scarce these days (you can call one, but good luck hailing one from a corner), but **Uber, Lyft,** and **pedicabs** are available, and there's decent public transportation. Indeed, a streetcar ride is as much entertainment as a means of getting around. Driving and parking can be a hassle—many streets are narrow, pot-holed, crowded, and one-way, and outside the French Quarter, streets angle in logic-defying directions to accommodate the curvy Mississippi. Paid street parking is minimal in the Quarter and CBD (and parking enforcement is strict); parking lots, especially at hotels, are fiendishly expensive.

That said, all the major **car-rental agencies** have a presence in New Orleans, with offices at the airport and around town. Rates vary widely according to company and seasonal demand. Plan in advance, and shop around. Insurance and taxes are almost never included in quoted rental-car rates in the U.S., and they can be significant. You'll pay a premium to pick up a rental at the airport, but it may be worth the convenience.

To rent a car you need a valid driver's license and a major credit card. Foreign visitors will need a passport (foreign driver's licenses are usually recognized, but it's wise to get an international one if your home license is not in English). The minimum age is usually 25, but Avis, Budget, Enterprise, and Hertz will rent to younger people for an added charge; they may also require proof of ability to pay (such as paycheck stubs or utility bills). It's a good idea to buy insurance coverage unless you're sure your own insurance is sufficient.

If you're in town for a while, download the **ParkMobile App.** Once you complete the annoying setup, you can conveniently pay for street parking via smartphone (and add meter time from afar—a huge plus). You can also pay by text on your phone—just know it won't be quick; you'll have multiple fields to fill out (license plate, name, address, credit card, and so forth). Or, *if* there's a meter, you could just use a credit card (feeding a meter with coins has gone extinct). Some paid parking lots use other apps (couldn't they all decide on one?).

Generally, gas costs in New Orleans tend to be at or below the U.S. average (shockingly so, if you're from California or Hawaii). Gas stations are readily available on major streets, but there are none within the French Quarter.

When driving in New Orleans, **right turns on a red light** are legal except where NO RIGHT TURN ON RED signs are posted (and not always prominently, so look closely). Sneaky **red-light cameras** abound (as do **speed cameras,** especially in school zones). Many major intersections restrict left turns. Drive past the intersection, make a U-turn at the next allowable place, then double back and turn right (a maneuver often called the "Louisiana left"). We recommend **looking both ways before proceeding** through a stop sign or green light; intersecting drivers often run the light, or simply don't pay attention. In the Quarter, be alert for pedestrians, who tend to forget the streets are open to cars.

Streetcars run down the center of Canal Street and St. Charles, Carrollton, and Loyola avenues, and drivers have to cross their paths frequently. **Look both ways for streetcars,** yield the right of way to them, and allow ample time to cross the tracks. They'll brake if you're in their way, of course, but it's best not to get stuck on the tracks and impede their progress.

It is illegal to have an open container of alcohol, including "go-cups," in a moving car, and, of course, driving while under the influence of alcohol is a serious offense. Keep car doors locked and never leave belongings, packages, or gadgets visible in parked cars.

By Taxi or Rideshare

Taxis used to be plentiful in New Orleans; these days, don't expect to hail one (except at the airport). Calling one isn't easy either (you may be on hold a while). The only semi-recommended taxi company in New Orleans is **United Cab** (no website; ✆ **504/522-9771**); meter rates vary. While the Curb app is the best option for taxis, **Uber** and **Lyft** are readily available (downloading the app and setting up your account is required). *Tip:* In the midst of big events (like Mardi Gras) or dense locations (like Bourbon or Frenchmen streets), you're better off walking a block or so to the corner of a more open street nearby for pickup. At times, rideshare apps may require you to move outside a specific "zone" to get picked up—and likewise may limit where you can be dropped off. From the French Quarter to a restaurant or club Uptown or in the Bywater, expect to spend $15 to $35 depending on traffic; surge pricing may add more. One thing you can almost always count on is a good conversation with a rideshare driver, so make small talk. They're often happy to share their local recommendations, too.

On Foot

We can't stress this enough: Walking is by far the best way to see New Orleans in the daytime (besides, you need to walk off all those calories!). You'll miss the many unique and sometimes glorious sights if you whiz past them. Slow down, stroll, and take it in. Say hello to people you pass by, especially if they're sitting on their porches. If it's just too hot, humid, or rainy, seek the shelter of balconies and galleries, or pop into locally owned cafes and bars, and support the business by buying a cold one. Hydration, y'all. Roaming the streets at night isn't the best idea, however, unless you're with others in well-lit busy areas.

By Streetcar

Besides being a National Historic Landmark, the **St. Charles Streetcar** (No. 12) is a convenient, scenic, and fun way to get from downtown to uptown and back. Its iconic green cars click and clack for 6½ miles, 24 hours a day, at frequent intervals, getting crowded on weekends (with visitors) and rush hours (business and school). Board at Canal and Carondelet streets (directly across Canal from Bourbon St. in the French Quarter) or anywhere along the line. The tracks wind beyond the point where St. Charles Avenue bends into Carrollton Avenue, ending at Marsalis Harmony Park (S. Claiborne Ave.). The original cars used on the St. Charles line are not air-conditioned, and only three of the cars are wheelchair-accessible. All other lines have A/C and lifts.

The **UPT-Riverfront** car (No. 49) runs the length of the French Quarter, from the French Market near Esplanade to Canal Street (a great foot saver). Its spiffy bright-red cars turn onto Canal Street and transfer to the **Canal Street** lines. Check the sign on the front of the Canal line cars—CEMETERIES (No. 47) goes to several of the older cemeteries (daily 5am-4:13am), while CITY PARK (No. 48, 5:11am-11:09pm) goes along Carrollton Avenue through Mid-City to City Park/the New Orleans Museum of Art. *Note:* At press time the Rampart Street/St. Claude line remained closed for reconstruction; the St. Claude/Arabi bus No. 8 fills in. Service is expected to resume in 2024.

The **fare** for any streetcar line is $1.25; transfers are free. All streetcars take the RTA's Le Pass app ticket by scan, a **JazzyPass** (see box, p. 298), or cash (exact change only). Expect holidays and parades to impact regular schedules and routes.

By Bike & Scooter

Biking is also a great way to see the city. The terrain is flat, the breeze feels good, there are bike paths, and you can cover ground pretty swiftly on two wheels. Streets can be busy, bumpy, and potholed, however, so it's a plus if you're experienced in city riding. And while driver awareness has improved, this ain't Amsterdam: Stay aware at all times.

Operated by the community-based nonprofit Blue Krewe, the convenient **Blue Bikes** bikesharing system has 500 "pedal-assist e-bikes" available to rent, located in "hubs" around the city. After downloading the mobile app and choosing a plan and payment form (factor in some time), you can locate a bike nearby, scan the QR code, unlock for $1 and pay-as-you-go for 15¢ a minute (monthly plans available for frequent riders). Lock the bike back at a hub or at any rack (for an extra $2) within the service area, then snap and submit a photo to end the ride. Bikes have lights and a lock but no helmets (not required but recommended in NOLA). Maps and details are on the website and app (www.bluebikesnola.com). Be careful not to lock it up outside the service area (which doesn't extend that far uptown); you'll get hit with a $25 fee. Bikes can be in short supply during an event when (and where) demand is high.

Long-established **Bicycle Michael's,** 622 Frenchmen St. (www.bicycle michaels.com; ✆ **504/945-9505**) has a fleet of good-quality multi-gear hybrids and mountain bikes (no cruisers) starting at $30 for a half-day (4 hr.), $45 per day; road bikes cost a bit more. The bikes (bearing nicknames like "King Tim" or "Chicken Tenders") must be picked up and returned during shop hours (closed Wed). If you're staying Uptown, hit **Mike the Bike Guy,** $30 per day (4411 Magazine St.; www.mikethebikeguy.com; ✆ **504/899-1344**). Rates include a lock, lights, and usually a helmet; both offer longer-term rentals; multi-day minimums may apply during Mardi Gras or Jazz Fest. Also see "Bicycle & Other Wheeled Tours," p. 201.

Another fun, easy way to get around is on a GB50 motor scooter from **Avenue Scooters,** 8840 Oak St. (www.avenuescooters.com; ✆ **504/609-3838**). Rates start at $60 for 3 hours, $80 per full day including helmet. They get up to about 35 mph, so you ride in car lanes (and get no love from four-wheeled drivers). Follow all traffic rules, and watch those potholes!

By Pedicab

These rickshaw-like tricycles will get two people from point A to B via pedal power (a driver's, not yours). They're relatively easy to hail in the French Quarter and occasionally seen in other tourist parts, or you can call to request one from **Bike Taxi Unlimited (**✆ **504/891-3441)** or **Need a Ride Pedicabs** (✆ **504/488-6565**). City-set rates are $5 for the first 6 blocks, $1 per block per person after that (plus tip for your hard-riding driver, especially if they make you a deal for a longer ride). It's a great option for fatigued feet or short hops when you want a little breeze (or breezy conversation).

By Ferry

The **Canal Street/Algiers Point Ferry** (www.norta.com; ✆ **504/248-3900**) is one of the city's great assets, for transportation to the old Algiers Point neighborhood (p. 181) and views of the city from the Mississippi River. It's a commuter ferry (pedestrians, bikes, and wheelchairs only, no cars), but it's atmospheric at night when the city's glowing skyline reflects on the water. The 25-minute ride from the foot of Canal Street costs $2 each way via Le

Discounted Rides with the JazzyPass

If you don't have a car in New Orleans, invest in a **JazzyPass,** which allows unlimited rides on all streetcar and bus lines (but not the ferry). It's a bargain at $3 for 1 day, $8 for 3 days, $15 for 7 days, or $45 for a full month (31 days). Purchase any of the passes on RTA's **Le Pass** app or at most Walgreens retail locations (call first, locations may not have all four types in stock). Time doesn't start until you first use the pass. You can also buy them (except the 1-month pass) at vending machines at the streetcar stops at Canal at Bourbon, N. Peters, White, or City Park streets, but they only accept cash. You can purchase a 1-day pass when boarding, with exact cash (drivers don't dispense change). Mail order in advance is another option, via the website, delivered in 5 to 10 business days. Youth, Senior, and Paratransit discount fares are available with ID. More info at **RTA** (www.norta.com; ☏ **504/248-3900**).

Pass app (scan upon entry) or exact cash. The ferry leaves the sparkling new, ADA-accessible Canal Street Ferry Terminal on the riverfront every 30 minutes beginning at 6:15am every day, with the last return ferry to downtown at 8:30pm on Sunday through Thursday, 10:30pm on Friday and Saturday. Check for schedule changes on holidays and special events; weather can affect the timing, too.

By City Bus

New Orleans has a good public bus system that many locals rely on, and the buses fill in when streetcars are down (usually due to track closure for an event). Chances are there's a bus that runs exactly where you want to go. Like the streetcars, the single-ride fare is $1.25 (including transfer). You must have exact change in bills or coins to pay upon entry, but you can buy fares and scan for entry via mobile phone using **Le Pass** app. For all-day or multiple rides, invest in a **JazzyPass** (see box, above). For route information, contact the **RTA** (www.norta.com; ☏ **504/248-3900**).

[FastFACTS] NEW ORLEANS

Area Codes The area code for New Orleans is **504.**

Business Hours Most stores don't open early in the morning—many open around 10am or noon and stay open until 5 or 6pm. Bars tend to stay open until the wee hours, even 24/7, and restaurants' hours vary depending on the types of meals they serve (most close around 9-11pm). Expect breakfast to start around 8am, lunch around 11am, and dinner at 6pm. Many are closed on Mondays.

Cellphones See "Mobile Phones," later in this section.

Crime See "Safety," later in this section.

Customs For U.S. Customs details and information on what you're allowed to bring home, consult your home country's customs agency. In the U.S., consult **U.S. Customs** at **U.S. Customs & Border Protection (CBP),** 1300 Pennsylvania Ave. NW, Washington, DC 20229 (www.cbp.gov; ☏ **877/227-5511**).

Doctors See "Health," below.

Drinking Laws The legal age for buying or consuming alcoholic beverages is 21; proof of age is required and often requested at bars, nightclubs, and restaurants, so bring physical ID with you (U.S. states' digital app IDs are acceptable, too). Nowadays pretty much everyone—even senior citizens—may get carded. Alcoholic beverages are available round-the-clock, 7 days a week. Bars can stay open all night in New Orleans (if they choose), and liquor is sold in grocery stores, liquor stores, or walk-up windows. You're allowed to drink in public, but not from a glass or bottle; bars will provide a plastic "go-cup" into which you can transfer your drink as you leave (save on waste with a sturdy, reusable one).

Warning: Although New Orleans has a reputation for tolerance, public intoxication and "drunk and disorderly" conduct are most definitely illegal, as many a jailed tourist can testify. Practice moderation, make smart decisions, and don't ever pee in the street. Don't even think about driving (car, motorcycle, or bicycle) while intoxicated: This is a zero-tolerance crime. Don't carry open containers of alcohol in your car or any public area that isn't zoned for alcohol consumption.

Electricity The United States uses 110-120 volts

AC (60 cycles), compared to 220-240 volts AC (50 cycles) in most of Europe, Australia, and New Zealand. Converters that change 220–240 volts to 110–120 volts are difficult to find in the U.S., so bring one with you.

Embassies & Consulates All embassies are in the nation's capital, Washington, D.C. Some have consulate offices in major U.S. cities; to find a consulate for your home country, check www.embassy.org/embassies.

Emergencies For fire, ambulance, and police, dial 📞 **911** from any phone (it is a free call).

Family Travel New Orleans offers plenty of activities and sights appropriate for children, who often get a real kick out of the city (and love Mardi Gras!). Summer months bring the heat but also the bargains, so weigh your family's tolerance levels for a visit during school vacation. See "Especially for Kids" on p. 202.

Gyms Most hotels have at least a nominal fitness center. Some offer day passes to local gyms. Otherwise, workout day passes can be had at two **Downtown Fitness** locations (www.downtownfitnesscenter.com): at 365 Canal St., 3rd floor, 📞 **504/525-2956;** or 2372 St. Claude Ave., 📞 **504/754-1101.** The storied **New Orleans Athletic Club** has an indoor pool and track, a library, and (yup) a bar (222 N. Rampart

St.; www.neworleansathletic club.com; 📞 **504/525-2375**; proof of stay and valid ID required). Members of the **Anytime Fitness** chain can find multiple locations. There are also lots of free or inexpensive drop-in workouts: **Move Ya Brass** (www.moveyabrass.com) gives stretch, bounce, hip-hop, HIIT, and group run workouts in Crescent Park and City Park; the international workout group **November Project** (www.Facebook.com/Nov ProjectNO) has free 6am workouts Wednesdays at Champions Square and Fridays at NOMA in City Park; the **Cabildo** (p. 161) and **Besthoff Sculpture Garden** (p. 172) offer yoga classes.

Health The most common annoyances are **pollen, sun, uneven sidewalks, overindulgence,** and **mosquitoes** (especially near swamps and bayous), so pack insect repellent, sunscreen, protective clothing, digestive aids, and antihistamines. For "Hospitals," see below. If you need a doctor for less urgent health concerns, try **Ochsner On Call** (www.ochsner.org/services/ochsner-on-call; 📞 **504/842-3155** or 800/231-5257; daily 24 hr.) or visit an **Ochsner Urgent Care** clinic (www.ochsner.org/services/urgent-care-services): 4100 Canal St. in Mid-City (📞 **504/218-4853**); 900 Magazine St. in the Warehouse District (📞 **504/552-2433**); or 4605 Magazine St. in Uptown (📞 **504/891-7676**); all open daily. The Louisiana Department of Health (www.ldh.la.gov; ℂ **225/342-9500**) offers information on COVID-19 testing locations, as does Ochsner On Call. Also see "Pharmacies," later in this section.

Hospitals   In an emergency, dial ℂ **911** from any phone to summon paramedics. Downtown emergency rooms are at **Tulane Medical Center,** 1415 Tulane Ave. (ℂ **504/988-5263**); and **University Medical Center,** 2000 Canal St. (ℂ **504/702-2128**); if you're uptown, try **Ochsner Baptist Medical Center,** 2700 Napoleon Ave. (ℂ **504/899-9311**); or **Touro LCMC Health,** 1401 Foucher St. (ℂ **504/269-3943**).

Insurance   Travel insurance is a good safety net if you think for some reason you may need to cancel or postpone your trip (or even if you don't). Most medical insurance policies cover you if you are on vacation, but check your policy before you depart.

Internet/Wi-Fi   Nearly all major hotels have free Wi-Fi in their lobbies, as do many cafes, bars, and all Starbucks (there's one at the edge of the French Quarter in The Sheraton on Canal, 500 Canal St.; ℂ **504/525-2500**). The vast majority of hotels also offer some form of in-room Internet access, usually high-speed wireless. Many now include the cost in the room charge; some add a daily surcharge. Barring that, simply boot up and see what signals you

get; or walk down any commercial street and look for "Free Wi-Fi" signs. A concierge or front desk attendant should be able to direct you to nearby public Wi-Fi locations. **Louis Armstrong New Orleans International Airport** has free Wi-Fi coverage in all passenger areas.

Language   English is spoken everywhere, while French and Spanish are heard occasionally in New Orleans.

Legal Aid   If you are pulled over by the police for a minor infraction (such as speeding), never attempt to pay the fine directly to an officer; this could be construed as attempted bribery, a much more serious crime. Pay fines by mail or directly into the hands of the clerk of the court. If accused of a more serious offense, say and do nothing before consulting a lawyer. Here in the U.S., the burden is on the state to prove a person's guilt beyond a reasonable doubt, and everyone has the right to remain silent, whether he or she is suspected of a crime or actually arrested. Once arrested, a person can make one telephone call to a party of his or her choice. The international visitor should call his or her embassy or consulate.

LGBTQ+ Travelers
New Orleans is a very welcoming town with an extensive and active LGBTQ+ community and many events specific to the community. The most fun you

can have is to roll in during **Southern Decadence,** aka Gay Mardi Gras (p. 33). Otherwise, just hit the bars and clubs (p. 230) or go online and talk with people. For resources, try *Ambush Magazine* (www.ambush mag.com), and the **Gulf South LGBTQ+ Chamber** (www.gslgbtchamber.org). The **Metropolitan Community Church of New Orleans,** 5401 S. Claiborne Ave. (www.MCCNew Orleans.com; ℂ **504/270-1622**), serves a primarily queer congregation. **Good Friends** (p. 231) bar is a hub. The **AllWays Lounge & Cabaret** (p. 230) has fab drag and burlesque shows and also holds an amazing monthly queer storytelling event. Go to **Oz** (p. 231) to get your late-night dance on. The local **LGBT Community Center** (www.lgbtccneworleans.org) lists events and info on its website and Facebook page.

Mail & Shipping   At press time, domestic postage rates were 48¢ for a postcard and 63¢ for a letter up to 1 ounce. For international mail, a first-class postcard or letter stamp costs $1.45. For more information, go to **www.usps.com**. Always include ZIP codes when mailing items in the U.S. Use the lookup tool at www.usps.com/zip4.

Convenient **FedEx Office** locations with full shipping (and printing) capabilities are at 801 Baronne St. (ℂ **504/581-2541**) and 901 Convention Center Blvd. (ℂ **504/585-5750**).

WHAT THINGS COST IN NEW ORLEANS	US$
Rideshare from airport to the Quarter	40.00 (for two people)
30-minute ride on a Blue Bike rental	5.50
One-way ride on bus or streetcar	1.25
1-day Jazzy Pass for bus/streetcar	3.00
Double room at the Four Seasons Hotel	350.00–450.00
Double at the Chimes Bed & Breakfast	144.00–200.00
Dorm bed at HI New Orleans Hostel	39.00–50.00
Order of three beignets at Café du Monde	3.85
Dinner at Commander's Palace (3 courses)	70.00 (per person)
Lunch buffet at Dooky Chase	19.95 (per person)
Small fried shrimp po' boy at Parkway Bakery & Tavern	10.99
Ticket to a show at Tipitina's (on average)	15.00–40.00
Cost of a Hurricane at Pat O'Brien's	11.50
Cost of a Pimm's Cup at Napoleon House	9.00

If you aren't sure what your address will be while in the U.S., mail can be sent to you, in your name, c/o General Delivery at New Orleans' main post office, 701 Loyola Ave. in the Warehouse District. The addressee must pick up mail in person, with proof of identity (such as driver's license or passport). Most post offices will hold mail for up to 30 days and are open weekdays 8am-4pm (Sat 9am–noon).

Medical Care See "Health," earlier in this section.

Mobile Phones Mobile (cell) phone and texting service in New Orleans is generally good, with the larger carriers all getting excellent coverage. Some dead zones still exist around the city and inside old brick buildings. International mobile phone service can be hit-or-miss (despite what you may have been told before you began your trip). If you plan to use your phone a lot while in New Orleans, it may be worthwhile to purchase a prepaid, no-contract phone locally. You can get hooked up at most **CVS** or **Walgreens** drugstores or **Walmart** (1901 Tchoupitoulas St.; ✆ **504/522-4142**). Compare the plans' sign-on offers, roaming and data use charges, usage requirements, and limitations to make sure you're not purchasing more extensive or longer-term services than you need.

If you have a computer and/or smartphone Internet service, consider using WhatsApp (www.whatsapp. com) or Zoom (www.zoom. us) for free international calls when both parties have the app.

Money & Costs Frommer's lists prices in U.S. dollars. The currency conversions quoted below were correct at press time. However, rates fluctuate, so before departing, consult a currency exchange website such as **www.xe.com**.

THE VALUE OF THE U.S. DOLLAR VS. OTHER POPULAR CURRENCIES

US$	C$	£	€	A$	NZ$
1.00	1.33	0.78	0.92	1.46	1.61

Costs in New Orleans are generally right in the middle of, and sometimes lower than, those in other midsize U.S. "destination" cities—less than New York, for example, but more than Phoenix. Prices have crept up over the last few years, so it's no longer the great value it once was, and costs vary greatly by season. In the heat of summer, you can often find good hotel and "Coolinary" restaurant deals, while prices can soar during big events. December's **prix-fixe Réveillon deals** can get you into restaurants for dinners that might otherwise be prohibitive.

With a few cash-only exceptions, **major credit cards** are accepted everywhere (some don't accept American Express, Discover, or Diner's Club). Cash is king on parade routes and holes-in-the-wall, but most food pop-ups and market vendors take Venmo and CashApp. Jazz Fest went cashless in 2023; we expect other major festivals to follow suit. ATMs are plentiful throughout the city (including inside many bars and souvenir shops). Expect a $3-$4 charge to use an ATM outside your network. To avoid the fee, many grocery and convenience stores will allow you to get a small amount of cash back with your purchase (from $10–$100, depending on store policy).

Beware hidden credit-card fees while traveling. Check with your bank before departing to see what fees, if any, will be charged for overseas transactions.

Newspapers & Magazines

The city has one local paper, the ***Times-Picayune/New Orleans Advocate*** (www.nola.com); most online stories are behind a paywall. ***Offbeat*** (www.offbeat.com) and ***Where Y'at*** (www.whereyat.com) are monthly entertainment guides with live music, art, and special-event listings. Both can usually be found in hotels and clubs and get scarce toward the end of the month. ***Gambit Weekly*** (www.nola.com/gambit), which comes out every Sunday, is a free alternative paper with a mix of local news and entertainment.

Packing

What to pack depends largely on when you'll be here and what you plan to do. Comfortable walking shoes are a must year-round (wear close-toed shoes on Bourbon St.). A compact umbrella is essential during the wetter months, as is a sunhat for long days outside (especially for a festival). A light outer layer or scarf is recommended even in the hottest weather, when indoor air-conditioning can get frigid. January to March, colder temps feel even colder due to humidity—hats, gloves, and an insulated jacket are saviors. Casual wear is the daytime norm, but cocktail wear is appropriate in nicer restaurants, and some of the old-liners require jackets for gentlemen.

Passports

Every air traveler entering the U.S. is required to show a valid passport (including U.S. citizens). Those entering by land and sea must also present a passport or other appropriate documentation. See **www.dhs.gov/cross-us-borders** for details. For more on passport requirements, contact the Passport Office of your home country. If you need to obtain or renew a passport, do so at least 6 months before your departure.

Pharmacies

Pharmacies (aka chemists or druggists) are easily found. The large chain pharmacies **CVS** and **Walgreens** operate throughout the city, including the French Quarter.

Police

Dial ✆ **911** for emergencies. This is a free call from any phone. Dial ✆ **311** for non-emergency help.

Safety

Unfortunately, it's true that New Orleans has a high crime rate. Much (not all) of the serious crime is drug- or theft-related and outside tourist areas. Still, we urge you to be very cautious about where you go, what you do, and with whom, particularly at night. Use the same street smarts you would in any big city: Travel in groups or pairs, take cabs or rideshares if you're not sure of a neighborhood, stay in well-lit areas with plenty of street and pedestrian traffic, don't hook up with strangers, and follow your instincts if something seems "off." Stay alert and walk with confidence; avoid looking distracted, confused, or (sorry) drunk. In fact, avoiding *being* drunk (and loud) are good general rules. One way to ensure that you will look like a tourist—and thus, a target—is to wear Mardi Gras beads any time or place outside of a parade where you caught them.

iPhones have become a target of grab-and-run thieves, especially since users are often distracted. If you must check something on your phone, stop into a hotel lobby, bar, or shop.

When it's not in use, put that expensive camera out of sight. Use camera cases and purses with a shoulder strap, carried diagonally over the shoulder. Consider using a money belt or other hidden wallet. For clubbing, invest in a shoulder-strappy bag, one you can dance with rather than leave on your seat. Never leave valuables in the outside pocket of a backpack. Use that hotel safe, and if you must store belongings in a car, store them in the trunk. Leave expensive-looking jewelry and other conspicuous valuables at home. And by all means, **don't look for or buy drugs or engage in any illegal activity.**

On the **Bourbon Street** party blocks, be careful when socializing with strangers, and be alert to distractions by potential pickpocket teams or someone handing you a gift (it never is). Use busy Bourbon, Decatur, or Royal streets to walk from the Quarter to Frenchmen Street (you may encounter unhoused people, but they're generally not dangerous). Better yet, call a car. Never visit cemeteries at night, unless you're with a tour.

Sections of **Central City** and the **Seventh Ward** are transitional and may be considered sketchy by tourists; as are some bits of the **Tremé, Bywater, Marigny,** and the **Irish Channel** section of the Lower Garden District. This shouldn't dissuade you from a destination spot, but keep on your toes.

Single Travelers Single tourists and conventioneers are plentiful in New Orleans; single women, men, and non-binary travelers should feel comfortable here. People are generally friendly and many restaurants, including some of the city's finest, serve meals at the bar—a personal favorite spot when dining solo, Still, single travelers in particular should heed the warnings under "Safety," above.

Smoking The city council instituted a broad-reaching law in 2015, banning smoking indoors almost everywhere including hotels, restaurants, casinos, nightclubs, and bars (cigar and vape bars are excepted). Places with patios or courtyards can designate them as smoking areas, but not all do. It's okay to light up on the street a few feet from restaurant or shop entrances, and in most parks. Though **marijuana** has been decriminalized in Louisiana, it's still illegal to smoke it in public places. A 2021 law made possession of up to 14 grams of marijuana—a half-ounce—a misdemeanor crime carrying a fine of no more than $100 (even for repeat offenses).

Taxes The United States has no value-added tax (VAT) or other indirect tax at the national level, but states, counties, and cities may levy their own taxes, which will not appear on price tags. The **sales tax** in New Orleans is 9.45%; **hotel room tax** is 16.35% plus $1–$2 per room per night.

International travelers who purchase goods in Louisiana to take back to their home countries can often get the sales tax refunded in full. When you make your purchase, keep your receipt and request a "tax back" voucher (you'll be asked to show your passport). Before you leave the state, bring your receipts, vouchers, and travel ticket (of fewer than 90 days duration) to a **Refund Center** in the Riverwalk Outlet mall (p. 236); Canal Place (p. 235); or the **Tax Free** counter at Louis Armstrong International Airport (Level 2, allow time before your flight). You'll be rebated in cash up to $500. Larger rebates are mailed; see **www.louisianataxfree.com** for instructions and more information. Not all stores participate, so ask first.

Also, many original works of art purchased in New Orleans are tax-exempt. Do inquire, as this applies in designated cultural districts only.

Telephones Hotel costs for long-distance and local calls made from guest room phones vary widely, from free to astronomically expensive—if you intend to use the room phone, ask about phone charges. You may be better off using a mobile phone or a prepaid calling card. Public pay-phones are rare, but some (for example, at airports) accept credit cards. Most long-distance and international calls can be dialed directly from any phone. Calls to area codes **800, 888, 877, 866, 855,** and **833** are free. **To make calls within the United States and to Canada,** dial **1** followed by the area code and the seven-digit number. **For other international calls,** dial **011** followed by the country code, city code, and the number you are calling. For **directory assistance** in the U.S. and Canada, dial ✆ **411.** For other phone services, dial **0** to reach an operator within the U.S.; dial **00** for assistance with international calls. Also see "Mobile Phones," p. 301.

Time New Orleans is in the Central Time Zone (CT), which is 6 hours earlier than Greenwich Mean Time. When it's noon in New Orleans, it's 10am in Los Angeles (PT); 1pm in New York City (ET); 6pm in London (GMT); and 5am the next day in Sydney.

Daylight savings time (summer time) is in effect from 2am on the second Sunday in March to 2am on the first Sunday in November, except in Arizona, Hawaii, the U.S. Virgin Islands, and Puerto Rico. Daylight saving time moves the clock 1 hour ahead of standard time.

Tipping In the U.S., tips are not a bonus but an essential part of certain workers' incomes. Even if service is poor, most people leave a smaller tip rather than none at all. Feeling generous? Tip more than amounts shown here. In hotels, tip **bellhops** $1–$2 per bag ($3 if you have a lot of luggage) and tip **housekeepers** $5 and up per night (more if you've been extra messy). Tip the **doorman** or **concierge** if he or she has provided you with some service (for example, calling a cab or obtaining tickets or reservations), $5–$20 or more depending on complexity. Tip the **valet-parking attendant** $2–$5 every time you get your car, more if you're driving something you need to protect.

In restaurants, bars, and nightclubs, tip **service staff** and **bartenders** 20% of the check, tip **checkroom attendants** $2 per garment, and tip **valet-parking attendants** $2–$5. Some restaurants will automatically add a tip to the bill for larger parties (typically 18% for 6 or more guests). Check your bill or ask your server whether gratuity, sometimes labeled "service charge," has been included in your bill.

Tip **drivers** 15%–20% of the fare, tip **skycaps** at airports at least $2 per bag (more if you have a lot of luggage), and tip **hairstylists** and **barbers** 15%–20%.

Toilets You won't find public toilets or "restrooms" on the streets in most U.S. cities, so scout them out in hotel lobbies, bars, restaurants, museums, and railway and bus stations. Large hotels are often the best bet for clean facilities. Restaurants and bars may restrict their restrooms to paying patrons, but it never hurts to ask.

Travelers with Disabilities Most public places are required to comply with disability-friendly regulations. Almost all public establishments and at least some modes of public transportation provide wheelchair-accessible entrances and facilities. Still, some older properties, including some National Historic Landmarks, may be inaccessible, given exemptions due to their historic nature. Before you book a reservation, call and inquire based on your needs.

The city's bumpy, uneven, potholed, and sometimes cobblestoned sidewalks and streets can be challenging for those with mobility or visual differences, though most crossings have curb cuts. Three of the historic St. Charles streetcars are equipped with wheelchair lifts at the front and rear of each car. (Look for the universal accessibility icon on the front and side to determine if the car has lifts.) All other streetcar lines have wheelchair lifts. More accessibility information can be found at www.neworleans. com/plan/accessibility/faqs; or www.nolarolla.com, a **wheelchair user's guide** to New Orleans.

For paratransit information and reservations, contact **RTA Paratransit** (www.norta.com/ Accessibility/Paratransit; ℂ 504/827-8345).

Vaccinations & Inoculations
At press time, all mask mandates and requirements on COVID-19 proof of vaccination or negative test have been lifted, though private businesses can implement their own requirements (none do). Check regulations if you're arriving from an area known to have rates of certain other illnesses (particularly cholera, yellow fever, measles, and Ebola).

Visas
The U.S. State Department has a **Visa Waiver Program (VWP)** allowing citizens from a long list of countries to enter the U.S. without a visa for stays of up to 90 days. Even visitors from VWP countries (and others for whom a visa is not necessary) are required to have an e-passport, online registration through the Electronic System for Travel Authorization (ESTA), and an electronic application before departing for the U.S. Travelers not eligible for VWP are required to get a visa. Some travelers may also be required to present a round-trip air or cruise ticket upon arrival in the U.S. Canadian citizens may enter without visas but will need to show passports and proof of residence. Citizens of all other countries must have: (1) a valid passport that expires at least 6 months later than the scheduled end of their visit to the U.S., and (2) a tourist visa. All visa and passport information are subject to change. Check with the American Embassy in your home country at least 6 months before your planned departure and read up at travel.state.gov/ content/travel/en/us-visas/ tourism-visit/visa-waiver-program.html.

Visitor Information
Even a seasoned traveler should consider writing or calling ahead to **New Orleans and Company,** 2020 St. Charles Ave., New Orleans, LA 70130 (www. neworleans.com; ℂ **800/ 672-6124** or 504/566-5011). The friendly staff can offer advice and help with decision-making; if you have a special interest, they'll help you plan your visit around it—this is definitely one of the most helpful tourist centers in any major city.

At the **New Orleans Jazz National Historic Park,** temporarily at 916 N. Peters St. (www.nps.gov/ jazz/index.htm; ℂ **504/589-3882**), super-cool National Park Service rangers are full of info and guidance.

Bonus: They offer frequent free programs highlighting local culture, from musical performances to dance classes to lectures by local experts. The historical **Basin St. Station** building, 501 Basin St. (ℂ **504/293-2600;** daily 8:30am–5pm), in the Tremé neighborhood, has a welcome center with maps; community exhibits; booklets on restaurants, accommodations, and sightseeing; and a walking tour kiosk.

Be aware: Many of the concierges, tour offices, and visitor centers scattered around the city (including the biggie at Basin Street Station) are *for-profit* offices operated by tourism businesses hawking their own wares. If you feel you're being sold something that's not exactly right, you can always contact any tour company directly to buy tours. Or just use *Frommer's* most excellent, unbiased, carefully curated recommendations!

Water
Tap water is safe to drink in New Orleans, although bottled water tastes better (though not eco-friendly). Treated water from the Mississippi River is the main source of tap water, as is true for most cities along the Mississippi.

Index

See also Accommodations and Restaurant indexes, below.

General Index

Accommodations

Map List

Photo Credits

Frommer's New Orleans, 9th Edition

Published by
FROMMER MEDIA LLC

ISBN 978-1-62887-579-9 (paper), 978-1-62887-580-5 (e-book)

Editorial Director: Pauline Frommer
Editor: Holly Hughes
Production Editor: Cheryl Lenser
Cartographer: Andy Dolan
Photo Editor: Alyssa Mattei
Indexer: Cheryl Lenser
Compositor: Lissa Auciello-Brogan
Cover Design: Dave Riedy

For information on our other products or services, see www.frommers.com.

Frommer Media LLC also publishes its books in a variety of electronic formats. Some content that
appears in print may not be available in electronic formats.

Manufactured in Turkey

5 4 3 2 1

ABOUT THE AUTHORS

Tami Fairweather is a writer, communications consultant, connector, sometimes event planner, and lover of fresh air, travel, magic, little rituals, and the window seat. Born and raised bi-coastally in Massachusetts and Washington state, her chosen home is New Orleans, where she holds great reverence for the culture bearers who give the city all its soul. Her travel stories have appeared in *Off Assignment, Canadian Traveller, Wanderlust Magazine, South Writ Large, Adventure Travel News*, and more.

Lavinia Spalding is series editor of *The Best Women's Travel Writing*, author of *Writing Away*, and co-author of *With a Measure of Grace* and *This Immeasurable Place*. Her work appears in the *New York Times, Tin House, Longreads, AFAR*, and many other publications, and she co-hosts the podcast "There She Goes." Since moving to New Orleans in 2016, Lavinia has been making her way through the city's extraordinary array of sights, sounds, scents, and tastes. But it's the feeling of New Orleans she loves most—a warmth and spirit unlike anything she's experienced, in all her wanderings. She's here to stay.

ABOUT THE FROMMER TRAVEL GUIDES

For most of the past 50 years, Frommer's has been the leading series of travel guides in North America, accounting for as many as 24% of all guidebooks sold. I think I know why.

Though we hope our books are entertaining, we nevertheless deal with travel in a serious fashion. Our guidebooks have never looked on such journeys as a mere recreation, but as a far more important human function, a time of learning and introspection, an essential part of a civilized life. We stress the culture, lifestyle, history, and beliefs of the destinations we cover, and urge our readers to seek out people and new ideas as the chief rewards of travel.

We have never shied from controversy. We have, from the beginning, encouraged our authors to be intensely judgmental, critical—both pro and con—in their comments, and wholly independent. Our only clients are our readers, and we have triggered the ire of countless prominent sorts, from a tourist newspaper we called "practically worthless" (it unsuccessfully sued us) to the many rip-offs we've condemned.

And because we believe that travel should be available to everyone regardless of their incomes, we have always been cost-conscious at every level of expenditure. Though we have broadened our recommendations beyond the budget category, we insist that every lodging we include be sensibly priced. We use every form of media to assist our readers, and are particularly proud of our feisty daily website, the award-winning Frommers.com.

I have high hopes for the future of Frommer's. May these guidebooks, in all the years ahead, continue to reflect the joy of travel and the freedom that travel represents. May they always pursue a cost-conscious path, so that people of all incomes can enjoy the rewards of travel. And may they create, for both the traveler and the persons among whom we travel, a community of friends, where all human beings live in harmony and peace.

Arthur Frommer